Sultan, Caliph, and tl of the Faith

The *Tārīkh al-fattāsh* is one of the most important and celebrated sources for the history of pre-colonial West Africa, yet it has confounded scholars for decades with its inconsistencies and the questions surrounding its authorship. In this study, Mauro Nobili examines and challenges existing theories on the chronicle, arguing that much of what we have assumed about the work is deeply flawed. Making extensive use of previously unpublished Arabic sources, Nobili demonstrates that the *Tārīkh al-fattāsh* was in fact written in the nineteenth century by a Fulani scholar, Nūḥ b. al-Ṭāhir, who modified preexisting historiographical material as a political project to legitimize the West African Islamic state known as the Caliphate of Ḥamdallāhi and its founding leader, Aḥmad Lobbo. Contextualizing its production within the broader development of the religious and political landscape of West Africa, this study represents a significant moment in the study of West African history and of the evolution of Arabic historical literature in Timbuktu and its surrounding regions.

MAURO NOBILI is Assistant Professor at the Department of History and the Center for African Studies at the University of Illinois. A historian of pre-colonial and early colonial West Africa, he has published on West African chronicles and Arabic calligraphies including in the journal *History of Africa*. He has been the recipient of several prestigious awards, including a National Endowment for Humanities grant.

African Studies Series

The African Studies series, founded in 1968, is a prestigious series of monographs, general surveys, and textbooks on Africa covering history, political science, anthropology, economics, and ecological and environmental issues. The series seeks to publish work by senior scholars as well as the best new research.

Editorial Board

David Anderson, *University of Warwick*
Catherine Boone, *London School of Economics and Political Science*
Carolyn Brown, *Rutgers University, New Jersey*
Christopher Clapham, *University of Cambridge*
Michael Gomez, *New York University*
Richard Roberts, *Stanford University, California*
David Robinson, *Michigan State University*
Leonardo A. Villalón, *University of Florida*

Other titles in the series are listed at the back of the book.

Sultan, Caliph, and the Renewer of the Faith

Aḥmad Lobbo, the *Tārīkh al-fattāsh* and the Making of an Islamic State in West Africa

MAURO NOBILI
University of Illinois, Urbana-Champaign

CAMBRIDGE
UNIVERSITY PRESS

CAMBRIDGE
UNIVERSITY PRESS

University Printing House, Cambridge CB2 8BS, United Kingdom

One Liberty Plaza, 20th Floor, New York, NY 10006, USA

477 Williamstown Road, Port Melbourne, VIC 3207, Australia

314-321, 3rd Floor, Plot 3, Splendor Forum, Jasola District Centre, New Delhi - 110025, India

103 Penang Road, #05-06/07, Visioncrest Commercial, Singapore 238467

Cambridge University Press is part of the University of Cambridge.

It furthers the University's mission by disseminating knowledge in the pursuit of education, learning and research at the highest international levels of excellence.

www.cambridge.org
Information on this title: www.cambridge.org/9781108789820
DOI: 10.1017/9781108804295

First published 2020
First paperback edition 2022

A catalogue record for this publication is available from the British Library

Library of Congress Cataloging in Publication data
Names: Nobili, Mauro, author.
Title: Sultan, caliph and the renewer of the faith : Ahmad Lobbo, the Tarikh alfattash and the making of an Islamic state in West Africa / Mauro Nobili.
Other titles: African studies series ; 148.
Description: Cambridge, United Kingdom ; New York, NY : Cambridge University Press, 2020. | Series: African studies series ; 148 | Includes bibliographical references and index.
Identifiers: LCCN 2019034626 | ISBN 9781108479509 (hardback) | ISBN 9781108789820 (paperback) | ISBN 9781108804295 (ebook)
Subjects: LCSH: Shehu Ahmadu Lobbo, 1775 or 1776–1844 or 1845. | Nūḥ ibn al-Ṭāhir, –1857 or 1858. | Tārīkh al-fattāsh. | Fula (African people) – Kings and rulers – Historiography. | Islam and state – Sudan (Region) – History – 19th century. | Macina – History – 19th century. | Hamdallahi (Mali) – History. | Inland Niger Delta (Mali) – History – 19th century. | Sudan (Region) – History – 19th century. | Macina – Historiography. | Sudan (Region) – Historiography.
Classification: LCC DT551.65 .N63 2020 | DDC 966.201–dc23
LC record available at https://lccn.loc.gov/2019034626

ISBN 978-1-108-47950-9 Hardback
ISBN 978-1-108-78982-0 Paperback

To Adama Ba and Mohamed Diagayeté,
who made me love, in very different ways,
the history of the Fulani

Contents

Figures

Maps

Tables

Acknowledgments

In the name of God, the Most Gracious and the Most Merciful, who guided me toward the daunting task of completing this book. I would have never been able to achieve this goal if I had not been lucky enough to have around me a supportive community of scholars and friends scattered across three continents who followed me during the many years of research that lie behind this work. So many people read parts of the book, discussed ideas, helped me in reading or locating primary sources, or simply supported me, that it is impossible to list them all in this acknowledgment. I apologize in advance for the people I have neglected.

I would like to start at the end, by thanking those who provided priceless support in the last part of the process: Charles C. Stewart (University of Illinois at Urbana-Champaign) and Bruce S. Hall (University of California, Berkeley) who read the first full draft of the manuscript; Carol Symes (University of Illinois at Urbana-Champaign), who edited the entire manuscript of the book twice, prior to its submission and again to publication; and Charlie English, who gave a final reading to the book. My thanks also go to Amir Syed (University of Pittsburgh), for the friendship and insights that he gave me throughout the writing process. I would like to acknowledge his wonderful family too: the time I spent with them provided me with the human warmth that was required to turn a rough draft into a book. Special mention goes also to Abubakar Abdulkadir (University of Alberta), Mohamed Diagayeté (Institut des Hautes Etudes et de Recherches Islamiques Ahmed Baba de Tombouctou – IHERI-ABT), and Hienin Ali Diakité (Hill Museum and Manuscript Library, Saint John's University), who helped read and translate several Arabic manuscripts while I was working on this project.

I completed this book while working at the University of Illinois at Urbana-Champaign, but the initial ideas were sketched far from the USA, in Cape Town, South Africa. During several working-night sessions with M. Shahid Mathee (University of Johannesburg), at his house, and with the logistical and emotional support of his wife Gadija Ahjum (University of Cape Town) and the kids, the intriguing first details of the story I tell in this book were disentangled. Many other people helped me in South Africa during the early stages of research, while I was a University Research Committee (URC) Post-Doctoral Fellow at the University of Cape Town: Shamil Jeppie and Andrea Brigaglia, co-principal investigators of my Post-Doctoral Fellowship; my friends and colleagues at the Tomb*ouct*ou Manuscripts Project, Rifqah Kahn, Susana Molins Lliteras, Samaila Suleiman, and Chapane Mutiua (the last two, currently at Bayero University – Kano, and University of Hamburg), who made my time there both productive and highly entertaining. Lastly, Andrea Brigaglia's family who had the patience to host me for two long years in Cape Town, and Abdul-Aleem Somers, on whose friendship and knowledge I relied so much during my time in South Africa.

I must also acknowledge the help of my colleagues in Mali: Abdulkadri Maiga, who was director of the IHERI-ABT during most of the writing of this book and gave me access to their manuscript collection; Sidi Allimam Maiga (IHERI-ABT), Saadou Traore, and Cheikh Hammou. Thanks are also due to my friend Seydou Traore: without him and his scooter I would not have known how to get around Bamako.

Several trips in other West African countries were required to collect all the materials I have used in my research. In Senegal, my deepest gratitude goes to the Coulibaly family, who hosted me several times in their Dakar home. At University Cheikh Anta Diop, the staff of the Laboratoire d'Islamologie at the Institut Fondamental d'Afrique Noire, Djim Dramé, Souleymane Gaye, and Oumou Kalsoum Ka, enabled my research. In Côte d'Ivoire, I was assisted by Moussa Konate (University Félix Houphouët–Boigny de Cocody) and Alfa Mamadou Diallo Lélouma; in Ghana, by Mohammed Amin Mahmud. In Nigeria and Mauritania, which I could not visit while working on the book, Salisu Bala (Ahmadu Bello University) and Mohameden Ahmed Salem Ahmedou proved to be wonderful supporters from afar.

At one point or another, all my colleagues at the University of Illinois at Urbana-Champaign have supported me during the writing process, especially during numerous sessions of our Pre-

Modern World Reading Group. Specifically, I want to mention our former chairs of the Department of History, Diane P. Koenker and Clare H. Crowston; the current occupant of that post, Dana Rabin, as well as Tariq O. Ali (now at Georgetown University), Teresa Barnes, Antoinette Burton, Jim R. Brennan, Ken M. Cuno, Behrooz Ghamari-Tabrizi (now at Princeton University), Marc A. Hertzman, Brian J. Jefferson, Craig M. Koslofsky, Wataru Morioka, Robert M. Morrisey, John Randolph, Maria Todorova, Roderick I. Wilson, Charlie D. Wright; my mentor Jerri Dávila; our Department of History staff, especially Tom L. Bedwell; our Library staff, Laila Hussein Moustapha, Celestina Savonius-Wroth, and Atoma Batoma; Maria Gillombardo in the Office of the Vice Chancellor for Research in Arts, Humanities, and Related Fields; and our Center for African Studies vice-director, Maimouna A. Barro, and the Office Support Specialist, Terri Gitler. Among the other US-based colleagues who have provided insights on my field of research, I must mention Rudolph "Butch" Ware (University of California, Santa Barbara), Graziano Krätli (Yale University), Scott S. Reese (University of Northern Arizona), and Muhammad Shareef (The Sankore' Institute of Islamic-African Studies International).

Other colleagues based in Europe also helped me while researching and writing this book, including Dmitry Bondarev and Darya Ogornodnikova (University of Hamburg), Jan Jansen and Warner Tjon Sie Fat (Leiden University), Ann Mayor (University of Geneva), Paulo F. de Moraes Farias and Paul Naylor (University of Birmingham), and Bernard Salvaing (University of Nantes).

I also want to mention Gregory Mann and Mamadou Diouf (Columbia University), Robert Launay and Rebecca Shereikis (Northwestern University), Benedetta Rossi (University of Birmingham), Toby Green (King's College London), Ousmane O. Kane and Matthew Steele (Harvard University), and Roberto Zaugg (University of Bern) – all of whom invited me to present my work in symposiums, conferences, and invited lectures.

Several institutions and centers have financially supported parts of the research for the book: the Tomb*ouct*ou Manuscripts Project of the University of Cape Town; the West African Research Association; at the University of Illinois at Urbana-Champaign, the Department of History, the Center for African Studies, the Center for Advanced

Studies, the Office of the Vice Chancellor for Research in Arts, Humanities, and Related Fields; and the National Endowment for Humanities.

Finally, I would like to thank my parents, my brother and his family, who continue to inspire me however far I roam from their Italian shore.

Notes on Orthography and Other Conventions

Transliteration

For transliteration from Arabic I have used the system employed by the *International Journal of Middle East Studies*, except for the *alif maqṣūra* (ى), which is transliterated as *à* instead of *ā*. Another exception to standard transliteration in English regards the word "chronicle" (تاريخ). Notwithstanding the common transliteration in Western scholarship of the Arabic term as *ta'rīkh*, the infinitive of the second form, the most correct one, which I use in my book, is *tārīkh*, with the long a instead of the *hamzat al-qaṭ'* (see Ibn Manẓūr, *Lisān al-'arab* [Cairo, Dār al-Ma'ārif, n.d.], vol. 1, 58).

As for the Fulfulde, I use the transliteration standards found in Donald W. Osborn, David J. Dwyer, and Joseph I. Donohoe, *Lexique Fulfulde (Maasina)–Anglais–Français: une compilation baséee sur racines et tirée de sources existantes suivie de listes en Anglais–Fulfude et Français–Fulfulde = A Fulfulde (Maasina)–English–French Lexicon: A Root-Based Compilation Drawn from Extant Sources Followed by English–Fulfulde and French–Fulfulde Listings* (East Lansing: Michigan State University Press, 1993).

Toponyms

Place names follow the conventions of respective countries. For instance, Malian places will normally follow French standards, whereas Nigerian ones follow English spellings. However, a few exceptions have been made, i.e. Timbuktu in place of Tombouctou, Masina for Macina, Azawād in place of Azaouad. In the cases of toponyms in Arabic manuscripts that no longer exist, or that I could not locate, I use the transliteration from the Arabic.

Names of People

Referring to names of people from sources written in many languages and different standards of spelling and transliterations represents a challenge. Trying as much as possible to avoid inaccuracies and inconsistencies, and for sake of identification and searchability, I have used for names of known Muslim scholars from West Africa the form recorded in the reference work John O. Hunwick et al., *The Arabic Literature of Africa*, 5 vols. (Leiden and Boston: Brill, 1993–) in the first instance, and later on in abbreviated forms. Regarding names of scholars from the larger Islamic world, for the same reasons, I use the form of the *Encyclopaedia of Islam*, 2nd edition, edited by P. J. Bearman et al. (Leiden: Brill, 1954–2007).

Two names require special attention: those of the two most referred characters of the book, Aḥmad Lobbo and Nūḥ b. al-Ṭāhir. Aḥmad Lobbo's full name appears in *The Arabic Literature of Africa* as Aḥmad B. Muḥammad Būbū b. Abī Bakr b. Sa'īd al-Fullānī. In the Middle Niger Aḥmad Lobbo is normally referred to as Seeku Aamadu, an adaptation of the Arabic title *shaykh* in Fulfulde and the rendering in the same language of the name Aḥmad. I have preferred the form Aḥmad Lobbo, which is the most widespread in the English literature on West African history. As for Nūḥ b. al-Ṭāhir, locally referred as Alfa Nuhu Tayrou, from the honorific title *alfa* and the Fulfulde rendering of his Arabic name, I have preferred to keep his name in Arabic, Nūḥ b. al-Ṭāhir, in line with the form that appears in the manuscripts and also approximating the form in *The Arabic Literature of Africa*.

For names that do not appear in *The Arabic Literature of Africa* and in the *Encyclopaedia of Islam*, I have employed the forms that is available in the Arabic manuscripts I refer to. An exception was made for the name Gelaajo, which figures with a very unstable form in the Arabic sources which struggle to reproduce Fulani names. The form "Gelaajo" follows my choice of spelling Fulani names that do not appear in Arabic sources according to the norms of transliterations referred to in the abovementioned *Lexique Fulfulde (Maasina)*.

Dates

I have normally only used Gregorian dates, except when citing a source that is dated according to the Islamic calendar. In this latter case I use both dates, with the Islamic calendar first, followed by the appropriate conversion in Gregorian.

Translations

I have consistently used available translations into English of texts from other languages. Mine are the translations from texts that are not available in English.

References to Manuscripts

Referencing manuscripts that normally show different systems of foliation or pagination is problematic. I used the existing references, to either folios (f.) or pages (p.) when available in the manuscript. In the absence of existing foliation or pagination, I have numbered myself the pages, starting with the one that includes the incipit of the text (thus not numbering frontispieces).

Introduction

This book is a study of the West African chronicle known as the *Tārīkh al-fattāsh* (The Chronicle of the Inquisitive Researcher) and its role in advancing a political project, the legitimation of the Caliphate of Ḥamdallāhi (1818–1862), located in what is now the Republic of Mali.[1] In reconstructing this story, I have brought together two bodies of literature that have often crossed paths, but whose relationship has not been fully explored until now. The first is the critical scholarship produced over the past hundred years or more on the *Tārīkh al-fattāsh*. The second is the scholarly literature on the eighteenth- and nineteenth-century West African Islamic revolutions and the Caliphate of Ḥamdallāhi.

Based on a thorough analysis of extant manuscript materials, my study contributes to a new understanding of the *Tārīkh al-fattāsh* and the events that called it into being. Since the time of its "discovery" by European travelers and scholars in the late nineteenth century, the chronicle has been understood to be a sixteenth- or seventeenth-century work that was subjected to later textual manipulation. In fact, as the research presented here will show, the *Tārīkh al-fattāsh* is a fully fledged nineteenth-century chronicle written by Nūḥ b. al-Ṭāhir (d. 1857–8), a Fulani scholar belonging to the elite of Ḥamdallāhi, who composed it to enhance the legitimacy of the founding ruler of the caliphate, Aḥmad Lobbo (d. 1845), during a time of competing claims to authority in the Middle Niger. Nūḥ b. al-Ṭāhir did not, however, compose the *Tārīkh al-fattāsh* from scratch, but produced it by modifying an older chronicle, which I have named the *Tārīkh Ibn al-Mukhtār*, or "The Chronicle of Ibn al-Mukhtār," after the author

[1] As explained below, the *Tārīkh al-fattāsh* only exists in printed form in a flawed edition (Octave V. Houdas and Maurice Delafosse [ed. and trans.], *Tarikh el-fettach par Mahmoud Kati et l'un de ses petit fils ou Chronique du chercheur pour servir à l'histoire des villes, des armées et des principaux personnages du Tekrour* [Paris: Ernest Leroux, 1913] [henceforth *La chronique du chercheur*]).

who wrote it during the second half of the seventeenth century. Nūḥ b. al-Ṭāhir transformed the *Tārīkh Ibn al-Mukhtār* into a new work by extensively refashioning its text and introducing an authoritative prophecy dating to the time of the Songhay Empire (1468–1591), which "foretells" the advent of Aḥmad Lobbo. Eventually, he ascribed the complete work to the sixteenth-century scholar Maḥmūd Ka'ti b. al-Ḥājj al-Mutawakkil Ka'ti al-Kurminī al-Tinbuktī al-Wa'kurī, known more simply as Maḥmūd Ka'ti (d. 1593).[2]

My unmasking of this very skillful textual manipulation represents the first historiographical contribution of my book: I unravel the complex history of the *Tārīkh al-fattāsh*, which has caused scholars to spill much ink since the 1890s, when the French journalist Albert Félix Dubois (d. 1945) first heard of it while in West Africa. However, as Marc Bloch underlines in his classic meditation, *The Historian's Craft*:

> To establish the fact of forgery is not enough. It is further necessary to discover its motivations ... Above all, a fraud is, in its way, a piece of evidence. Merely to prove that the famous charter of Charlemagne to the church of Aix-la-Chapelle is not authentic is to avoid an error, but not to acquire knowledge. On the other hand, should we succeed in proving that the forgery was committed by the followers of Frederick Barbarossa, and that it was designed to implement dreams of imperial grandeur, we open new vistas upon the vast perspectives of history.[3]

In the case of the *Tārīkh al-fattāsh*, simply identifying the sections of the chronicle that were forged to support Aḥmad Lobbo will prevent scholars from using these nineteenth-century passages as evidence for earlier history. Moreover, a serious inquiry into the history of the *Tārīkh al-fattāsh* can do much more than correct potential anachronisms. The very fact of the chronicle's production in the nineteenth century triggers a set of new historical questions: Why did a supporter of Aḥmad Lobbo and of the caliphate manipulate older

[2] With the generous support of a National Endowment for Humanities – Scholarly Editions and Translations grant, I am currently preparing, with Ali H. Diakité, (Hill Museum and Manuscript Library, Saint John's University) and Zachary Wright (Northwestern University in Qatar) a new critical edition and translation of the *Tārīkh Ibn al-Mukhtār* and of the *Tārīkh al-fattāsh*.

[3] Marc Bloch, *The Historian's Craft: Reflections on the Nature and Uses of History and the Techniques and Methods of Those Who Write It*, trans. Peter Putnam (New York: Vintage Books, 2009), 93.

texts? Why was Aḥmad Lobbo in need of this intervention? And what kind of state did he rule over? Answering these questions opens new windows on the history of the Caliphate of Ḥamdallāhi, and on wider issues of legitimacy, authority, and the status of literacy and its political functions in nineteenth-century West Africa – with further implications for a broader understanding of the region within the Islamic ecumene. In addition to proving that the *Tārīkh al-fattāsh* is a nineteenth-century chronicle written to bolster the Caliphate of Ḥamdallāhi, *Sultan, Caliph, and the Renewer of the Faith* seeks to answer these other historical questions.[4]

The Caliphate of Ḥamdallāhi

Because this book is a study of the *Tarīkh al-fattāsh* and its production in a specific context, the Caliphate of Ḥamdallāhi, I begin with a brief historical survey of this state, which is still quite sparsely documented. To date, the most comprehensive studies are the classic work by Amadou Hampaté Ba and the French ichthyologist Jacques Daget, *L'empire peul du Macina, 1818–1853*, first published in 1955;[5] and the study of the historian Bintou Sanankoua, entitled *Un empire peul au XIXe siècle: la Diina du Maasina*, published in 1990.[6] In addition to these monographs, another important, but unpublished contribution is the 1969 Ph.D. dissertation of William A. Brown, "The Caliphate of

[4] I expand here on a theory that I have already sketched in Mauro Nobili and M. Shahid Mathee, "Towards a new study on the *Tārīkh al-fattāsh*," *History in Africa* 42 (2015): 37–73; Mauro Nobili, "A propaganda document in support of the 19th century Caliphate of Ḥamdallāhi: Nūḥ b. al-Ṭāhir al-Fulānī's 'Letter on the appearance of the twelfth caliph' (*Risāla fī ẓuhūr al-khalīfa al-thānī 'ashar*)," *Afriques* 7 (2016) [http://journals.openedition.org/afriques/1922]; and Mauro Nobili, "New reinventions of the Sahel: reflections on the *tārīḫ* genre in the Timbuktu historiographical production, seventeenth to twentieth centuries," in *Landscapes, Sources and Intellectual Projects of the West African Past: Essays in Honour of Paulo Fernando de Moraes Farias*, edited by Toby Green and Benedetta Rossi (Leiden and Boston: Brill, 2018), 201–219.

[5] *L'empire peul* was first published in 1955 (Amadou Hampaté Ba and Jacques Daget, *L'empire peul du Macina, 1818–1853* [Dakar: Institut Français d'Afrique Noire, 1955]) and then reprinted several times. In this book, I used a 1980s reprint (Amadou Hampâté Ba and Jacques Daget, *L'empire peul du Macina, 1818–1853* [Abidjan: Les Nouvelles Éditions Africaines, 1984] [henceforth *L'empire peul*]).

[6] Bintou Sanankoua, *Un empire peul au XIXe siècle: La Diina du Maasina* (Paris: Karthala/ACCT, 1990).

Hamdullahi, ca. 1818–1864: A Study in African History and Tradition."[7] These three studies, which only provide cursory references to the *Tārīkh al-fattāsh*, differ substantially from each other.[8] *L'empire peul du Macina* is a problematic account of the history of the caliphate, in which source-driven narratives are often intertwined with more imaginative reconstructions by the authors.[9] Sanankoua's work is an expansion of her Ph.D. dissertation and, although much less comprehensive, *Un empire peul* remains a valuable account of the caliphate that dedicates ample space to its administration.[10] Brown's dissertation is a very different type of work. Rough, sometimes resembling a series of extensive notes, it offers a thematic history that provides an indispensable foundation for any study of Ḥamdallāhi. [MAPS 1 and 2]

All of these works employ different names for the state founded by Aḥmad Lobbo, which extended over much of the Middle Niger, a region that can be roughly defined as the strip of land along the Niger between the Malian towns of Ké-Macina (65 miles east of Segou) and Gourma Rharous (72 miles east of Timbuktu).[11] Hampaté Ba and

[7] William A. Brown, "The Caliphate of Hamdullahi, ca. 1818–1864: A Study in African History and Tradition" (Ph.D. dissertation, University of Wisconsin, 1969). Another important contribution, although much more limited in scope and length, is Marion Johnson's article on the economic foundations of the caliphate, which focuses on taxation, trade, and production: Marion Johnson, "The economic foundations of an Islamic theocracy: The case of Masina," *Journal of African History* 17/4 (1976): 481–495. See also the short biographies of Aḥmad Lobbo: Mamadou Diallo, "Sekou Amadou," in *Culture et civilisation islamiques: Le Mali*, edited by Abdelhadi Boutaleb (Casablanca: Organisation islamique pour l'éducation, les sciences et la culture, 1408), 163–166; Mohamed Diagayeté, "Aḥmad Lobbo (1776–1845): His works and correspondence," *Annual Review of Islam in Africa* 12/2 (2015): 67–70.

[8] For references to the *Tārīkh al-fattāsh* in these works, see *L'empire peul*, 280; Brown, "The Caliphate of Hamdullahi," 7; Sanankoua, *Un empire peul*, 84.

[9] On this aspect of Hampaté Ba and Daget's work, see Bernard Salvaing, "La question de l'influence de la Qādiriyya sur les débuts du califat de Ḥamdullāhi" (unpublished paper).

[10] Bintou Sanankoua-Diarrah, "L'organisation politique du Maasina (Diina), 1818–1862" (Ph.D. dissertation, Paris I – Sorbonne, 1982).

[11] The Middle Niger was a multi-ethnic region inhabited by the semi-nomadic river folk usually referred to as Bozo, the Somono, who were boatmen, the agriculturalist Bambara, Dogon, and Marka (the latter also devoted to trade), as well as the herdsman Fulani, Arabs and Tuareg, and the Songhay, who specialize in different occupations. Good introductions to the geography and the people of the Middle Niger are Jean Gallais, *Le delta intérieur du Niger: étude de géographie régionale*, 2 vols. (Dakar: IFAN, 1967); Roderick J. McIntosh, *The Peoples of the Middle Niger: The Island of Gold* (Malden, MA: Blackwell,

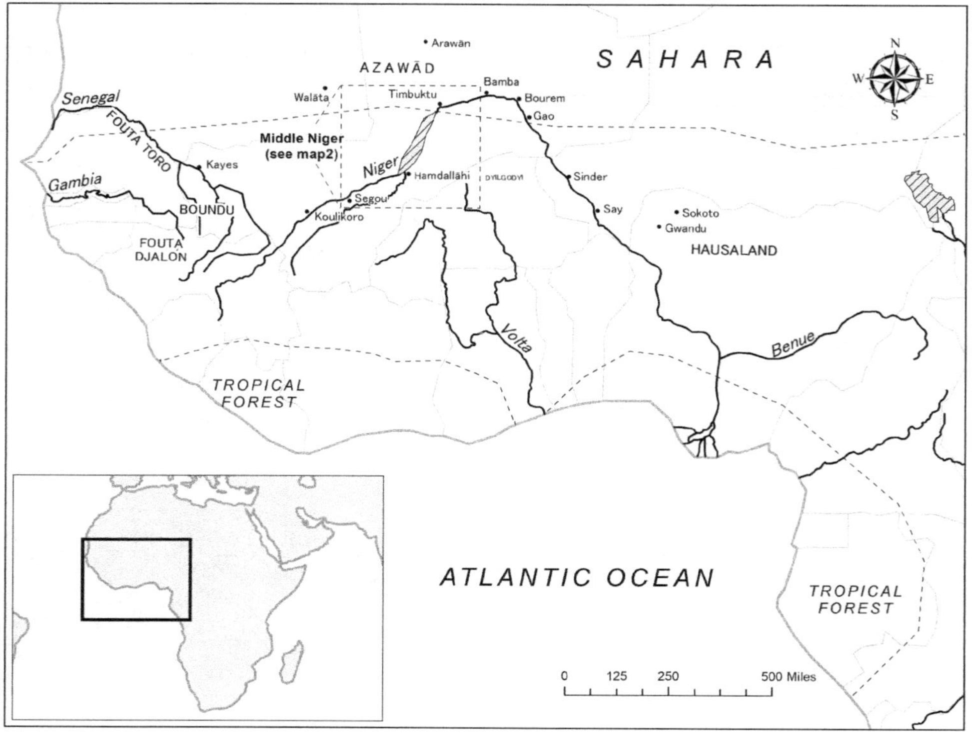

Map 1: West Africa (Copyright Wataru Morioka)

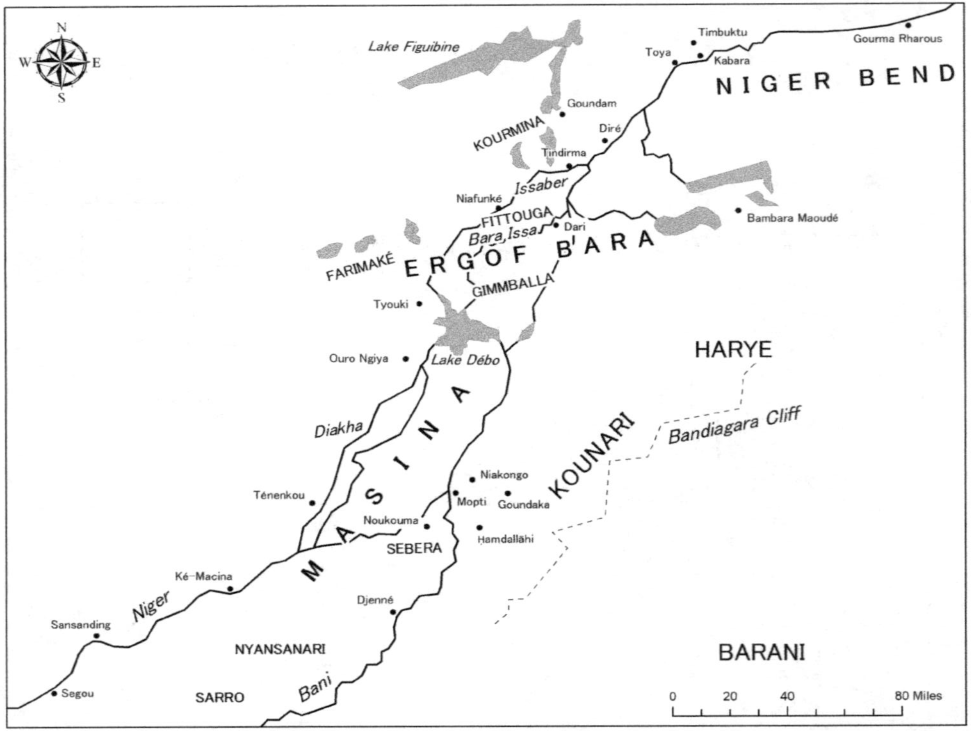

Map 2: The Middle Niger (Copyright Wataru Morioka)

Daget name it the Fulani Empire of Masina, with explicit reference to the ethnicity of Aḥmad Lobbo and many of his followers, the Fulani, and to the region in which the movement emerged, Masina, a toponym often used in reference to the floodplain of the Inland Delta Niger.[12] Sanankoua adopts the term Diina, from the Arabic *dīn* (religion), which is the name preferred by the people of central Mali. Brown chooses the term Caliphate of Ḥamdallāhi, from the name of its capital.[13] I have aligned myself with Brown's choice, aware that the term "caliphate" and its definition are contentious in Islamic history.[14] Although originally designed to refer to the ultimate Muslim authority, as Mervyn Hiskett points out, "the title *khalīfa* became somewhat devalued in the course of the Middle Ages, in that it was used increasingly frequently by local Muslim rulers who had no serious claim to worldwide authority."[15] In nineteenth-century West Africa "the true significance" of the terms "caliph" and "caliphate" lies "in the fact that both of them imply absolute rejection of the secular and profane *mulk/malik*," i.e. "kingship" and "king."[16] Therefore, the name

1998); and Roderick J. McIntosh, *Ancient Middle Niger: Urbanism and the Self-Organizing Landscape* (Cambridge: Cambridge University Press, 2005).

12 The approximate limits of the modern Inland Delta Niger are Ké-Macina and the lakes Débo and Korientzé, with a total of about 21,000 square miles. The rise of the water in the Inland Delta is the result of the increased flow rate of the Niger and of the Bani as a consequence of the rainfalls upstream of the floodplain, in the Guinea highlands and in northwestern Côte d'Ivoire. Thus, while in the Inland Delta the river stays in its riverbed during the rainy season of June–September, its water then starts to increase, and reaches its highest levels in December and January, during the coldest time of the year. Later, in February, the level of the river decreases, and eventually, in May, during the hot season, the water reaches its lowest level. For a description of the seasonal cycle of the Middle Niger and of the water regime of the river, see Gallais, *Le delta intérieur*, vol. 1, 73–76.

13 The name of the capital was in fact Ḥamdallāhi, a Fulanized version of the Arabic al-ḥamdu li-[A]llāhi, "praise be to God" (Sanankoua, *Un empire peul*, 78).

14 In a recent study on the shifting definition of the caliphate, Hugh Kennedy underlines that "there is no one way, no single template or legal framework that defines caliphate ... There has never been one generally agreed view of what powers the office should have, who is qualified to be caliph and how caliphs should be chosen" (Hugh Kennedy, *Caliphate: The History of an Idea* [New York: Basic Books, 2016], xvi–xvii).

15 Mervyn Hiskett, *The Development of Islam in West Africa* (London: Longman, 1987), 172.

16 Hiskett, *The Development of Islam*, 173. On the terms "caliph" and "caliphate," see D. Sourdel, A. K. S. Lambton, F. De Jong, and P. M. Holt, s.v.

that Brown employs captures the central claim made in the *Tārīkh al-fattāsh* that Aḥmad Lobbo was a West African caliph.

The establishment of the caliphate in the early nineteenth century put an end to a period of political fragmentation in the Middle Niger begun with the Moroccan conquest of the Songhay Empire in 1591.[17] By 1618 the Moroccan sultans stopped appointing the *pāshā*s, North African delegates who ruled the Middle Niger from their new capital in Timbuktu, and ceased sending replacements for the army – a clear sign of diminished interest in their territorial possession in West Africa. Eventually, by 1660, the one-time Moroccan "colony" became a de facto independent state on the Niger between Masina and Gao, usually referred to by historians as the Pāshālik of Timbuktu. The period of the pāshālik was characterized by the rule of more or less autonomous cities with garrisons under military leaders (*qā'id*), who were selected by the Arma, the descendants of Moroccan soldiers who had settled in the sub-Saharan region and intermarried locally, developing into a warrior class of mestizo Songhay.[18] The Arma garrisons' commandants acknowledged, at least formally, the authority of the *pāshā* of Timbuktu, but

"Khalīfa," in *Encyclopaedia of Islam 2nd edition*, edited by P. J. Bearman et al. (Leiden: Brill, 1954–2007) (henceforth EI^2), 937–953.

17 For a study of the Moroccan conquest and of the Songhay resistance, see Lansine Kaba, "Archers, musketeers, and mosquitoes: The Moroccan invasion of the Sudan and the Songhay resistance (1591–1612)," *Journal of African History* 22 (1981): 457–75. The fall of the Songhay state and period that followed are analyzed in detail in Michel Abitbol, *Tombouctou et les arma: de la conquête marocaine du soudan nigérien en 1591 à l'hégémonie de l'empire peulh du macina en 1833* (Paris: G.-P. Maisonneuve et Larose, 1979); and Elizabeth Hodgkin, "Social and Political Relations on the Niger Bend in the Seventeenth Century" (Ph.D. dissertation, Birmingham University, 1987). See also Fatima Harrak and El Houssain El Moujahid (eds.), *Le Maroc et l'Afrique subsaharienne aux débuts des temps modernes: les Sa'adiens et l'empire Songhay: actes du colloque international organisé par l'Institut des études africaines, Marrakech, 23–25 octobre 1992* (Rabat: Publication de l'Institut des Études Africaines, 1995).

18 Scholars, starting with Paul Marty, *Islam et les tribus du Soudan*, vol. 2:*La région de Tombouctou (Islam Songaï): Dienné, le Macina et dépenances (Islam Peul)* (Paris: Leroux, 1920), 7, derive the term "Arma" from the Arabic *al-rumāt*, plural form of *al-rāmin*, "rifleman." Hodgkin advances an alternative hypothesis, derived from a note by Paulo F. de Moraes Farias in a personal communication, according to which "in Spanish and Portuguese arma means not only weapons but also each of the different corps within the army, the infantry, artillery, etc. In this context it should be remembered that Spanish was the lingua franca of the Arma, at least in the early years" (Hodgkin, "Social and Political Relations," 19, n. 1).

the *qā'id*s enforced an indirect rule in these city-states, leaving the administration mainly in the hands of traditional authorities. No real influence was established outside these Arma-ruled cities of the Middle Niger and the Niger Bend, such as Djenné, Timbuktu, Bamba, and Gao.

Among the territories under the Arma's dominion, Masina was only loosely controlled. In fact, the emergence of the pāshālik overlapped in the area with that of nomad Fulani warrior aristocracies. Each Fulani clan was led by a chief, or *arɗo* in Fulfulde, and all the *arɗo*s, in turn, recognized the authority of the *arɗo mawɗo*, or "great *arɗo*." The latter was the chief of Masina, and belonged to the military elite of the Dikko, a sub-clan of the Jalluɓe, who gravitated around the area of Ouro Ngiya, southwest of the Lake Débo. The Fulani elites never really imposed a centralized state in the region, but remained satisfied with their nomadic lifestyle. More concrete control was exercised, starting from the eighteenth century, by the Bambara *fama*s ("kings" in Bambara) of Segou, first with Biton Koulibaly (r. 1712–1755) and then under the Diarra dynasty (1766–1861).[19]

By the late 1810s the rising discontent over the political situation of Masina, characterized by the dominion of the powerful Bambara *fama*s and the local Fulani warrior aristocracy, led an increasingly large number of followers to rally around Aḥmad Lobbo, a member of the Sangaré-Bari sub-clan of the Fittooɓe, and future caliph of Ḥamdallāhi. Initially, Aḥmad Lobbo avoided entering into conflict with the local military elites, but he had an increasingly tense relationship with the religious establishment of Djenné, the most important scholarly center of the southern Middle Niger. However, the stronger the opposition of the religious authorities was, the larger the group of Aḥmad Lobbo's partisans became.[20] The composition of his

19 On the Bambara state of Segou, see the classic Charles Monteil, *Les Bambara du Segou et du Kaarta: étude historique, ethnographique et litteraire d'une peuplade du Soudan Français* (Paris: Maisonneuve, 1977), 3–102; Louis Tauxier, *Histoire des Bambara* (Paris: P. Geuthner, 1942); or the more recent Richard L. Roberts, *Warriors, Merchants, and Slaves: The State and the Economy in the Middle Niger Valley, 1700–1914* (Stanford: Stanford University Press, 1987), 21–71; and Sundiata A. Djata, *The Bamana Empire by the Niger: Kingdom, Jihad, and Colonization, 1712–1920* (Princeton: Markus Wiener, 1997).

20 For an analysis of the socio-economic discontent of the people of the southern Middle Niger at the dawn of Ḥamdallāhi, see Brown, "The Caliphate of Hamdullahi," 110–116.

supporters – rural scholars, Fulani not belonging to the warrior aristocracy, and Marka communities – indicates that Aḥmad Lobbo had gathered around him those with a shared animosity toward the Djenné elite, the Fulani nobility, and the Bambara overlords.[21] At the time, a reciprocal relationship existed between the Muslim scholars of Djenné, the Arma, the Fulani Dikko, and the Bambara overlords, all of whom supported and legitimized each other to maintain the status quo. The tension between the scholarly elite of Djenné and Aḥmad Lobbo eventually translated into his followers' open hostility toward the Fulani military aristocracies and the Bambara of Segou. This hostility crystallized in the aftermath of the "incident of Simay," which took place sometime in 1816–17.

According to oral traditions, this event took place after the ruler of Djenné ordered Aḥmad Lobbo and his followers to abandon his house there. While Aḥmad Lobbo was delaying his departure, one of his disciples met Arɗo Giɗaaɗo, son of Arɗo Aamadu, the acting *arɗo mawɗo* of the Middle Niger, in the market of Simay, a village located just north of Djenné. There, Arɗo Giɗaaɗo mistreated Aḥmad Lobbo's disciple and urged him to tell his master to leave the area. To add insult to injury, Arɗo Giɗaaɗo stole the disciple's robe. Aḥmad Lobbo, who had gained strong support among the inhabitants of the region, then directly challenged the authority of the *arɗo*. He sent another of his disciples, Ali Giɗaaɗo, to the same market the next week, with the charge of asking the *arɗo* to give back the robe he had stolen. He further instructed that, if Arɗo Giɗaaɗo was unwilling, he should be killed. As expected, Arɗo Giɗaaɗo refused to return the stolen robe and began to insult Aḥmad Lobbo, provoking Ali Giɗaaɗo to kill the *arɗo*.

At this point, open conflict between Aḥmad Lobbo's followers and the Fulani warrior elite was inevitable. Arɗo Aamadou successfully sought the support of Da (d. 1827), the Bambara king of Segou, as

21 Scholars often describe the Caliphate of Ḥamdallāhi as the result of a Fulani upheaval (see, for example, Madina Ly-Tall, "Massina and the Torodbe (Tukuloor) Empire until 1878," in *General History of Africa*, vol. 6: *Africa in the Nineteenth Century until the 1880s*, edited by J. F. Ade Ajayi [Paris: UNESCO, 1989], 600–635, 601; and Murray Last, "Reform in West Africa: The jihād movements of the nineteenth century," in *History of West Africa*, vol. 2, edited by J. F. Ade Ajayi and Michael Crowder [Harlow: Longman, 1987], 1–47, 33). However, the inter-ethnic composition of the movement led by Aḥmad Lobbo was built around the need to challenge the local authorities, both religious and political, and to revoke Segou overlordship from the area.

well as other Fulani warriors, including Gelaajo, the *pereejo* (chief) of the Sidibe military aristocracy of Kounari.[22] Their combined army moved against Aḥmad Lobbo and his followers, who had retreated to Noukouma (about 18 miles southwest of Mopti). On Saturday 21 March 1818 the Bambara soldiers attacked before the arrival of Arɗo Aamadu and Gelaajo. Under circumstances that remain unclear, and which tradition depicts as heroic, if not divinely ordained, the Bambara soldiers were defeated. Discouraged by this, the Fulani chiefs decided to abandon the war. By contrast, the ranks of Aḥmad Lobbo swelled substantially after the victory at Noukouma, allowing his followers to pursue and defeat their enemies, so that by mid-May 1818 Aḥmad Lobbo emerged as the leader of a new state centered in Masina.

By the mid-1820s Aḥmad Lobbo had consolidated his control over the southern Middle Niger and the plains between the Niger and the Bandiagara cliff, as well as the Erg of Bara and the rocky region of Hayre east of it. His capital at Ḥamdallāhi (about 13 miles southeast of Mopti), which was founded around 1821, developed as the administrative center of this new state.[23] The history of this caliphate is characterized by

22 Equivalent to *arɗo*, the title *pereejo* is used for the chiefs of the Sidibe clan (Donald W. Osborn, David J. Dwyer, and Joseph I. Donohoe, *Lexique Fulfulde (Maasina) –Anglais–Français: une compilation basée sur racines et tirée de sources existantes suivie de listes en Anglais–Fulfude et Français–Fulfulde = A Fulfulde (Maasina) –English–French Lexicon: A Root-Based Compilation Drawn from Extant Sources Followed by English–Fulfulde and French–Fulfulde Listings* [East Lansing: Michigan State University Press, 1993], 87).

23 The foundation of the new capital, Ḥamdallāhi, was symbolic and strategic. From a symbolic point of view, the foundation of the city, dedicated to God's glory, marked a break with the hostile old centers of power, such as Djenné or the main *arɗo* settlement of Ouro Ngiya. However, practical concerns were also part of the decision to build the new capital. Ḥamdallāhi occupied a strategic location. It stood on the slope of a hill about 918 feet high, in thorny grassland. It was protected by the floodplain on its western side; but at the same time, from this side, it was close enough to the River Bani, which gave the capital access to the riverine transportation network. The Bandiagara plateau protected the city to the south and southeastern side, as did the rocky region of Kounari in the north. Unlike other cities of the region, such as Djenné, Segou, and Timbuktu, Ḥamdallāhi was not visited by any European traveler, and no direct account of it exists. Furthermore, in spite of its role as capital of the caliphate, it has never been subjected to any detailed study, with the exception of a section in Sanankoua's Ph.D. dissertation, later shortened in a chapter of her *Un empire peul* and a separate article (Sanankoua, "L'organisation politique," 122–174; Sanankoua, *Un empire peul*, 77–92; Bintu Sanakoua, "Hamdallaahi, capitale de la Diina," in *Boucle du Niger: approches multidisciplinairs*, edited by Junzo Kawada [Tokyo: Institut de Recherches sur les Langues et Cultures d'Asie

constant warfare until after Aḥmad Lobbo's death. Conflict with Segou continued on its western and southwestern fronts, as well as with smaller Bambara states such as Sarro and Nyansanari. This mostly consisted of intermittent skirmishes and raids. The conflict that emerged with the Bambara state of Kaarta, however, was more serious. In 1843–44, the army of Aḥmad Lobbo, led by his son Aḥmad b. Aḥmad b. Muḥammad Lobbo (d. 1853; henceforth Aḥmad II) suffered several losses. Thereafter, the borderland between the caliphate and the Bambara-dominated areas remained contested, although further Bambara attempts to penetrate the region controlled by the caliphate resulted in defeat. Every attempt by the caliphate to expand westward proved equally futile, thanks to the strength of states such as Segou and Kaarta.

On the southeastern front the policy of Ḥamdallāhi was much more aggressive and successful, most likely due to the absence of such centralized polities. The army of Ḥamdallāhi thus expanded into the region of Barani (Burkina Faso), which marked the southernmost limit of the caliphate. Ḥamdallāhi also attempted to extend its border further east and north, though the results were inconclusive. Several efforts were made to control the Fulani-dominated area of Dyilgodyi (Burkina Faso). Likewise, northeast of the Erg of Bara the expansionist policy of Ḥamdallāhi sought to secure control over the Niger Bend. After the first conquest of the region in 1826, the Arma and the Tuareg who inhabited the regions of Timbuktu and Azawād rebelled several times, trying to escape the imposition of direct rule by the caliphate. Control over these two regions remained weak enough for the local chiefs of Dyilgodyi and the Niger Bend, although they recognized the suzerainty of Ḥamdallāhi, to remain almost politically independent.

The caliphate founded by Aḥmad Lobbo, who died in 1845, lasted for almost half a century. His successors were his son Aḥmad II and his

et d'Afrique, 1990], 311–327); and of a few excavations carried on between the end of the 1980s and the early 1990s by the Mission Archéologique et Ethnoarchéologique Suisse en Afrique de l'Ouest – MAESAO (for a full bibliography of the MAESAO publications, see Alain Gallay et al., *Hier et aujourd'hui, des poteries et des femmes: céramiques traditionnelles du Mali: catalogue d'exposition, juin–oct. 1996; Genève, Muséum d'histoire naturelle* [Geneva: Département d'anthropologie et d'écologie de l'Université, 1996], 135–140). I thank Anne Mayor, who kindly shared this exhibition catalogue, as well as the MAESAO's publication Alain Gallay et al., *Hamdallahi, capitale de l'empire peul du Massina, Mali: première fouille archéologique, études historiques et ethnoarchéologiques* (Stuttgart: F. Steiner, 1990).

grandson Aḥmad b. Aḥmad b. Aḥmad b. Muḥammad Lobbo (d. 1862; henceforth Aḥmad III), who was captured and executed by another Fulani leader, 'Umar b. Sa'īd b. al-Mukhtār b. 'Alī b. al-Mukhtār, known as al-Ḥājj 'Umar (d. 1864), after his conquest of Ḥamdallāhi in 1862. However, the fact that the caliphate lasted until the early 1860s does not mean that Aḥmad Lobbo's authority had gone uncontested. On the contrary, his rule was characterized by challenges from different actors: the Fulani military aristocracies, the religious establishment of the Middle Niger, and the leaders of neighboring polities, including the powerful Fodiawa family who ruled over the Caliphate of Sokoto.

My study of the *Tārīkh al-fattāsh* locates the chronicle within the context of Aḥmad Lobbo's contested authority, which its text was devised to legitimate. Part of that contestation was directly connected to the historical dynamics in which Aḥmad Lobbo emerged, as an outsider, to challenge the established Fulani military aristocracies and the scholarly elites of the Middle Niger. But another part of the resistance to the rise of Ḥamdallāhi is connected to a broader transformation of the West African political landscape during this era, and the turmoil caused by a series of revolutions that enabled groups of Muslim scholars to seize political power.

The Islamic Revolutions in West Africa

The Caliphate of Ḥamdallāhi belongs to a series of revolutions led by Muslim scholars (*'ulamā'*) in West Africa during the eighteenth and nineteenth centuries.[24] The study of these movements, often referred to as *jihād*s, is almost as old as the academic discipline of African History.[25] It was inaugurated by Abdullahi (H. F. C.) Smith in

[24] As Rudolph T. Ware III points out, the terms "scholars" and its Arabic equivalent *'ulamā'* "carry a strong connotation of textual scholarship that does not fully capture the social role of learned people in earlier eras in West Africa" (Rudolph T. Ware III, *The Walking Qur'an: Islamic Education, Embodied Knowledge, and History in West Africa* [Chapel Hill: University of North Carolina Press, 2014], 78). I here use the terms "scholar" and *'ālim* with the broader meaning of a person who is literate in Arabic, with different degrees of advancement, and puts his knowledge to the service of his community, often receiving some kind of compensation in return.

[25] For a critique of the simplistic use of the term *jihād* in this literature, see Amir Syed, "Between jihād and history: Re-conceptualizing the Islamic revolutions of West Africa" in *Handbook of Islam in Africa*, edited by

a 1961 article, in which he described these movements as "neglected" because historians had mainly focused, at that time, on the growth of European imperialism in Africa.[26] A few years later, in 1967, Murray Last's classic monograph *The Sokoto Caliphate* and John R. Willis's article on the doctrinal basis of these movements marked the emergence of a series of works on the topic.[27] While studies on the Caliphate of Ḥamdallāhi are few, the body of literature on the West African revolutions today is so large that Benjamin F. Soares has called their study a "sub-discipline" of African History.[28]

Scholars have long debated whether these revolutions were related to one another.[29] The first one took place in the Senegal valley, beginning

Fallou Ngom, Mustapha Kurfi, and Toyin Falola (London: Palgrave, forthcoming).

26 H. F. C. [Abdullahi] Smith, "A neglected theme of West African history: The Islamic revolutions of the 19th century," *Journal of the Historical Society of Nigeria* 2/2 (1961): 169–185, 169.

27 Murray Last, *The Sokoto Caliphate* (New York: Humanities Press, 1967); John R. Willis, "*Jihād fī sabīl Allāh*: Its doctrinal basis in Islam and some aspects of its evolution in nineteenth-century West Africa," *Journal of African History* 8/3 (1967): 395–415. Crucial introductions on the topic of West African Islamic revolutions are Aziz A. Batran, "The nineteenth-century Islamic revolutions in West Africa," in *General History of Africa*. vol. 6: *Africa in the Nineteenth Century until the 1880s*, edited by J. F. A. Ajayi (Berkeley: UNESCO/University of California, 1989), 537–554; Peter B. Clarke, *West Africa and Islam: A Study of Religious Development from the 8th to the 20th Century* (London: Arnold, 1984), 77–152; Mervyn Hiskett, "The nineteenth-century jihads in West Africa," in *The Cambridge History of Africa*, vol. 5: *From c. 1790 to c. 1870*, edited by John E. Flint (Cambridge: Cambridge University, 1976), 125–169; Hiskett, *The Development of Islam*, 138–193 and 227–243; Last, "Reform in West Africa"; Murray Last, "The Sokoto Caliphate and Borno," in *General History of Africa*, vol. 6, 555–599; Roman Loimeier, *Muslim Societies in Africa: A Historical Anthropology* (Bloomington: Indiana University Press, 2013), 108–129; Ly-Tall, "Massina and the Torodbe (Tukuloor) Empire"; David Robinson, "Revolutions in the Western Sudan," in *The History of Islam in Africa*, edited by Nehemia Levtzion and Randall L. Pouwels (Athens: Ohio University Press, 2000), 131–152; J. Spencer Trimingham, *A History of Islam in West Africa* (London: Oxford University Press, 1970), 155–218. In what follows, the focus is on the major monographs on the topic, leaving aside countless relevant articles, book chapters, and unpublished dissertations, as the overview of the monographs is in fact representative of the overall production on the topic.

28 Benjamin F. Soares, "The historiography of Islam in West Africa: An anthropologist's view," *Journal of African History* 55/1 (2014): 27–36, 29.

29 Different opinions are expressed, for example, by Philip D. Curtin, who argues for such continuity, and Hiskett and Loimeier, who have rejected this idea and suggested that the movements emerged in fact independently (Philip D. Curtin,

in the second half of the seventeenth century, as the result of a movement started by a Moorish scholar called Nāṣir al-Dīn (d. 1674), who created a fragile state on both sides of the river that lasted until around 1677. Possibly related to this movement is one that led to the foundation of a new state in Boundu (Senegal) during the late 1600s. In the following century two further revolutions were led by Fulani Muslim scholars, first in and in the Fouta Djalon plateau (Republic of Guinea) in the 1720s and then in Fouta Toro (Senegal) in the 1770s. These last three states persisted, with mixed fortunes, until the second half of the nineteenth century and the arrival of French colonial occupation. In Hausaland, roughly the territories dominated by Hausa-speaking population between the modern republics of Nigeria and Niger, another Fulani leader, ʿUthmān b. Muḥammad Fodiye b. ʿUthmān b. Ṣāliḥ Fūdī (d. 1817; henceforth ʿUthmān b. Fūdī) waged war against the king of Gobir and established another state centered around the newly built capital Sokoto in the early nineteenth century. The Sokoto Caliphate, governed by the descendants of ʿUthmān b. Fūdī, starting with his son, Muḥammad Bello b. ʿUthmān b. Muḥammad Fodiye (d. 1837), then expanded into the territories of modern Nigeria, Niger, and Cameroon, and lasted until British colonial conquest in 1903. Last in this series of revolutions, apart from the one led by Aḥmad Lobbo, is that by yet another Fulani scholar, al-Ḥājj ʿUmar, who started his movement in Fouta Djalon in the 1850s and then sought to expand into the Senegal valley. Stopped by the French, he moved eastward and conquered the kingdom of Segou and eventually the Caliphate of Ḥamdallāhi.[30]

A common feature of these Islamic revolutions was the foundation of states alternatively described as "empires," "imamates," or "caliphates," among other terms.[31] They were characterized by a certain

"Jihad in West Africa: Early phases and interrelations in Mauretania and Senegal," *Journal of African History* 12/1 [1971]: 11–24, 14; Hiskett, *The Development of Islam*, 157; Loimeier, *Muslim Societies in Africa*, 109–110).

30 To this list, some scholars add the movement led by Samori Toure, in a vast area covering the territories of contemporary eastern Guinea and Sierra Leone, southern Mali and Burkina Faso, and northern Côte d'Ivoire, as well as "a late series of lesser jihāds in the Senegambian region [... which] were directly linked to the dynamics of European expansion": Loimeier, *Muslim Societies in Africa*, 108. (See also Clarke, *West Africa and Islam*, 137–149; Hiskett, *The Development of Islam*, 232–243.)

31 Robinson, "Revolutions in the Western Sudan," 131.

degree of conformity to *siyāsa shar'iyya*, governance in accordance with various interpretations of Islamic law. However, each political system developed different structures along a "spectrum of expressions of rule" rather than modeling an ideal "Islamic state."[32] I will refer to these polities as "theocracies," by which I mean, quoting the old but still useful description by J. Spencer Trimingham, "the rule of a man or a clerical organization which lays claim to having a mandate from God."[33] A common factor in these revolutions was that Muslim scholars seized power and established, according to Rudolph T. Ware, "distinct forms of clerical rule."[34] As consequence of this phenomenon, in the words of John O. Hunwick, "*religious authorities* . . . become the government and attempt to exercise *secular power* with the weapons of religious ideology."[35] By "secular power" Hunwick means

> the power – grounded in (but not solely dependent on) access to armed might – to govern, that is to order society with hierarchies of power, to raise revenue, to defend itself and those it governs and, in some sense, to "provide" for its people. The term "secular" is used in the sense of an approach to power that is essentially pragmatic, that is not dictated by a religious or other ideology. Though it may accept and operate within the general culture of a religion, it is guided in most matters by principles of efficacy in carrying out the tasks of government it considers necessary to perform, and in maintaining itself in power.[36]

By "religious authority" – intended in this book as Islamic – Hunwick means

> an assumed authority to guide and order people's social – and to varying extents economic and political – lives in accordance with an interpretation of what the holders of such authority claim to be divine authority, which overrides authority established by "secular" powers. The authority, although characterized as "assumed," is nevertheless grounded in the ability of those

32 Loimeier, *Muslim Societies in Africa*, 108.
33 Trimingham, A History of Islam in West Africa, 160.
34 Rudolph T. Ware, "Slavery and Abolition in Islamic Africa, 1776–1905," in *The Cambridge World History of Slavery*, vol. 4: *AD 1804–AD 2016*, edited by David Eltis, Stanley L. Engerman, Seymour Drescher, and David Richardson (Cambridge: Cambridge University Press, 2017), 344–372, 348.
35 John O. Hunwick, "Secular power and religious authority in Muslim society: The case of Songhay," *Journal of African History* 37/2 (1996): 175–194, 178 (italics mine).
36 Hunwick, "Secular power and religious authority," 176.

who claim it to convince their fellowmen of their special access to "divine" authority and to be acting as agents for it.[37]

Hunwick's dichotomy between the "secular power" and the "religious authority" is obviously anachronistic – hence the use of quotation marks. As Talal Asad points out, "this separation of religion from power is a modern Western norm, the product of a unique post-Reformation history."[38] Therefore, it does not represent a priori reality. However, it comes close to describing the context of West African Islamic history in which Muslim scholars had, for a long time before the eighteenth century and often still until today, preferred to remove themselves from politics.[39]

Lamin Sanneh, in his *Beyond Jihad*, captures the normative position of these *'ulamā'*: "The clerics abjured political office for themselves and required rulers to recognize this clerical neutrality."[40] James Searing, too, observes of many West African jurists that they

> become the protectors of the Muslim community and wield substantial influence over something very much like "civil society" through their role as interpreters of Islamic law as long as they do not directly challenge the dynasties in power. The goal is the autonomy of Islam and Muslim communities under the guidance of religious scholars, not political power.[41]

Applying these correctives, it is possible to reframe Hunwick's dichotomy as between political and religious authority, but also to make explicit the difference between authority and power. Following Michael G. Smith's classic study of Zaria, *authority* refers to "the [perceived] right to make a particular decision and to command obedience."[42] As such, it is different from *power*, which is "the ability

37 Hunwick, "Secular power and religious authority," 176.

38 Talal Asad, *Genealogies of Religion: Discipline and Reasons of Power in Christianity and Islam* (Baltimore: Johns Hopkins University Press, 1993), 28.

39 In the *longue durée* history of African kingship, on the contrary, political authority had been often invested with a religious legitimacy attached to different types of African traditional religions; see, for example, Hanne Haour, *Rulers, Warriors, Traders, Clerics: The Central Sahel and the North Sea, 800–1500* (Oxford: Oxford University Press for the British Academy, 2007), 61.

40 Lamin O. Sanneh, *Beyond Jihad: The Pacifist Tradition in West African Islam* (New York: Oxford University Press, 2016), 8.

41 James Searing, "Islam, slavery and jihad in West Africa," *History Compass* 4/5 (2006): 761–779, 773.

42 Michael G. Smith, *Government in Zazzau, 1800–1950* (London: Oxford University Press, 1964), 18.

to act effectively on persons or things, [and] to take or secure decisions."[43] The normative position of the Muslim scholars was not therefore devoid of power; but that power was not exercised directly in the political sphere, which belonged to other kind of elites.

The separation of Muslim scholars from political power was the result of the clerics' incorporation into local social structures characterized by the presence of endogamous groups often referred to as "castes."[44] In the words of Tal Tamari, West African "castes form one of three social categories. The others are the 'nobles' or 'freeborn', and the slaves."[45] Muslim scholars eventually became one of these "castes," but with the capacity to incorporate their disciples within their ranks.[46] Ware points out that "endogamy," "social segregation," and "hierarchy" were the major characteristics of such groups.[47] I would add that a feature of such castes was also their exclusion from political power. As Tamari underlines, "caste persons are not allowed to exercise political power (except indirectly, as advisors to . . . nobles)."[48] Indeed, those Muslim scholars who did associate themselves with wielders of political power had done so mainly in the role of counsellor with different degrees of influence, as described in Nehemia Levtzion's classic study on the Volta Basin, *Muslims and Chiefs in West Africa*; and as Hunwick, Lansine Kaba, and Levtzion himself have brilliantly shown with regard to the *'ulamā'* of Timbuktu and the Songhay rulers.[49]

As Ware points out, "the difference between 'casted' people (griots, blacksmiths, leatherworkers, and so on) and [the] wellborn or nobles

[43] Smith, *Government in Zazzau*, 18.

[44] See Tamari's excellent study on the topic: Tal Tamari, *Les castes de l'Afrique occidentale: artisans et musiciens endogames* (Nanterre: Société d'ethnologie, 1998).

[45] Tal Tamari, "The development of caste systems in West Africa," *Journal of African History* 32/2 (1991): 221–250, 223.

[46] Ware, *The Walking Qur'an*, 83. [47] Ware, *The Walking Qur'an*, 82.

[48] Tamari, "The development of caste systems," 237.

[49] Hunwick, "Secular power and religious authority"; Lansine Kaba, "The pen, the sword, and the crown: Islam and revolution in Songhay reconsidered, 1464–1493," *Journal of African History* 25/3 (1984): 241–256; Nehemia Levtzion, *Muslims and Chiefs in West Africa: A Study of Islam in the Middle Volta Basin in the Pre-Colonial Period* (Oxford: Clarendon Press, 1968); Nehemia Levtzion, "Islam in West African politics: Accommodation and tension between the *'ulamā'* and the political authorities," *Cahiers d'Études Africaines* 18/3 (1979): 333–345.

was understood to be an embodied distinction."[50] Likewise, different spheres of authority were embodied in different groups. Scholars came to embody, in the eyes of Muslims and many non-Muslims, religious authority. Meanwhile, throughout the post-1591 history of the Middle Niger, political power was in the hands of what can best be defined as "warrior elites," such as the Bambara of Segou, the Dikko and Sidibe Fulani, and the Arma on the eve of Ḥamdallāhi's rise.[51] It was this long-standing division that was to be challenged by the Islamic revolutions: the bodily separation of political and religious authority. These two spheres of authority now came to be combined in the same person, whom one could call a scholar-ruler, represented by individuals such as Muḥammad Bello in Sokoto and by Aḥmad Lobbo in Ḥamdallāhi. I therefore use the term "revolution" for these movements. As Searing posits, "labeling jihad as 'revolutionary' ... emphasizes the exceptional character of jihad in West Africa."[52] These revolutions were not movements of revival, as Willis has argued.[53] They were not focused on the restoration of a preexisting conflation of political and religious authority, but on a novel change in which these two forms of authority became embodied in the same individual. Therefore, in order to understand these revolutions, one must go beyond a *histoire événementielle* of each, the biographies of their leaders, and the analysis of their writings or study of the administration of the theocracies they founded. Scholars should explore the foundations of these new leaders' authority and the legitimization processes behind it.

Old and New Approaches to Islamic Revolutions

Most of the works on West African Islamic revolutions approach the topic from the point of view of political history. Masterpieces of this

50 Ware, *The Walking Qur'an*, 82.

51 This expression was coined by Richard L. Roberts, who refers to Segou as a "warrior state" (Roberts, *Warriors, Merchants, and Slaves*, 22 *et passim*). Roberts's concept can be extended to other states of the time, since "warfare was an inseparable component of the political economy of the Middle Niger valley" (Roberts, *Warriors, Merchants, and Slaves*, 17).

52 Searing, "Islam, slavery and jihad," 771.

53 Willis, "*Jihād fī sabīl Allāh*," 395. As Soares notes, instead of understanding the militarization and direct involvement in politics of Muslim scholars as a break with tradition, this phenomenon has been described as a form of normative relationship between Muslim scholars and political authorities, to the detriment of other historical experiences, both more ancient as well as contemporary (Soares, "The historiography of Islam in West Africa," 30).

genre are the above-mentioned monograph by Last and a complementary work by R. E. Adeleye.[54] Together, they provide indispensable analyses of the Sokoto Caliphate and describe the structures of the theocracy established by 'Uthmān b. Fūdī. Similar in depth and scope is David Robinson's work on the movement led by al-Ḥājj 'Umar, which sketches the history of this leader's rise to power, combining elements of economic and military history.[55] Madina Ly-Tall's study of al-Ḥājj 'Umar is also focused on politics, although she provocatively represents this movement as an anti-colonial one.[56] Slightly different from these works is Joseph P. Smaldone's military history of warfare and state formation in Sokoto, which argues that the state's structure was effectively shaped by the organization of the army, and vice versa.[57]

Another approach to the history of West African Islamic revolutions has focused on the biographies of their great leaders. To this trend belongs the study on al-Ḥājj 'Umar by Willis, as well as the work on 'Uthmān b. Fūdī by Hiskett, who places these leaders in the intellectual context in which these leaders were formed and to which they substantially contributed.[58] In the past three decades there have been more studies on revolutionary leaders' roles as intellectuals, an approach mainly developed with respect to the members of the Fodiawa family of 'Uthmān b. Fūdī. An excellent overview of the intellectual contributions made by the family of Sokoto's leaders is provided by Ahmad M. Kani.[59] Other similar works focus on individual Fodiawa scholars, such as the introduction to the works of 'Uthmān b. Fūdī by

[54] Last, *The Sokoto Caliphate*; Rowland A. Adeleye, *Power and Diplomacy in Northern Nigeria, 1804–1906: The Sokoto Caliphate and its Enemies* (London: Longman, 1977).

[55] David Robinson, *The Holy War of Umar Tal: The Western Sudan in the Mid-Nineteenth Century* (Oxford: Oxford University Press, 1985).

[56] Madina Ly-Tall, *Un Islam militant en Afrique de l'ouest aux XIX siècle: la Tijaniyya de Saïku Umar Futiyu contre les pouvoirs traditionnels et la puissance coloniale* (Paris: L'Harmattan, 1991).

[57] Joseph P. Smaldone, *Warfare in the Sokoto Caliphate: Historical and Sociological Perspectives* (Cambridge: Cambridge University Press, 1977).

[58] Mervyn Hiskett, *The Sword of Truth: The Life and Times of the Shehu Usuman Dan Fodio*, 2nd ed. (Evanston: Northwestern University Press, 1994); John R. Willis, *In the Path of Allah Umar: An Essay into the Nature of Charisma in Islam* (London: Frank Cass, 1989).

[59] Ahmad M. Kani, *The Intellectual Origin of Islamic Jihad in Nigeria* (London: al-Hoda, 1988).

Seyni Moumouni.[60] This book parallels the contemporary efforts of Sidi M. Mahibou, who reconstructed the intellectual biography of 'Uthmān b. Fūdī's erudite brother 'Abd Allāh b. Muḥammad Fodiye b. 'Uthmān Muḥammad b. Ṣāliḥ (d. 1829; henceforth 'Abd Allāh b. Fūdī) with particular emphasis on his political thought.[61] Oddly, no published work yet exists on the second ruler of Sokoto, Muḥammad Bello.[62] By contrast, extensive research has been carried out on Muḥammad Bello's sister, the prolific daughter of 'Uthmān b. Fūdī, Asmā' bt. 'Uthmān b. Muḥammad Fodiye, known as Nana Asmā'u (d. 1864).[63]

Yet this extensive literature seems to neglect what Robinson has called the "the fundamental problem faced by all of these movements ... the question of legitimation: who had the authority to declare a jihad and to take charge of an emerging Islamic state?"[64] When scholars have touched sporadically on the issue of authority, they have made vague references to the Weberian idea of "charisma."[65] A case in point is Willis's monograph on al-Ḥājj 'Umar.[66] Likewise, John H. Hanson's excellent study of the states that originated from al-Ḥājj 'Umar's movement takes charisma as a starting point of his

60 Seyni Moumouni, *Vie et oeuvre du Cheik Uthmân Dan Fodio, 1754–1817: de l'Islam au Soufisme* (Paris: L'Harmattan, 2008).

61 Sidi M. Mahibou, *Abdullahi Dan Fodio et la théorie du gouvernement Islamique* (Paris: L'Harmattan, 2010).

62 Several Ph.D. dissertations provide intellectual sketches of Muhammad Bello; see, for example, M. T. M. Minna, "Sultan Muhammad Bello and his Intellectual Contribution to the Sokoto Caliphate" (Ph.D. dissertation, School of Oriental and African Studies, 1992), which I cite in this book.

63 Jean Boyd, *The Caliph's Sister: Nana Asma'u 1793–1865. Teacher, Poet and Islamic Leader* (London: Frank Cass, 1989); Jean Boyd and Beverly B. Mack, *Collected Works of Nana Asma'u, Daughter of Usman Dan Fodiyo (1793–1864)* (East Lansing: Michigan State University Press, 1997); Beverly B. Mack and Jean Boyd, *One Woman's Jihad: Nana Asma'u, Scholar and Scribe* (Bloomington: Indiana University Press, 2000).

64 Robinson, "Revolutions in the Western Sudan," 132.

65 Amir Syed, "al-Ḥājj 'Umar Tāl and the Realm of the Written: Mastery, Mobility and Islamic Authority in 19th Century West Africa" (Ph.D. dissertation, University of Michigan, 2016), 17–18. For a discussion on the applicability of the Weberian concept of authority to Islamic African contexts, see Donal B. Cruise O'Brien, "Introduction," in *Charisma and Brotherhood in African Islam*, edited by Donal B. Cruise O'Brien and Christian Coulon (Oxford: Clarendon Press, 1989), 1–31.

66 Willis, *In the Path of Allah*.

inquiry.[67] But as for the legitimization of such authority, research is nearly non-existent.

To quote from Bloch's influential study of authority in medieval Europe, *The Royal Touch*:

> In order to understand what monarchies were in former times ... it will not be enough to enter into the most minute details of the workings of the administrative, judicial and financial organization which they imposed upon their subjects. Neither will it be enough to conduct an abstract analysis, nor to attempt to extract from a few great theories the concepts of absolutism or divine right. We must also fathom the beliefs and fables that grew up around the princely houses.[68]

Bloch's focus on the belief systems surrounding rulers called for a *histoire des mentalités* that encompassed political, intellectual, and religious domains. In our case, such an inquiry includes exploration of the foundations of authority and the mechanisms of legitimization that characterized West African Islamic revolutions and the theocracies that emerged from them. This calls for a more sophisticated understanding of local Islamic epistemologies. As intellectual historian Quentin Skinner underlines, historians need seriously to engage "what different peoples at different times may have had good reasons by their lights for holding true, regardless of whether we ourselves believe that what they held true was in fact the truth."[69]

This issue has been recently tackled by Scott S. Reese, who stresses, in his *Imperial Muslims*, the need to pay attention to the "agency of the 'unseen'."[70] By "unseen," Reese refers to the spiritual concept of *ghayb*: "what is hidden, inaccessible to the senses and to reason – thus, at the same time absent from human knowledge and hidden in divine wisdom," which could be translated as "Divine Mystery."[71] He notes that most available studies that try to incorporate religious beliefs into their analyses of historical causality always result in an effort to

[67] John H. Hanson, *Migration, Jihad and Muslim Authority in West Africa: The Futanke Colonies in Karta* (Bloomington: Indiana University Press, 1996).

[68] Marc Bloch, *The Royal Touch: Sacred Monarchy and Scrofula in England and France*, trans. J. E. Anderson (Abingdon and New York: Routledge, 2015), 4.

[69] Quentin Skinner, *Visions of Politics*, vol. 1: *Regarding Methods* (Cambridge: Cambridge University Press, 2015), 52.

[70] Scott S. Reese, *Imperial Muslims: Islam, Community and Authority in the Indian Ocean, 1839–1937* (Edinburgh: Edinburgh University Press, 2018), 2.

[71] D. B. MacDonald and L. Gardet, s.v. "al-Ghayb," in *EI*², vol. 2, 1025.

understand the palpable effects of the unseen in such works, "agency only occurs within the context of social interactions between human beings. As such, the significance of the unseen is presumed to be entirely material or tangible."[72] This runs the risk of reducing religious discourses to political ones. As Asad posits:

> [Any] attempt to understand Muslim traditions by insisting that in them religion and politics (two essences modern society tries to keep conceptually and practically apart) are coupled must, in my view, lead to failure. At its most dubious, such attempts encourage us to take up an a priori position in which religious discourse in the political arena is seen as a disguise for political power.[73]

Reese accordingly warns that "it is important to recognize that the engagement with the unseen may have less to do with the advantage to be gained in this world and more about one's relationship with and understanding of the next."[74]

Applying Reese's observations to the present study of the *Tārīkh al-fattāsh* and its project of legitimization of Ḥamdallāhi, the religious discourses that encircle the figure of Aḥmad Lobbo, including those employed by Nūḥ b. al-Ṭāhir in the chronicle, cannot be simply interpreted as attempts to deceive the caliphate's subjects and rivals, and to convince them of his authority on false grounds. On the contrary, they are based on an epistemology that was shared by the writer, the caliph, and his intended audience. As Anthony Grafton argues in his influential work on forgeries, one of the most persistent motives for the fabrication of texts is the need to bolster existing beliefs.[75] For instance, in the case of forgeries dating to the Hellenistic period and the early Roman Empire, they were produced by defeated peoples of the Mediterranean basins whose "authors sincerely believed ... that they were descended from races and cultures older than the Greeks and the Romans."[76]

Nineteenth-century Islamic West Africa, as I will show, was a world full of saints, prophecies, and eschatological expectations. Therefore, a study that dismisses the religious legitimacy of Aḥmad Lobbo's political authority can only partially understand the history of

72 Reese, *Imperial Muslims*, 11. 73 Asad, *Genealogies of Religion*, 29.
74 Reese, *Imperial Muslims*, 11.
75 Anthony Grafton, *Forgers and Critics: Creativity and Duplicity in Western Scholarship* (Princeton: Princeton University Press, 1990), 40.
76 Grafton, *Forgers and Critics*, 41.

Ḥamdallāhi and, by extension, other West African Islamic revolutions. More broadly, my work attends to the intersections of political and religious discourses in Islamic societies whose political order is believed to be divinely sanctioned. In this, it follows in the footsteps of recent scholarship that goes beyond a superficial understanding of the religious and the political in pre-modern societies. For instance, in *The Millennial Sovereign*, A. Afzar Moin studies the Mughal dynasty of India (1526–1857) and the Safavid dynasty in Persia (1501–1722) to show that rulers' "claims of political power became inseparable from claims of saintly status."[77] Likewise, Hussein Fancy's study of the Muslim mercenary horsemen who were employed by the Christian rulers of the kingdom of Aragon during the later Middle Ages shows that "the sovereign ambitions of the Aragonese kings were grounded in tightly imbricated and inseparable ideas of law and theology."[78]

The intertwined stories of the Caliphate of Ḥamdallāhi and the *Tārīkh al-fattāsh* represent a perfect case study for such an approach. *Sultan, Caliph, and the Renewer of the Faith* will demonstrate that the authority of Aḥmad Lobbo, as articulated in the chronicle but also expressed in other ways, rested on a complex network of claims that were political as well as religious in nature, including claims of the ruler's scholarly knowledge, sainthood, and divine investiture. Indeed, the *Tārīkh al-fattāsh* portrays Aḥmad Lobbo as sultan, the authoritative ruler of West Africa, and the last of a long line of legitimate rulers modeled on Askiyà al-Ḥājj Muḥammad b. Abī Bakr (d. 1538) – or simply Askiyà Muḥammad, the most famous of the emperors of the Songhay;[79] as the twelfth of the caliphs under whom the Islamic community would thrive, according to a *ḥadīth* ascribed to the Prophet; and as the *mujaddid*, or "renewer" of Islam, who, according to another

77 A. Azfar Moin, *The Millennial Sovereign: Sacred Kingship and Sainthood in Islam* (New York: Columbia University Press, 2014), 4.

78 Hussein A. Fancy, *The Mercenary Mediterranean: Sovereignty, Religion, and Violence in the Medieval Crown of Aragon* (Chicago: University of Chicago Press, 2016), 151.

79 The title *askiyà*, its pronunciation, use, and emergence are still very controversial. See John O. Hunwick, *Timbuktu and the Songhay Empire: al-Sa'dī's Ta'rīkh al-Sūdān down to 1613, and Other Contemporary Documents* (Leiden and Boston: Brill, 2003), 335–337; and Paulo F. de Moraes Farias, *Arabic Medieval Inscriptions from the Republic of Mali: Epigraphy, Chronicles and Songhay–Tuāreg History* (Oxford: Oxford University Press for the British Academy, 2003), xcvii–cvi § 192–219.

Prophetic tradition, is sent by God to prevent the Muslim community going astray. In order to study and fully appreciate such claims, I draw attention to a new archive of mostly untapped primary sources: the large number of Arabic manuscripts that constitute the so-called Islamic Library of West Africa.

From the Colonial Library to the Islamic Library of West Africa

In his inspiring work *The Invention of Africa*, the philosopher Valentin Y. Mudimbe stresses that "Africanism," or the discourse about Africa, is based on the "Colonial Library."[80] Mudimbe borrows the concept of "library" from Michel Foucault.[81] The latter describes a library as a site of discourse "which includes not only the books and treatises traditionally recognized as valid, but also all the observations and case-histories published and transmitted, and the mass of statistical information ... that can be supplied" in a specific field.[82] But one should not regard the process of producing such a "library" as having erased Africans' agency. As Frederick Cooper points out, "Europe's ambivalent conquests ... made the space of empire into a terrain where concepts were not only imposed but also engaged and contested."[83] Africans were an integral part of the colonial library's creation, at various levels of engagement.

A fitting example of such participation in the construction of this library is that of the missionary-trained Anglican bishop Samuel Ajayi Crowther (d. 1891). Yoruba by birth but educated at the Fourah Bay College in Freetown (Sierra Leone), Crowther was very active in reinforcing, as Mudimbe argues, the stereotypes of the African "savage" and the need for the "regeneration" of local cultures.[84] Many other

80 Valentin Y. Mudimbe, *The Invention of Africa: Gnosis, Philosophy, and the Order of Knowledge* (Bloomington: Indiana University Press, 1988).

81 Ousmane O. Kane, *Non-Europhone Intellectuals*, trans. Victoria Bawtree (Dakar: Codesria, 2012), 63.

82 Michel Foucault, *The Archaeology of Knowledge and The Discourse on Language*, trans. A. M. Sheridan Smith (New York: Pantheon, 1972), 51–52.

83 Frederick Cooper, *Colonialism in Question: Theory, Knowledge, History* (Berkeley: University of California Press, 2009), 4. For case studies pointing to African agency in colonial contexts, see Femi J. Kolapo and Kwabena O. Akuran-Parry (eds.), *African Agency and European Colonialism: Latitudes of Negotiations and Containment* (Lanham, MD: University Press of America, 2007).

84 Mudimbe, *The Invention of Africa*, 48.

African players were involved as cultural brokers who collected information on behalf of colonial administrators and served to facilitate the administration of European empires. As Robinson argues, regarding French production of colonial knowledge in West Africa, "the most obvious fact about the French archival material is the mediation of Africans. African clerks made and kept most of the records and controlled access to the Europeans. Interpreters, chiefs, and marabouts provided a framework for understanding local situations."[85] This created a space for African actors to navigate the colonial system and bend it to the advantage of their communities – or even to advance personal goals, as for example in the case of the interpreter Wangrin, the protagonist of the renowned semi-historical novel by Hampaté Ba.[86] However, the knowledge generated by local actors was eventually used to produce Eurocentric hegemonic discourses that framed Africa as the epitome of otherness, justifying European domination of its peoples.

To move beyond the Colonial Library and begin a reevaluation of African experiences, Mudimbe suggests, among other things, interrogating Islamic sources.[87] External Islamic sources produced by Muslim geographers, historians, and travelers to sub-Saharan Africa have been taken into consideration by historians for a long time.[88] However, as Ousmane O. Kane has recently pointed out, another library is available to scholars, equipped with the necessary linguistic and epistemological tools: the Islamic Library of West Africa, i.e. the texts in Arabic and in *'ajamī* (African languages written in an adapted Arabic alphabet) produced by local Muslims themselves.[89]

Yet the Islamic Library of West Africa, while localized and peculiar to the region, was not disconnected from the rest of the Islamic world.

[85] David Robinson, *Paths of Accommodation: Muslim Societies and French Colonial Authorities in Senegal and Mauritania, 1880–1920* (Oxford: James Currey, 2001), 50.

[86] Amadou Hampaté Ba, *The Fortunes of Wangrin*, trans. Aina Pavolini Taylor (Bloomington: Indiana University Press, 1973).

[87] Mudimbe, *The Invention of Africa*, 181.

[88] For example, classic works such as Tadeusz Lewicki, *Arabic External Sources for the History of Africa to the South of Sahara*, trans. Marianna Abrahamowicz (Wrocław: Zaklad narodowy im. Ossolińskich, 1969); Joseph M. Cuoq, *Recueil des sources arabes concernant l'Afrique occidentale du VIIIe au XVIe siècle (Bilād al-Sūdān)* (Paris: Éditions du Centre national de la recherche scientifique, 1975); and J. F. P. Hopkins and Nehemia Levtzion, *Corpus of Early Arabic Sources for West African History*, 2nd ed. (Princeton: Markus Wiener, 2000).

[89] Kane, *Non-Europhone Intellectuals*, 4.

West African discourses were not produced in an intellectual vacuum, but always in connection with the Islamic "discursive tradition," a concept first employed by Asad.[90] As Roman Loimeier explains:

> We should visualize Islam as a great pool or corpus of texts, of prescriptions concerning the faith and/or everyday life, of shared rituals and festivals, of norms and values, as well as teaching traditions that were based on a number of key texts such as the Quran, the compilations of the sunna of the Prophet, as well as a large number of legal and theological texts.[91]

Therefore, the production of the Islamic Library of West Africa was, and continues to be, "dialogical – informed by the core texts but also locally produced – and situational – deployed as a response to local spiritual and social contexts," in Reese's words.[92] West Africans, like Muslims all over the globe and throughout Islamic history, have reinterpreted their faith in ways that made it useful and meaningful to them, in their own contexts.

The Islamic Library of West Africa mainly survives in the form of Arabic manuscripts. Kane stresses that "many commendable" efforts have been made, in the past couple of decades, to reevaluate these sources.[93] He defines these activities as "Timbuktu Studies," meaning the efforts expended by scholars "mapping the intellectual field – essentially the collection, archiving, cataloguing, digitizing, and translation into European languages of the Islamic archives of West Africa."[94] Certainly, these efforts represent a starting point for any serious study of African Muslim societies. However, despite the abundance of manuscripts produced in West Africa, celebrated in both academic studies and in journalism, and despite there being a large number of projects devoted to the preservation and digitization of these manuscripts, little effort has been made to study them.[95]

90 Talal Asad, *The Idea of an Anthropology of Islam* (Washington, DC: Center for Contemporary Arab Studies – Georgetown University, 1986).

91 Loimeier, *Muslim Societies in Africa*, 19.

92 Scott S. Reese, "Islam in Africa/Africans and Islam," *Journal of African History* 55/1 (2014): 17–26, 23.

93 Ousmane O. Kane, *Beyond Timbuktu: An Intellectual History of Muslim West Africa* (Cambridge, MA, and London: Harvard University Press, 2016), 25.

94 Kane, *Beyond Timbuktu*, 18.

95 Laudable efforts are the classical series Fontes Historiae Africanae (www.britac.ac.uk/fontes-historiae-africanae-new-series-sources-african-history), which used to have a sub-series called Series Arabica (www.britac.ac.uk/fontes-historiae-africanae-original-series), but that continues publishing sporadically

The lack of actual work on these manuscripts is surely a reflection of the fact that philology, to quote Edward Said in an essay that calls for a return to this methodology, "is just about the least with-it, least sexy, and most unmodern of any of the branches of learning associated with humanism."[96] It also reflects, in the polemical words of Sheldon Pollock, "profound changes in the nature of humanistic learning [... namely] the hypertrophy of theory ... the devaluation of the strictly textual in favor of the oral and the visual; the growing indifference to and incapacity in foreign languages, especially historical languages, worldwide; and the shallow presentism of scholarship and even antipathy to the past as such."[97] Pollock's words may seem to have been directed to African historiography, but in fact they are not. Indeed, it is in Africanist scholarship that the critique advanced by Pollock is mostly evident. For example, it is still easy to find, in an authoritative study of slavery, statements such as the following:

> African societies, by and large, remain predominantly oral in their modes of cultural production and transmission ... We must add here that there are also some things that can only be said through the deeply encoded language of the drum and the dance. This presents researchers in African history and culture with unresolved challenges. Among them is the challenge of developing a new kind of literacy, the ability and skills to read and interpret

translation of Arabic materials, such as de Moraes Farias, *Arabic Medieval Inscriptions*; the now defunct VECMAS (Valorisation et édition critique des manuscrits arabes subsahariens), which published some editions and translations into French of West African manuscripts (http://vecmas-tombouctou.ens-lyon.fr/); and the Brill series African Sources for African History (https://brill.com/view/serial/ASAH) which has also published some Arabic texts and translations, such as Cornelia Giesing and Valentin F. Vydrin, *Ta:rikh Mandinka de Bijini (Guinée-Bissau): la mémoire des Mandinka et Sòoninkee du Kaabu* (Leiden and Boston: Brill, 2007). In this context of the neglect of studies based on Arabic manuscripts from sub-Saharan Africa, an exception is represented by northern Nigeria and the abundant study of local Arabic sources in the form of manuscripts. These materials have been extensively studied since the early post-colonial period, as the region's Islamic heritage was immediately mobilized to form a cohesive Muslim identity for the northern regions of the country (see Samaila Suleiman, "The Nigerian History Machine and the Production of Middle Belt Historiography" [Ph.D. dissertation, University of Cape Town, 2015], 93–96).

96 Edward Said, "The return to philology," in *Humanism and Democratic Criticism* (New York: Columbia University Press, 2004), 57–84, 57.

97 Sheldon Pollock, "Future philology? The fate of a soft science in a hard world," *Critical Inquiry* 35/4 (2009): 931–961, 934–935.

a range of sources: not only written texts, but also sources created by Africans themselves.[98]

Such a perspective denies that African Muslims have been writing texts themselves, for centuries – and this does not diminish the importance of oral traditions and other forms of expressions adopted by Africans. However, as the philosopher Souleymane Bachir Diagne proclaims, "it is time to leave what we could call a *griot paradigm* that identifies Africa with orality, in order to envisage a history of (written) erudition in Africa."[99] This is particularly evident in the case of Mali, and of Timbuktu, where the number of manuscripts claimed to have been produced and preserved sometimes reaches astronomical and unlikely figures.[100] Yet scholars have not utilized these manuscripts to their full historical potential.[101] Bruce Hall's study on local ideas of race in Saharan and Sahelian West Africa is the only recent study that capitalizes on the availability of Arabic manuscripts from Timbuktu archives.[102]

The present book follows in the footstep of Hall's work by centering its analysis on West African Arabic manuscripts from Mali, engaging these sources as complex discourses of power rather than as positivist repositories of facts. In the words of Benedetta Rossi and Toby Green:

> Where previous generations of historians may have mined sources produced in Africa for "hard evidence," new frameworks of historiography recognise the significance of the political circumstances surrounding a source's

98 Kofi Anyidoho, "Foreword: Beyond the printed word," in *African Voices on Slavery and the Slave Trade*, edited by Alice Bellagamba, Sandra E. Greene, and Martin A. Klein (Cambridge: Cambridge University Press, 2016), xvii–xxii, xviii.

99 Souleymane Bachir Diagne, *The Ink of the Scholars: Reflections on Philosophy in Africa* (Dakar: Codesria, 2016), 57 (italics in original text).

100 See, for example, the analysis of this numbers in Jean-Louis Triaud, "Tombouctou ou le retour du mythe: l'exposition médiatique des manuscrits de Tombouctou," in *L'Afrique des savoirs au sud du Sahara (XVIe–XXIe siècle): acteurs, supports, pratiques*, edited by Daouda Gary-Tounkara and Didier Nativel (Paris: Karthala, 2012), 201–222.

101 An overview of most of the available editions and translations of works produced by West African Muslim scholars is Bernard Salvaing, "À propos d'un projet en cours d'édition de manuscrits arabes de Tombouctou et d'ailleurs," *Afriques – Eclectiques, Sources* (2015) (http://afriques.revues.org/1804).

102 Bruce Hall, *A History of Race in Muslim West Africa, 1600–1960* (Cambridge: Cambridge University Press, 2011).

production. This approach takes the decolonizing of the history of Africa a step further: here is recognition of the complex intellectual pasts and historical engagements of members of ... African intelligentsias, those "source-producers" who have shaped current historiographical overviews of the ... African past.[103]

My book follows this methodological turn, which moves away from the Orientalist approach identified by Said, considering the text an object of study per se to produce positive knowledge about "other" cultures.[104] My approach is particularly indebted to the seminal work by Paulo F. de Moraes Farias, *The Arabic Medieval Inscriptions from the Republic of Mali*, as well as to many other of his more synthetic pieces; and also to the lesser-known works of archaeologist Augustin F. C. Holl on the *Dīwān salāṭīn Barnū* (King List of Borno).[105] Both de Moraes Farias and Holl's studies of Western and Central African Arabic sources approach these documents as sophisticated works of local intellectuals with precise rhetorical plans and authorial intentions. This new appreciation of the written records produced by Muslim intellectuals does not apply only to the historiography of African Islamic societies. A very similar approach is taken, for instance, by Manan A. Asif's recent *A Book of Conquest*.[106] In his innovative

103 Toby Green and Benedetta Rossi, "Introduction. Thick contextualization: Interpreting West African landscapes, sources, and projects," in *Landscapes, Sources and Intellectual Projects of the West African Past: Essays in Honour of Paulo Fernando de Moraes Farias*, edited by Toby Green and Benedetta Rossi (Leiden and Boston: Brill, 2018), 1–22, 2.

104 Edward W. Said, *Orientalism* (New York: Vintage Books, 1979), 52.

105 On de Moraes Farias's studies on the topic, see de Moraes Farias, *Arabic Medieval Inscriptions*; Paulo F. de Moraes Farias, "Barth, fondateur d'une lecture reductrice des chroniques de Tombouctou," in *Heinrich Barth et l'Afrique*, edited by Mamadou Diawara, Paulo F. de Moraes Farias, and Gerd Spittler (Cologne: Köppe, 2006), 215–224; and Paulo F. de Moraes Farias, "Intellectual innovation and the reinvention of the Sahel: The seventeenth-century chronicles of Timbuktu," in *The Meanings of Timbuktu*, edited by Shamil Jeppie and Souleymane B. Diagne (Cape Town: HSRC Press, 2008), 95–109; For Holl's contributions, see Augustin F. C. Holl, *The Diwan Revisited: Literacy, State Formation and the Rise of Kanuri Domination (AD 1200–1600)* (London and New York: Kegan Paul International, 2000); and Augustin F. C. Holl, "New perspectives on the Diwan: State formation and the rise of Kanuri domination in the Central Sudan (AD 1200–1600)," in *Land, Literacy and the State in Sudanic Africa*, edited by Donald Crummey (Trenton, NJ: Africa World Press, 2005), 45–76.

106 Manan A. Asif, *A Book of Conquest: The Chachnama and Muslim Origins in South Asia* (Cambridge, MA: Harvard University Press, 2016).

study of the popular thirteenth-century *Chachnama* (The Book of Chach), which parallels my work on the *Tārīkh al-fattāsh*, Asif convincingly argues that this work, often portrayed as a history of Sindh in the seventh and eighth centuries, "in reality is a work of political theory" rather than a chronicle.[107]

Sultan, Caliph, and the Renewer of the Faith is accordingly based on locally produced Arabic manuscript sources, the indigenous and ingenious works of West African Muslim intellectuals, which expand our understanding of the *Tārīkh al-fattāsh*, its creation, political agenda, and role in the history of the Caliphate of Ḥamdallāhi. Ultimately, it aims to shed light on strategies for the legitimation of authority in the nineteenth-century West African Islamic revolutions.

The Case of Ḥamdallāhi and Its Archive

The study of the *Tārīkh al-fattāsh* and of the Caliphate of Ḥamdallāhi has rarely been informed by the large number of available manuscripts. To date, all the research produced on the chronicle derives from the colonial edition and translation into French by Octave V. Houdas (d. 1916) and Maurice Delafosse (d. 1926), published in 1913. The existing scholarship on the Caliphate of Ḥamdallāhi is mainly based on oral traditions collected in the colonial and post-colonial periods, and on the sporadic use of Arabic documents.[108] This is paradoxical,

[107] Asif, *A Book of Conquest*, 20.

[108] *L'empire peul*, 13; Brown, "The Caliphate of Hamdullahi," 1; Sanankoua "L'organisation politique," II). Apart from the information contained in these studies, an extensive body of collections of oral sources, in the form of oral epics and of oral histories, exist on the Caliphate of Ḥamdallāhi (see, for example, Yero Arsoukoula, *Notes de ma guitare: Sékou Amadou* [Bamako: Ed. du Mali, n.d.], Christiane Seydou, *Silâmaka et Poullôri: recit epique peul* [Paris: Armand Colin, 1972]; Christiane Seydou, *La geste de Ham-Bodêdio ou Hama le Rouge* [Paris: Classiques africains, 1977]; Christiane Seydou, *Les guerres du Massina: récits épiques peuls du Mali* [Paris: Karthala, 2014]; Christiane Seydou, *Héros et personnages du Massina: récits épiques peuls du Mali* [Paris: Karthala, 2014]; and Almamy Maliki Yattara and Bernard Salvaing, *Almamy*, vol. 2: *L'âge d'homme d'un lettré malien* [Brinon-sur-Sauldre: Grandvaux, 2003]). For this study, I have used oral traditions only via this secondary literature. This choice reflects my expertise, but also can be explained by the recent upheavals in Mali, especially the crisis that erupted in 2012, which has left the rural areas of Mali in a state of constant danger, and this impacted my opportunity for conducting fieldwork and collecting new interviews in the region once controlled by the caliphate.

considering that the works of Ba, Brown, and Sanankoua clearly show that the spread of Arabic literacy within the lands controlled by Aḥmad Lobbo was one of the most significant achievements of the Caliphate of Ḥamdallāhi.

Regarding Ḥamdallāhi, the scholarly landscape is slowly changing. The recent *L'inspiration de l'Éternel: éloge de Shékou Amadou, fondateur de l'empire peul du Macina par Muḥammad b. ʿAlī Pereejo*, edited under the direction of George Bohas, represents the first step toward a serious evaluation of the caliphate's literary heritage.[109] This work, with an erudite foreword by Bernard Salvaing, is an edition and translation of the hagiographical account of Aḥmad Lobbo's life, the *Fatḥ al-Ṣamad fī dhikr shayʾ min akhlāf shaykhinā Aḥmad* (The Inspiration of the Eternal in Remembrance of some of the Exemplary Peculiarities of our Shaykh Aḥmad; henceforth *Fatḥ al-Ṣamad*) by Muḥammad b. ʿAlī Pereejo (*fl.* 1840). Another important work, Aḥmad Lobbo's own *al-Iḍṭirār ilà Allāh fī ikhmād baʿḍ mā tawaqqada min al-bidaʿ wa-iḥyāʾ baʿḍ mā indarasa min al-sunan* (The Essential Necessity of God to Extinguish some Ignited Innovations and to Revive some Traditions at the Verge of Extinction; henceforth *Kitāb al-Iḍṭirār*) remains unpublished in Ali H. Diakité's MA thesis.[110]

[109] Georges Bohas, Abderrahim Saguer, and Bernard Salvaing (ed. and trans.), *L'inspiration de l'Éternel: éloge de Shékou Amadou, fondateur de l'empire peul du Macina, par Muḥammad b. ʿAlī Pereejo* (Brinon-sur-Sauldre: Grandvaux/VECMAS, 2011) (henceforth *Fatḥ al-Ṣamad*).

[110] Hienin Ali Diakite (ed. and trans.), "Édition et traduction du *Kitāb al-Iḍṭirār* de Aḥmad Lobbo" (MA thesis, École Normale Supérieure de Lyon, 2011) (henceforth *Kitāb al-Iḍṭirār*). Other important texts on the history of Ḥamdallāhi are available in translation, but date to later times, to the reigns of Aḥmad II and Aḥmad III. Most famous is the Sidi M. Mahibou and Jean Louis Triaud (ed. and trans.), *Voilà ce qui est arrivé: Bayân mâ Waqaʿa d'al-Ḥâ ğğ ʿUmar al-Fûtî: plaidoyer pour une guerre sainte en Afrique de l'Ouest Au XIXe siècle* (Paris: CNRS, 1983). Others are unpublished, namely the Ph.D. dissertations by Diakité and Ismail Traore that include translations of very important documents related to the Caliphate of Ḥamdallāhi (Ismail Traore [ed. and trans.], "Les relations épistolaires entre la famille Kunta de Tombouctou et la Dina du Macina (1818–1864)" [Ph.D. dissertation, École Normale Supérieure de Lyon, 2012]; Hienin Ali Diakite [ed. and trans.], "al-Mukhār b. Yerkoy Talfi et le Califat de Hamdallahi au XIXe siècle: édition critique et traduction de Tabkīt al-Bakkay. À propos d'une controverse inter-confrérique entre al-Mukhtār b. Yerkoy Talfi (1800–1864) et Aḥmad al-Bakkay (1800–1866)" [Ph.D. dissertation, École Normale Supérieure de Lyon, 2015]).

Still, the extraordinary amount of manuscript materials generated during the caliphate calls for a new study of both Ḥamdallāhi and the *Tārīkh al-fattāsh*. To this end *Sultan, Caliph, and the Renewer of the Faith* continues the meticulous work on Arabic primary sources carried on by Bohas's team and by Diakité in order to answer larger historical questions about the nature of authority, legitimacy, and the politics of literacy in West Africa. The bulk of the sources employed here are preserved in the Institut des Hautes Études et de Recherches Islamiques Ahmed Baba de Tombouctou (IHERI-ABT).[111] The two other major manuscript repositories explored in this book are those housed at the Bibliothèque nationale de France (BnF) and the Institut de France (IF). The former hosts the private collection of Aḥmad al-Kabīr al-Madanī (d. 1898), son and successor of *al-ḥājj* ʿUmar in Segou, which was looted by Colonel Louis Archinard (d. 1932) after the French conquest of the city in 1890.[112] This collection, alternatively known as Bibliothèque ʿUmarienne or the Fonds Archinard, is of

[111] Formerly known as the Institut des Hautes Études et de Recherches Islamiques Ahmed Baba and (before 2000) as the Centre de Documentation et de Recherches Ahmed Baba, the center was created in 1970, following a 1967 UNESCO meeting of African history specialists in Timbuktu, where participants advocated the establishment of a repository for local written sources to serve as a research center. A report of this meeting is available in English translation in John O. Hunwick, "Report of the UNESCO meeting of experts on the utilisation of written sources for the history of Africa held at Timbuktu, 30 November–7 December 1967," *Research Bulletin – Centre of Arabic Documentation, University of Ibadan* 4 (1968): 52–69. On the history of the institute, a comprehensive introduction is Muhammad Ould Youbba, "The Ahmed Baba Institute of Higher Islamic Studies and Research," in *The Meanings of Timbuktu*, edited by Shamil Jeppie and Souleymane B. Diagne (Cape Town: HSRC Press, 2008), 287–302. The institute opened in 1973, and today hosts a collection of 43,182 manuscripts (Mohamed Diagayeté, personal communication, 6 June 2019). During the 2012–2013 crisis in northern Mali, some 27,000 of these were relocated to Bamako, with the result that the holdings of the institute are now divided between these two cities: the old buildings in Timbuktu and the new one in the capital city (Mohamed Diagayeté, personal communication, 8 March 2017). A handlist of 9,000 of the IHERI-ABT manuscripts is Sidi Amar Ould Ely et al., *Fihris mahkhṭuṭāt Markaz Aḥmad Baba li-l-wathāʾiq wa-l buḥuth al-ārikhiyya bi-Timbuktu /Handlist of the Manuscripts in the Centre de Documentation et de Recherches Historiques Ahmad Baba, Timbuktu, Mali*, 5 vols. (London: al-Furqan Islamic Heritage Foundation, 1995–1998).

[112] On this collection, see Noureddine Ghali, Sidi Mohamed Mahibou, and Louis Brenner, *Inventaire de la Bibliothèque ʿUmarienne: conservée à la Bibliothèque nationale, Paris* (Paris: CNRS, 1985).

relevance for the present study because Aḥmad al-Kabīr al-Madanī seems to have incorporated the manuscripts that were once in the library of Ḥamdallāhi into his father's library.[113] The other Paris-based collection is hosted at IF under the name Fonds de Gironcourt. This is a small collection of twelve bound volumes containing separate folders of manuscripts brought to Paris in 1912 by the French agronomist Georges de Gironcourt (d. 1960), who traveled extensively in the Middle Niger collecting, among other texts, several manuscripts from Masina and from the cities of Djenné and Timbuktu.[114]

Apart from these repositories, a few manuscripts from other collections have also been used in the research for this book, namely those of the Ahl Sīdiyya Library in Boutilimit (Mauritania), accessed in microfilm copy at the University of Illinois at Urbana-Champaign Library (USA); the Institut Fondamental d'Afrique Noire (IFAN) in Dakar and the private collection of Aliou Ndiaye in the village of Adeane in Casamance (Senegal); the Bibliothèque de manuscrits de Djenné (accessed via the Endangered Archives Program, "Major project to digitise and preserve the manuscripts of Djenné, Mali [EAP488]": https://eap.bl.uk/project/EAP488; "Project to digitise and preserve the manuscripts of Djenné and surrounding villages [EAP690]": https://eap.bl.uk/project/EAP690; and "Continued digitisation and preservation of the Arabic manuscripts of Djenné and surrounding villages [EAP879]": https://eap.bl.uk/project/EAP879), the private collection of Almami Maliki Yattara in Bamako, and the Maktabat Muḥammad al-Bukhārī in the village of Banikan in the province of Niafounké (Mali); the Institut des recherches en sciences humaines (IRSH) de Niamey (Niger); the British Library (UK); the National Archives in Kaduna (accessed via the Endangered Archives Program, "Northern Nigeria: Precolonial documents preservation scheme – major project (EAP535)": https://eap.bl.uk/project/EAP535) and the Northern History Research Scheme (NHRS) Unit at the Ahmadu Bello University in Zaria (Nigeria); and manuscripts from the Malian Arabic Manuscripts Microfilming Project (henceforth MAMMP).

113 Yattara and Salvaing, *Almamy*, vol. 2, 214.
114 Mauro Nobili, *Catalogue des manuscrits arabes du Fonds de Gironcourt (Afrique de l'Ouest) de l'Institut de France* (Rome: Istituto per l'Oriente C. A. Nallino, 2013).

Outline of the Book

Although a work of history, *Sultan, Caliph, and the Renewer of the Faith* adopts an interdisciplinary approach and employs methods and tools from literary criticism, religious studies, philosophy, and analytical bibliography. My book is an exploration of a chronicle, the *Tārīkh al-fattāsh*, which has been widely misunderstood by contemporary scholars, but it is not a study of this work per se. The *Tārīkh al-fattāsh* is here used as a tool to investigate historical questions regarding authority and legitimacy in nineteenth-century West Africa, with an emphasis on the case of the Caliphate of Ḥamdallāhi – of which this book also provides the first in-depth study in English. To better present this complex case study, I have abandoned chronology as an organizational framework. Instead, I move back and forth between time periods, from the late fifteenth century to the present. To facilitate this narrative, the book is divided, in addition to this introduction, into three parts followed by a conclusion.

Part I addresses crucial historiographical, philological, and historical questions in order to clarify the nature of this widely circulated, yet misinterpreted, text. This section takes the reader on a trip across the centuries, between the late fifteenth century and the early 2000s, passing through the colonial period to explore first the historiography of the *Tārīkh al-fattāsh* and then to clarify the history of production of the chronicle in the nineteenth century. Here, I show that the text edited by Houdas and Delafosse in 1913, and translated under the name *La chronique du chercheur*, conflates two different works. The first of these was composed in the seventeenth century by Ibn al-Mukhtār. The second, the only one entitled *Tārīkh al-fattāsh*, was composed in the first half of the nineteenth century by the Fulani scholar Nūḥ b. al-Ṭāhir, but ascribed apocryphally to the sixteenth century and to Maḥmūd Ka'ti. This latter work was produced to legitimize the rule of Aḥmad Lobbo and the Caliphate of Ḥamdallāhi. It creates a metahistorical connection between Aḥmad Lobbo and his putative ancestor, Askiyà Muḥammad, the famous emperor of Songhay, who is reinvented by Nūḥ b. al-Ṭāhir as an ideal West African ruler who combines both political and religious authority.

After proving that the chronicle is a nineteenth-century work, Part II is, in Foucauldian terms, an "archaeology" of the *Tārīkh al-fattāsh*.[115]

115 On the concept of "archaeology," see Foucault, *The Archaeology of Knowledge*, 7.

In other words, in this part I investigate the historical context that made the chronicle both possible and necessary. I explore the emergence of new claims to authority by Aḥmad Lobbo and his entourage in which the religious and political spheres were conflated. However, Aḥmad Lobbo's claims to a legitimate authority were resisted by many of his contemporaries: first, by the traditional Fulani military aristocracies, then by the prestigious Kunta scholarly family of the Middle Niger and Azawād, as well as by the Fodiawa family of the powerful neighboring Sokoto Caliphate. While the old Fulani elite was eliminated by Aḥmad Lobbo, the influential Kunta leaders (*shaykh*s) had to come to terms with the rule of Ḥamdallāhi, accepting Aḥmad Lobbo's function as the political authority, though they resisted his claims on the religious sphere. Much broader were the objections of the Fodiawa leaders, who asserted that Ḥamdallāhi was in fact a province of Sokoto, as the result of an early pledge of allegiance sworn by the Fulani leader to the founder of Sokoto, 'Uthmān b. Fūdī. The Fodiawa thus contested every aspect of Aḥmad Lobbo's leadership. It was in response to this multi-faceted resistance that Nūḥ b. al-Ṭāhir composed his *Tārīkh al-fattāsh*.

Part III returns to focus on the chronicle and represents, using D. F. McKenzie's terminology, an exercise in the "sociology of texts."[116] It explores the circulation of the *Tārīkh al-fattāsh*, the impact it had on its audience, its reception and rejection in the region, and its continued use and misuse up until the present day. It examines in detail how the complex literary manipulation accomplished in the *Tārīkh al-fattāsh* circulated within and beyond the borders of the caliphate, and how it was received in the Middle Niger and further afield, focusing in particular on the refutation of Ḥamdallāhi's claims by the Sokoto elite. I also show how, in the eschatologically loaded context of the Middle Niger in the nineteenth century, the chronicle's narrative, comprising saints, miracles, prophesied caliphs etc., which have been superficially dismissed by contemporary scholars as "unlikely," reflects the local Islamic epistemology of the time. This part continues by showing how the project supported by *Tārīkh al-fattāsh* eroded after Aḥmad Lobbo's death, to the extent that the text almost disappeared. It was only with the arrival of French colonialism that the chronicle resurfaced, and was

[116] Donald F. McKenzie, *Bibliography and the Sociology of Texts* (Cambridge: Cambridge University Press, 1999).

then used to advance a very different kind of project: the production of knowledge of the past of the colonized people that could be put to the service of the colonial administration. Eventually, in the problematic shape of Houdas and Delafosse's 1913 *La chronique du chercheur*, the chronicle become one of the most influential primary sources for West African history.

The conclusion focuses on three broader lessons that can be drawn from the connected stories of the *Tārīkh al-fattāsh* and of the Caliphate of Ḥamdallāhi: (1) The writing of history in West Africa cannot be divorced from its political motivations and intentions. (2) West African Muslim scholars, such as Aḥmad Lobbo and Nūḥ b. al-Ṭāhir, were far from isolated from the rest of the Islamic world – on the contrary, they engaged with the Islamic discursive tradition by using tropes, such as that of the caliph or the renewer of the faith, and applied them to a local context. (3) The role of the written word in nineteenth-century West Africa, as a tool of power and a license to access elite circles, that challenges widespread characterizations of the region as a place dominated by orality or by a very limited use of literacy, was crucial.

In sum, *Sultan, Caliph, and the Renewer of the Faith* is more than a study of the intertwined histories of the *Tārīkh al-fattāsh* and of Ḥamdallāhi. It is also a methodological manifesto for a different approach to the study of Africa's Muslim societies, which demonstrates the potential for producing new histories based on critical analyses of the Islamic Library of West Africa.

PART I

A Nineteenth-Century Chronicle in Support of the Caliphate of Ḥamdallāhi: Nūḥ b. al-Ṭāhir's Tārīkh al-fattāsh

> It happens to both books and men. Some lead a quiet and respectable life, domestically confined in the well-defined space that bibliographers have assigned to them. Others, on the contrary, resistant to any type of order, keep on living across the centuries an eventful life, adventurous, exhausting, as if their effervescent nature, which not even time can defeat, prevents them from keeping quiet and remaining still within the enclosed space to which decorum, norm, or fashion want to relegate them.
>
> *René R. Khawam,* Les milles et une nuits *(Paris: Phébus, 1986), vol. 1, 13*

The complicated story of the *Tārīkh al-fattāsh* could begin in the nineteenth century, at the time of Nūḥ b. al-Ṭāhir, Aḥmad Lobbo, and the Caliphate of Ḥamdallāhi; or in the seventeenth century, after the establishment of the Pāshālik of Timbuktu, when the last events recorded in the chronicle took place; or even further back in time, during the golden age of the Songhay Empire in the fifteenth and sixteen centuries, when Askiyà Muḥammad ruled over the Middle Niger. However, the confused reception of the chronicle in African historiography, which ripped the *Tārīkh al-fattāsh* from its context of production – the political project to legitimize Ḥamdallāhi – dates to the time of French colonialism. Therefore, I will start my analysis with the colonial period: not to impose a Eurocentric view on the history of the chronicle, but to disprove the dominant theories that depend on a flawed reconstruction of the text that was produced in the colonial period.

Shortly after the French conquest of Timbuktu in 1893, the journalist Albert Félix Dubois visited the fabled city and was introduced to its rich textual culture. He was the first Westerner to hear about the *Tārīkh al-fattāsh*, but he could not locate a copy of the work. Less than twenty years later, the well-known Arabist Octave V. Houdas and his son-in-law, the famous colonial scholar Maurice Delafosse, succeeded where Dubois had failed. They collated three manuscripts which had been identified (wrongly, as I will prove) as different copies of the chronicle, edited the resulting Arabic text, and translated it into French in 1913 under the title of *La chronique du chercheur*. However, Houdas and Delafosse, like Dubois before them, were tricked by Nūḥ b. al-Ṭāhir's apocryphal ascription of the *Tārīkh al-fattāsh* to Maḥmūd Ka'ti, a sixteenth-century scholar of the court of the Songhay Empire. Accordingly, Houdas and Delafosse attributed their conflated text, *La chronique du chercheur*, to Maḥmūd Ka'ti.

The publication of *La chronique du chercheur* represents a crucial moment in African historiography, since the text edited by Houdas and Delafosse soon became one of the most widely used sources for the history of West Africa.[1] Reprinted several times, it is also included in the *Collection UNESCO d'oeuvres représentatives Série africaine*.[2] Its Arabic text has served as the basis for three further Arabic commented editions.[3] The French translation was used for the only existing rendering of the text into English.[4] However, after more than a century of continuous use, ongoing scholarship has cast serious doubts on the reliability and authenticity of this text. To put it in the words of Madina Ly, "who does not experience a sense of discomfort reading the text, notwithstanding the precise footnotes that should

1 For example, on the back cover of the classic study on the Songhay state by Sékéné Mody Cissoko, *Tombouctou et l'empire Songhay*, the *Tārīkh al-fattāsh* and the *Tārīkh al-Sūdān* are described as "the two crucial sources for the history of the Soudan" (Sékéné Mody Cissoko, *Tombouctou et l'Empire Songhay: épanouissement du Soudan nigérien aux XVe–XVIe siècles* [Dakar: Les Nouvelles Editions Africaines, 1975]).

2 www.unesco.org/culture/lit/rep/pop.php?fnc=record&lng=en_GB&record=6070.

3 Ḥamā' Allāh Wuld Sālim (ed.), *Tārīkh al-fattāsh* (Beirut: Dār al-Kutub al-'Ilmiyya, 2013); Ādam Bambā (ed.), *Tārīkh al-fattāsh* (Damascus: Risāla, 2014); A. A. S. Maiga et al. (eds.), *Tārīkh al-fattāsh* (Bamako: Imprimerie Mangane et Fils, 2014).

4 Christopher Wise and Hala Abu Taleb (ed. and trans.), *Ta'rīkh al fattāsh: The Timbuktu Chronicles, 1493–1599* (Trenton, NJ: Africa World Press, 2011). This work is essentially meant for a wider, non-specialized audience, but is, in the words of de Moraes Farias, "a flawed, in places misleading rendering of the chronicle," especially of its French translation (Paulo F. de Moraes Farias, Review of *Ta'rīkh al-fattāsh* by Christopher Wise and Hala Abu Taleb [eds. and trans.], *Islamic Africa* 4/2 [2013]: 249–256).

clarify it?"[5] This "discomfort" is the result of scholars' failure to understand that *La chronique du chercheur* unintentionally severed the *Tārīkh al-fattāsh* from its author, Nūḥ b. al-Ṭāhir; from its historical context, the nineteenth-century Middle Niger; and from the ruler it aimed to legitimize, Aḥmad Lobbo.

Part I aims to present a new contribution to the small corpus of critical scholarship that can be defined as "*Tārīkh al-fattāsh* studies" – borrowing from the title of a series of articles on the topic by Hunwick.[6] It comprises two chapters that guide the reader through the scholarship on the *Tārīkh al-fattāsh*, highlight its problems, and move toward a new analytical approach to the history of the chronicle that reconnects it to the Caliphate of Ḥamdallāhi. It will demonstrate that the current understanding and uses of this text are radically impaired by scholars' dependence on what I will prove to be a defective colonial confection that passes as a critical edition. In place of this problematic text, Part I points to the availability of manuscript sources that, once interrogated critically, will render *La chronique du chercheur* obsolete and present the reader with the real *Tārīkh al-fattāsh*: an indispensable source for understanding the Middle Niger in the nineteenth century. It exposes Nuḥ b. al-Ṭāhir's skillfulness in embedding new pieces of writing into an older chronicle, the seventeenth-century *Tārīkh Ibn al-Mukhtār*, in order to produce a masterful work in support of his patron, Aḥmad Lobbo.

[5] Madina Ly, "Quelques remarques sur le Tarikh el-Fettach," *Bulletin de l'Institut Fondamental d'Afrique Noire, Série B – Sciences Humaines* 34/3 (1972): 471–492, 471.

[6] See John O. Hunwick, "Studies in the *Ta'rīkh al-Fattāsh*, I: Its authors and textual history," *Research Bulletin, Centre of Arabic Documentation – University of Ibadan* 5 (1969): 57–65; John O. Hunwick, "Studies in the *Ta'rīkh al-Fattāsh*, II: An alleged charter of privilege issued by Askiyà al-Ḥājj Muḥammad to the Descendants of Mori Hawgāro," *Sudanic Africa* 3 (1992): 133–148; John O. Hunwick, "Studies in the *Ta'rīkh al-Fattāsh*, III: Ka'ti origins," *Sudanic Africa* 12 (2001): 111–114.

1 A Century of Scholarship

This chapter reconstructs the different trends within the studies of the *Tārīkh al-fattāsh* and then advances the novel theory that the chronicle as a whole is a nineteenth-century work. Since the publication of *La chronique du chercheur* and up to the present time, most scholars have accepted not only the text published by Houdas and Delafosse, but their thesis that the *Tārīkh al-fattāsh* is a sixteenth-century text produced by Maḥmūd Ka'ti.[1] Later, according to their reconstruction, the chronicle was updated by a grandson of Maḥmūd Ka'ti, known as Ibn al-Mukhtār QNBL – which they read as Gombélé, who compiled the final version in the second half of the seventeenth century by incorporating notes left by other members of the Ka'ti family. Eventually, Houdas and Delafosse concluded, the first chapter of the chronicle was "slightly modified" in the early nineteenth century on behalf of Aḥmad Lobbo, the ruler of the Caliphate of Ḥamdallāhi. This theory was further complicated, first by Joseph Brun and then by Hunwick, who argued for the existence of two scholars by the name of Maḥmūd Ka'ti, both of whom were involved in the writing of chronicle.[2] In recent years, the number of Maḥmūd Ka'tis who allegedly contributed to the chronicle has gone up to three, thanks to a peculiar theory advanced in the introduction of a new edition published by a team of scholars of the IHERI-ABT.[3] The only alternative theory on the genesis of this text has been advanced by Levtzion, according to whom the *Tārīkh al-fattāsh* was a seventeenth-century work written by Ibn al-Mukhtār, later manipulated in the nineteenth century.[4]

[1] *La chronique du chercheur*, vii–xx.

[2] Joseph Brun, "Notes sur le 'Tarikh-El-Fettach'," *Anthropos* 9-3/4 (1914): 590–596; Hunwick, "Studies in the Ta'rīkh al-Fattāsh, I."

[3] Maiga et al. (eds.), *Tārīkh al-fattāsh*, 1–37.

[4] Nehemia Levtzion, "Was Maḥmūd Ka'tī the author of the *Ta'rīkh al-fattāsh*?" *Bulletin de l'Institut Fondamental d'Afrique Noire. Série B, Sciences Humaines*

All these theories assume the existence of an original chronicle polluted by later additions. Accordingly, scholars have remained fixated on a quest for the discovery of a pristine sixteenth- or seventeenth-century chronicle from which any sign of later textual manipulation must be cleansed. This supposition has occluded the existence of different layers of writing, and has thus hindered a full understanding of the history of the *Tārīkh al-fattāsh*. By employing Genette's classic study, *Palimpsests: Literature in the Second Degree*, I deconstruct Houdas and Delafosse's *La chronique du chercheur.*[5] I prove that this work is a conflated text, not a reliable edition, and that the manuscripts they employed do not represent different recensions of the same text, but two different works. Moreover, the differences between these two texts are more extensive than previously imagined by scholars. Following the methodological approach advanced in de Moraes Farias's study of the seventeenth-century "Timbuktu chronicles" and Holl's work on the *Dīwān salāṭīn Barnū*, which invite us to focus on the rhetorical construction and authorial intention of West and Central African chronicles instead of mining them for information, I uncover two distinct chronicles collapsed in Houdas and Delafosse's edition: the seventeenth-century *Tārīkh Ibn al-Mukhtār* and the nineteenth-century *Tārīkh al-fattāsh*. Since the dawn of the colonial period, however, these two chronicles have remained trapped together in the pages of *La chronique du chercheur.*[6]

Félix Dubois and the "Phantom Book of the Sudan"

On 16 December 1893 the skyline of Timbuktu presented some unfamiliar features to the gaze of contemporary viewers: the tricolored

4-1/2 (1970): 1–12; Nehemia Levtzion, "Mahmūd Ka'tī fut-il l'auteur de *Ta'rīkh al-fattāsh*?" *Bulletin de l'Institut Fondamental d'Afrique Noire. Série B, Sciences Humaines* 33 (1971): 665–674; Nehemia Levtzion, "A seventeenth-century chronicle by Ibn al-Mukhtār: A critical study of *Ta'rikh al-fattāsh*," *Bulletin of School of Oriental and African Studies* 34/3 (1971): 571–593.

5 Gérard Genette, *Palimpsests: Literature in the Second Degree* (Lincoln: University of Nebraska, 1997).

6 On de Moraes Farias and Holl's approach, see de Moraes Farias, *Arabic Medieval Inscriptions*; de Moraes Farias, "Barth"; de Moraes Farias, "Intellectual innovation"; Holl, *The Diwan Revisited*; Holl, "New perspectives."

French flag flew high above the city's buildings.[7] A platoon of French naval commandos, led by Lieutenant H. Gaston M. L. Boiteaux (d. 1897), had entered Timbuktu the previous night and negotiated its surrender without facing any resistance from the local population. However, the French forces were extremely small in number and were scattered widely: some in the city, others on the barges on the backwaters south of Timbuktu, and still others manning the gunboats *Niger* and *Mage* on the main branch of the River Niger, about 7.5 miles to the south. In all, there were fewer than forty soldiers armed with rifles, and just three cannons.

Lieutenant Boiteaux had entered Timbuktu on his own initiative, without the authorization of French military authorities, but he could not hold the city alone. Although the Tuareg lords of the region had not prevented the occupation of Timbuktu, they responded immediately afterward by putting the city under virtual siege. They also attacked and killed midshipman Léon Aube (d. 1893), who had been left in charge of the gunboats, as well as eighteen of his men stationed at Our-Oumaira, halfway between the river and Timbuktu. Alarmed by the Our-Oumaira attack, Colonel Eugène É. Bonnier (d. 1894) hastened to the Niger Bend from upstream, transporting an entire column of 400 men on local pirogues. They arrived on 10 January 1894 and Boiteaux, accused of insubordination for having taken Timbuktu without the approval of his superiors, was relieved of his command.

Bonnier was also destined to disappear from the scene. Setting out with a group of French and West African troops, he aimed to scout the route between Goundam and Timbuktu, as a second column of French soldiers was arriving by land from Segou, under the command of Colonel Joseph J. C. Joffre (d. 1931), a future hero of the Great War. At dawn on 15 January, in a place called Tacoubao, west of Timbuktu near Lake Figuibine, Bonnier was ambushed by the Tuareg and killed along with most of his men: more than eighty were slaughtered and

[7] Daniel Grévoz, *Les canonnières de Tombouctou: les Français à la conquête de la cité mythique, 1870–1894* (Paris: L'Harmattan, 1992) represents the best synthesis of the events that led to the conquest of Timbuktu, on which I base my reconstruction of Timbuktu's conquest. For a more general analysis of the French colonization of West Africa, see A. S. Kanya-Forstner, *The Conquest of the Western Sudan: A Study in French Military Imperialism* (Cambridge: Cambridge University Press, 1969).

only a few managed to escape.[8] Joffre and his soldiers arrived in Tacoubao on 8 February, where they buried their dead, and eventually reached Timbuktu four days later. From his base in the city, Joffre launched a series of campaigns against the Tuareg, to punish those involved in the Tacoubao events around the area of Goundam and later to the north of Timbuktu. In so doing, he became one of the main protagonists in the so-called pacification of the Sahara, in fact a series of brutal campaigns against the local inhabitants that continued into the 1930s.

Though the French did not yet have firm control over the Niger Bend, the news of the conquest of Timbuktu – the exotic city which for centuries had been the object of European desire – soon arrived in France.[9] The editor of the newspaper *Le Figaro*, Antonin Périvier (d. 1924), quickly invited two prominent journalists to visit and document the newly conquered prize: Jules Huret (d. 1915) and Dubois. Huret declined the offer, but Dubois, already an experienced traveler in Egypt, Palestine, Panama, and tropical Africa – he had covered the Brosselard–Faidherbe mission that had defined the border between French Guinea and British Sierra Leone in 1891 – accepted with enthusiasm.[10] By August 1894 Dubois was in Senegal. Two months later, in October, he left Dakar for Timbuktu. He arrived in January 1895, one year after the Tacoubao events, at the end of a grueling trip that involved a railway, a steamboat, porters, and a pirogue journey from Koulikoro. When Dubois returned to France six months later, his newspaper printed a special supplement entitled *Le Figaro à Tombouctou*.[11] In the following year, 1896, Dubois published his bestselling book, *Tombouctou la mystérieuse*.[12]

[8] For a description of the Tacoubao event from the point of view of the Tuareg, see Jacques Hureiki, "La version Touarègue de la bataille de Taqinbawt (Tacoubao) (15 janvier 1894)," *Journal des Africanistes* 73/1 (2003): 127–136.

[9] The genesis of the myth of Timbuktu is narrated in Eugenia W. Herbert, "Timbuktu: A case study of the role of legend in history," in *West African Culture Dynamics: Archaeological and Historical Perspectives*, edited by B. K. Swartz and R. E. Dumett (The Hague: Mouton, 1980), 431–454.

[10] On Dubois, see Yves-Jean Saint-Martin, *Félix Dubois, 1862–1945: grand reporter et explorateur, de Panama à Tamanrasset* (Paris: L'Harmattan, 1999).

[11] The special issue *Le Figaro à Tombouctou* (July 27, 1895) is available at http://gallica.BnF.fr/ark:/12148/bpt6k272818g.

[12] Félix Dubois, *Tombouctou la mystérieuse* (Paris: Flammarion, 1897). I used the English translation by Diana White (Félix Dubois, *Timbuctoo the Mysterious*, trans. Diana White [London: William Heinemann, 1897]).

The journalist's triumphalist tone and his explicit support for the French *mission civilisatrice* in Africa might deceive the casual reader into dismissing this work as a simple "travelogue," as *Tombouctou la mystérieuse* has recently been characterized.[13] Along with the German traveler Heinrich Barth (d. 1865), who had visited Timbuktu in 1853-4, Dubois can rightly be considered a pioneer among Western scholars in the history and philology of West Africa.[14] While in Timbuktu, he inspected several works in manuscript format and was impressed by the local scholars' libraries, filled with "ancient manuscripts," both "large" and "marvelous."[15] He was delighted with the idea, expressed in the racist language of the time, that "the learned doctors were, to use an expression which may appear strange when applied to Negroes, bibliophiles."[16] Hyperbolically, he concluded that "the libraries of Timbuctoo may be said to have included almost the whole of Arabian literature."[17]

During the weeks that he spent in Timbuktu, Dubois collected an astonishing amount of information on the written heritage of the town, thanks to his collaboration with local scholars who used to entertain him night and day in his courtyard:

> My visitors sat crouched upon their heels, while I occupied a solitary chair, with a little table and some blank paper before me ... It was a class, in fact, with the proportion reversed, the professors being the many and the pupil the one. The deliberate and picturesque phraseology of the Oriental flowed on unceasingly, recitations being succeeded by readings from the old chronicles of Timbuctoo.[18]

[13] Wise and Abu Taleb (ed. and trans.), *Ta'rīkh al-fattāsh*, ix.

[14] On the role of Barth in African historiography, see Mamadou Diawara, Paulo F. de Moraes Farias, and Gerd Spittler (eds.), *Heinrich Barth et l'Afrique* (Cologne: Köppe, 2006). The German traveler's work was published in 1857 both in English (Heinrich Barth, *Travels and Discoveries in North and Central Africa: Being a Journal of an Expedition Undertaken under the Auspices of H.B. M.'s Government in the Years 1849–1855*, 5 vols. [London: Longman, Brown, Green, Longmans and Robert, 1857]) and in German (Heinrich Barth, *Reisen und Entdeckungen in Nord- und Central-Afrika in den Jahren 1849 bis 1855: Tagebuch seinerim Auftrag der brittischen Regierung unternommenen Reise*, 5 vols. [Gotha: Justus Perthes, 1857]).

[15] Dubois, *Timbuctoo the Mysterious*, 276, 277, and 287.

[16] Dubois, *Timbuctoo the Mysterious*, 288.

[17] Dubois, *Timbuctoo the Mysterious*, 288.

[18] Dubois, *Timbuctoo the Mysterious*, 220.

Dubois was thus in a position to introduce his European audience to some of the most relevant works produced in the region of Timbuktu.[19] Among them was one that attracted his special attention: the *Tārīkh al-fattāsh*, which he called the *Fettassi*.[20] He described it as having been written by a then unknown scholar by the name of Maḥmūd Ka'ti:

[19] Among the works that the Dubois refers to in his book is the *Tārīkh al-Sūdān*, the famous seventeenth-century Timbuktu chronicle written by the historian al-Sa'dī (Dubois, *Timbuctoo the Mysterious*, 312–316 *passim*). The Arabic text is edited and translated into French in Octave V. Houdas (ed. and trans.), *Tarikh es-Soudan par Abderrahman ben Abdallah ben 'Imran bn 'Amir es-Sa'di*, 2 vols. (Paris: Ernest Leroux, 1898–1900). An English translation of the first twenty-seven chapters plus the thirtieth can be found in Hunwick, Timbuktu and the Songhay Empire, 1–270. On the *Tārīkh al-Sūdān*, see John O. Hunwick, *Arabic Literature of Africa*, vol. 4: *The Writings of Western Sudanic Africa* (Leiden and Boston: Brill, 2003) (henceforth *ALA* IV), 40–1, item 1. Dubois also refers to the *Ajwibat 'an as'ilat al-amīr Askiyà al-ḥājj Muḥammad*, the legal replies written at the turn of the sixteenth century by the Saharan jurist al-Maghīlī to the king of the Songhay Empire, Askiyà Muḥammad (Dubois, *Timbuctoo the Mysterious*, 299). On this work, edited and translated into English in John O. Hunwick, *Sharī'a in Songhay: The Replies of al-Maghīlī to the Questions of Askia al-Ḥājj Muḥammad* (London and New York: Oxford University Press for the British Academy, 1985), see John O. Hunwick, *Arabic Literature of Africa*, vol. 2: *The Writings of Central Sudanic Africa* (Leiden: Brill, 1995) (henceforth *ALA* II), 21, item 1. Dubois also mentions the anonymous biographical dictionary of the *pāshā*s of Timbuktu, the *Tadhkirat al-nisyān fī akhbār mulūk al-Sūdān*, edited and translated into French in Octave V. Houdas (ed. and trans.), *Tedzkiret en-nisiān fi akhbar molouk es-Soudān* (Paris: Ernest Leroux, 1901) (Dubois, *Timbuctoo the Mysterious*, 316; for the *Tadhkirat al-nisyān*, see *ALA* IV, 41–42, item 1); the *Dhikr al-wafāyāt wa-mā ḥadatha min al-umūr al-'iẓām wa-l-fitan* by Mūlāy al-Qāsim, a work written around 1800 including several necrologies and reports on historical events (Dubois, *Timbuctoo the Mysterious*, 316–317; on Mulāy al-Qāsim's *Dhikr al-wafāyāt*, translated into French as Michel Abitbol, *Tombouctou au milieu du XVIIIe siècle, d'après la chronique de Mawlay al-Qâsim b. Mawlay Sulaymân* [Paris: Maisonneuve et Larose, 1982], see *ALA* IV, 42, item 1); and the *fatwà* on slavery titled *Mi'rāj al-Ṣu'ūd ilà nayl ḥukm mujallab al-sūd* by the famous Timbuktu scholar Aḥmad Bābā, who lived between the sixteenth and the seventeenth century (Dubois, *Timbuctoo the Mysterious*, 309); on the *Mi'rāj al-Ṣu'ūd*, see *ALA* IV, 26, item 38. The work is edited and translated into English in John O. Hunwick and Fatima Harrak (ed. and trans.), *Mi'rāj al-Ṣu'ūd: Aḥmad Bābā's Replies on Slavery* (Rabat: Manshūrāt Ma'hd al-Dirāsāt al-Ifrīqīya, 2000).

[20] The name "Fettassi" is recorded by Dubois according to the local pronunciation of the Arabic *fattāsh* – which suppresses the voiceless palato-alveolar fricative *shīn* in favor of the voiceless dental fricative *sīn*; see *La chronique du chercheur*, xvi.

> Under the title of *Fettassi*, Koti [Maḥmūd Ka'ti] edited a history of the kingdoms of Ganata, Songhoi, and Timbuctoo, from their origins until 1554 (950 of Hegira). In spite of the most persistent research, I have not been able to procure more than fragments of this important work. Everyone knows all about it, but no one possesses it; it is the phantom book of the Sudan.[21]

Maḥmūd Ka'ti, according to local reports, was a famous and pious scholar, also remembered as a performer of miracles.[22] Despite the fact that Dubois failed to locate a copy of the *Tārīkh al-fattāsh*, he managed to collect some information that represents, in the words of de Moraes Farias, the very beginning of "critical inquiry into the *Ta'rīkh al-fattāsh*."[23]

Dubois's account of the chronicle was mainly based on oral information gleaned from a Timbuktu notable whom he described as being "very well informed," and who even claimed to be a descendant of Maḥmūd Ka'ti.[24] The notable convinced Dubois that the *Tārīkh al-fattāsh* had

> never been so well known as the other histories of the Sudan because it dealt with the concerns of many peoples and many men. Families, since grown rich and powerful, and the chiefs of various countries, were shown in it with very humble origins, sometimes being the offspring of slaves. The book caused great annoyance to many people on this account, and those interested bought all the copies they could procure and destroyed them.[25]

A single copy of *Tārīkh al-fattāsh* had escaped destruction, according to Dubois: this, the "original" manuscript, had been secretly hidden by his informant's ancestors. However, in the early nineteenth century a new threat to the manuscript had appeared on the horizon: Aḥmad Lobbo. At the time of the Caliphate of Ḥamdallāhi, Dubois's informant continued,

21 Dubois, *Timbuctoo the Mysterious*, 302. The name of the author of the work is given by Dubois as "Koti," elsewhere as "Mahmoud Koutou (or Koti)," "Mohaman Koti or Koutou" or even as "Ahmadou Koti" (Dubois, *Timbuctoo the Mysterious*, 135, 301, and 330).

22 Dubois, *Timbuctoo the Mysterious*, 302.

23 De Moraes Farias, *Arabic Medieval Inscriptions*, lxxi § 109.

24 Dubois, *Timbuctoo the Mysterious*, 303.

25 Dubois, *Timbuctoo the Mysterious*, 303.

> one of my great-aunts, living in Tindirmah, had inherited it [the manuscript of the *Tārīkh al-fattāsh*], and guarded it jealously. To avoid unpleasantness, and at the same time preserve the book from destruction, she had it placed in a wooden box and buried under a hillock close to her house. My aunt was a widow, and among other charms she possessed was the gift of conversation. Her house was the centre of frequent gatherings, and when she was asked, "What is this mound in your garden?" she always replied, "It is Ahmadou [*sic*] Koti, my venerable ancestor, who is buried there." Her friends never failed to say a short prayer over the mound, for Koti had left a great reputation for piety and wisdom behind him.[26]

The wily great-aunt zealously protected the buried manuscripts until, eventually,

> a Foulbe [i.e. Fulani] succeeded in becoming so intimate with my aunt that she imparted her secret to him. He immediately left Tindirmah, and went to his king, Cheikou Ahmadou [Aḥmad Lobbo], to reveal to him the existence of a complete copy of the *Fettassi*. Shortly afterwards the king sent a troop of soldiers to dig up the mound and discover its precious treasure; but as they were returning to Hamdallai, the bearer of the priceless volume capsized his canoe and the book was lost to the world forever.[27]

In Timbuktu, Dubois also collected some written documents – or "fragments," as he described them – that allowed him to expand further his reconstruction of the history of the chronicle. These documents, eventually donated to the Bibliothèque nationale de France, "amply" proved, according to Dubois, the "inestimable value" of the chronicle.[28] Since he calls them "fragments," one is tempted to believe that he had found pieces of lengthier manuscripts preserving the text of the *Tārīkh al-fattāsh*. However, his description reveals that they were, in fact, copies of another document altogether:

[26] Dubois, *Timbuctoo the Mysterious*, 303.
[27] Dubois, *Timbuctoo the Mysterious*, 303–304.
[28] Dubois, *Timbuctoo the Mysterious*, 303. This document is very common in West African collections. Hunwick refers to it as the *Risāla fī ẓuhūr al-khalīfa al-thānī ʿashar*, or *Epistle on the Arrival of the Twelfth Caliph* and its author, the "influential" but anonymous scholar mentioned by Dubois, is Nūḥ b. al-Ṭāhir b. Mūsà, no other than the one who composed the *Tārīkh al-fattāsh* (see *ALA* IV, 213, item 1). Dubois donated two copies of the letter to the BnF, accessible under the inventory number BnF, manuscript arabe, 5259, ff. 74a–78b and BnF, manuscript arabe, 5259, ff. 79a–84b. On this epistle, see Chapter 6.

An Arabian work ... a little pamphlet of propaganda, written and disseminated by an influential marabut at the instigation of Cheikou Ahmadou. The author pompously addresses himself to the whole of Africa; "... The twelve of the regenerating Khalifs, he after whom the Mahdi comes, is born. He is the Sheik, the Emir of the Faithful, Ahmadou ben Mohammed [Aḥmad Lobbo], who is risen to restore the faith of the Lord and do battle for God in the Sudan."[29]

According to Dubois, the unnamed author of the pamphlet justified his claims by embedding a forged episode in an apparently genuine story: the late fifteenth-century pilgrimage to Mecca made by the renowned ruler of the Askiyà dynasty of the Songhay Empire, Askiyà Muḥammad.[30] In Dubois's view, the original narrative employed in the pamphlet would have come from the *Tārīkh al-fattāsh*. The first part of the story of the king's visit to the sacred places of Islam, Dubois asserts, "is accurate enough and fairly approximates the history, but after this we enter the region of fable, the mythical facts of interested trickery."[31]

The "trickery" to which the French journalist refers was a prophecy inserted in the document "under the pretence of [being a] quotation" from the *Tārīkh al-fattāsh*. It "foretold" the ascent of Aḥmad Lobbo and was ascribed to the fifteenth-century Egyptian polymath Jalāl al-Dīn al-Suyūṭī (d. 1505).[32] Dubois immediately spotted a forgery: "it can scarcely be necessary to explain that this prophecy is not to be found in the *Fettassi*, but was invented to assist the cause of Cheikou Ahmadou and the Foulbes."[33] Dubois was technically correct to identify this insertion as a conscious, politically motivated anachronism. However, by summarily dismissing this nineteenth-century manipulation of the historical text, Dubois inaugurated a problematic

29 Dubois, *Timbuctoo the Mysterious*, 135.
30 *Askiyà* is the royal title of the second dynasty of the Songhay Empire. In spite of a folk etymology provided in the *Tārīkh al-Sūdān* that locates the emergence of the title to the second half of the fifteenth century (Houdas [ed. and trans.], *Tarikh es-Soudan*, Arabic text 72/French text 118; Hunwick, *Timbuktu and the Songhay Empire*, 103), epigraphic evidence shows that the title was in use as early as the thirteenth century, originally given to "a headgroom and Master of Horse" and later developed into "a military commander close to the ruler" (de Moraes Farias, *Arabic Medieval Inscriptions*, xcix § 199).
31 Dubois, *Timbuctoo the Mysterious*, 136.
32 Dubois, *Timbuctoo the Mysterious*, 135.
33 Dubois, *Timbuctoo the Mysterious*, 137.

approach to the study of the *Tārīkh al-fattāsh* that erased the nineteenth century from the history of the chronicle and which all later scholars of the chronicle have inherited, including Houdas and Delafosse, who produced the widespread 1913 edition and French translation called *La chronique du chercheur*.

La chronique du chercheur

A few years after Dubois first reported news of the *Tārīkh al-fattāsh* in France, the explorer Albert L. M. J. Bonnel de Mézières (d. 1942) started the collection of the manuscript corpus that eventually allowed Houdas and Delafosse to publish *La chronique du chercheur*.[34] Between 1911 and 1913, Bonnel de Mézières was commissioned by the governor of the Federation of French West Africa, François Joseph Clozel (d. 1918), to undertake a series of missions in the region of Timbuktu and Walāta (Islamic Republic of Mauritania). During these missions, Bonnel de Mézières collected seventy-six Arabic manuscripts, most of which are, unfortunately, untraceable today.[35]

One of these manuscripts, found in 1911 in Timbuktu, attracted the explorer's attention. It was an incomplete manuscript, lacking its beginning, "believed in Timbuktu to be the only surviving copy of a very important work on the history of the Soudan."[36] Unwilling to part with this precious manuscript, the owner had a copy made for Bonnel de Mézières.[37] Eventually, this manuscript would be identified, mistakenly, as a copy of the *Tārīkh al-fattāsh* which had been described by Dubois in 1895–6. In fact, a note written on the false guard-leaf of the manuscript proves that the manuscript was not actually acknowledged as such by its owner:

[34] For a short biography of Bonnel de Mézières, see Numa Broc, *Dictionnaire illustré des explorateurs et grands voyageurs français du XIXe siècle* (Paris: Éditions du CTHS, 1988), 35–36.

[35] Albert Bonnel de Mézières, "Note sur ses récentes découvertes, d'après un télégramme adressé par lui, le 23 mars 1914, à M. le gouverneur Clozel," *Comptes rendus des séances de l'Académie des Inscriptions et Belles-Lettres* 58/3 (1914): 253–257. These manuscripts are briefly described in Maurice Delafosse, "Notes sur les manuscrits acquis en 1911 et 1912 par M. Bonnel de Mézières dans la région de Tombouctou-Oualata (Haut-Sénégal et Niger)," *Annales et Mémoires de l'Afrique-Occidentale Française* (1916): 120–129.

[36] *La chronique du chercheur*, viii.

[37] *La chronique du chercheur*, viii.

Book of collection of biographies of the kings of Songhay and a fragment of the report on the kings of the Sūdān and the kings who predate the Songhay, such as the Sultan Kayama'a or the Sultan of Mali KNK Mūsà. I did not find the name of the author because of the loss of one or two pages at the beginning.[38]

Although incomplete, the manuscript made for Bonnel de Mézières was judged to be very important, and Clozel ordered it to be sent to the École des langues orientales where it was examined by a professor of Arabic and prominent French Orientalist of the time, Houdas.[39] Among Houdas's diverse interests were the Arabic writings of West African scholars.[40] In 1912, when Houdas received the manuscript, he had already published the edition and the French translation of the *Tadhkirat al-nisyān* (The Reminder for the Forgetful) (1890) and the *Tārīkh al-Sūdān* (The Chronicle of the Sudan) (1898–1900).[41]

Houdas immediately recognized the relevance of the new chronicle, which "constituted a document of primary relevance for the history of the French Sudan and fortunately provided supplementary information to the one provided by the *Tārīkh al-Sūdān*."[42] However, because the manuscript was incomplete, he insisted that Bonnel de Mézières attempt to find a complete copy. The latter sent a letter to the Timbuktu notable who owned the original manuscript. He was unable to satisfy this request, but along with the letter in which he informed Bonnel de Mézières of his failed search, he enclosed his own manuscript of the work, i.e. the one used weeks earlier to copy the work for the

38 See BnF, 6651, False guard-leaf. "KNK" is normally read in Africanist historiography as "Kankan" (see, for example, Hunwick, *Timbuktu and the Songhay Empire*, 9). I preferred to leave this name unvocalized, as no agreement has been reached by scholars on its pronunciation.

39 For a short biography of Houdas, see Louise Delafosse, *Maurice Delafosse: le Berrichon conquis par l'Afrique* (Paris and Abbeville: Société française d'histoire d'outremer, 1977), 289–293; and Jean-Louis Triaud, "Haut-Sénégal-Niger, un modèle 'positiviste'? De la coutume à l'histoire: Maurice Delafosse et l'invention de l'histoire africaine," in *Maurice Delafosse. Entre orientalisme et ethnographie: l'itinéraire d'un Africaniste, 1870–1926*, edited by Jean-Loup Amselle and Emmanuelle Sibeud (Paris: Maisonneuve et Larose, 1998), 210–232, 213–215.

40 Apart from his translations of the Timbuktu chronicles, Houdas is well known for his translation of works on Islamic law, the history of Morocco, the calligraphies of the Islamic West, and Arabic grammar.

41 Houdas (ed. and trans.), *Tarikh es-Soudan* and Houdas (ed. and trans.), *Tedzkiret en-nisiān*.

42 *La chronique du chercheur*, ix.

French explorer.[43] Houdas labeled this latter manuscript MS A, because it was the older of the two, while the copy made for Bonnel de Mézières, he labeled MS B.[44]

In the summer of 1912, during a retreat with his family at Sancergues in central France, Houdas was busy editing the Arabic text of these manuscripts when he was joined by his son-in-law, Delafosse, who had studied Arabic under Houdas at the École des langues orientales and had eventually married Alice Houdas in 1907.[45] Now a famous scholar who occupied prestigious positions such as that of Professor of Sudanese languages at the École des langues orientales, the École colonial, the École des sciences politiques, and the École d'ethnographie, Delafosse was a very versatile intellectual, as proven by his 1912 *Haut-Sénégal-Niger*.[46] This is a work that covers several different disciplines and uses a wide range of sources, confirming Delafosse's location of his expertise "between Orientalism and Ethnography."[47]

When Houdas had started working, he did not know either the title or the author of the chronicle he was working on. However, late in 1912, Bonnel de Mézières found a single leaf recording a short legend about the origins of the Songhay that one of his local informants, unfortunately unidentified, told him was from the *Tārīkh al-fattāsh*. This legend was identical to one isolated leaf that was attached to MS A. Assuming that this isolated leaf was part of the beginning of the chronicle, and learning that Bonnel de Mézières's leaf had allegedly come from the *Tārīkh al-fattāsh*, Houdas and Delafosse began to

[43] *La chronique du chercheur*, x. The original manuscript included three isolated leaves with different texts, two of which Houdas thought might have come from the missing beginning of the manuscript; the third was a fragment of the *Tārīkh al-Sūdān* (*La chronique du chercheur*, x).

[44] *La chronique du chercheur*, ix–x.

[45] See the detailed biography of Delafosse, written by his daughter (Delafosse, *Maurice Delafosse*).

[46] Maurice Delafosse, *Haut-Sénégal-Niger*, 3 vols. (Paris: Larose, 1912). As underlined by Jean-Louis Triaud, who has studied the correspondence between Delafosse and Charles Monteil (d. 1949), Delafosse joined Houdas when the latter had already partially edited and translated the text, and contributed substantially to the critical apparatus of their translation (Triaud, "De la coutume à l'histoire," 225).

[47] I have borrowed the title of the collection of essays devoted to Delafosse: Amselle and Sibeud (eds.), *Maurice Delafosse, Entre orientalisme et ethnographie*.

suspect that their text was the Timbuktu chronicle long sought by Dubois. "Our supposition was soon confirmed," they wrote.[48]

By the end of 1912, Jules Brévié (d. 1964), a colonial administrator and a specialist in Arabic and West African history, previewed part of Houdas and Delafosse's translation.[49] Brévié recognized several passages as being like those from a manuscript he had bought in Kayes, which was a copy of the *Tārīkh al-fattāsh*. This manuscript had been copied on 29 May 1912 from "an original, very old and in bad condition."[50]

Brévié sent this manuscript to Houdas and Delafosse, which they labeled MS C.[51] After having analyzed it, the two scholars assumed that it contained the complete text of the first manuscript provided by Bonnel de Mézières, MS B: "[MS C] is in fact the same work discovered by M. Bonnel de Mézières, but complete, with its *true title* ... and the name of its *author* Maḥmūd Ka'ti."[52] By collating these three manuscripts, they produced what they thought to be a reliable edition of the entire work: "We find ourselves in the possession of all the elements necessary to reconstruct, more or less completely, a first order work on the history of the Soudan."[53]

According to Houdas and Delafosse, the chronicle they had "reconstructed" was initiated in 1519 by Maḥmūd Ka'ti.[54] Its full title was *Tārīkh al-fattāsh fī akhbār al-buldān wa-l-juyūsh wa-akābir al-nās*, which they translated as *La chronique du chercheur pour servir à l'histoire des villes, des armées et des principaux personnages du Tekrour*.[55] This chronicle, they reported, was then updated on the basis of notes left by members of the Ka'ti family, by one of Maḥmūd Ka'ti's grandsons, known only as "the son of al-Mukhtār" – Ibn al-Mukhtār, around 1664–5.[56] In summarizing their argument, Houdas

48 *La chronique du chercheur*, x.

49 Robert Cornevin, "Jules Brévié," in *Hommes et destins*, vol. 5: *Expansion coloniale* (Paris: Académie des sciences d'outre-mer, 1975), 86.

50 *La chronique du chercheur*, xi. This copy displays the wrong date, 1335/1917 (*La chronique du chercheur*, Arabic text 184). This should read 1330/1912, as the copyist mixed the use of Arabic and Indian numerals, confusing ٥ with 0 – or alternatively Houdas and Delafosse read the manuscript wrongly (١٣٣٥ in place of ١٣٣٠).

51 *La chronique du chercheur*, x–xi.

52 *La chronique du chercheur*, xi (italics mine).

53 *La chronique du chercheur*, xiii.

54 *La chronique du chercheur*, xvii.

55 *La chronique du chercheur*, xvi.

56 *La chronique du chercheur*, xix.

and Delafosse stated: "It is to the collaboration of the grandfather, uncles, and grandson that the *Tārīkh al-fattāsh* is due. The real compiler of the work was the grandson of Maḥmūd Ka'ti [i.e. Ibn al-Mukhtār], who was the first inspiration."[57]

After Ibn al-Mukhtār had completed the chronicle, according to Houdas and Delafosse's theory, its first chapter was "slightly modified" in the early nineteenth century by the addition of the prophecy aimed at conferring religious and political legitimacy on Aḥmad Lobbo – confirming the argument that Dubois had already advanced on the basis of oral sources in his *Tombouctou la mysterieuse*.[58] However, Houdas and Delafosse, like Dubois before them, dismissed the importance of the prophecy as "an *hors-d'oeuvre* within the work we are dealing with, more bizarre than actually interesting."[59] That said, the nineteenth-century intervention helped them to explain the discrepancies among MSS A, B, and C. MS A is incomplete and lacks a beginning. MS B, being a copy of MS A, also preserves the work only partially. Hence, the editors reasoned, both copies contained a version of the chronicle that did not conform to the nineteenth-century *vulgata* because it had not included the prophecy; both, they argued, were therefore deprived of their beginnings due to censorship by the agents of Aḥmad Lobbo. By contrast, they further reasoned, MS C was complete and therefore represented the whole text, including the prophecy. They concluded that, although MS C also includes other passages which do not appear in the other two copies of the chronicle, the three manuscripts preserved different recensions of the same text.

Another, final, manuscript came into the hands of Houdas and Delafosse. In September 1913, when *La chronique du chercheur* was already in press, Bonnel de Mézières bought another manuscript from Timbuktu.[60] It was an incomplete chronicle written on behalf of an *askiyà* of Timbuktu named Askiyà Dawūd b. Hārūn (r. 1657–1669), who had ruled under the Arma.[61] According to Houdas and Delafosse, this work – which reproduced verbatim several passages of the text they had edited – was a draft of the original chronicle compiled by Ibn

57 *La chronique du chercheur*, xix. 58 *La chronique du chercheur*, xii.
59 *La chronique du chercheur*, xii. 60 *La chronique du chercheur*, 326.
61 The second appendix was in the hands of Delafosse until at least 1916 when he wrote a note on the manuscripts purchased by Bonnel de Mézières (Delafosse, "Notes sur les manuscrits," 129). Unfortunately, I could not locate this manuscript and I can only rely on the Houdas and Delafosse French translations.

al-Mukhtār that was eventually updated to produce in the final version of the *Tārīkh al-fattāsh*.[62] Sensing the importance of this chronicle, they published its French translation as the second appendix to *La chronique du chercheur*.

As it emerges from their introduction, Houdas and Delafosse recognized that the *Tārīkh al-fattāsh* had gone through several textual manipulations. Nonetheless, displaying an almost blind confidence in the authenticity of *La chronique du chercheur* as a whole, they had little doubt about the authenticity of the chronicle they had edited and translated.

Tārīkh al-fattāsh Studies

The complicated textual history of *La chronique du chercheur* could have not failed to attract the attention of scholars. In 1914, just one year after its publication, P. Joseph Brun, a Christian missionary in Algiers, produced a careful book review that spurred a continuous tradition of critical studies.[63] After that, for more than fifty years – while both scholars and colonial administrators continued to use this work extensively – there were no further contributions to its critique, with the exception of a few remarks by Charles Monteil in his work on the medieval Empire of Mali.[64] It was the late 1960s and early 1970s that saw the resurgence of scholarship on *La chronique du chercheur*.

Hunwick inaugurated a series of articles whose latest installment was published in the early 2000s.[65] Between 1970 and 1971 Levtzion published three articles that revolutionized the understanding of the chronicle.[66] In 1972, Ly published a detailed review of all the problematic issues characterizing the chronicle as represented by this edition.[67] Later, Michel Abitbol briefly contributed to the topic in his

62 *La chronique du chercheur*, French text 326.
63 Brun, "Notes sur le 'Tarikh-El-Fettach'."
64 Charles Monteil, *Les empires du Mali* (Paris: Larose, 1930).
65 Hunwick, "Studies in the *Ta'rīkh al-Fattāsh*, I"; Hunwick, "Studies in the *Ta'rīkh al-Fattāsh*, II"; Hunwick, "Studies in the *Ta'rīkh al-Fattāsh*, III."
66 Levtzion, "Was Maḥmūd Ka'tī the author"; Levtzion, "Mahmūd Ka'tī fut-il l'auteur de *Ta'rīkh al-fattāsh*?"; Levtzion, "A seventeenth-century chronicle."
67 Ly, "Quelques remarques," 471. Ly did not have access to Levtzion's article when she published her contribution, as confirmed by a personal communication by Levtzion to Dramani-Issufou dated 17 July 1973: "Mme Ly told me in a letter that she has read my article only after her article was already

study of Timbuktu under Arma rule.[68] In the early 2010s, with the approach of the centennial of the publication of *La chronique du chercheur*, a revived interest in the chronicle was catalyzed by Christopher Wise and Hala Abu Taleb, who in 2011 published a translation into English, based largely on the French translation.[69] In the following year came a new edition of the Arabic text as edited by Houdas and Delafosse, equipped with new annotations by Ḥamā' Allāh Wuld Sālim.[70] Finally, in 2014, two new Arabic editions, also based on *La chronique du chercheur*, were published by West African scholars: one by a team attached to the IHERI-ABT and the second by Ādam Bambā.[71]

What follows is a systematic review of this existing scholarship, organized according to the main issues raised by the work of Houdas and Delafosse: authorship, textual history and interpolation, title, and the second appendix.

Authorship

The issue of the authorship of the chronicle is inextricably related to the unlikely extent of Maḥmūd Ka'ti's lifespan, as reported in *La chronique du chercheur*, which has raised the suspicion of several scholars: if Maḥmūd Ka'ti really was born in 1468, he would have been 125 years old when he died in 1593.[72] His purported dates come from different, and often contradictory, sources. His date of birth is derived from the text of *La chronique du chercheur*, in which Maḥmūd Ka'ti states that he was twenty-five years old in 898/1492–3, the year in which Askiyà Muḥammad defeated his predecessor, and the last ruler of the Sonni dynasty, Sonni Bāru.[73] As for his death, it is recorded in an obituary

with the editor" (Zakari Dramani-Issifou, *L'Afrique noire dans les relations internationales au XVIe siècle: analyse de la crise entre le Maroc et le Sonrhai* [Paris: Karthala/Centre de Recherches Africaines, 1982], 31, n. 27).

68 Abitbol, *Tombouctou et les Arma.*

69 Wise and Abu Taleb (ed. and trans.), *Ta'rīkh al-fattāsh.*

70 Wuld Sālim (ed.), Tārīkh al-fattāsh.

71 Bambā (ed.), *Tārīkh al-fattāsh*; Maiga et al. (eds.), *Tārīkh al-fattāsh.*

72 *La chronique du chercheur*, xvii.

73 *La chronique du chercheur*, French text 113/Arabic text 58. Different forms of the title Sonni occur in the sources. According to a comparative study of such forms by Hunwick, it seems that the correct pronunciation would be "sõṅyi" (Hunwick, *Timbuktu and the Songhay Empire*, appendix 2, 333–334). In spite of that, and in spite of the fact that the form *shī* is the one that appears in the

included in the *Tārīkh al-Sūdān* as 1 Muḥarram 1002/ 26 September 1593.[74] However, local variant traditions were reported by Dubois. First, the date of birth of Maḥmūd Ka'ti was given as 1460.[75] According to the same source, Maḥmūd Ka'ti would have survived Askiyà Muḥammad by fourteen years.[76] This means that he finally passed away in 958/1551, since Askiyà Muḥammad died in 944/ 1538, as reported by the *Tārīkh al-Sūdān.*[77]

The first theory put forward by scholars to solve the problem of Maḥmūd Ka'ti's age was advanced by Brun, who argued for the existence of two men of the same name who were involved in the production of the chronicle.[78] According to his hypothesis, Maḥmūd Ka'ti I was born in 1468, as recorded in *La chronique du chercheur*, and died in 1553–4, following the tradition recorded by Dubois mentioned above.[79] Maḥmūd Ka'ti I was the author of the original chronicle, but his work was then built upon by his descendants. A homonymous relative of Maḥmūd Ka'ti I, whom Brun called Maḥmūd Ka'ti II, was among those who reworked the original chronicle. He was born during the reign of Askiyà Muḥammad, i.e. 1493–1529, and died in 1593.[80] The birth date of Maḥmūd Ka'ti II comes from Brun's critique of a sentence in the Houdas and Delafosse translation. The Arabic text has "wulida fī ayyām Askià Muḥammad, Muḥammad b. Muḥammad b. Sa'īd ... wa-l-faqīh al-qāḍī Maḥmūd b. al-ḥājj al-Mutawakkil Ka'ti."[81] The sentence is translated by Houdas and Delafosse as "du vivant de l'*askia* Mohammed naquirent: Mohammed ben Mohammed ben Saïd ... [et] le juriconsulte et câdi Mahmoûd ben El-Hâjj El-Motaouakkel Kâti" – or, in English, "during the life of Askiyà

Tārīkh al-fattāsh, I decided to use the form *sonni* throughout, as it is the one most used in current scholarship.

74 Houdas (ed. and trans.), *Tarikh es-Soudan*, Arabic text 211/French text 322; Hunwick, *Timbuktu and the Songhay Empire*, 260.

75 Dubois, *Timbuctoo the Mysterious*, 302.

76 Dubois, *Timbuctoo the Myserious*, 302.

77 Houdas (ed. and trans.), *Tarikh es-Soudan*, Arabic text 94/French text 156; Hunwick, *Timbuktu and the Songhay Empire*, 135–136.

78 Wise and Abu Taleb (ed. and trans.), *Ta'rīkh al-fattāsh*, completely neglect this issue.

79 However, here Brun miscalculates the date of death of Maḥmūd Ka'ti: Fourteen years of the Islamic calendar after 1538, the death of Askiyà Muḥammad would be 1551 and not 1553/4.

80 Brun, "Notes sur le 'Tarikh-El-Fettach'," 596.

81 *La chronique du chercheur*, Arabic text 82.

Muḥammad were born: Muḥammad b. Muḥammad b. Saʿīd . . . [and] the jurist and *qāḍī* Maḥmūd b. al-Ḥājj al-Mutawakkil Kaʿti."[82] Brun, along with Hunwick and Levtzion later on, notes a mistranslation here, since the expression *fī ayyām*, when associated with the name of a ruler, means "during the reign" and not "during the life."[83] Brun concluded, here still following Houdas and Delafosse, that a descendant of both Maḥmūd Kaʿtis, Ibn al-Mukhtār, was the "final redactor" of the chronicle in the form represented by the edited text.[84]

Hunwick accepted Brun's theory of the existence of two Maḥmūd Kaʿtis and substantiated it with reference to further evidence that had escaped Brun's scrutiny.[85] According to the *Tārīkh al-Sūdān*, Maḥmūd Kaʿti I was a student of Aḥmad b. Muḥammad al-Saʿīd, a scholar born in 1523–4.[86] If there had been only one Maḥmūd Kaʿti, born in 1468, he would have studied with Aḥmad b. Muḥammad al-Saʿīd at the ripe old age of more than eighty-five, "hardly an age at which to come and sit at the feet of anyone, let alone a man so young."[87] Hunwick concludes that it was Maḥmūd Kaʿti II, the younger, who could have attended Aḥmad b. Muḥammad al-Saʿīd's lessons. Furthermore, during the reign of Askiyà Dāwūd (r. 1549–1583), Maḥmūd Kaʿti went to Gao to see the *askiyà* and asked for gifts for his daughters, who were getting married, and for his son, who was completing his studies.[88] If Maḥmūd Kaʿti had been born in 1468, he would have been between 81 and 115 years old, "too advanced in years to be travelling about on behalf of daughters of marriageable age (i.e. 14–15)."[89] In her contribution to the topic, Ly mainly follows the same path as Brun and

[82] *La chronique du chercheur*, French text 153.
[83] Brun, "Notes sur le 'Tarikh-El-Fettach'"; Hunwick, "Studies in the *Ta'rīkh al-Fattāsh*, I"; Levtzion, "A seventeenth-century chronicle."
[84] Brun, "Notes sur le 'Tarikh-El-Fettach'."
[85] Hunwick, "Studies in the *Ta'rīkh al-Fattāsh*, I." It is not clear why Hunwick refers to Maḥmūd Kaʿti I as "Kaṭe" (Hunwick, "Studies in the *Ta'rīkh al-Fattāsh*, I," 57). Ḥamā' Allāh Wuld Sālim embraces the theory of the two Kaʿtīs (Wuld Sālim [ed.], *Tārīkh al-fattāsh*).
[86] Houdas (ed. and trans.), *Tarikh es-Soudan*, Arabic text 35/French text 57; Hunwick, *Timbuktu and the Songhay Empire*, 49. On the birth of Aḥmad b. Muḥammad al-Saʿīd, see Houdas (ed. and trans.), *Tarikh es-Soudan*, Arabic text 43/French text 71; Hunwick, *Timbuktu and the Songhay Empire*, 62.
[87] Hunwick, "Studies in the *Ta'rīkh al-Fattāsh*, I," 58.
[88] *La chronique du chercheur*, Arabic text 118/French text 217.
[89] Hunwick, "Studies in the *Ta'rīkh al-Fattāsh*, I," 58–59.

Hunwick, with two Maḥmūd Ka'tis involved in the writing of the chronicle and Ibn al-Mukhtār defined as a mere "compiler."[90]

An alternative theory was advanced by Levtzion, who argued that the *Tārīkh al-fattāsh* is a seventeenth-century work written exclusively by Ibn al-Mukhtār.[91] He contended that, among the three manuscripts used by Houdas and Delafosse, only two represent the original chronicle: MS A and its copy, MS B.[92] By carefully analyzing the edited Arabic text of *La chronique du chercheur*, Levtzion argued that all the passages absent from these two manuscripts, but present in MS C, were later forged interpolations.[93] As the result of this theory, he convincingly suggested that Maḥmūd Ka'ti did not have a life of extreme length. Employing exclusively evidence from MS A, the "original chronicle" according to Levtzion, and from the *Tārīkh al-Sūdān*, a more plausible biography of Maḥmūd Ka'ti emerges: a scholar born sometime during Askiyà Muḥammad's reign, most likely in the 1510s, associated with Askiyà Dāwūd, who died in 1593 at the age of seventy or eighty.[94] Moreover, Maḥmūd Ka'ti, concluded Levtzion, was not the author of the chronicle, not even of its first section, as advanced by other scholars.[95] Rather, the *Tārīkh al-fattāsh* is a "coherent work of history" written by "one author – Ibn al-Mukhtār, of the second half of the seventeenth century – and not a product of three successive generations" or more, as accepted by other scholars.[96] This theory was eventually introduced to an Arabic-speaking audience by the detailed introduction of Bambā's edition.[97]

More recently, a new theory has been advanced in the introduction to the new Arabic edition of the IHERI-ABT team, by Harouna Almahadi Maiga.[98] There were not only two Ka'tis (as advanced by Brun, Hunwick, and Ly): there were three of them engaged in compiling the *Tārīkh al-fattāsh*, but it was only the third one, Maḥmūd Ka'ti b. al-Mukhtār al-QNBL (*sic*) – read as Kombèle – who wrote the chronicle around 1664.[99] Maiga relies on the fascinating story of the

90 Ly, "Quelques remarques," 492.
91 Levtzion, "A seventeenth-century chronicle," 579.
92 Levtzion, "A seventeenth-century chronicle," 573.
93 Levtzion, "A seventeenth-century chronicle," 578.
94 Levtzion, "A seventeenth-century chronicle," 575.
95 Levtzion, "A seventeenth-century chronicle," 577.
96 Levtzion, "A seventeenth-century chronicle," 579.
97 Bambā (ed.), *Tārīkh al-fattāsh*. 98 Maiga et al. (eds.), *Tārīkh al-fattāsh*.
99 Maiga et al. (eds.), *Tārīkh al-fattāsh*, 33.

Ka'ti family as advanced by Ismael Diadié Haïdara, the curator of the Timbuktu-based Fondo Kati Library, according to which Maḥmūd Ka'ti was a descendant of Muslim Visigoths who had left Andalusia in 1467 and settled in West Africa, where they left notes on the history of their family in the margins of their family collection of manuscripts.[100] Unfortunately, this complex and fascinating story cannot survive academic scrutiny.[101] In 2015, Susana Molins Lliteras

[100] The popularity of this story dates to a 2001 article by Hunwick (Hunwick, "Studies in the *Ta'rīkh al-Fattāsh*, III"). He described the recent discovery of an apparently amazing manuscript in a Timbuktu collection that was soon to become known worldwide: the Fondo Kati, the collection of the alleged descendants of Maḥmūd Ka'ti. It was a copy of the very popular biography of the Prophet Muḥammad, *Kitāb al-shifā' bi-ta'rīf ḥuqūq al-Muṣṭafà* (Healing by the Recognition of the Reality of the Chosen One), by the twelfth-century Andalusian scholar known as Qāḍī 'Iyād. What made this manuscript unique was the presence of a marginal note dated July–August 1468, recording a purchase of the manuscript by one 'Alī b. Ziyād al-Qūṭī, i.e. the Goth, while on his way from his native Andalusia to West Africa. The offspring of this 'Alī b. Ziyād al-Qūṭī was Maḥmūd Ka'ti, who would consequently be of Andalusian descent. This note is just one of the many found in the Fondo Kati. It is these marginalia, or notes written in the margins of manuscripts, that make this collection special in the crowded library landscape of Timbuktu. On the basis of these notes, the current curator of the Fondo Kati, I. D. Haïdara, provides a narrative that purports to add new information on the personality of Maḥmūd Ka'ti, based on oral traditions in his family and on the marginalia of the Fondo Kati collection which have been recently brought together in a book he co-authored with Manuel Pimentel (Ismaël Diadié Haïdara and Manuel Pimentel, *Tombuctú: Andalusíes en la ciudad perdida del Sáhara* [Córdoba: Almuzara, 2015]). Maḥmūd Ka'ti's ancestors, according to I. D. Haïdara's reconstruction, were Muslim descendants of the last Visigoth king of Spain before the Arab conquest, Witiza (r. 700–710). One of Witiza's descendants, 'Alī b. Ziyād, left his hometown, Toledo in Andalusia, after the "Fuego de la Magdalena," the 1467 revolt of local Muslims and Jews, to escape the Christians' revenge. 'Alī b. Ziyād al-Qūṭī eventually arrived in sub-Saharan Africa where he settled in the Western Niger Bend ca. 1471. There, he intermarried with the local population, marrying Khadīja of the Soninke Silla clan, who was the niece of the Songhay king Sonni 'Alī and the eldest sister of Askiyà Muḥammad. Slowly the Andalusian Visigoths became, according to I. D. Haïdara, assimilated with the Soninke, from which the *nisba* Wa'kurī, i.e. Wa'kore – or Soninke in Arabic – arose, but they kept their Andalusia Gothic descent inscribed in their other *nisba*, Ka'ti, which would be a version of al-Qūṭī. Maḥmūd Ka'ti was the firstborn African son of 'Alī b. Ziyād al-Qūṭī.

[101] The first study of the Kati family, by Albrecht Hofheinz, was not based on the study of the manuscripts themselves, but on I. D. Haïdara's narrative plus "several notes John Hunwick photographed during his visit in Timbuktu in 1999" (Albrecht Hofheinz, "Goths in the Lands of the Blacks: A preliminary survey of the Ka'ti Library in Timbuktu," in *The Transmission of Learning in*

concluded the first in-depth study of this collection in her Ph.D. dissertation.[102] On the basis of her personal interviews with I. D. Haïdara, as well as the study of his publications in Spanish and of the marginalia found on a set of images from the Fondo Kati library, Molins Lliteras found that these notes are problematic from several points of view, from codicological (paper, inks, and decorations), to paleographic and chronological, thus concluding that "the marginalia from the Kati collection, said to date from the fifteenth and sixteenth centuries, ostensibly could not have been written on those purported dates."[103] The marginal notes seem to date from the nineteenth century at the earliest, but more probably from the late twentieth century. Therefore, once I. D. Haïdara's fascinating story is disproved, the theory advanced by Maiga is unsustainable.[104]

Textual History and Interpolations

Almost all the scholars who have worked on *La chronique du chercheur* have agreed that the work, and the manuscripts on which it was based, has a complex textual history comprising several layers of authorship and interpolation. Brun cast the first doubts that the edited chronicle corresponds to the original one.[105] For him, the original

Islamic Africa, edited by Scott S. Reese [Leiden and Boston: Brill, 2004], 154–183, 171, n. 37).

102 Susana Molins-Lliteras, "Africa Starts in the Pyrenees: The Fondo Kati, between al-Andalus and Timbuktu" (Ph.D. dissertation, University of Cape Town, 2015).

103 Molins-Lliteras, "Africa Starts in the Pyrenees," 224–225.

104 A bizarre theory on the authorship of the *Tārīkh al-fattāsh* is tangentially provided in Elias Saad, *Social History of Timbuktu: The Role of Muslim Scholars and Notables, 1400–1900* (Cambridge and New York: Cambridge University Press, 1983). Saad advances the idea that the original author was the famous Timbuktu scholar Maḥmūd b. ʿUmar Aqīt al-Ṣanhājī al-Masūfī (d. 1548) or somebody from his family (Saad, *Social History of Timbuktu*, 46; on Maḥmūd b. ʿUmar Aqīt, see *ALA* IV, 13–14). According to Saad, the chronicle was appropriated by Maḥmūd Kaʿti's family when one of the latter's sons, Ismaʿīl, incorporated Maḥmūd b. ʿUmar Aqīt's chronicle into its own historiographical work, which he called *Tārīkh al-fattāsh* and was then finalized by a son of Ismaʿīl's sister, known as Ibn al-Mukhtār Qunbul – Saad's reading of the unvocalized Arabic name QNBL (Saad, *Social History of Timbuktu*, 50). Unfortunately, Saad adds in a footnote that "[a] full discussion of this issue lies beyond the scope" of his work, leaving his interesting theory unsubstantiated (Saad, *Social History of Timbuktu*, 262, n. 135).

105 Brun, "Notes sur le 'Tarikh-El-Fettach'," 590.

chronicle written by Maḥmūd Ka'ti I corresponds only to the first five or six chapters of the edited text.[106] However, these chapters did not survive in their original form, but only in the one that Ibn al-Mukhtār gave them when he completed the text in the seventeenth century.[107] In composing his own version of the chronicle, Ibn al-Mukhtār employed the original work of Maḥmūd Ka'ti I plus other sources, including first-hand accounts of events of his time as well as information that he collected from Maḥmūd Ka'ti II, his uncles Yūsuf, Ismā'il, and al-Amīn, as well as from his father, al-Mukhtār.[108] In other words, according to Brun, *La chronique du chercheur* as it survives today was compiled from heterogeneous sources by Ibn al-Mukhtār, among them an original chronicle written by Maḥmūd Ka'ti I, which roughly corresponds to the first part of the edited text.

There is no mention in Brun's study of the post-seventeenth-century textual manipulation that had been noted by Houdas and Delafosse in their introduction. By contrast, Hunwick devoted ample space to this topic and suggested that, after the work was completed by Ibn al-Mukhtār, two major manipulations occurred.[109] First was the addition of the prophecy concerning the twelfth caliph, already exposed as a nineteenth-century forgery by Dubois, Houdas, and Delafosse; second was some information on the servile status of certain endogamous groups of the Middle Niger that had escaped the attention of previous scholars.[110] Briefly dismissing the prophecy as a textual stratagem to legitimize Aḥmad Lobbo's power, Hunwick's attention focused on the issue of the servile groups. Without offering further proof, he stated that these references were part of the original sixteenth-century chronicle, expurgated from it sometime in the eighteenth century "by some one other than Shaikh Aḥmad [i.e. Aḥmad Lobbo]."[111] Thus, MS A was a copy of the original chronicle, with references to servile groups expunged. These passages were removed, he argues, because people of previously servile origins had obtained positions of prominence after the Moroccan conquest of the Songhay state in 1591,

106 Brun, "Notes sur le 'Tarikh-El-Fettach'," 591.
107 Brun, "Notes sur le 'Tarikh-El-Fettach'," 592.
108 Brun, "Notes sur le 'Tarikh-El-Fettach'," 596.
109 Hunwick, "Studies in the *Ta'rīkh al-Fattāsh*, I."
110 Hunwick, "Studies in the *Ta'rīkh al-Fattāsh*, I," 60–62.
111 Hunwick, "Studies in the *Ta'rīkh al-Fattāsh*, I," 63.

in accordance with an oral testimony recorded by Dubois.[112] At the time when the new first chapter including the prophecy in support of Aḥmad Lobbo was added, the manuscript employed included the passages on servile castes removed from MS A. Thus, this information reemerged in the nineteenth-century version of the text.[113]

As result of his analysis, Hunwick advanced a theory of about five different stages of textual manipulation. Originally, a chronicle "covering the first six chapters at least ... and perhaps the first ten (down to 1549)" was written by Maḥmūd Ka'ti I.[114] A second "edition" of the work was realized by Maḥmūd Ka'ti II before the end of the sixteenth century. Sometime in the second half of the seventeenth century, Ibn al-Mukhtār updated the chronicle. After this date, but prior to the early nineteenth century, the passages regarding the servile status of certain groups were expurgated from the text. Eventually, the resulting text was extended by the addition of the prophecy in chapter 1 and the reincorporation of the passages on servile groups, during the time of Aḥmad Lobbo.[115] Ly goes further in this direction, and her long analysis of *La chronique du chercheur* focuses on ascribing different sections to different authors.[116] More recently, the IHERI-ABT team simply dismissed the parts of the texts that were inserted in the nineteenth century as "fictional accounts."[117]

It was Levtzion who advanced a completely different theory on the textual manipulation of the chronicle. He argued that the chronicle is, in essence, the result of two separate moments of production: a seventeenth-century work exclusively written by Ibn al-Mukhtār, as already highlighted above, plus some textual interpolations added on behalf of Aḥmad Lobbo and thus dating to the first half of the nineteenth century.[118] Levtzion suggested that the different manuscripts

112 Hunwick, "Studies in the *Ta'rīkh al-Fattāsh*, I," 63.

113 Hunwick, "Studies in the *Ta'rīkh al-Fattāsh*, I," 64. Hunwick stresses this point in a private correspondence with Dramani-Issifou: "I do not think that *all* the materials relating [to] the servile groups is purely a 19th century forgery. I[t] must have had some basis in the realities of an earlier period" (private correspondence between Hunwick and Dramani-Issifou, October 1974, quoted in Dramani-Issifou, *L'Afrique noire*, 30, n. 23; italics in the original).

114 Hunwick, "Studies in the *Ta'rīkh al-Fattāsh*, I," 64.

115 Hunwick, "Studies in the *Ta'rīkh al-Fattāsh*, I," 64.

116 Ly, "Quelques remarques," 480–492.

117 Maiga et al. (eds.), *Tārīkh al-fattāsh*, 15–16.

118 Levtzion, "A seventeenth-century chronicle."

used by Houdas and Delafosse embody these two moments of production. While MS A and MS B represent an incomplete copy of the original chronicle by Ibn al-Mukhtār, MS C represents the new version circulated in the early nineteenth century by Aḥmad Lobbo's entourage, as already advanced by Houdas and Delafosse in their introduction.[119] Levtzion concludes that he "regard[s] the chronicle in its present form – published and translated by Houdas and Delafosse – as a combination of two texts: (i) the text which appears in all MSS (i.e. A, B, C); (ii) the text which appears in MS C only."[120] In other words *La chronique du chercheur* is the result of the combination of the original seventeenth-century chronicle plus some added passages dating to the nineteenth century.[121]

Levtzion also provided a detailed analysis of the sections of the edited text that appear only in MS C.[122] He identifies two main motivations for the interpolations: the claims made for the legitimacy of the caliphate and the mention of servile groups. Levtzion briefly argues that the insertion of the prophecy is to be understood in the context of contemporary tensions over the designation of the legitimate caliph of West Africa at the time of the West African Islamic revolutions.[123] Crucial to the credibility of the prophecy, according to Levtzion, was Maḥmūd Ka'ti's association with a chronicle whose main aim was be a reliable "eyewitness" to the prophecy foretelling Aḥmad Lobbo's role as rightful caliph of West Africa:

> The author of the additional sections of MS C . . . laboured hard to make the TF [i.e. *Tārīkh al-fattāsh*] bear evidence on the expected coming of the twelfth caliph, namely Shehu Ahmadu [i.e. Aḥmad Lobbo], an heir to the eleventh caliph, Muḥammad Askiyà. In order to render the evidence about the prophecy more convincing, the [alleged] author MK [i.e. Maḥmūd Ka'ti] should have been in the company of Muḥammad Askiyà in Mecca.[124]

While some of the above analyses highlight the fact that the nineteenth-century chronicle has undergone extensive manipulation, scholars have in the main neglected to investigate the identity of the nineteenth-

119 Levtzion, "A seventeenth-century chronicle," 573.
120 Levtzion, "Was Maḥmūd Ka'tī the author," 2.
121 Levtzion, "A seventeenth-century chronicle," 579.
122 Levtzion, "A seventeenth-century chronicle," 583–586.
123 Levtzion, "A seventeenth-century chronicle," 587–588.
124 Levtzion, "A seventeenth-century chronicle," 576.

century "forger." When Dubois visited Timbuktu, he referred to "an influential marabout" as the inventor of the prophecy at the "the instigation of" Aḥmad Lobbo.[125] Only Abitbol advances the hypothesis that the forger was the Fulani scholar named Nūḥ b. al-Ṭāhir, a prominent figure in the Caliphate of Ḥamdallāhi. He does so on the basis of Nūḥ b. al-Ṭāhir's propaganda pamphlet in support of Aḥmad Lobbo, which extensively quotes from the nineteenth-century text: "The responsibility of the latter [Nūḥ b. al-Ṭāhir] in the manipulations of the *Fattash*, especially in regard to the legal status of the servile tribes and the prophecy on the arrival of the last Caliph of Islam, is beyond doubt after reading several pamphlets that he wrote at the beginning of the 19th century."[126] Abitbol's opinion has been reproduced, sometimes cautiously, by other scholars.[127] Only recently has Bambā devoted ample space to the figure of Nūḥ b. al-Ṭāhir in the introduction to his edition of the *Tārīkh al-fattāsh*.[128] However, the sole association of this scholar with propaganda in support of Aḥmad Lobbo does not prove that it was Nūḥ b. al-Ṭāhir who produced what Robinson, endorsing Abitbol's theory, has defined as "one of the boldest manipulations that West African history has ever witnessed."[129]

Title and Second Appendix

Two final issues remain to be addressed: the issue of the work's title and the status of the texts reproduced in the second appendix. According to Brun, the title belongs to the original work by Maḥmūd Ka'ti I, who was "undisputedly the author of a book titled *Tarikh-el-fettash*."[130] This title was eventually appropriated by Ibn al-Mukhtār.[131] Hunwick is apparently of the same opinion, since he argues that, despite the fact that the first chapter had been rewritten at the time of Aḥmad Lobbo, the section in which the author discloses his identity and the title *Tārīkh*

125 Dubois, *Timbuctoo the Mysterious*, 135.
126 Abitbol, *Tombouctou et les Arma*, 12.
127 Robinson, *The Holy War*, 81; *ALA* IV, 213; Hofheinz, *Goths in the Land of the Blacks*, 70.
128 Bambā (ed.), *Tārīkh al-fattāsh*, 55–60.
129 Robinson, *The Holy War*; David Robinson, "Breaking new ground in 'pagan' and 'Muslim' West Africa," *Canadian Journal of African Studies/Revue Canadienne des Études Africaines* 42/2-3 (2008): 300–313, 309.
130 Brun, "Notes sur le 'Tarikh-El-Fettach'," 596.
131 Brun, "Notes sur le 'Tarikh-El-Fettach'," 591.

al-fattāsh belongs to the original chronicle: "The passage in which the author sets out his aims ... is nevertheless genuine."[132] As for Wuld Sālim, he argues without any evidence that the title is not original to Maḥmūd Ka'ti I, but belongs to Maḥmūd Ka'ti II.[133]

Levtzion appeared skeptical about the nature of the title. In his first publication on the topic, a work-in-progress report, he infers that the title might belong to the section added in the nineteenth century. Yet "perhaps, for convenience only we may continue to use this title, until a more authentic title will be discovered."[134] Eventually, it seems that Levtzion decided to avoid the discussion entirely, since the issue of the title is not raised in his more complete final article on the *Tārīkh al-fattāsh*.[135] Ly's article is, on the contrary, the only contribution to explicitly suggest that *Tārīkh al-fattāsh* is not the name of the original chronicle, but part of the nineteenth-century interpolation.[136]

As for the second appendix of *La chronique du chercheur*, this crucial text has not attracted enough attention from scholars. The most debated issue has been whether or not the text reproduced in it was written by the author of *La chronique du chercheur*. According to Brun, who follows Houdas and Delafosse, the second appendix includes the preface to Ibn al-Mukhtār's work, which would have been eventually replaced by Ibn al-Mukhtār himself at the beginning of the work of Maḥmūd Ka'ti.[137] Levtzion, by comparing the second appendix with MS A, shows that the two texts overlap in most of their passages, often verbatim.[138] Furthermore, the beginning of the text reproduced in the appendix covers the events that chronologically precede the section where MS A starts, i.e. the history of the Songhay dynasties of the Zā and Sonni, in the midst of which MS A begins its narrative.[139] Levtzion thus suggests that "it is very likely that the first

132 Hunwick, "Studies in the *Ta'rīkh al-Fattāsh*, I," 64.
133 Wuld Sālim (ed.), *Tārīkh al-fattāsh*, 6.
134 Levtzion, "Was Maḥmūd Ka'ti the author," 6.
135 Levtzion, "A seventeenth-century chronicle."
136 Ly, "Quelques remarques," 473.
137 Brun, "Notes sur le 'Tarikh-El-Fettach'," 592.
138 Levtzion, "A seventeenth-century chronicle," 581.
139 Like the titles *sonni* and *askiyà*, *Zā* also presents some problems of etymology and reading. According to Hunwick, "the dynastic title Zā, conventionally so spelt since Barth first discussed the history of Songhay, is most probably a *vox nihil* ... The title of this dynasty was, in fact, Zuwā/Juwā, perhaps actually pronounced Žᵘwa, with a central vowel so short that

part of the appendix represents the first missing first part of MS A."[140] Any remaining differences between the two texts can be explained by the fact that the appendix "might represent an earlier version of the chronicle, which was later revised."[141]

Monteil and Hunwick both argue against this theory.[142] According to Monteil, the second appendix is a fragment of an anonymous chronicle that used the work by Maḥmūd Ka'ti extensively, but differs from it.[143] Hunwick advances a stronger argument based on his analysis of the so-called *Kitab al-ḥūrma* (Document of Immunity), a charter of privileges allegedly granted by Askiyà Muḥammad to the descendants of a local scholar named Mori Hawgāro (*fl.* 1450) and reproduced in *La chronique du chercheur*.[144] According to Hunwick, the author of the second appendix, who wrote this chronicle at the request of Askiyà Dāwūd b. Hārūn, would have not cited the *Kitab al-ḥūrma*, a document which is strongly critical of the behavior of the *askiyà*s of his own day in regard to their attitude toward slavery, accusing them of illegally selling Mori Hawgāro's descendants.[145] Thus, following Hunwick's reasoning, it is unlikely that the author would write a work in which he overtly criticizes his patron.

The above review of a century's critical scholarship on *La chronique du chercheur* shows that scholars have not been able to provide a satisfactory solution to the problematic aspects of the conflated text bearing this title. Moreover, most of the people who have explored the history of this work have followed the approach inaugurated by Dubois, Houdas, and Delafosse, which erases the nineteenth-century layer of writing, focusing only on the search for the "original text." As a consequence, Nūḥ b. al-Ṭāhir, Aḥmad Lobbo, and the Caliphate of Ḥamdallāhi rarely figure in the scholarship on *La chronique du chercheur*. Even worse, many scholars continue to ignore the truly problematic nature of the text published by Houdas and Delafosse.[146] Among

it could sound much like Ža" (Hunwick, *Timbuktu and the Songhay Empire*, appendix 2, 332 [italics in the original text]).

140 Levtzion, "A seventeenth-century chronicle," 580.

141 Levtzion, "A seventeenth-century chronicle," 582.

142 Monteil, Les empires du Mali; Hunwick, "Studies in the *Ta'rīkh al-Fattāsh*, II."

143 Monteil, *Les empires du Mali*, 79.

144 Hunwick, "Studies in the *Ta'rīkh al-Fattāsh*, II."

145 Hunwick, "Studies in the *Ta'rīkh al-Fattāsh*, II," 148.

146 For example, in his influential study of the Songhay Empire, Jean-Pierre Olivier de Sardan completely neglects the problematic nature of the edited text of *La*

them are the translators of *La chronique du chercheur* into English, who completely neglect all the scholarly literature on the topic.[147]

As Levtzion remarked: "[A] critical study of TF should take us back to the manuscripts used by the editors in collating the published text. Unfortunately nothing is known about the location of the two more important manuscripts-MS A and MS C."[148] Indeed, the assumption has been that MS A and MS C have both been lost, while MS B – less important insofar as it is a copy of MS A – was known to be at the BnF under the shelf mark Ms. Arabe 5561.[149] This is only partially true. During my research at IHERI-ABT, I identified MS A as IHERI-ABT 3927 – henceforth referred to as MS A/IHERI-ABT 3927.[150] Regrettably, MS C's whereabouts are still unknown. Last documented in 1916, it may have been destroyed during World War II, along with many other documents owned by Delafosse.[151] However, it is possible to reconstruct its text from the critical apparatus of *La chronique du chercheur*, thus producing a sort of virtual text of this manuscript.[152]

chronique du chercheur and uses passages fabricated in the nineteenth century to depict practices of slavery in the late Middle Ages (Jean-Pierre Olivier de Sardan, "Captifs ruraux et esclaves impériaux du Songhay," in *L'esclavage en Afrique précoloniale*, edited by Claude Meillassoux [Paris: F. Maspero, 1975], 99–134). Likewise, Ferran I. Vernet does not discuss the complexity of Houdas and Delafosse's edition, in spite of the fact that *La chronique du chercheur* is the major source for his study of the Songhay (Ferran I. Vernet, "Dispute au sujet du caractère de la propriété au Songhay au XVIe siècle," in *Le Maroc et l'Afrique subsaharienne aux débuts des temps modernes: les Sa'adiens et l'empire Songhay: actes du colloque international organisé par l'Institut des études africaines, Marrakech, 23–25 octobre 1992*, edited by Ahmed Touqif [Rabat: Publication de l'Institut des Études Africaines, 1995, 47–63]. More recently, Michael A. Gomez, while acknowledging the problematic nature of *La chronique du chercheur*, also continues using the chronicle as a genuine work written by Maḥmūd Ka'ti (Michael A. Gomez, *African Dominion* [Princeton: Princeton University Press, 2018]).

147 Wise and Abu Taled (ed. and trans.), *Ta'rīkh al-fattāsh*.

148 Levtzion, "A seventeenth-century chronicle," 573.

149 The copy at the BnF has been known since 1913 (*La chronique du chercheur*, Texte Arabe, Avertissement).

150 Nobili and Mathee, "Towards a new study," 51–54.

151 On the pillage of Delafosse's archives, see Delafosse, *Maurice Delafosse*, 2, 13, 253. The last mention of the manuscript is in Delafosse, "Notes sur les manuscrits," 120–129.

152 Although Houdas and Delafosse's analysis of the textual history of the chronicle is completely misleading, their scholarly rigor is excellent, thus making their critical apparatus reliable.

Deconstructing *La chronique du chercheur*

Among the different scholars who have worked on *La chronique du chercheur*, only Levtzion has advanced a convincing theory to explain the relationship between the two families of manuscripts employed by Houdas and Delafosse, i.e. MS A/IHERI-ABT 3927 and its copy MS B/ BnF 6651, plus the family represented only by MS C. He suggested, as detailed above, that forged sections were inserted in MS C to manipulate the text originally reproduced in MS A/IHERI-ABT 3927. The following analysis, which does not consider MS B, insofar as it is a copy of MS A/IHERI-ABT 3927, takes Levtzion's study as its starting point but reveals that the relationships among these texts are far more complicated than he previously fathomed.

Genette's *Palimpsests: Literature in the Second Degree* provides an effective theoretical framework and terminology for explicating the complexity of manuscript transmission.[153] The relationship between MS A/IHERI-ABT 3927 and MS C is one of *hypertextuality*, which refers to "any relationship uniting a text B (which I shall call the *hypertext*) to an earlier text A (I shall call it *hypotext*) upon which it is grafted."[154] In the present case, MS C – containing obvious extensive nineteenth-century interpolations – is the hypertext of an older hypotext, which is MS A/IHERI-ABT 3927.

According to Genette, a hypotext becomes a hypertext via a process of "transformation" that can be of several types.[155] In the present case, the text of MS A/IHERI-ABT 3927 underwent transformations by "*extension*," i.e. "augmentation by massive addition[s]."[156] A clear example of extension is the addition, in MS C, of a full biography of Sonni ʿAlī (d. 1492), the king who reigned over the Songhay before

[153] See Genette, *Palimpsests*. Charles D. Wright's study of the *Apocalypse of Thomas* has inspired me into approaching the *Tārīkh al-fattāsh* by employing Genette's theory (see Charles D. Wright, "Rewriting (and re-editing) the Apocalypse of Thomas," *in Écritures et réécritures: la reprise interprétative des traditions fondatrices par la littérature biblique et extra-biblique*, edited by Claire Clivaz [Leuven: Peeters, 2012], 441–453). I am grateful to him for having shared his thoughts with me, and his work.

[154] Genette, *Palimpsests*, 5 (italics in the original text). For *commentary*, Genette means a relationship that "unites a given text to another, of which it speaks without necessarily citing it (without summoning it), in fact sometimes even without naming it" (Genette, *Palimpsests*, 4).

[155] Genette, *Palimpsests*, 5.

[156] Genette, *Palimpsests*, 254–269 (italics in the original text).

Askiyà Muḥammad, which is reproduced verbatim from the *Tārīkh al-Sūdān* and is not found in MS A/IHERI-ABT 3927.[157] This process is the one brilliantly described by Levtzion in his seminal contributions to the *Tārīkh al-fattāsh*.[158] However, Levtzion underestimated the complexity of the relationship between MS A/IHERI-ABT 3927 and MS C, considering the latter simply an extended version of the former, to which forged textual interpolations were added. In Levtzion's words, "all the text of MS A is incorporated in MS C, but the latter includes also additional sections, passages and phrases."[159]

Levtzion did not recognize the second and opposite process of transformation that MS A/IHERI-ABT 3927 underwent to become MS C. According to Genette's terminology, this was a substantial "*reduction*" by "*trimming*."[160] In reworking MS A/IHERI-ABT 3927 to produce MS C, not only were new passages added – some up to several printed pages long, as Levtzion suggested – but sometimes whole sentences and entire lengthy paragraphs of MS A/IHERI-ABT 3927 were expurgated from MS C. An example of trimming occurs at the end of MS A/IHERI-ABT 3927: a whole section, totaling almost two pages of the edited text, has been removed from MS C. This section comprises a story about a miracle performed by 'Umar b. Maḥmūd b. 'Umar b. Muḥammad Aqīt (d. after 1594), *qāḍī* of Timbuktu, during his deportation to Marrakesh after the Moroccan conquest of the city. It continues with the often-quoted statement by the author, that Timbuktu became like "a body without the soul" after the deportation of its *'ulamā'* in 1593. The section concludes with the description of an encounter between the *qāḍī* of Timbuktu, Muḥammad Baghayogho, and the Moroccan *pāshā* of the city, Maḥmūd b. Zarqūn (d. 1595).[161]

157 *La chronique du chercheur*, French text 98, line 3/Arabic text 50, line 18). The editors decided not to publish the biography of Sonni 'Alī, as it was a duplicate of the text of the *Tārīkh al-Sūdān* (*La chronique du chercheur*, Arabic text 50, n. 3); the text of the biography is in Houdas (ed. and trans.), *Tarikh es-Soudan*, Arabic text 64–71/French text 103–116; Hunwick, *Timbuktu and the Songhay Empire*, 91–101.

158 Levtzion, "A seventeenth-century chronicle."

159 Levtzion, "A seventeenth-century chronicle," 573.

160 Also referred to by Genette as "*pruning*" (Genette, *Palimpsests*, 230; italics in the original text). On trimming and other possible types of reductions, see Genette, *Palimpsests*, 229–254.

161 *La chronique du chercheur*, Arabic text 174–176/French text 307–309.

As these examples show, the processes of extension and reduction can occur in different parts of the text. They can also take place simultaneously, in the latter case generating a transformation described by Genette as "*substitution*."[162] The story of the foundation of Tindirma illustrates another such case. MS A/IHERI-ABT 3927 briefly sketches the event, reporting that Tindirma was founded under Askiyà Muḥammad in 902/1496–7.[163] MS C provides a completely different account: here, the story of the foundation of Tindirma as reported in MS A/IHERI-ABT 3927 is removed and replaced with another, much longer account.[164] In this case, a short section of MS A/IHERI-ABT 3927, just a few lines, is replaced by a long account of almost two pages of the edited text.

Table 1 displays the major differences found in MS A/IHERI-ABT 3927 and MS C, providing the reference to the pages of the edition and the translation of *La chronique du chercheur*, and the description of the type of transformation.

In fourteen instances, the texts of two manuscripts differ substantially. There are eight cases of extension, four substitutions, one trimming, and one instance in which it is difficult to determine the type of substitution, due to lacunae in the available manuscripts.[165] As Genette underlines, "to reduce or augment a text is to produce another text … which derives from it, but not without altering it in various manners."[166] Therefore, it is more appropriate to treat the texts preserved by MS A/IHERI-ABT 3927 and MS C not as two recensions of the same work, but as two different works altogether. By contrast, scholars have remained, since the times of Dubois, Houdas, and Delafosse, romantically engaged in a quest for the original old chronicle, neglecting the importance of later layers of writings as historical sources per se. Denigrating additions to the chronicle as "mere" forgeries polluting an "original" work is characteristic of a traditional European philological approach that is reflected broadly in Western

162 Genette, *Palimpsests*, 259–267 (italics in the original text).
163 *La chronique du chercheur*, Arabic text 62/French text 119.
164 *La chronique du chercheur*, Arabic text 62–63/French text 119–121.
165 One cannot rule out that some of these differences are, in fact, the result of some accident in the chain of transmission of the two chronicles. However, the analysis below seems to suggest the opposite.
166 Genette, *Palimpsests*, 229 (italics in the original text).

Table 1 ***Main Textual Differences between the Manuscripts of*** **La chronique du chercheur**

MS A/IHERI-ABT 3927	MS C	Transformation
-	Arabic text 9–32, l. 15/French text 6, l. 1–56, l. 4	(A lacuna in the manuscripts of MS A/MS 3972 prevents definition of this transformation)
-	Arabic text 50, l. 18/French text 98, l. 3	Extension
-	Arabic text 53, l. 12–58, l. 19/French text 102, l. 14–114, l. 1	Extension
Arabic text 59, l. 2–59, l .4/ French text 114, l. 7–l. 10	59, n. 1/French text 114	Substitution
59, l. 13–61, l. 13/French text 115, l. 19–118, l. 4	Arabic text 59, l. 11–59, l. 13/French text 115, l. 15–l. 18	Substitution
Arabic text 62, l. 2–62, l. 4/ French text 118, l. 15–119, l. 2	Arabic text 62, l.4 – 63, l.16 / French text 119, l. 2–121 l.17	Substitution
Arabic text 64, n. 1/124, n. 3	Arabic text 62, l. 16–68, l. 15/French text 119, l. 3–131, l. 13	Substitution
-	Arabic text 70, l. 18–71, l. 10/French text 136, l. 4–137, l. 12	Extension
-	Arabic text 116, l. 12–117, l. 19/French text 212, l. 21–215, l. 9	Extension
-	Arabic text 123, l. 7–123, l. 19/French text 224, l. 31–225, l. 24	Extension
-	Arabic text 140, l. 10–141, l. 9/French text 255, l. 6–256, l. 9	Extension
-	Arabic text 143, l. 9–144, l. 10/French text 258, l. 29–260, l. 16	Extension
-	Arabic text 149, l. 4–149, l. 18/French text 266, l. 25–268, l. 19	Extension
Arabic text 174, l. 13–176, l. 3/French text 307, l. 12–309, l. 13	-	Trimming

scholarship on African written sources. As Holl notes, studies on African written sources have been

> characterized by a heavy reliance on textual evidence which is studied following above all a philological approach. The approach aims to retrieve the original or archetypal frame of historical documents which are, therefore, considered to have been corrupted by a lengthy series of interpolations and/or copyists' mistakes. In doing so, inconsistencies and contradictions discovered are relegated to the status of accidents in the chain of transmission of historical information.[167]

Most of the time, textual modifications are not "accidents," but hide more complex historical dynamics. Indeed, in the case of *La chronique du chercheur*, the differences between the two manuscripts are not only quantitative, i.e. in the number of transformations the first text underwent to become the second. Rather, the transformations modify these texts' rhetorical constructions and authorial intentions. It is to these often-neglected features of West African chronicles that de Moraes Farias has drawn the attention of scholars, in his seminal *Arabic Medieval Inscriptions from the Republic of Mali.*[168] In reference to the seventeenth-century chronicles of Timbuktu, de Moraes Farias has warned about "a tendency toward historical reductionism."[169] By this, he means that these chronicles have been approached as "mere agglutinative repositories of information";[170] or, in other words, as a "repository of hard facts, not as creative and artful reconstruction[s] of a past."[171] Scholars have therefore treated the chronicles as "disorganized bundles of raw information, not as rather well cooked writerly production[s]."[172] De Moraes Farias's argument is echoed by Holl, in his critique of Africanist historians' approach to Arabic written sources mentioned above: "Instead of proceeding from isolated 'facts', be they phonemes, words, sentences, toponyms, ethnonyms, titles, etc. [each] document [has to be] considered in its totality as a complex internal system of nested levels of meanings."[173]

167 Holl, "New perspectives," 46.
168 De Moraes Farias, *Arabic Medieval Inscriptions.*
169 De Moraes Farias, *Arabic Medieval Inscriptions*, xlviii § 48.
170 De Moraes Farias, *Arabic Medieval Inscriptions*, lxxxv § 149.
171 De Moraes Farias, *Arabic Medieval Inscriptions*, xlviii–xlix § 48.
172 De Moraes Farias, *Arabic Medieval Inscriptions*, lxxi § 107.
173 Holl, "New perspectives," 47.

De Moraes Farias has revolutionized the approach to these chronicles by stressing their "literariness" and "constitutive rhetoric," and by characterizing their authors as "text craftmen and ideological agents."[174] He stresses the importance of understanding "the politico-ideological agenda of the chronicle[s], and about how this agenda might have influenced the historical reconstruction of the text."[175] By following these suggestions and approaching the texts conflated in *La chronique du chercheur* in a holistic way, it emerges that MS A/IHERI-ABT 3927 and MS C contain different works. The first preserves an untitled chronicle composed in the seventeenth century by the "son of al-Mukhtār," in confirmation of Levtzion's theory referred above – I thus refer to this work as the *Tārīkh Ibn al-Mukhtār* (The Chronicle of the Son of *al-Mukhtār*). The text of the *Tārīkh Ibn al-Mukhtār* is very different from the one preserved in MS C – the only manuscript bearing the title *Tārīkh al-fattāsh*. The next chapter will focus on this latter chronicle and on its production, which involved a substantial rewriting of the earlier *Tārīkh Ibn al-Mukhtār*. I will show that the *Tārīkh al-fattāsh* is a metahistorical narrative written in support of Aḥmad Lobbo by Nūḥ b. al-Ṭāhir, a famous West African scholar belonging to the ruling elite of Caliphate of Ḥamdallāhi, but then apocryphally ascribed by him to Maḥmūd Ka'ti.

[174] De Moraes Farias, *Arabic Medieval Inscriptions*, lxix § 101, lxx § 104.
[175] De Moraes Farias, *Arabic Medieval Inscriptions*, xlvii § 44.

2 *The* Tārīkh al-fattāsh*: A Nineteenth-Century Chronicle*

This chapter completes the work of deconstruction of Houdas and Delafosse's *La chronique du chercheur* that I started in the previous one and complicates the simplistic understanding of the *Tārīkh al-fattāsh* as an original document, plus textual interpolations. By focusing on the authorial intention and rhetorical construction of the two texts subsumed in *La chronique du chercheur*, I show that MS C, i.e. the *Tārīkh al-fattāsh*, is substantially different from its hypotext, the *Tārīkh Ibn al-Mukhtār* included in MS A/IHERI-ABT 3927. The key document, and the point of departure for my analysis, is a draft of the *Tārīkh al-fattāsh* that explicitly connects the writing of the chronicle to Nūḥ b. al-Ṭāhir.

As Grafton highlights, the work of every forger consists of "imagination and corroboration," i.e. "the creation of the forgery and the provision of its pedigree."[1] The draft of the *Tārīkh al-fattāsh*, which narrates the story of the fifteenth-century Pilgrimage made by the king of the Songhay Empire, Askiyà Muḥammad, and the prophecy concerning the arrival of Aḥmad Lobbo as legitimate ruler of West Africa, represents the imaginative work of Nūḥ b. al-Ṭāhir, and is the focus of the first part this chapter. After providing a biography of Nūḥ b. al-Ṭāhir, a prominent West African intellectual who has escaped the attention of scholars so far, the rest of the chapter focuses on the "corroboration" of the narrative included in the draft of the *Tārīkh al-fattāsh*. Such corroboration consisted in Nuḥ b. al-Ṭāhir's translation of his text into the realm of "plausible" history. This process took place by incorporating the fictional narrative of Askiyà Muḥammad's Pilgrimage, during which Aḥmad Lobbo's arrival was predicted, into the earlier *Tārīkh Ibn al-Mukhtār*. As result, the whole narrative structure of this latter text would be transformed to create the complete *Tārīkh al-fattāsh*, whose aim was to construct a prophetic and

[1] Grafton, *Forgers and Critics*, 50.

historical basis for Aḥmad Lobbo's claims to be considered a sultan, the twelfth caliph predicted by the Prophet, and a "renewer" of Islam.

Borrowing from Abdelfattah Kilito's study of forgeries in classical Arabic literature, one can say that Nūḥ b. al-Ṭāhir was the "real author" of the *Tārīkh al-fattāsh*, the one who actually wrote the chronicle.[2] However, to complete his forgery and add credibility to his claims, he apocryphally credited the authorship of the resulting chronicle to Maḥmūd Ka'ti, an earlier scholar who had actually lived at the time of the Askiyà Muḥammad. Therefore, under the pen of Nūḥ b. al-Ṭāhir, Maḥmūd Ka'ti becomes, again using Kilito's terminology, the "true author" of the *Tārīkh al-fattāsh*, or the only name to which the chronicle is attributed and from which it derives its "true" authority.[3]

This complex story has remained mainly unexplored until now, proving another of Kilito's points that "by the time a book becomes successful and widely distributed, it is almost impossible to separate it from the name customarily attached to it."[4] To finally rectify the understanding of the *Tārīkh al-fattāsh*, it is necessary to look back to early twentieth-century Sinder, a town upstream from today's capital of the Republic of Niger, Niamey, where a local Songhay scholar and book collector met a French explorer with an unparalleled passion for West African Arabic manuscripts and inscriptions.[5]

A Draft of a Nineteenth-Century Chronicle

In the 1890s, roughly at the same time as the French conquered Timbuktu and Dubois visited the city, a Songhay Muslim scholar named Yūsuf b. al-Khalīl was spending a few years in Sokoto, where he put together a collection of Arabic manuscripts.[6] He then returned

[2] Abdelfattah Kilito, *The Author and His Doubles: Essays on Classical Arabic Culture* (Syracuse: Syracuse University Press, 2001), 65.

[3] Kilito, *The Author and His Doubles*, 65.

[4] Kilito, *The Author and His Doubles*, 71.

[5] The town of Sinder should not be confused with the well-known city of Zinder, located further east.

[6] Georges de Gironcourt, *Missions de Gironcourt en Afrique occidentale, 1908/1909–1911/1912: documents scientifiques, publiès avec le concours de l'Acadèmiedes sciences (Fonds Bonaparte), de l'Acadèmie des inscriptions et belles-lettres, et de la Sociètè de gèographie* (Paris: Société de géographie, 1920), 149. The name of Yūsuf b. al-Khalīl figures in de Gironcourt's writing as "Isoufi

to his hometown of Sinder, where he became a locally renowned scholar and his collection of manuscripts grew. A few years later, in the summer of 1912 – while Houdas and Delafosse were working on the text of *La chronique du chercheur* – a foreigner knocked on his door: the French agronomist de Gironcourt.[7]

Sponsored by French Ministry of the Colonies, the Ministry of Public Education, and the Académie des Inscriptions et Belles-Lettres, de Gironcourt was in West Africa on a mission aimed at compiling a corpus of Arabic inscriptions from the French West African colonies.[8] However, throughout his almost two-year trip, he also had several Arabic manuscripts copied for him by local scribes, along with a few "originals" he managed to bring back to France.[9]

On 3 June, after several months in West Africa, de Gironcourt entered Yūsuf b. al-Khalīl's precious library in Sinder, which the French explorer described as "sizable."[10] There, Yūsuf b. al-Khalīl's disciples copied about twenty manuscripts for the French agronomist. The connection between de Gironcourt and Yūsuf b. al-Khalīl continued after the former left Sinder. The Songhay scholar traveled with de Gironcourt to the neighboring town of Say, and negotiated with local Muslim scholars to gain access to their own manuscripts.[11] On his side, de Gironcourt tried to obtain for Yūsuf b. al-Khalīl the French *Ordre des Palmes Académiques.*[12]

Two days after de Gironcourt's arrival in Sinder, a talented local Songhay pupil of Yūsuf b. al-Khalīl, whose name the French agronomist spelled as "Harouna Alfaga," copied a short chronicle concerning the history of the Middle Niger. This manuscript, which displays the

Alilou." The Arabic form of the name appears in several manuscripts of the Fonds de Gironcourt (Nobili, *Catalogue des manuscrits arabes*, 43).

7 On de Gironcourt's stay in Sinder and in the surrounding region, as well as his meeting with Yūsuf b. al-Khalīl, see Nobili, *Catalogue des manuscrits arabes*, 43–45.

8 De Gironcourt's reproduction of West African inscriptions are preserved at the Institut de France (IF, Objects d'art n. 60, Estampages d'inscriptions lithiques rassemblées par de Gironcourt; IF, Fonds de Gironcourt, 2417/II, *Inscriptions à faible relief reproduites au trait*).

9 De Gironcourt's *modus operandi* is described in Nobili, *Catalogue des manuscrits arabes*, 19–20.

10 Georges de Gironcourt, "Report," *Comptes rendus des séances de l'Académie des inscriptions et belles-lettres* (1912): 428–432, 429.

11 De Gironcourt, *Missions de Gironcourt*, 149.

12 IF, Fonds Henri Cordier, MS 5456, *Correspondance d'Henri Cordier*, n. 197.

copyist's elegant handwriting, was eventually deposited at the Institut de France late in 1912, under the shelf mark MS 2410 (174), along with all the others that de Gironcourt had brought from West Africa.[13] [Figure 1] The chronicle opens with the pious invocation of the name of God (*basmala*), and continues:

This is the chronicle of the needful one, Nūḥ b. al-Ṭāhir b. Mūsà, disciple of Shaykh Sīdi al-Mukhtār al-Kuntī. He call it *Tārīkh al-fattāsh fī akhbār al-buldān wa-l-juyūsh wa-akābir al-nās wa-dhikr waqā'i al-Takrūr wa-'aẓā'im al-umūr wa-tafrīq ansāb al-'abīd min al-aḥrār* [The Chronicle of the Inquisitive Researcher on the Information of the Lands and Armies, the Elite, and the Mention of the Incidents of Takrūr, the Relevant Events and the Differentiation of the Lineages of Slaves from the Freeborn].[14]

The incipit of this chronicle confirms Abitbol's assumption that Nūḥ b. al-Ṭāhir was involved in manipulating the text edited as *La chronique du chercheur*. But in fact, it does more than that. It points to Nūḥ b. al-Ṭāhir as the real author of a chronicle titled *Tārīkh al-fattāsh*. The contents of this chronicle are well known: it is the account of the late fifteenth-century Pilgrimage of the newly enthroned king of the Songhay Empire, Askiyà Muḥammad.

Nūḥ b. al-Ṭāhir presents Askiyà Muḥammad as the caliph of his time: "there was a consensus of all the scholars of that age that he was a caliph."[15] The author lists the authorities who had recognized the Songhay king as caliph, namely, a fictional *sharīf* of the Ḥasānid dynasty of Mecca called Mūlāy al-'Abbās, the Egyptian polymath al-Suyūṭī, the Saharan reformer Muḥammad b. 'Abd al-Karīm al-Maghīlī (d. 1504–5), and the king of the *jinn*, Shamharūsh.[16] According to the chronicle, while in Mecca the *askiyà* encountered the non-existent *sharīf* Mūlāy al-'Abbās, who invested the Songhay king as caliph of

[13] IF, Fonds de Gironcourt, 2410 (174) (see Nobili, *Catalogue des manuscrits arabes*, 217–218, item 92; following *ALA* IV, 213, item 1, I classified the work, imprecisely, as a copy of Nūḥ b. al-Ṭāhir's *Risāla fī ẓuhūr al-khalīfa al-thānī 'ashar*, on which see Chapter 6).

[14] IF, Fonds de Gironcourt, 2410 (174), p. 1.

[15] IF, Fonds de Gironcourt, 2410 (174), p. 1.

[16] IF, Fonds de Gironcourt, 2410 (174), p. 1. Mūlāy al-'Abbās is a fictional character. As underlined by Hunwick, at the time of the visit to Mecca by Askiyà Muḥammad, the *sharīf* was Muḥammad b. Barakāt (r. 1454/5–1497/8) and "there never was a *sharīf* of Mecca called al-'Abbās" (John O. Hunwick, "Aḥmad Bābā and the Moroccan invasion of the Sudan [1591]," *Journal of the Historical Society of Nigeria* 2/3 [1962]: 311–328, 327).

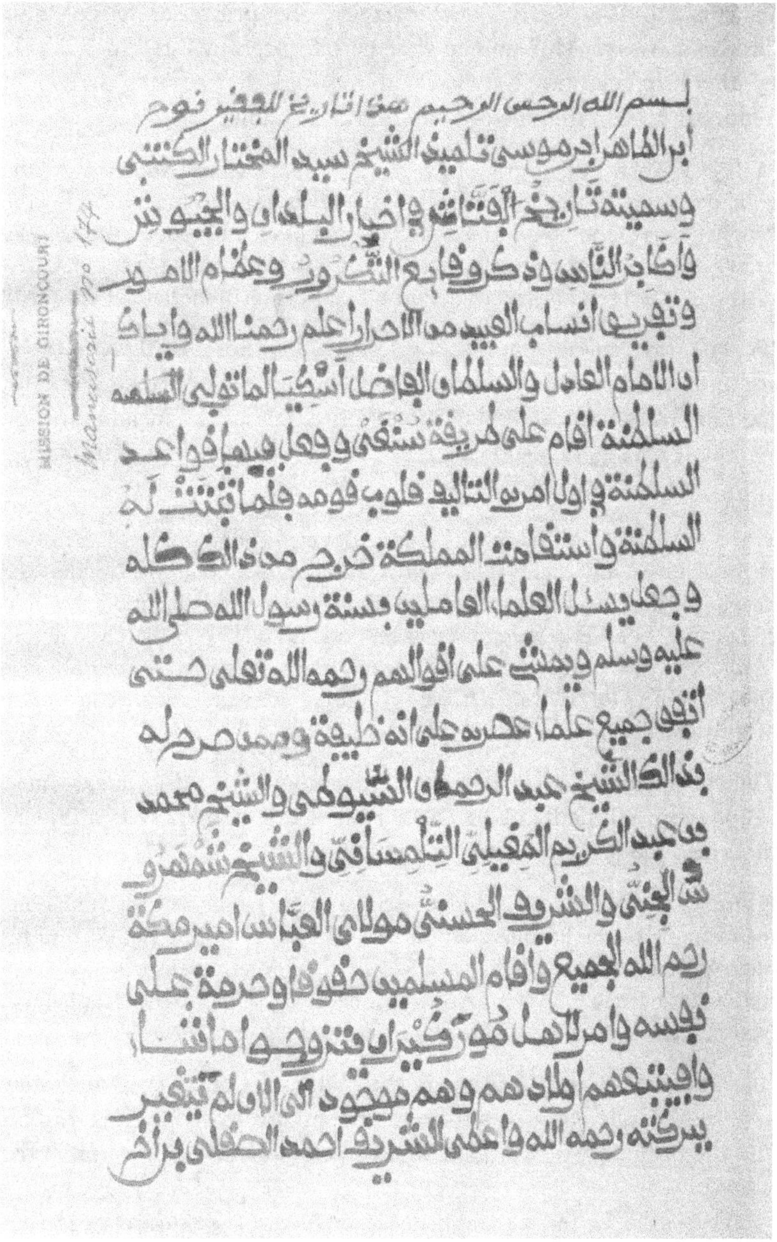

بسم الله الرحمن الرحيم هذا التاريخ للفقير نوح
ابن الطاهر ابن موسى تلميذ الشيخ سيد المختار الكنتي
وسميته تاريخ الفتاش في اخبار البلدان والجيوش
واكابر الناس وذكر وقايع التكرور وعظائم الامور
وتفريق انساب العبيد من الاحرار اعلم رحمنا الله واياك
ان الامام العادل والسلطان الفاضل اسكيا المتولي السلطنة
السلطنة اقام على طريقة سنية وجعل فيها قواعد
السلطنة في اول امره التاليف قلوب قومه فلما ثبتت له
السلطنة واستقامت المملكة خرج من ذلك كله
وجعل يسال العلماء العاملين بسنة رسول الله صلى الله
عليه وسلم ويمشي على اقوالهم رحمه الله تعالى حتى
اتفق جميع علماء عصره على انه خليفة وممن صرح له
بذلك الشيخ عبد الرحمن السيوطي والشيخ محمد
بن عبد الكريم المغيلي التلمساني والشيخ شمهروش
الجني والشريف الحسني مولاي العباس امير مكة
رحم الله الجميع واقام المسلمين حقوقا وحرمة على
نفسه وامر لاهل مور كيري ان تتزوجوا ماشاء
واتبعهم اولادهم وهم موجودون الى الان لم تتغير
ببركته رحمه الله واعطى الشريف احمد الصقلي برا

Figure 1: Institut de France, Fonds de Gironcourt, 2410 (174), a draft of the *Tārīkh al-fattāsh* (Copyright Institut de France)

Takrūr, i.e. West Africa.[17] Moreover, the prince of Mecca also informed Askiyà Muḥammad that he had been invested in this role by the Prophet himself, who had foretold the *askiyà*'s arrival in a famous *ḥadīth*. In the words of Nūḥ b. al-Ṭāhir:

Mūlāy al-'Abbās, the prince of Mecca, gave him [Askiyà Muḥammad] the good news that he was the eleventh of the twelve caliphs mentioned [by the Prophet – may God honor him and grant him peace]. He put on the *askiyà*'s head a green hat and a white turban, and also gave him a sword and declared in front of the attending crowd that he was the caliph of the land of Takrūr.[18]

On his way back from the Pilgrimage, the short *Tārīkh al-fattāsh* continues, Askiyà Muḥammad stopped in Cairo, where he met with the famous scholar al-Suyūṭī and enquired about the meaning of the Prophetic saying. In response to the *askiyà*'s request, al-Suyūṭī clarified the words of Mūlāy al-'Abbās:

When he [Askiyà Muḥammad] got to Egypt, he found Shaykh 'Abd al-Raḥmān al-Suyūṭī there. The *askiyà* asked him about the caliphs, the Prophet – may God honor him and grant him peace – mentioned would come after him. The *shaykh* answered saying: "They are twelve: five in Medina, two in Cairo, one in the Levant, and two in Iraq – They all have already come. Only two are left, who will come from the Takrūr. You are one of the two. The other will come after you."[19]

The chronicle then provides clear indications to identify this awaited caliph with Aḥmad Lobbo. Nūḥ b. al-Ṭāhir reports that al-Suyūṭī described the prophesied twelfth caliph thus:

A virtuous, knowledgeable, and active man, who will follow the Sunna [i.e. the example of the Prophet], will arrive. His name will be Aḥmad and his reign will emerge in some island of Sebera in the Masina. His tribe will be of the Sangaré. He will be your [Askiyà Muḥammad's] heir to the Caliphate, in justice, virtues, generosity, devotion, piety and victory.[20]

The association of this Aḥmad with Aḥmad Lobbo is immediately apparent, as the latter was from the Fulani group of the Sangaré-Bari and the Caliphate of Ḥamdallāhi emerged in Sebera, the region at the

17 On the name Takrūr, see 'Umar al-Naqar, "Takrur: The history of a name," *Journal of African History* 10/3 (1969): 365–374.
18 IF, Fonds de Gironcourt, 2410 (174), p. 2.
19 IF, Fonds de Gironcourt, 2410 (174), p. 2.
20 IF, Fonds de Gironcourt, 2410 (174), p. 2.

intersection of the Niger and Bani Rivers, where Aḥmad Lobbo had a decisive victory over his enemies at Noukouma.

After this clear reference to Aḥmad Lobbo, the draft of the *Tārīkh al-fattāsh* narrates that Askiyà Muḥammad was also in possession of some "tribes" (*qabā'il*) which the *askiyà* had inherited as slaves of the crown from the previous king of the Songhay, Sonni Bāru. Finally, the chronicle concludes abruptly with Askīyà Muḥammad enforcing his rule over the members of these "twelve tribes" which he had "inherited" from the previous Songhay king, after al-Maghīlī confirmed the juridical opinion of al-Suyūṭī: "This happened after he had asked Shaykh Muḥammad b. 'Abd al-Karīm al-Maghīlī about the status of these tribes and the latter told him exactly as Shaykh 'Abd al-Raḥmān al-Suyūṭī and their words were the same as the footprints of two horseshoes."[21]

The reader acquainted with the West African historiographical tradition will easily recognize that the contents of this short chronicle appear verbatim in the conflated text of *La chronique du chercheur*.[22] However, its first lines, which were not reproduced in the manuscripts used to produce *La chronique du chercheur*, have so far eluded attention: the lines that unambiguously ascribe its authorship and the title *Tārīkh al-fattāsh* to Nūḥ b. al-Ṭāhir. This ascription reveals the clear authorial intent of the short *Tārīkh al-fattāsh*, which is to create a metahistorical narrative that celebrates Askiyà Muḥammad as the rightful West African ruler of the late fifteenth and early sixteenth centuries, and to extend his legitimacy to his belated successor, easily identifiable as Aḥmad Lobbo. But what was the connection between the latter and the author of the short *Tārīkh al-fattāsh*?

21 IF, Fonds de Gironcourt, 2410 (174), p. 7.

22 Most likely for this reason, scholars have generally ignored the manuscript that de Gironcourt had copied from Yūsuf b. al-Khalīl's collection, although it had been well known to them, as references to it by Abdullahi Smith, Hunwick and Hassan I. Gwarzo, and Levtzion prove (Abdullahi [H. F. C.] Smith, "Source material for the history of the western Sudan," *Journal of the Historical Society of Nigeria* 1/3 [1958]: 238–247, 242–243; John O. Hunwick and Hasan I. Gwarzo, "Another look at the de Gironcourt Papers," *Research Bulletin – Centre of Arabic Documentation, University of Ibadan* 3/2 [1967], 74–99, 94–95, Minor ta'rīkhs and pseudo-histories item 1; and Levtzion, "A seventeenth-century chronicle," 572, n. 6).

The Life and Times of Nūḥ b. al-Ṭāhir

Nūḥ b. al-Ṭāhir was a prominent figure in nineteenth-century West Africa, in particular among the notables of the Caliphate of Ḥamdallāhi.[23] His full name was Nūḥ b. al-Ṭāhir Belko b. Abī Bakr b. Mūsà al-Fulānī, of the Dibanaɓe sub-clan of the Yirlaɓe Fulani.[24] According to the traditions collected by Ali Koullogo Diallo, which will be proven to be sometimes inaccurate and shrouded in a mythical aura, Nūḥ b. al-Ṭāhir was born in 1738 to an affluent and powerful Muslim family in Dari, a town east of Niafounké. He learned the Qur'ān from young age in the local Qur'ān school (*kuttāb*), and then became a shepherd and a warrior, following the traditional Fulani customs. One day, at the age of forty, while grazing his flock around Timbuktu, he decided to pursue the path of empirical knowledge (*'ilm*) and intuitive insight (*ma'rifa*). He shaved his head and moved to the town of Arawān, where he became a student of the leader of the Qādiriyya brotherhood in the region, 'Alī b. al-Najīb. He subsequently attached himself to one of the latter's pupils, al-Mukhtār b. Abī Bakr al-Kuntī al-Wāfī (d. 1811; henceforth al-Mukhtār al-Kabīr), the Kunta scholar who elevated his clan to notoriety in the late eighteenth century. After having completed his training under the Kunta *shaykh*'s tutelage, Nūḥ b. al-Ṭāhir decided to undertake the Pilgrimage in around 1808. On his way to Mecca he stopped in Hausaland and became, for three years, a student of the founding leader of the Sokoto Caliphate, 'Uthmān b. Fūdī. There, Nūḥ b. al-Ṭāhir became famous for his knowledge, receiving the Fulfulde

[23] The only biographical sketch is available in secondary sources that are unfortunately difficult to access: Ali Koullogo Diallo's chapter in the ISESCO volume *Culture et civilisation islamique: Mali* and Diagayeté's Ph.D. dissertation in Arabic, "al-Fulāniyyūn wa-ishāmuhum fī ḥaḍāra al-Islāmiyya bi-Mālī" (The Fulani and their role in the Islamic culture in Mali). Ali Koullogo Diallo, "Alpha Nuhu Taahiru," in *Culture et civilisation islamiques: Le Mali*, edited by Abdelhadi Boutaleb (Casablanca: Organisation islamique pour l'éducation, les sciences et la culture, 1408 [1988]): 221–228; and Muḥammad Diagayeté [Jakāyatī], "al-Fulāniyyūn wa-ishāmuhum fī ḥaḍāra al-Islāmiyya bi-Mālī" (Ph.D. dissertation, Zaytūna University, 1427–1428/2007), 109–110. A very short profile based on oral traditions is also provided by Hampaté Ba and Daget (*L'empire peul*, 114–117).

[24] Diagayeté [Jakāyatī], "al-Fulāniyyūn," 109. Brown suggests that Nūḥ b. al-Ṭāhir was part Songhay and part Fulani, without citing his source (Brown, "The Caliphate of Hamdullahi," 171, n. 39).

honorific of *ngel binndi* from the Sokoto leader, translated by Hampaté Ba and Daget as "the master of literacy."[25]

Around 1811, 'Uthmān b. Fūdī instructed Nūḥ b. al-Ṭāhir to go to Masina – an order that contradicted the latter's original decision to travel to Mecca and finally perform the Pilgrimage. 'Uthmān b. Fūdī allegedly foretold that a new Islamic movement was about to emerge in Masina, and that Nūḥ b. al-Ṭāhir himself was destined to play a key role in it. When he left Sokoto, however, Nūḥ b. al-Ṭāhir returned instead to al-Mukhtār al-Kabīr. When the latter died a few months later, Nūḥ b. al-Ṭāhir remained with al-Mukhtār al-Kabīr's famous son and heir, Muḥammad b.al-Mukhtār b. Aḥmad b. Abī Bakr al-Kuntī al-Wāfī (henceforth Muḥammad al-Kuntī, d. 1826). In 1820, Muḥammad al-Kuntī sent Nūḥ b. al-Ṭāhir to serve as an advisor to Gelaajo, the Fulani chief of Kounari, who had by then acknowledged the dominance of the nascent Caliphate of Ḥamdallāhi. One of Nūḥ b. al-Ṭāhir's services to the chief of Kounari was to manage the official correspondence of his patron, a duty in which he excelled. It was in this capacity that he caught the personal attention of Aḥmad Lobbo, who appointed Nūḥ b. al-Ṭāhir as his advisor and confidant after Gelaajo's rebellion of 1824–5. On his arrival in Ḥamdallāhi, Nūḥ b. al-Ṭāhir's knowledge and piety made him, in Koullogo Diallo's words, "the second most influential personality" in the caliphate after Aḥmad Lobbo.[26]

In the above account of his career, the early life of Nūḥ b. al-Ṭāhir is revealed as more of a mythical narrative than a biography. In particular, his early life is shrouded in mystery. The date of his death is 1274/1857–8, according to written sources.[27] But according to the traditional date of his birth, in 1738, Nūḥ b. al-Ṭāhir would have died at the

[25] *L'empire peul*, 114, n. 3. [26] Diallo, "Alpha Nuhu Taahiru," 223.

[27] The date of Nūḥ b. al-Ṭāhir's death comes from a shared passage in two important chronicles of the Middle Niger, that are unpublished today: The first, the *Dhikr mā waqa'a fī al-qarn al-thalith 'ashar* (The Memory of What Happened in the Thirteenth Century) was initiated by one 'Abd Allāh b. al-Muṣṭafà and completed by another unknown author by the name of Ibrāhīm al-Ra'īs b. Ismā'īl (IF, Fonds de Gironcourt, 2406 [75] [henceforth *Dhikr*]); the second, titled *Mā waqa'a fī al-Takrūr al-sūdāniyya mimmā bayna Tinbuktū wa-Janna* (What Happened in the Sudanese Takrūr between Timbuktu and Jenne), often known as known as the *Tārīkh Fittuga*, was authored by Ismā'īl b. al-Mukhtār (IHERI-ABT 281 [henceforth *Mā waqa'a*]); two more copies of this work are available, one, incomplete, is IHERI-ABT 411, and the second is IFAN, Fonds Veillard, Cahier n. 4. On the death of Nūḥ b. al-Ṭāhir, see *Dhikr*, p. 4; and *Mā waqa'a*, pp. 8–9.

unlikely age of 120 – a strange parallel between the implausibly lengthy life of Maḥmūd Kaʿtī, the "true" author of the *Tārīkh al-fattāsh*, and Nūḥ b. al-Ṭahir, the "real" author of the chronicle. Furthermore, he would have studied with ʿUthmān b. Fūdī in his early seventies and then joined Aḥmad Lobbo at the advanced age of eighty-two. All this evidence pushes the actual birth date of Nūḥ b. al-Ṭāhir to later in the eighteenth century, sometime around the 1770s. In this way, at the age of about thirty, he could well have been a pupil of al-Mukhār al-Kuntī (but not of ʿAlī b. al-Najīb) at the turn of the nineteenth century, then joining the Caliphate of Ḥamdallāhi in his early fifties: a mature age that would have made him suitable for the important positions he occupied under Aḥmad Lobbo. Likewise, the story of Nūḥ b. al-Ṭāhir's education in Sokoto is an episode that seems to be unsupported, except by the oral traditions recorded by Hampaté Ba and Daget, which might have embellished the biography of the Fulani scholar by making him not only a student of the Kunta, but also of the Fodiawa. In fact, it seems that Nūḥ b. al-Ṭāhir was sent to ʿUthmān b. Fūdī, but not as a student, as it was the latter who transmitted the litany (*wird*) of the Qādiriyya brotherhood to the founder of the Sokoto Caliphate.[28]

Documentary sources indicate that, in the early nineteenth century, Nūḥ b. al-Ṭāhir was already active in the region of Djenné, specifically an anonymous chronicle known as *Tārīkh Karamoko Ba* or "The Chronicle of Karamoko Ba" on the history of the Jakhanke clerical lineage of the Jābi-Gassama.[29] This historical account references a famous scholar from Fouta Djalon, Sālim Jābi-Gassama, also known as Karamoko Ba (d. 1824 or 1829), studying in Djenné under Nūḥ b. al-Ṭāhir: "In Djenné, he [Karamoko Ba] met numerous scholars, among whom were Alfa Nuhu [i.e. Nūḥ b. al-Ṭāhir], a Masina Fulani. He studied numerous branches of the Islamic sciences under this man whose greatness as a *shaykh* and teacher

28 Aziz A. Batran, "Sīdī al-Mukhtār al-Kuntī and the Recrudescence of Islam in the Western Sahara and the Middle Niger, c. 1750–1811" (Ph.D. dissertation, University of Birmingham, 1971), 347.

29 The chronicle, entitled in English *The Noble Account concerning the Exalted History of the Doings of Karamokho Ba and his Ancestors (may God be pleased with them)*, is only available in the English translation provided in Lamin Sanneh, "Futa Jallon and the Jakhanke clerical tradition, Part II: Karamokho Ba of Touba in Guinea," *Journal of Religion in Africa* 12/2 (1981): 114–123. On this chronicle, see *ALA* IV, 527, item iv.

was well known."[30] That Karamoko Ba did indeed study with Nūḥ b. al-Ṭāhir is confirmed by several other Jakhanke sources. For example, the poem *Kitāb fī amr shaykh al-ḥājj Ṭūbā* (Writing concerning *shaykh al-ḥājj* of Touba) lists one Nūḥ b. al-Ṭāhir among Karamoko Ba's teachers.[31] A marginal note on a manuscript of the widespread commentary of the Qur'ān known as the *Tafsīr al-jalalayn* (The Commentary of the Two Jalāls) stresses that all the knowledge that Karamoko Ba possessed derived from Nūḥ b. al-Ṭāhir.[32] The unpublished *Kitāb al-bushrà: sharḥ mirqāt al-kubrà* (Book of Good News: Commentary on the Great Ladder) by al-Ḥājj Ibrāhīm b. Karamoko Sankoung Gassama (d. after 1973), adds a more precise detail: that Karamoko Ba was also initiated in the Qādiriyya Muslim brotherhood by Nūḥ b. al-Ṭāhir, who gave him the Qādirī litany (*wird*).[33]

Sometime after Karamoko Ba studied in Djenné, most likely in the early nineteenth century, he relocated to Kankan (Guinea). Nūḥ b. al-Ṭahir then joined the emerging reform movement led by Aḥmad Lobbo. A letter from Muḥammad al-Kuntī to Aḥmad Lobbo suggests that Nūḥ b. al-Ṭāhir was already associated Aḥmad Lobbo at the very beginning of his mission. It is dated 12 Jumādà II/8 April 1818, a few weeks after the battle of Noukouma, which marks the emergence of the Caliphate of Ḥamdallāhi. It includes advice on good governance from the Kunta *shaykh* to Aḥmad Lobbo, but also a final request to extend Muḥammad al-Kuntī's regards to one Muḥammad al-Rashīd

30 Translated in Sanneh, "Futa Jallon and the Jakhanke," 116. On Sālim Jābi-Gassama, see *ALA* IV, 523–524.

31 British Library, OR 6473, p. 3.

32 Private collection of Aliou Ndiaye, village of Adeane in Casamance, Senegal, vol. 2, 15. I thank Darya Ogorodnikova for having informed me about this manuscript and the one containing the *Kitāb fī amr shaykh al-ḥājj Ṭūbā* and for having shared with me digital images of these documents.

33 Cited in Sanneh, "Futa Jallon and the Jakhanke," 114. Karamoko Ba was not the only student who received the Qādirī litany from Nūḥ b. al-Ṭāhir, witnessing the adherence of the Fulani scholar to this brotherhood. The colonial administrator Paul Marty records two scholars active in the region of Nampala, northwest of Mopti, close to the modern border between Mali and Mauritania, who either received the *wird* directly from Nūḥ b. al-Ṭāhir himself, such as Alfa Seidou Sammba Ba (b. ca. 1838), or by some of his disciples, such as Hammadi Kébé Ba (b. ca. 1870) (Paul Marty, *Études sur l'Islam et les tribus du Soudan*, vol. 4: *La région de Kayes, le pays bambara, le Sahel de Nioro* [Paris: Leroux, 1920], 154 and 156).

b. Muhammad al-Muṣṭafà b. Muḥammad al-Bashīr, as well as to Nūḥ b. al-Ṭāhir.[34]

Another letter from Muḥammad al-Kuntī seems to clarify the events in Nūḥ b. al-Ṭāhir's biography for the late 1810s–early 1820s.[35] In this document, internally datable to before 1822, Muḥammad al-Kuntī refers to Aḥmad Lobbo as having already involved Nūḥ b. al-Ṭāhir in his project of religious reform in the Middle Niger at that time – a task that the Kunta *shaykh* discouraged his pupil from accepting.[36] According to this letter, it was Aḥmad Lobbo who put Nūḥ b. al-Ṭāhir in charge of the alliance between Ḥamdallāhi and Gelaajo, and not Muḥammad al-Kuntī, as suggested by the oral traditions.[37]

From this point on, Nūḥ b. al-Ṭāhir became a scholar who played a crucial role in the history of the Caliphate of Ḥamdallāhi. He was the "doyen" of the Great Council (Fulfulde *batu mawd'o*), the institution composed of 100 scholars that ruled Ḥamdallāhi along with the caliph.[38] Among the forty scholars sitting permanently on the Great Council, Nūḥ b. al-Ṭāhir was also one of the two permanent counselors of the caliph.[39] Within the council, Nūḥ b. al-Ṭāhir occupied several important positions. He was among the scholars in charge of discussing the selection of the regional chiefs with Aḥmad Lobbo.[40] He mediated the disputes between the Great Council and the military authorities.[41] He was in charge of the educational system of Ḥamdallāhi.[42]

The influence of Nūḥ b. al-Ṭāhir became even stronger in Ḥamdallāhi with the approach of Aḥmad Lobbo's death, as some traditions recorded by Hampaté Ba and Daget suggest. It is claimed that Nūḥ b. al-Ṭāhir chaired the assembly of scholars that chose Aḥmad II, the son of Aḥmad Lobbo, as successor to the caliphate, settling the dispute with the other candidate, the caliph's nephew Baalobbo (d. after 1878–90), and his supporters.[43] After the death of

[34] IF, Fonds de Gironcourt, 2405 (25), p. 12.

[35] Partial French translation of this letter in Abdallah Wuld Maulûd Wuld Daddah, "Šayh Sîdi Muhammed Wuld Sîd al-Muḫtar al-Kunti (1183H/ 1769–70–2 Šawwâl 1241/12 Mars 1826): Contribution à l'histoire politique et religieuse de Bilâd Šinqîṭ et des régions voisines, notamment d'après les sources arabes inédites" (Ph.D. dissertation, Université de Paris – Sorbonne, 1977), 156–162.

[36] On the date of this letter, see Wuld Daddah, "Šayh Sîdi Muhammed," 157, n. 1.

[37] Wuld Daddah, "Šayh Sîdi Muhammed," 157 and 161.

[38] *L'empire peul*, 64. [39] *L'empire peul*, 251, n. 3. [40] *L'empire peul*, 74.

[41] *L'empire peul*, 70. [42] *L'empire peul*, 49. [43] *L'empire peul*, 248–251.

Aḥmad Lobbo, Nūḥ b. al-Ṭāhir washed the caliph's body.[44] Furthermore, Hampaté Ba and Daget record an ensuing crisis caused by Aḥmad II, who felt inadequate to fill in his father's position and abdicated in favor of Nūḥ b. al-Ṭāhir – but was convinced by him to accept the position and succeed Aḥmad Lobbo.[45] Nūḥ b. al-Ṭāhir continued to serve Aḥmad II, and also supported the latter's son Aḥmad III during the disputes around succession to the power. Nūḥ b. al-Ṭāhir eventually retired in 1852 to Niakongo, a village northeast of Mopti, where he died, as mentioned above, in 1857–8.

After Nūḥ b. al-Ṭāhir's death in Niakongo his body was returned to Ḥamdallāhi, where he was buried next to Aḥmad Lobbo and Aḥmad II, as explicitly requested by the founder of the caliphate himself.[46] Even the third generation of leaders of the caliphate recognized the importance of Nūḥ b. al-Ṭāhir, as epitomized by an anecdote recorded by Brown: "At death, Alfa Nuh [Nūḥ b. al-Ṭāhir]'s body was carried from Niakongo to Hamdullahi on the backs of the machube [slaves] while the nobles rode horseback. When 'Ahmad (III) saw this, he criticized the nobles for having failed to obtain a blessing by having carried the body of Alfa Nuh themselves."[47] [Figure 2]

The analysis of extant sources provides a clearer picture of the life of Nūḥ b. al-Ṭāhir as a notable of Ḥamdallāhi, but he was also a famous scholar, with interest in several branches of knowledge. According to Brown, Nūḥ b. al-Ṭāhir stood out among the *'ulamā'* of Ḥamdallāhi, and was the only one who was well known beyond the borders of the caliphate, along with al-Mukhtār b. Wadī'at Allāh al-Māsinī, known as Yirkoy Talfi (d. ca. 1862).[48] However, no research has been hitherto conducted on his writings.

Nūḥ b. al-Ṭāhir's Writings

Despite Nūḥ b. al-Ṭāhir's fame as an accomplished scholar, his intellectual contributions to Islamic scholarship in nineteenth-century West Africa remain obscure, and none of his work has been analyzed or published so far – except, of course, for his unacknowledged authorship

[44] *L'empire peul*, 252. [45] *L'empire peul*, 254.
[46] *L'empire peul*, 48. On Aḥmad Lobbo explicitly requesting Nuḥ b. al-Ṭāhir to be buried next to him, see *L'empire peul*, 251–252.
[47] Brown, "The Caliphate of Hamdullahi," 189, n. 54.
[48] Brown, "The Caliphate of Hamdullahi," 104.

Figure 2: The mausoleum of Aḥmad Lobbo, Nūḥ b. al-Ṭāhir, and Aḥmad II in Ḥamdallāhi (Copyright Alfa Mamadou Diallo Lélouma).

of the *Tārīkh al-fattāsh*.[49] Some of his writings have survived in manuscript format. For example, he authored a commentary (*sharḥ*) on the *Lāmiyyat al-af'āl* (The Verbal Structures in *Lām* Rhyme) Ibn Mālik (d. 1274), a work on Arabic morphology (*ṣarf*) very popular in West Africa.[50] [Figure 3] This proves Nūḥ b. al-Ṭāhir's

[49] An exception is represented by my translation of the *Risāla fī ẓuhūr al-khalīfa al-thānī 'ashar* (Mauro Nobili [ed. and trans.], "Letter on the appearance of the twelfth caliph [*Risāla fī ẓuhūr al-khalīfa al-thānī 'ashar*]: Edition of the Arabic text with English translation," *Afriques* 7 [2016] [http://journals.openedition.org/afriques/1958]). The list of Nūḥ b. al-Ṭāhir's works provided in *ALA* IV, 213 is incomplete.

[50] This work is available in two manuscripts copies: IHERI-ABT 3126 and IRSH 2036. I could not access the IRSH copy, which is apparently complete and consists of sixteen pages (Mawlāy Ḥasan and Ayman Fu'ād Sayyid, *Fihris al-makhṭūṭāt al-Islāmīya al-mawjūda bi-Ma'had al-abḥāth fī al-'ulūm al-insānīyah, al-Nayjar/Catalogue of Islamic Manuscripts at the Institut des Recherches en Sciences Humaines [IRSH], Niger* [London: al-Furqan Islamic Heritage Foundation, 2004], vol. 5, 45–46). On the importance of the *Lāmiyyat al-af'āl* in West Africa, see Bruce S. Hall and Charles C. Stewart, "The historic 'core curriculum' and the book market in Islamic West Africa," in *The*

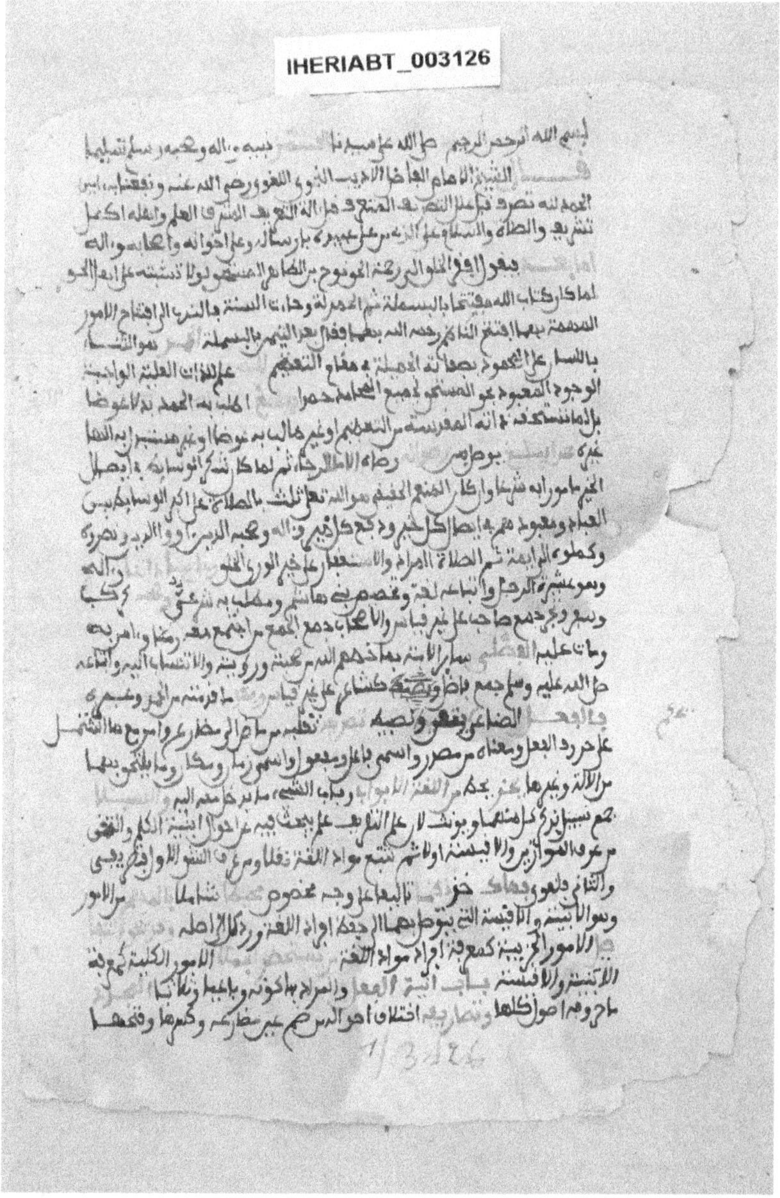

Figure 3: IHERI-ABT 3126, Nūḥ b. al-Ṭāhir, *Sharḥ al-lāmiyya* (Copyright IHERI-ABT).

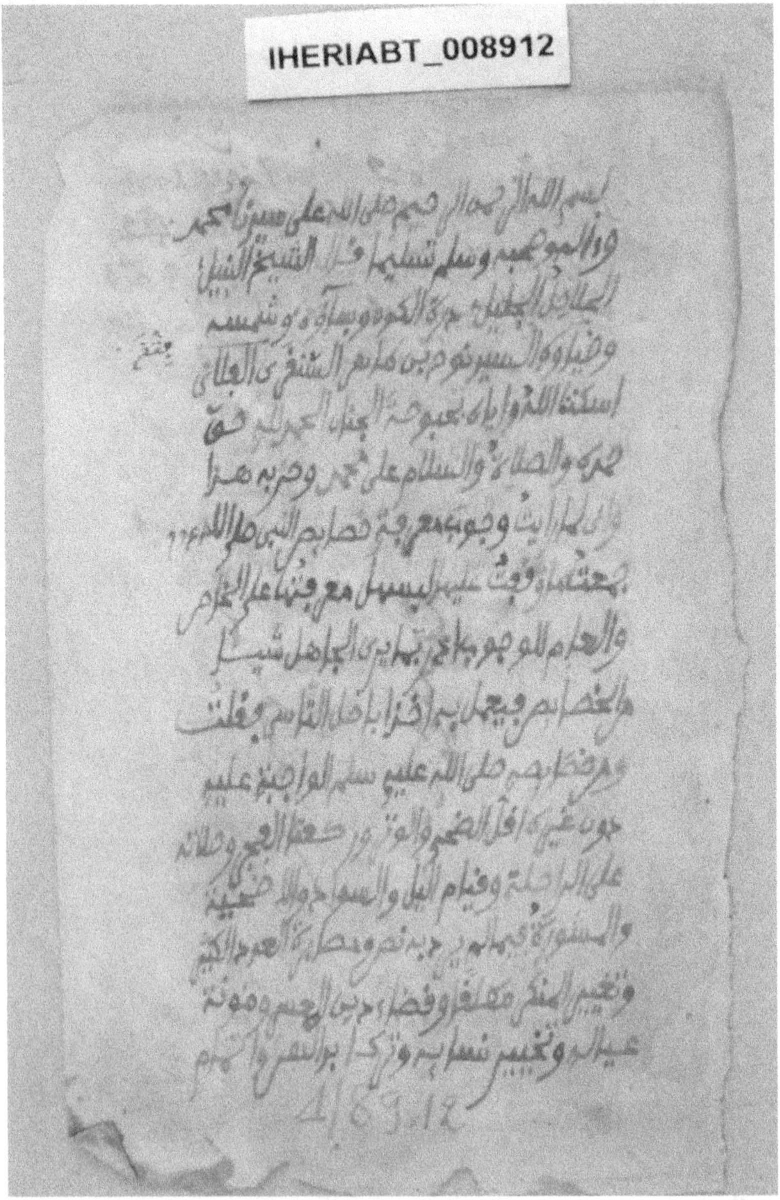

Figure 4: IHERI-ABT 8912, Nūḥ b. al-Ṭāhir, *Maktūb fī khaṣā'iṣ al-Nābī* (Copyright IHERI-ABT)

mastery of Arabic grammar, but the discipline that most interested the Fulani scholar was history. In this domain, Nūḥ b. al-Ṭāhir wrote a short treatise on the distinctive features of the Prophet (*khaṣā'is al-Nabī*), which inscribes itself in the tradition of biographical works on the Prophet (*sirā*).[51] [Figure 4] However, the fame of Nūḥ b. al-Ṭāhir's interest in history went beyond his own writings, as testified by the spurious ascription to him of a posthumous manuscript retailing a very common tradition regarding the origins of the Fulani and a list of Fulani rulers of the Middle Niger – which extends well beyond Nūḥ b. al-Ṭāhir's lifetime.[52]

Among Nūḥ b. al-Ṭāhir's historical writings is the short draft of the *Tārīkh al-fattāsh* discussed above, but this text does not seem to be a complete work. The only existing copy, totally unknown to local scholars, is the manuscript that Haruna Alfaga copied for de Gironcourt in 1912. However, it seems that this text had not circulated in the form of an independent work. A note on the frontispiece of the manuscript, which de Gironcourt compiled based on his observations and on information collected by Yūsuf b. al-Khalīl, records that the chronicle was sketched as a note in the last pages of another work. In de Gironcourt's words, "Writing occupying the last two pages of a book 'khamous' [i.e. *qāmūs*, Arabic for 'dictionary'] of 22/33.5 cm that looks like about fifty years old [thus dating back to around the 1860s]. On unlaid paper. It was received from a marabout from the Masina."[53]

De Gironcourt's note suggests that the short chronicle was, in fact, a draft not meant for circulation, sketched for personal use in the final pages of a dictionary. Therefore, its text would have remained hidden in that manuscript if not for de Gironcourt's zeal in collecting local histories. Furthermore, the dictionary that originally contained the

Trans-Saharan Book Trade: Manuscript Culture, Arabic Literacy, and Intellectual History in Muslim Africa, edited by Graziano Krätli and Ghislaine Lydon (Leiden and Boston: Brill, 2011), 109–174, 121.

51 IHERI-ABT 8912.

52 Almamy Maliki Yattara Collection 34. This manuscript comes from the private collection of Almamy Maliki Yattara, who copied it from a manuscript owned by one Alfa Barké Kondo of Ténenkou. Yattara's manuscript was photographed and listed by Bernard Salvaing, who kindly shared it with me along with the unpublished list.

53 IF, Fonds de Gironcourt, 2410 (174), f. 112a (fiche signaletique).

copy was itself copied from the last pages of a manuscript that, according to Yūsuf b. al-Khalīl, was bought by its previous owner who had come from Masina around the 1860s. Is it possible that the original owner of the manuscript was Nūḥ b. al-Ṭāhir himself, and that the text at the end of it was his own draft? The evidence makes this hypothesis plausible.

Nūḥ b. al-Ṭāhir's narrative, although it provides "proofs" of Aḥmad Lobbo's legitimacy as the prophesied West African ruler and heir to the Songhay king, Askiyà Muḥammad, would have seriously threatened the very ingenuity of the legitimization project if circulated in the form of the short *Tārīkh al-fattāsh*. The unconcealed ascription of the narrative to Nūḥ b. al-Ṭāhir, which represents the "imaginative" part of the work of any forger as described by Grafton, would have revealed the author's tendentiousness and exposed his ploy. Thus, this narrative could have not circulated in this format. Instead, again in Grafton's terminology, it was necessary also to produce "corroboration": Nūḥ b. al-Ṭāhir had to validate his inventive story to transform it into a reliable source. To achieve this, he embedded his narrative into the older *Tārīkh Ibn al-Mukhtār*.

The Chronicle of the "Son of al-Mukhtār"

The *Tārīkh Ibn al-Mukhtār* exists today only in two related copies: MS A/IHERI-ABT 3927 and its copy MS B/BnF 6651.[54] Both manuscripts are incomplete, lacking several pages at the chronicle's beginning. Corroborating the work of Levtzion, my comparison of this text with Houdas and Delafosse's second appendix suggests that the latter might be the French translation of another, also incomplete, copy of the *Tārīkh Ibn al-Mukhtār* – a third one.[55] The second appendix includes the first part of the work that is missing in MS A/IHERI-ABT 3927 and MS B/BnF 6651. Therefore, a complete text of the *Tārīkh Ibn al-Mukhtār* can now be reconstructed.

This chronicle was written under the patronage of Askiyà Dāwūd b. Hārūn, thus between 1657 and 1669. The incipit of this chronicle starts with: "This historical note was composed at the request of the

[54] A composite manuscript hosted at IHERI-ABT, with the call number 2221, contains another short fragment of the *Tārīkh Ibn al-Mukhtār*.

[55] See Levtzion's arguments in Levtzion, "A seventeenth-century chronicle," 580.

honorable and brave Askiyà Dāwūd, the son of Askiyà Hārūn, son of Askiyà al-Ḥājj, son of Askiyà Dāwūd, son of the commander of the believers, Askiyà al-Ḥājj Muḥammad."[56] Its author provides us with another detail that allows for the dating of the chronicle, narrating an episode occurring in 1664–5 as "witnessed with my own eyes."[57] This reference establishes 1664–5 as the *terminus post quem* for the writing of the chronicle.

As explicitly stated in its introduction, this is intended to be a chronicle of the Askiyà dynasty:

> This is a historical note in which I provide the biography of the princes of Takrūr, who bear the title of *askiyà*, from Askiyà al-Ḥājj Muḥammad b. Abī Bakr until our time, in chronological order. In the biography of each prince, I will mention the event that happened during his time related to the eminent religious figures and the scholars.[58]

In addition, the work briefly covers, in chronological order, the history of the first two Songhay dynasties, the Zā and the Sonni; and ends in the year 1599, after the Moroccan conquest of 1591.[59] In spite of that, the Askiyà dynasty remains the central focus of the chronicle, to the point that Ferran I. Vernet and Michael A. Gomez have also noted how the dynasty's legitimization is a priority in the author's political agenda.[60] However, like its contemporary text the *Tārīkh al-Sūdān*, the *Tārīkh Ibn al-Mukhtār* is mainly an "exercise in catastrophe management," in the words of de Moraes Farias.[61] Far from being nostalgic for the era of imperial Songhay, both texts offer an explanation for the Moroccan invasion of the Niger Bend in 1591 and call for acceptance of the new political order. The chroniclers "sermonize on the link between the Soŋoy independence and the sinfulness of the last Askiya sovereigns and their kin."[62] They explain the fall of the Songhay

[56] *La chronique du chercheur*, French text 328. Interestingly, the manuscript MS A/IHERI-ABT 3927 also comprises, apart from the main text of the *Tārīkh Ibn al-Mukhtār*, a few folios, written in the same hand, from the *Tārīkh al-Sūdān* covering the events of Askiyà Dāwūd b. Hārūn's reign (IHERI-ABT 3927, unnumbered f. 70).

[57] *La chronique du chercheur*, Arabic text 75/French text 142.

[58] *La chronique du chercheur*, French text 327.

[59] *La chronique du chercheur*, Arabic text 184/French text 320.

[60] Vernet, "Dispute au sujet du caractère de la propriété," 56; Gomez, *African Dominion*, 176.

[61] De Moraes Farias, *Arabic Medieval Inscriptions*, lxxii § 111.

[62] De Moraes Farias, *Arabic Medieval Inscriptions*, lxxiii § 117.

state and the Moroccan invasion in metaphysical terms, as God's punishments for the moral decay of the Askiyà family. This "meta-historical symbolism" prepares the ground for the acceptance of the new Arma aristocracy and builds a "bridge over the gap between the invaders and the other social categories."[63] The authors of the *Tārīkh al-Sūdān* and the *Tārīkh Ibn al-Mukhtār* endorse the descendants of the Moroccan invasion, the Arma, and, at the same time, advance a scenario in which the previous political elite, the Askiyà family, and the Timbuktu Muslim patriciate, as the repositories of religious authority, can both participate in the political arena along with the new Arma regime.

Very little is known about the author of the *Tārīkh Ibn al-Mukhtār*. The given name (*ism*) is not mentioned in his chronicle. He identifies himself only by his patronymic (*nasab*) as the son of al-Mukhtār

Table 2 *A Tentative Family Tree of the Ka'ti and QNBL Families*

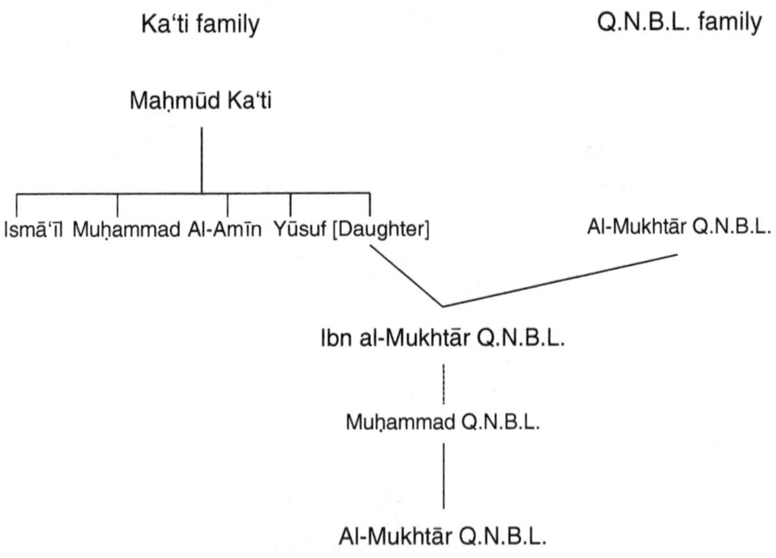

QNBL: "I have heard this account from my father al-Mukhtār QNBL"[64] However, Ibn al-Mukhtār does provide some further

[63] De Moraes Farias, *Arabic Medieval Inscriptions*, lxxiv § 119, lxxv § 121.
[64] *La chronique du chercheur*, Arabic text 70/French text 135.

information about himself directly. He was, as emerges from the following passage, the grandson of Maḥmūd Ka'ti: "I reported all of this from what my grandfather Alfa' Maḥmūd b. al-Ḥājj al-Mutawakkil said, as written down by one of his students."[65] Maḥmūd Ka'ti was therefore his maternal grandfather, since Ibn al-Mukhtār refers to the *qāḍī* Isma'īl Ka'ti, to the *faqīh* and *qāḍī* Muḥammad al-Amīn Ka'ti, and the *faqīh* Yūsuf Ka'ti – all sons of Maḥmūd Ka'ti – as his maternal uncles.[66]

It seems that Ibn al-Mukhtār, nephew and grandson of *qāḍīs*, also initiated a lineage of other Muslim judges. The *Tadhkirat al-nisyān* records information on two other QNBLs, most likely son and grandson of Ibn al-Mukhtār: a certain Muhammad QNBL and al-Mukhtār QNBL.[67] The first was *qāḍī* in Tindirma, and died on 12 December 1710.[68] The second, his son, succeeded the father as *qāḍī* of the same town.[69]

A study of the available contemporary sources and scholarship suggests that Ibn al-Mukhtār and his chronicle were not well known in the region. For example, he does not appear in the *Fatḥ al-shakūr fī ma'rifat a'yān 'ulamā' al-Takrūr* (Victory of the Most Appreciative in Educating about the Notable Scholars of the Takrūr), in which Muḥammad b. Abī Bakr al-Ṣiddīq al-Bārtaylī (d. 1805) records several biographies of scholars from Timbuktu and the surrounding area.[70] In this work, al-Bārtaylī pays special attention to chroniclers, recording a biography of 'Abd al-Raḥmān b. 'Abd Allāh b. 'Imrān b. 'Āmir al-Sa'dī, the author of the *Tārīkh al-Sūdān*.[71] However, he does not record any information about Ibn al-Mukhtār. Likewise, no

65 *La chronique du chercheur*, Arabic text 48/French text 92.

66 *La chronique du chercheur*, Arabic text 72, 89, 142/French text 138, 168, 257.

67 In the text the name is left unvocalized, but in this case Houdas read the name as "Qanbel" (Houdas [ed. and trans.], *Tedzkiret en-nisiān*, Arabic text 96/French text 155, n. 1).

68 Houdas (ed. and trans.), *Tedzkiret en-nisiān*, Arabic text 137/French text 222.

69 Houdas (ed. and trans.), *Tedzkiret en-nisiān*, Arabic text 96/French text 155.

70 On the *Fatḥ al-shakūr*, see *ALA* IV, 1540, item 4. The *Fatḥ al-shakūr* is translated into French in Chouki El Hamel, *La vie intellectuelle islamique dans le sahel ouest-africain, XVI–XIX siècles: une étude sociale de l'enseignement islamique en mauritanie et au nord du mali (XVI–XIX siècles) et traduction annotée de Fatḥ ash-shakūr d'al-Bartilī al-Walātī (mort en 1805)* (Paris: L'Harmattan, 2002), 141–420.

71 El Hamel, *La vie intellectuelle*, 371. Al-Sa'dī's name is misspelled in the *Fatḥ al-shakūr* as al-Sa'īdī.

information on the author of the *Tārīkh Ibn al-Mukhtār* is available in two important twentieth-century works, the *Izālat al-rayb wa-l-shakk wa-l-tafrīṭ fī dhikr al-'ulamā' al-mu'allifīn min ahl al-Takrūr wa-Ṣaḥrā'* (Removal of Doubt, Uncertainty, and Neglect in the Mentions of the Authored Scholars from the Takrūr and the Sahara) by Aḥmad b. Mbārak b. Barka b. Muḥammad al-Mūsā-ū-'Alī al-Takanī al-Wādnūnī al-Sūsī al-Timbuktī, known as Aḥmad Būl'arāf (d. 1955);[72] and the *Sa'āda al-abadiyya fī ta'rīf 'ulamā' Tinbuktu al-bahiya* (Eternal Felicity through the Introduction of the Brilliant Scholars of Timbuktu) by Mūlāy Aḥmad (b.) Bābēr al-Arawānī (d. 1997).[73] Both works, written by Timbuktu-based scholars, record important information on the history of the town and its scholars, using local sources extensively, but they remain silent on Ibn al-Mukhtār and the chronicle he authored.

The obscurity of the *Tārīkh Ibn al-Mukhtār* stands in contrast to the other seventeenth-century chronicle of the region, the *Tārīkh al-Sūdān*, which is often quoted. For example, the *Fatḥ al-shakūr* uses al-Sa'dī's work extensively in 37 out of 215 biographical entries.[74] Furthermore, copies of the *Tārīkh al-Sūdān* have been found in different parts of North and West Africa, witnessing the chronicle's extensive circulation in the region.[75] Indeed, it may well be that relative obscurity of the *Tārīkh Ibn al-Mukhtār* is what attracted Nūḥ b. al-Ṭāhir's attention: here was a useful and detailed seventeenth-century work recording the biographies of the Askiyàs, the kings of the Songhay Empire, into which he could insert and disguise the narrative that he himself had invented regarding Askiyà Muḥammad's Pilgrimage. Precisely because the *Tārīkh Ibn al-Mukhtār* was not a famous work, like its contemporary, the *Tārīkh al-Sūdān*, Nūḥ b. al-Ṭāhir was able to manipulate this

[72] al-Hādī al-Mabrūk al-Dālī (ed.), *Izālat al-raiyb wa-al-shšakk wa-al-tafrīṭ fī dhikr al-'ulamā' al-mu'allifīn min ahl al-Takrūr wa-al-Ṣaḥrā'* (n.p.: n.d.). On the *Izālat al-rayb*, see *ALA* IV, 54, item 7.

[73] IHERI-ABT 2752. On the *Sa'āda al-abadiyya*, see *ALA* IV, 63, item 8.

[74] El Hamel, *La vie intellectuelle*, 49.

[75] Of the copies of the *Tārīkh al-Sūdān* employed by Houdas and more recently by Hunwick, one (MS A) comes from Segou (*TS*, xiv); four (MS B, MS E, MS F, and MS G) from Timbuktu (Houdas [ed. and trans.)], *Tarikh es-Soudan*, xiv; Hunwick, *Timbuktu and the Songhay Empire*, xviii); one (MS D) from Sokoto (Nobili, *Catalogue des manuscrits arabes*, 61–64, item 4); MS C, given to Houdas by René Basset in Algiers, has uncertain provenance e (*TS*, xiv–v). Another copy, never used by scholars, is in Djenné (Djenné manuscript Library, Fonds Djeitteye, 1).

text without anybody noticing the intervention, in order to construct a new chronicle: the *Tārīkh al-fattāsh*.

Askiyà Muḥammad, the Putative Ancestor of Aḥmad Lobbo

Unlike the seventeenth-century *Tārīkh Ibn al-Mukhtār*, which portrays itself as a chronicle of the Askiyà dynasty in general, Nūḥ b. al-Ṭāhir frames the *Tārīkh al-fattāsh* as a celebration of one particular *askiyà*, Askiyà Muḥammad. Although the chronicle does cover the history of the region until the initial period of Arma domination, the introduction to the work specifies that its goal is the glorification of Askiyà Muḥammad:

> God the Most High has blessed us by making manifest in our time the just caliph, the conqueror and victorious sultan, the upright Askiyà al-Ḥājj Muḥammad b. Abī Bakr, of Torodo origin, but resident in Gao. He illuminated our path through his righteous guide, after the darkness of misguidance, and chased away from us echoes of fear and destruction. By the glory of God the Most High, lands from east to west became open to him and delegations submitted to him individually or in groups. Kings became subject to him, by force or spontaneously. By His blessing, we are in good state and happiness after having been in difficulty and misery. God the Most High has replaced all of that with His favor just as He said to His best of creation, "So, truly with hardship comes ease, with hardship comes ease [Qur'ān 94: 5–6]." I wanted to collect, among the most important stories along with the memory of the cursed Shu'i [Sonni] 'Āli, what has been made easy for the hand and the tongue – to God the Most High I seek help.[76]

This celebration of Askiyà Muḥammad is a key rhetorical device in the pointed political propaganda designed to support the Caliphate of Ḥamdallāhi and its leading founder, Aḥmad Lobbo. Lauding a centuries-old ruler had little meaning per se, but Askiyà Muḥammad fulfills two narrative roles within Nūḥ b. al-Ṭāhir's plan: he is a symbol of the rightful Muslim ruler par excellence and, in that capacity, the putative ancestor of Aḥmad Lobbo.

Nūḥ b. al-Ṭāhir constructs the opening passages of the *Tārīkh al-fattāsh* around the concept of God's delegation of authority to the caliphs and the institution of the caliphate as the continuation of the

[76] *La chronique du chercheur*, Arabic text 10–11/French text 9–10.

Prophet's mission. This first concept is expressed in Nūḥ b. al-Ṭāhir's own words: "He [God] entrusted the caliphs with authority, so that in them He gives shelter to the outcast and through them He bends the disobedient opponent. He made them [the caliphs] His shadow on the earth."[77] To buttress the second concept, Nūḥ b. al-Ṭāhir turns to the often-quoted *ḥadīth*, "This affair started with the Prophethood and mercy, and then it will continue with the caliphate and mercy."[78] In other words, the doxology is an invitation for Muslims to follow the ruler, as in the Qur'ānic passage, "Obey God and obey the Messenger and those among you who have authority" (Qur'ān 4: 59). This is made explicit in Nūḥ b. al-Ṭāhir's statement that "those who follow them [the caliphs] are on the right path and will be successful; those who turn away from them are astray and will fail."[79]

Yet the invocation of the doxology should not deceive the reader into believing that the *Tārīkh al-fattāsh* is an invitation for political passivity. Nūḥ b. al-Ṭāhir does not just invite us to follow *any* ruler; he invites us to follow Askiyà Muḥammad, who becomes the embodiment of the caliph in the chronicle. To achieve this aim, Nūḥ b. al-Ṭāhir first works on ennobling the *askiyà*'s origins. Stephan Bühnen has showed that Askiyà Muḥammad's *nisba* "al-Tūrī," used in the *Tārīkh Ibn al-Mukhtār* and the *Tārīkh al-Sūdān*, refers to Fouta Toro and not to the widespread surname Toure, as is sometimes still argued.[80] However, in the *Tārīkh al-fattāsh*, the Songhay king is described as "al-Turūdī," which refers to the Torodbe clerisy.[81] Since it has been established that the Torodbe clerisy emerged in Fouta Toro, characterizing the *askiyà* as a "Turūdī" is anachronistic; it is another invention of Nūḥ b. al-Ṭāhir, because the Torodbe clerisy seems to have only emerged in Fouta Toro in the late seventeenth century, i.e. more than a hundred years after the death of Askiyà Muḥammad.[82] Most likely, Nūḥ b. al-Ṭāhir wanted to link the *askiyà* to the Torodbe who had

77 *La chronique du chercheur*, Arabic text 9/French text 6.
78 *La chronique du chercheur*, Arabic text 10/French text 7. The *ḥadīth* comes from Abū Bakr Aḥmad b. al-Ḥusayn al-Bayhaqī, *al-Sunan al-kubrà* (Mecca: Maktaba Dār al-Bāz, 1994), vol. 8, 159, no. 16407.
79 *La chronique du chercheur*, Arabic text 9/French text 6.
80 Stephan Bühnen, "Askiya Muḥammad I and his *qabīla*: Name and provenance," *Sudanic Africa* 16 (2005): 83–90.
81 *La chronique du chercheur*, Arabic text 10/French text 9.
82 On the origins of the Torodbe, see John Ralph Willis, "The Torodbe clerisy: A social view," *Journal of African History* 19/2 (1978): 195–212, 200.

become the religious leadership of the Senegal River region, and from whom many leaders of Islamic revolutions were descended.[83]

Furthermore, Nūḥ b. al-Ṭāhir intervenes in the identification of the Songhay king's maternal ancestors. According to the *Tārīkh Ibn al-Mukhtār*, Askiyà Muḥammad's mother descended from the famous Companion of the Prophet, Jābir b. ʻAbd Allāh al-Anṣārī (d. 697). However, Ibn al-Mukhtār was very cautious in reporting this information: "I have seen some people who reconnect his [Askiyà Muḥammad's] genealogy to Jābir b. ʻAbd Allāh al-Anṣārī."[84] In order to make the genealogy of the *askiyà* more prestigious, Nūḥ b. al-Ṭāhir therefore replaces the skepticism of Ibn al-Mukhtār with a precise genealogy of Askiyà Muḥammad's mother that goes back twenty-two generations to Jābir b. ʻAbd Allāh al-Anṣārī.[85]

Nūḥ b. al-Ṭāhir also had to confront the traditions – circulating, arguably, in both oral and written forms – which held that Askiyà Muḥammad continued to rule according to traditional Songhay royal customs. For example, an isolated fragment preserved with MS A/IHERI-ABT 3927 records several of these customs, among them that the subjects of the king would sprinkle their heads with dust in the *askiyà*'s presence, a tradition that goes back to the time of the emperor of Ghāna.[86] Unable to eradicate the memory of these traditions, Nūḥ b. al-Ṭāhir incorporated them into the *Tārīkh al-fattāsh*, following verbatim the fragment of MS A/IHERI-ABT 3927:

> Askiyà Muḥammad observed the Songhay way and made it the foundation of the state. Nobody in his army was allowed to sit in his presence except for the *Djenné-koi*. All of them covered their heads with dust in front of him, except for the *Djenné-koi* who would only sprinkle flour on themselves. All of them had to remove their hats when they poured dust on themselves, with the exception of the *Kourmina-Fāri*. None of them could tell the truth to him, except for the *Dendi-Fāri*. Only the *Bara-koi* could hold back from an order and the *askiyà* had to accept it, whether he liked it or not. Nobody among them could enter his palace on horseback, except for the *Dirma-koi*. In his land, only the *qāḍī* could summon a servant of the *askiyà* and send him for some business and he could not refuse. Nobody in his gatherings could call the *askiyà* by his name except for the *Gesere-dunka*. Nobody, except for a *sharīf*, could sit by

83 Willis, "The Torodbe clerisy," 195.
84 *La chronique du chercheur*, Arabic text 59/French text 114.
85 *La chronique du chercheur*, Arabic text 59, n. 1/French text 114, n. 4.
86 IHERI-ABT 3927, unnumbered f. 68.

his side on the podium. The *askiyà* ordered that, whenever the *qāḍī* visited him, a prayer mat should be unfolded for them. He decided that the eunuchs of his house must remain to his left. He decided that he would not stand up for anybody but the scholars and the pilgrims when they return from Mecca. He chose that only the scholars, the *sharīf*s and their sons, and the *sans*, even young, could eat with him. God have mercy on him.[87]

However, he then comments that "this was at the beginning of his rule to draw near in enticement the hearts of his people. Then, when his authority became firm and the kingdom became upright, he left all of that. He began asking the scholars who act on the teaching of the Prophet."[88] In other words, Nūḥ b. al-Ṭāhir redeems Askiyà Muḥammad from his association with traditional Songhay royal customs, suggesting that he eventually abandoned them.

Nūḥ b. al-Ṭāhir also reimagines the story of Askiyà Muḥammad's 1493 coup d'état against the Sonni dynasty and transforms it into a legitimate *jihād* against an unjust ruler. He could count at the time on al-Maghīlī's *a posteriori* legitimization of the *askiyà*'s war against the Sonnis, a consequence of his anathemization of the figure most representative of them, Sonni 'Alī.[89] However, Nūḥ b. al-Ṭāhir further strengthens the legitimate character of the *askiyà*'s war. He achieves this task indirectly, first by the vilification of the Sonnis, and in particular of Sonni 'Alī. As Gomez has recently pointed out, the portrait of this ruler in *Tārīkh Ibn al-Mukhtār* was not completely negative: "What emerges most saliently [in relation to Sonni 'Alī] is the recognition, if not celebration, of an imperialism that equates with greatness and glory."[90] Therefore, to darken Ibn al-Mukhtār's portrayal of Sonni 'Alī, Nūḥ b. al-Ṭāhir inserts an entire chapter of the *Tārīkh al-Sūdān*, which takes a stronger stand against the Sonni ruler, into the *Tārīkh al-fattāsh*.[91] Furthermore, Nūḥ b. al-Ṭāhir wraps the narrative of Askiyà

87 *La chronique du chercheur*, Arabic text 11/French text 13–14.
88 *La chronique du chercheur*, Arabic text 11–12/French text 14–15.
89 In his *Replies* to the Askiyà al-Ḥājj Muḥammad, al-Maghīlī had defined Sonni 'Alī as belonging to one of the three categories of unbelievers against which it is legitimate to conduct *jihād*: "He who claims to be a Muslim and whom we judge to be an unbeliever because he has committed an outward action such as none but an unbeliever would, as you mentioned concerning Sunni 'Alī" (Hunwick, *Sharī'a in Songhay*, Arabic text 19/English text 47).
90 Gomez, *African Dominion*, 183–184.
91 The chapter, which is not translated by Houdas and Delafosse, is located in *La chronique du chercheur*, Arabic text 50/French text 98.

Muḥammad in a legal discourse of legitimacy. He introduces a long story concerning three messengers sent by Asikyà Muḥammad to Sonni Bāru, who invite the latter to convert to Islam and to pledge allegiance to the *askiyà*. According to this story, it was only after the refusal of the *sonni* that Askiyà Muḥammad attacked and defeated him.[92] This episode aims at legitimizing the Askiyà Muhammad's war, according to the example of the Prophet, who set the precedent for Muslim leaders to first summon enemies to convert or accept the terms of a pact before launching war – otherwise the war would be considered illegitimate.[93]

Ennobling Askiyà Muḥammad's origins, detaching him from the traditional royal habits of Songhay kings, and legitimizing his coup against the *sonni* are just a few of the interventions that make up Nūḥ b. al-Ṭahir's transfiguration of the *askiyà*. It is around the Pilgrimage of Askiyà Muḥammad that Nūḥ b. al-Ṭāhir works hardest to achieve his goal. Here, the narrative of the investiture of the Songhay king by Mūlāy al-'Abbās, which he had originally sketched in the short draft *Tārīkh al-fattāsh*, is inserted verbatim at the beginning of the long *Tārīkh al-fattāsh* – with the exception, of course, of the work's ascription to Nūḥ b. al-Ṭāhir. Moreover, the narrative is enriched with several new elements. The encounter between Askiyà Muḥammad and Mūlāy al-'Abbās is especially embellished: contrary to the scanty description of events in the short *Tārīkh al-fattāsh*, the long version of the chronicle describes the investiture of Askiyà Muḥammad as a veritable rite of passage that transforms the Songhay king into a West African caliph. While sitting near the Ka'ba, the prince of Mecca reveals to the *askiyà* that he is the eleventh caliph prophesied by the Prophet. However, he explains that Askiyà Muḥammad could not be declared as such because kingship with temporal power (*mulk*) could not be combined with the caliphate (*khilāfa*). Thus, Mūlāy al-'Abbās urges Askiyà Muḥammad to renounce his temporal power, which the king does by giving all of his royal insignia to the prince of Mecca. Then Mūlāy al-'Abbās went into retreat for three days and, once returned, turbaned the *askiyà* as caliph of West Africa.[94]

92 *La chronique du chercheur*, Arabic text 53–55/French text 102–106.
93 Hunwick, *Timbuktu and the Songhay Empire*, 107, n. 32.
94 *La chronique du chercheur*, Arabic text 12/French text 16.

Another episode related to Mūlāy al-'Abbās, on which the *Tārīkh al-fattāsh* spends several pages, further strengthens the investiture of Askiyà Muḥammad, this time *in absentia*. In Mecca, several years after the *askiyà*'s visit, Mūlāy al-'Abbās meets his nephew Aḥmad al-Ṣaqlī, and sends him to Timbuktu, justifying his choice by saying that "there lives the caliph of our ancestor, the Messenger of God," Askiyà Muhammad.[95]

Once the transfiguration of Askiyà Muḥammad into the ideal caliph is completed, Nūḥ b. al-Ṭāhir connects him to Aḥmad Lobbo by incorporating the entire section concerning al-Suyūṭī originally sketched in the draft of the chronicle. However, to further strengthen this connection, in the final version of the *Tārīkh al-fattāsh*, Nūḥ b. al-Ṭāhir expands on some characters who are only mentioned marginally in the short version and who take on the role of foretellers of Aḥmad Lobbo's advent.

The first of these is Shamharūsh, the *jinn*.[96] According to the story elaborated in the *Tārīkh al-fattāsh*, two scholars in the entourage of Askiyà Muḥammad, Mūḥammad TL and Ṣāliḥ Diawara, along with the latter's young son Mūsà, met a group of *jinn* at an oasis between Alexandria and Cairo.[97] Among these *jinn* was Shamharūsh, who told the followers of the *askiyà*:

Askiyà Muḥammad is a pious man. I heard the Prophet – may God honor him and grant him peace – saying: "The caliphs are twelve, all from the Quraysh." I think that he [Askiyà Muḥammad] is one of them. Ten have already arrived and two are left. Perhaps, he is one of them. The last will

[95] *La chronique du chercheur*, Arabic text 21/French text 35.

[96] Also known as Sīdī Shamharūsh al-Ṭayār ("the flyer"), this *jinn* is very popular in North African traditions, and especially in Morocco, where locals identify a place in Fez as the cave where he used to hold his meetings with other *jinn*. Shamharūsh is said to have converted to Islam at the time of the Prophet and to have become a scholar, a judge, and one of the seven kings of the *jinn*; on Shamharūsh, see Edward Westermarck, *Ritual and Belief in Morocco* (London: Macmillan, 1926), vol. 1, 283–285; Mohammed Maarouf, *Jinn Eviction as a Discourse of Power: A Multidisciplinary Approach to Moroccan Magical Beliefs and Practices* (Leiden: Brill, 2007), 107–108; and Robert W. Lebling, *Legends of the Fire Spirits: Jinn and Genies from Arabia to Zanzibar* (London: I. B. Tauris, 2010), 86–87.

[97] Askiyà Muḥammad also meets with one of the disciples of Shamharūsh, Damīr b. Ya'qūb, of whom the Songhay king asks questions about the origin of the Songhay, the Soninke, the Wangara, the Sorko, and the Berbers (*La chronique du chercheur*, Arabic text 24–29/French text 40–48).

arrive in the thirteenth century [of the Hegira/nineteenth century Gregorian]. The Prophet – may God honor him and grant him peace – also told me that I will live until the ninth century and that I will be contemporary with the eleventh caliph. Then he will have authority over *jinn* and men. At that time, I will die.[98]

Shamharūsh confirms the elevation of Askiyà Muḥammad as legitimate ruler of West Africa and as eleventh caliph of Islam. He also returns to the connection between the *askiyà* and his putative descendant Aḥmad Lobbo, although the *jinn* does not explicitly mention the name of the caliph of Ḥamdallāhi, but only his century.

Another character who is used to connect Askiyà Muḥammad to Aḥmad Lobbo in the *Tārīkh al-fattāsh* is the North African jurist ʻAbd al-Raḥmān al-Thaʻālibī (d. 1479). He is credited with a spurious statement, allegedly quoted by Maḥmūd Kaʻti, in which he predicts, again without explicit mention of the name, the arrival of Aḥmad Lobbo in the thirteenth century of the Islamic calendar as well as the resistance that he would experience from his contemporaries:

The *faqīh* Maḥmūd [Kaʻti] said, giving strength to the words of *imām* [al-Suyūṭī] and in agreement with what is attributed to the latter, that Shaykh ʻAbd al-Raḥmān al-Thaʻālibī stated that at the end of the time there will be two caliphs from the land of Takrūr. The first will appear at the end of the ninth century, the second at the beginning of the thirteenth. The people of their time will reject them as caliphs and will declare their

98 *La chronique du chercheur*, Arabic text 66/French text 127. While Shamharūsh is in the *Tārīkh al-fattāsh* only one of the many authorities who recognized Askiyà Muḥammad as caliph, in the oral traditions collected by Hampaté Ba and Daget, he becomes the only reference to the *askiyà*'s investiture as caliph; Shamharūsh is the one who explains to Askiyà Muḥammad the tradition of the twelve caliphs; and he is the one who prophesies the arrival of Aḥmad Lobbo (*L'empire peul*, 17–19). The importance of Shamharūsh in the *Tārīkh al-fattāsh* reflects the prominent role occupied by this *jinn* in the Middle Niger. According to oral traditions collected at the beginning of the twentieth century from the "chief of the Bozo of the region of Jenne," whose name is recorded as "Ousman Kontao," Shamharūsh indicated to the Bozo and the Nono/Marka the place to build the city of Djenné (Charles Monteil, *Une cité soudanaise: Djénné, métropole du Delta Central du Niger* [Paris: Éditions Anthropos, 1971], 35). Furthermore, continues Ousman Kontao, Shamharūsh was also the architect of al-Ḥājj ʻUmar's victories (Monteil, *Djénné*, 35). At that time, the *jinn* was living in Noyna, southwest of Djenné, but according to Ousman Kontao, he had disappeared since the arrival of the French (Monteil, *Djénné*, 35).

actions to be the result of injustice and falsehood, but God will suppress every ignorant one who denies and every jealous *'ālim*. The two caliphs will be equal in every laudable quality except in knowledge. God will lavishly pour on them abundant wealth protected from sight that the two will spend on what pleases God.[99]

However, the most explicit connection between the *askiyà* and Aḥmad Lobbo is constructed around the figure of al-Maghīlī. In a very interesting passage that is worth quoting in its entirety, the Saharan scholar urges Askiyà Muḥammad to write a letter to his putative descendant, Aḥmad Lobbo:

He [Askiyà Muḥammad] wrote: "This is the letter of the *amīr al-mu'minīn*, the one who stood against the impious and the infidels, Askiyà al-Ḥājj Muḥammad b. Abī Bakr, to his legitimate inheritor, the one who will continue his work, the supporter, *amīr al-mu'minīn* Aḥmad b. Muḥammad [the full name of Aḥmad Lobbo], the victorious. Peace is more desirable than all desired things and honor more illuminating and splendid than the pearl, especially for you; may it cover all of your ancestors and descendants with essence and sweetness. Accordingly, the motivation for writing to you, dear righteous and pious brother, is to inform and give you the glad tidings that you are the last of the caliphs and the one to subdue the enemies and the guide of the successful believers by the consensus of the scholars. We request from you supplication and I hope to be in your noble company on the Day of Resurrection; likewise we beseech God's protection from the tests and trials of our times and hope from God – glorified be He – to place us in the company of the best of creation. Amīn." Then the *shaykh* prayed for the *askiyà* so that God [will] deliver this letter by any means. He ordered those present to pray.[100]

Once Askiyà Muḥammad has been transformed into an ideal West African ruler, Nūḥ b. al-Ṭāhir, via the expedient of the prophecy, attaches Aḥmad Lobbo to him. He thus sets the pace for the achievement of his real purpose, that is, to construct Aḥmad Lobbo's legitimacy on three levels: as legitimate sultan, inheritor of a long line of West African rulers; as twelfth caliph, under whom the Islamic community would thrive; and as renewer of the faith.

[99] *La chronique du chercheur*, Arabic text 16/French text 24–25.
[100] *La chronique du chercheur*, Arabic text 15/French text 23.

A Triple-Layered Legitimacy

Sultan: The Apogee of West African Royal Tradition

The first level of legitimacy that Nūḥ b. al-Ṭāhir attaches to the caliph of Ḥamdallāhi rests on the claim that Aḥmad Lobbo inherited from Askiyà Muḥammad the position of legitimate ruler of the Middle Niger. Such a position does not imply any claim of religious authority, and I have preferred to refer to it with the title of "sultan," a title that was given in Islamic history to "provincial or even quite petty rulers who had assumed a *de facto* power alongside the caliph" – i.e. a political ruler whose authority coexists with that of a Muslim religious authority.[101]

To achieve the aim of making Aḥmad Lobbo a legitimate "sultan," Nūḥ b. al-Ṭāhir expands on a rhetorical device set in place originally in the seventeenth-century chronicles of Timbuktu and reconstructed by de Moraes Farias.[102] These chroniclers had managed to make sense of the 1591 Moroccan invasion of the Niger Bend and the following disruption of the local political order by "constructing narratives of the past that were apparently free of gaps, that is, deploying writing strategies that prevented narrative breaks where evidence was missing."[103] Often having at their disposal very scarce information about the period they were covering, the authors achieved their history of the region by inventing a continuous narrative of the Middle Niger, a sort of universal history of the region, which connects the first, mythical dynasties of the region to the seventeenth-century Arma *pāshā*s. This artificial narrative of the Middle Niger's past lies at the core of the political project of the *tārīkh*s of Timbuktu. To justify the acceptance of the Arma, the chroniclers build a "bridge over the gap between the invaders and the other social categories."[104] Hence, in the

[101] *EI*², s.v. "Sulṭān," vol. 9, 849 (italics in original). Sultan as a title was not alien to the West African context. It was used widely with this connotation to refer to political rulers, for example in the *Tārīkh al-Sūdān*, to medieval empires of Ghāna and Mali, or to the Sonni kings of the Songhay (Houdas [ed. and trans.], *Tarikh es-Soudan*, Arabic text 3 *et passim*/French text 4 *et passim*; Hunwick, *Timbuktu and the Songhay Empire*, 5 *et passim*.

[102] De Moraes Farias, *Arabic Medieval Inscriptions*; and de Moraes Farias, "Intellectual innovation."

[103] De Moraes Farias, "Intellectual innovation," 100.

[104] De Moraes Farias, *Arabic Medieval Inscriptions*, lxxiv § 119, lxxv § 121.

seventeenth-century chronicles, the "pāshā line was not represented as alien oppressors" but as the continuation of the legitimate local royal tradition.[105]

In his *Tārīkh al-fattāsh*, Nūḥ b. al-Ṭāhir re-attaches Aḥmad Lobbo to the long tradition of legitimate temporal rulers of West Africa which had been invented by the seventeenth-century chronicles of Timbuktu via the prophecy that transforms the caliph of Ḥamdallāhi into the heir of Askiyà Muḥammad. Nūḥ b. al-Ṭāhir even depicts Aḥmad Lobbo as superior to Askiyà Muḥammad, insofar as Aḥmad Lobbo would succeed where the Songhay kings had failed – for example, in opening up the land of Borgo.[106] In the dialogue between al-Suyūṭī and Askiyà Muḥammad, the former says: "No region will escape your sovereignty except one called Borgo, with *bā'* with elongated *ḍamma*, *rā'* with *sukun* and after it *kāf* with elongated *ḍamma*. God the Most High will open up this place by the hand of the second caliph who will live after you."[107] Furthermore, Aḥmad Lobbo would revive the faith where Askiyà Muḥammad's descendants had destroyed it: "Then, he [Askiyà Muḥammad] also asked the *shaykh* if there would be from his offspring one who would revive the religion and restore his order. The *shaykh* replied to him: 'No, but a virtuous, knowledgeable, and active man, who will follow the Sunna will arrive.'"[108] But Aḥmad Lobbo would exceed the Songhay king in knowledge, as al-Suyūṭī makes clear in his dialogue with the *askiyà*: "He will surpass you in knowledge, for he will excel in several sciences, while you only know the rules of prayer, alms giving, and the fundamentals of creed. He will be the last of the caliphs mentioned."[109]

By re-attaching Aḥmad Lobbo to the long list of legitimate West African rulers, and by making him superior to the epitome of this lineage, Askiyà Muḥammad, Nūḥ b. al-Ṭāhir's narrative transfigures Aḥmad Lobbo into the apogee of a millennium-old royal tradition in West Africa. However, Nūḥ b. al-Ṭāhir goes further than this, by attributing to Aḥmad Lobbo another type of authority grounded in solid Islamic sources: that of the twelfth caliph of Islam.

105 De Moraes Farias, *Arabic Medieval Inscriptions*, lxxvii § 129.
106 According to Houdas and Delafosse, Borgo is a region situated east of Mopti and north of Bandiagara (see *La chronique du chercheur*, French text 17, n. 2).
107 *La chronique du chercheur*, Arabic text 13/French text 17.
108 *La chronique du chercheur*, Arabic text 13/French text 18.
109 *La chronique du chercheur*, Arabic text 13/French text 18.

The Twelfth Caliph

In the *Tārīkh al-fattāsh*, Aḥmad Lobbo is also identified with the last of the twelve caliphs prophesied by Muḥammad in a famous *ḥadīth* to which both Mūlāy al-ʻAbbās and al-Suyūṭī implicitly refer.[110] This tradition, which exists in slightly different narratives in both the *Saḥīḥ* (Authentic Collections) of Muslim (d. 875) and the *Sunan* (Traditions) of Abū Dāwūd (d. 889), ascribes to the Prophet the statement that twelve caliphs would reign after him. The version of Abū Dāwūd, for instance, narrates, on the authority of Jābir b. Samura, that the Prophet said: "The religion will continue to be established until there are twelve caliphs over you, and the whole community will agree on each of them."[111] The same tradition, recorded via a different chain of transmitters, also adds the following: "When he came back to his home, the Quraysh came to him and said: Then what will happen? He said: Then turmoil will prevail."[112]

The first traces of this tradition in West Africa appear in Aḥmad Bābā b. Aḥmad b. al-Ḥājj Aḥmad b. ʻUmar b. Muḥammad Aqīt's *Istiṭrād al-ẓurafāʼ* (The Discursive Subjects of the Elegant Ones).[113] However, it is likely that this tradition reached West Africa with al-Suyūṭī's *Tārīkh al-khulafāʼ* (The History of the Caliphs), a work that circulated widely in the region and represented, according to Hall and Stewart, "the principal source of wider Islamic historical information about the early Islamic period."[114] The *Tārīkh al-khulafāʼ* contains an extensive discussion of the twelve caliphs and records several versions of the *ḥadīth*.[115] Al-Suyūṭī comments on the tradition of the twelve caliphs by referring to the interpretations of al-Qāḍī ʻIyād b. Mūsà (d. 1149)

110 The tradition of the twelve caliphs is strongly rooted in Sunni tradition, and should not be confused with the doctrine of the twelve Imāms, a basic belief of the Twelver branch of Shiʻite Islam. On the twelve Imāms, see EI^2, s.v. "Ithnā ʻashariyya," vol. 4, 277–279.

111 Abū Dāwūd [Sulaymān b. al-Ashʻath], *Sunan* (Riyadh: Dār al-Salām, 2008), vol. 4, 506, no. 4279.

112 Abū Dāwūd, *Sunan*, vol. 4, 507, no. 4281.

113 See *ALA* IV, 2, item 22. The work is lost and only known via a reference in Muḥammad al-Qādirī's biography of Aḥmad Bābā contained in the *Nashr al-mathānī li-ahl al-qarn al-ḥādī ʻashar wa-al-thānī* (A. Graulle and P. Meillard [ed. and trans.], *Nachr al-mathânî de Mouhammad al-Qâdirî* [Paris: Leroux, 1913, vol. 1, 271).

114 Hall and Stewart, "The historic ʻcore curriculum'," 121.

115 Henry S. Jarrett (trans.), *History of the Caliphs by Jalálu'ddín a's Suyúṭi* (Calcutta: Asiatic Society of Bengal, 1881), 8–11.

and Ibn Ḥajar al-ʿAsqalānī (d. 1449). Al-Qāḍī ʿIyād had argued that the tradition's reference to the agreement of the Islamic community means that, during the time of these caliphs, all Muslims recognized their legitimacy and there was no other Muslim ruler claiming caliphal authority. Thus, explains Ibn Ḥajar, following the argument of al-Qāḍī ʿIyād, all these caliphs had already existed: the Rightly Guided Caliphs Abū Bakr (d. 634), ʿUmar b. al-Khaṭṭāb (d. 644), ʿUthmān b. ʿAffān (d. 656), ʿAlī b. Abī Ṭālib (d. 661); and the Umayyad caliphs Muʿāwiya I (d. 680), Yazīd b. Muʿāwiya (d. 683), ʿAbd al-Malik b. Marwān (d. 705), al-Walīd b. ʿAbd al-Malik b. Marwān (d. 715), Sulaymān b. ʿAbd al-Malik (717), ʿUmar b. ʿAbd al-ʿAzīz (d. 722), Yazīd b. ʿAbd al-Malik (d. 724), and Hishām b. ʿAbd al-Malik (d. 743). In other words, the twelve caliphs were all the first rulers of the Islamic community, with the exception of Muʿāwiya II (d. 683) and Marwān b. ʿAbd al-Ḥakam (d. 685), caliphs during the civil war that saw Ibn al-Zubayr (d. 692) fighting against the Umayyads and declaring himself alternative caliph.[116] Ibn Ḥajar continues listing the other Umayyad caliphs until 743, the year in which the Umayyad dynasty was challenged and ultimately overthrown by the ʿAbbasids. Afterward, Ibn Ḥajar continues, al-Andalus had been declared an independent caliphate under ʿAbd al-Raḥmān b. Muʿāwiya (d. 788) and the unity of the Islamic community was lost forever. The disorder that occurred in the wake of the Umayyads' fall and the consequent proliferation of rulers claiming to be caliphs could be, according to Ibn Ḥajar, the "turmoil" referred to in the *ḥadīth* recorded by Abū Dāwūd.

This interpretation leaves no space for Aḥmad Lobbo to be the twelfth caliph, since all the caliphs predicted by the Prophet would have already arrived. However, al-Suyūṭī endorsed another interpretation of the tradition, which was also suggested as a possibility by Ibn Ḥajar. According to this alternative interpretation, "turmoil" might also refer to the chaos preceding the end of the world. If this was the case, not all the twelve caliphs had arrived, since the end of the world had not yet come. Here al-Suyūṭī expanded on Ibn Ḥajar and identified a different list of caliphs: Abū Bakr ʿUmar b. al-Khaṭṭāb,

[116] At that time, the Islamic community was split into two parts, one bound by an oath of allegiance to the Umayyads in Damascus and the other to Ibn al-Zubayr in his stronghold in Mecca. Only after the death of the latter did ʿAbd al-Malik b. Marwān manage to restore the unity of the *umma*. On Ibn al-Zubayr's revolt, commonly referred to as the Second Civil War, see H. A. R. Gibb, s.v. "ʿAbd Allāh b. al-Zubayr," *EI*^{2}, vol. 1, 54–55.

'Uthmān b. 'Affān, 'Alī b. Abī Ṭālib, al-Ḥasan b. 'Alī (d. 661), Mu'āwiya I, Ibn al-Zubayr, 'Umar b. 'Abd al-'Azīz, and the 'Abbasid caliphs al-Muhtadī (d. 870) and al-Ẓāhir bi-Amr Allāh (d. 1226). Al-Suyūṭī thus inserted some new names into the list provided by Ibn Ḥajar. The first, al-Ḥasan b. 'Alī, was, in fact, often inserted into the list of Sunni caliphs after the death of his father and the rise to the caliphate of Mu'āwiya I. The second new caliph in the list was Ibn al-Zubayr, preferred by al-Suyūṭī to his rival for the caliphate, Yazīd b. Mu'āwiya. As for the two 'Abbasid caliphs, al-Muhtadī and al-Ẓāhir, it was most likely that their piety and justice gained them a spot in al-Suyūṭī's list. The total number of caliphs enumerated by al-Suyūṭī therefore comprised only ten names out of twelve since, according to the Egyptian scholar, "there remain two who are to be awaited" before the end of the world.[117] It is this passage that most likely connects al-Suyūṭī's *Tārīkh al-khulafā'* to the work of Nūḥ b. al-Ṭāhir. Aware of al-Suyūṭī's pronouncement, Nūḥ b. al-Ṭāhir makes Mūlāy al-'Abbās and al-Suyūṭī agree that Askiyà al-Ḥājj Muḥammad was the eleventh of the caliphs mentioned by the Prophet and that Aḥmad Lobbo, the latter's heir, was to be the twelfth.

The *Tārīkh al-fattāsh* explicitly depicts Aḥmad Lobbo as a legitimate West African sultan and the twelfth caliph of Islam, thus combining both political and religious authority. However, the religious legitimacy of the caliph of Ḥamdallāhi was further equipped with another layer of legitimacy as *mujaddid*, or renewer of the faith.

Renewer of the Faith

The tradition of the *tajdīd*, or the renewal of the faith, and its derivative concept of the renewer of the faith, is very widespread in Islamic history.[118] Its source is another famous *ḥadīth* first recorded by Abū Dāwūd.[119] On the authority of Abū Hurayra, the *ḥadīth* has the

[117] Jarrett (trans.), *History of the Caliphs*, 11.

[118] For a detailed study of the *tajdīd* tradition, see John O. Hunwick, "Ignaz Goldziher on al-Suyūṭī," *The Muslim World* 67/2 (1978): 79–99, 85–86; and Ella Landau-Tasseron, "The 'cyclical reform': A study of the mujaddid tradition," *Studia Islamica* 70 (1989): 79–117.

[119] Abū Dāwūd, *Sunan*, vol. 4, 512, no. 4291. Larry Poston reports that al-Nasawī (d. 916), al-Ṭabarānī (d. 971), Ibn 'Adī (d. 976), al-Ḥākim (d. 1014), and al-Bayhaqī (d. 1066) record slightly different versions of the *ḥadīth* (Larry Poston, "The second coming of 'Isa: An exploration of Islamic premillennialism," *The Muslim World* 100/1 [2010]: 100–116, 101).

Prophet saying, "God will raise for this community at the end of every hundred years someone who will renovate its religion for it."[120]

This tradition is very well known in West Africa, where it was most likely introduced by the works of al-Suyūṭī and al-Maghīlī.[121] Al-Suyūṭī wrote extensively on the subject, and among his writings is a treatise specifically devoted to the topic, the *Risāla fī man yabʿath Allāh li-hādhihi al-umma ʿalà raʾs kull miʾat sana* (An Epistle on the One Sent by God to the Islamic Nation at the Beginning of Every Century) – also known as *al-Tanbīʾa bi-man yabʿathuhu Allāh ʿalà raʾs kull miʾat* (The Warning about the One Sent by God at the Beginning of Every Century). The whole purpose of this work, written in 1493, is to prove that al-Suyūṭī himself is the *mujaddid* of the incoming century, the tenth century of the Islamic calendar.[122] As for al-Maghīlī, he refers to this tradition in his famous *Ajwiba ʿan asʾilat al-amīr Askiyà al-Ḥajj Muḥammad* (The Replies to the Questions of Askiyà al-Ḥajj Muḥammad) when, in his answer about the role of the scholar, he says: "Thus it is related that at the beginning of every century God sends men a scholar who regenerates their religion for them."[123] Hassan I. Gwarzo has also suggested that al-Maghīlī, like al-Suyūṭī, was claiming the title of *mujaddid* for himself.[124]

The notion of *tajdīd*, however, gained prominence in West Africa later on. As Aziz A. Batran argues, "nowhere in dar al-Islam did the concept of

---

[120] Abū Dāwūd, *Sunan*, vol. 4, 512, no. 4291.

[121] Aziz A. Batran, "Mahdist manifestations in Muslim Africa," in *Islam and Revolution in Africa* (Brattleboro, VT: Amana Books, 1984), 22–43, 33. Usman Muhammad Bugaje, "The Tradition of *Tajdid* in Western Bilad al-Sudan: A Study of the Genesis, Development and Patterns of Islamic Revivalism in the Region, 900–1900 AD" (Ph.D. dissertation, University of Khartoum, 1991), deals with the phenomenon of *tajdīd* in West Africa until the beginning of the twentieth century.

[122] Hunwick, "Ignaz Goldziher on al-Suyūṭī," 87. Even though I have not found any copy of this work in West Africa, al-Suyūṭī's *al-Kashf ʿan mujāwazat hadhihi al-umma al-alf*, in which he summarizes the traditions of the *mujaddid*, is well known in the Western Sahara and south of the desert. At least four copies are available in West African collections: BnF, manuscript arabe 5350, ff. 163b–166; IF, Fonds de Gironcourt, 2413 (197); IHERI-ABT 3884; MAMMP, Reel 10.

[123] Hunwick, *Sharīʿa in Songhay*, 66. Several copies of the Replies exist in West African libraries: IFAN, Fonds Brevié 22 (copy in Kaduna O/AR12/1); IFAN, Fonds Brevié 23 (copy in Kaduna O/AR12/1); IRSH 540; Bnf 5259, ff. 39–44; Bnf 5259 ff. 48–65; Sokoto 4/58b/440.

[124] Hassan I. Gwarzo, "The Life and Teachings of al-Maghīlī, with Particular Reference to the Saharan Jewish community" (Ph.D. dissertation, University of London, 1972), 175 *et passim*.

Mujaddid have a more profound effect than in nineteenth century West Africa."[125] For example, al-Mukhtār al-Kabīr claimed, in more than one of his works, that he was the *mujaddid*.[126] For example, in his *Fiqh al-a'yān fī ḥaqā'iq al-Qur'ān* (The Understanding of the Notable Scholars on the Realities of the Qur'ān), he states, "The authorities of the time are unanimously agreed that the *mujaddid* of the thirteenth century is the author of this book."[127] The popularity of the Kunta *shaykh* must have substantiated his claims. Indeed, no official process has ever existed to certify the "election" of a *mujaddid*, but rather, as Hunwick suggests, it was mainly "a *vox populi*."[128]

That al-Mukhtār al-Kabīr claimed to be the *mujaddid*, and was most likely recognized as such by many, neither prevented nor excluded others from doing the same. Over time, scholars reached the conclusion that for each century there were many renewers. Ibn al-Athīr (d. 1232–3), for example, "made a list of all the *mujaddidūn*, systematically including for each century a caliph, jurists of all the schools and various countries, traditionists and even Imāmī Shi'ites."[129] Al-Mukhtār al-Kabīr himself believed in this multiplicity of *mujaddid*s and, in the abovementioned *Fiqh al-a'yān*, lists, for example, four renewers in the ninth century alone: al-Maghīlī, the Kunta ancestor 'Umar b. Aḥmad al-Bakkāy (d. 1552–3), al-Suyūṭī, Muḥammad b. Yūsuf al-Sanūsī (d. 1490), and Askiyà Muḥammad;[130] for the tenth, he names three West African *mujaddids*: Aḥmad Bābā, Muḥammad Baghayogho (d. 1594), and Bābā al-Mukhtār (d. 1749–50).[131]

In the thirteenth century of the Islamic calendar, al-Mukhtār al-Kabīr was not the only one in West Africa to claim to be the *mujaddid*. At least another self-proclaimed renewer achieved fame in the region – none other than 'Uthmān b. Fūdī. The rumors that he was the *mahdī* were widespread in the early nineteenth century among his disciples.[132]

125 Batran, "Mahdist manifestations in Muslim Africa," 33.
126 Batran, "Sīdī al-Mukhtār al-Kuntī," 164.
127 Quoted in Batran, "Sīdī al-Mukhtār al-Kuntī," 171. On the *Fiqh al-a'yān*, see *ALA* IV, 75, item 12.
128 Hunwick, "Ignaz Goldziher on al-Suyūṭī," 81.
129 Landau-Tasseron, "The 'cyclical reform'," 85.
130 Cited in Batran, "Sīdī al-Mukhtār al-Kuntī," 170.
131 Cited in Batran, "Sīdī al-Mukhtār al-Kuntī," 171.
132 On the eschatological turmoil in northern Nigeria at the beginning of the nineteenth century, see Muhammad A. al-Hajj, "The thirteenth century in

Thus, ʿUthmān b. Fūdī explicitly rejected this claim in his *Taḥdhīr al-ikhwān min ʿiddiʿā' al-mahdiyya al-mawʿūda ākhir al-zamān* (A Warning to the Brothers against Claiming the Mahdiyya Promised at the End of Time).[133] In another of his works, the *Maḥdhurāt fī ʿalamāt khurūj al-Mahdī* (The Dangers Surrounding the Emergence of the *Mahdī*), ʿUthmān b. Fūdī recurs to geomancy to reiterate his denial of being the *mahdī*.[134] However, in this work he does make the statement that he was the *mujaddid* of his century.[135]

It was in this context that Nūḥ b. al-Ṭāhir inscribed Aḥmad Lobbo into the list of West African renewers of the faith, along with al-Mukhtār al-Kuntī and ʿUthmān b. Fūdī – even though he does not support this claim with any evidence.[136] By assigning Aḥmad Lobbo the title of *mujaddid*, Nūḥ b. al-Ṭāhir completes in the *Tārīkh al-fattāsh* his enterprise of equipping his patron with a multi-layered legitimacy for the leadership of Ḥamdallāhi. Nūḥ b. al-Ṭāhir's final goal was to disguise his identity as the "real" author of the chronicle. He needed to find a reliable figure whom he could make the "true" author of his *Tārīkh al-fattāsh*. He found Maḥmūd Kaʿti to be the most suitable candidate.

An Apocryphal Ascription

The *Tārīkh al-fattāsh* opens, after the *basmala* and praises to the Prophet, with the words: "The *shaykh*, the scholar, the jurist, the man of letters, the judge, the just, the ascetic, the pious, the saint, the learned, the devout, the servant of God, Sīdī Maḥmūd Kaʿti, from the province of Kourmina but residing in Timbuktu, of Waʿkūrī origins, says [what follows]."[137] A few pages into the chronicle, another passage invented by Nūḥ b. al-Ṭāhir ascribes the purported date for the chronicle's

Muslim eschatology: Mahdist expectations in the Sokoto Caliphate," *Research Bulletin – Center of Arabic Documentation of the University of Ibadan* 3/2 (1967): 100–115.

133 Al-Hajj, "The thirteenth century in Muslim eschatology," 114. On the *Taḥdhīr al-ikhwān*, see *ALA* II, 72–73, item 71.

134 On the *Maḥdhurāt*, see *ALA* II, 64, item 35.

135 See Moumouni, *Vie et oeuvre*, 124–128.

136 The reference to the *tajdīd* is subtle in the *Tārīkh al-fattāsh* (*La chronique du chercheur*, Arabic text 5/French text 19), but explicit in the propaganda pamphlet in which the arguments of the chronicle are widely circulated (see Chapter 6).

137 *La chronique du chercheur*, Arabic text 9/French text 5.

initiation: "Then Mūlāy al-'Abbās ordered the son of his brother named Mūlāy al-Ṣaqlī to go there [to live at the court of Askià Muḥammad]. Mūlāy al-Ṣaqlī moved there in the year 925/1519. His establishment coincided with the period of the beginning of the writing [of this work]."[138]

These two passages achieve a crucial goal by putting the name of Maḥmūd Ka'ti in the incipit of the chronicle and ascribing it to the early sixteenth century. Here, Nūḥ b. al-Ṭāhir aims to clear away any possible doubt about the work's authorship and antiquity. However, Nūḥ b. al-Ṭāhir also transformed the figure of Maḥmūd Ka'ti substantially, both with respect to his role and his location in time. In order to understand this transformation, it is first necessary to reconstruct a biography, as yet incomplete, of Maḥmūd Ka'ti, expanding on a similar exercise already attempted by Levtzion.[139] This effort is based on the only sources that provide pre-nineteenth-century information: the *Tārīkh Ibn al-Mukhtār* and the *Tārīkh al-Sūdān.*[140]

Maḥmūd Ka'ti was born during the reign of Askiyà Muḥammad, thus between 1493 and 1538.[141] No information is available about the place in which he was born.[142] Likewise, the sources do not provide a clear picture of Maḥmūd Ka'ti's youth and training. The *Tārīkh al-Sūdān* only reports that he studied, along with other notables of Timbuktu, under the celebrated scholar Aḥmad b. Muḥammad al-

138 *La chronique du chercheur*, Arabic text 16/French text 26 and Arabic text 17/French text 27.

139 Expanding on Levtzion's tentative biography of Maḥmūd Ka'ti: see Levtzion, "A seventeenth-century chronicle," 573–576.

140 No information on Maḥmūd Ka'tī is available in the *Fatḥ al-shakūr* or in the *Izālat al-rayb*. The *Sa'āda al-abadiyya* does not report any interesting information except for the unusual date of the death of Maḥmūd Ka'ti as 1058 hijrī, i.e. 1647–8 CE (IHERI-ABT 2752, 6a and 16a). However, in this passage Aḥmad Bābēr mistakenly reports the date of death of another Maḥmūd Ka'ti – the son of 'Alī b. Ziyād – recorded in the *Tārīkh al-Sūdān* (Houdas [ed. and trans.], *Tarikh es-Soudan*, Arabic text 301/French text 456).

141 *La chronique du chercheur*, Arabic text 82/French text 153.

142 The only evidence suggesting the region of Kourmina, where the town of Tindirma is located, as his birthplace comes from the first lines of Nūḥ b. al-Ṭāhir's *Tārīkh al-fattāsh* (*La chronique du chercheur*, Arabic text 9/French text 6). As such, they are questionable. Most likely, as Maḥmūd Ka'ti exercised the function of *qāḍī* in the town of Tindirma, the only town, along with Timbuktu and Gao, in which seventeenth-century sources provide evidence of his activities, Nūḥ b. al-Ṭāhir may have chosen Kourmina his as possible hometown.

Sa'īd.[143] This teacher was active between 1552–3 and his premature death in 1568.[144] Yet he became renowned for his expertise in *ḥadīth* and, especially, jurisprudence: specializing in teaching the *Muwaṭṭā'* (The Trodden Path) of Mālik b. Anas (d. 795–6), the *Mudawwana* (The Corpus of Law) of Saḥnūn (d. 854–5), and *Mukhtaṣar* (Abridgment) of Khalīl b. Isḥāq (d. 1365). Therefore, it was most likely jurisprudence that Maḥmūd Ka'ti studied with Aḥmad b. Muḥammad al-Sa'īd. The period of time in which the teacher was active also suggests that Maḥmūd Ka'ti was born in the late 1520s, thus being about the same age as his teacher, or a bit younger.[145]

No further information is available on the emergence of Maḥmūd Ka'ti as a significant figure in the Songhay state. By the time Askiyà Dāwūd was king, between 1549 and 1582, he was important enough to serve, at least sporadically, at the *askiyà*'s court. He seems to have wielded special influence over a certain Bukar al-Anbārī (also spelled Bukar Lanbāru), the *askiyà-alfa* of Askiyà Dāwūd and Askiyà Isḥāq I (r. 1588–1592): a function carried out by a scholar specifically attached to the Songhay kings, who acted as their scribe and advisor.[146] Maḥmūd Ka'ti was also advisor to Askiyà Dāwūd at the time when a returning group of pilgrims stopped in Gao.[147] The esteem that the *askiyà* had for Maḥmūd Ka'ti materialized in several gifts from the Songhay king to the scholar: the *askiyà* helped Maḥmūd Ka'ti to marry his daughters, donating four rugs, four female slaves, and four veils, as well as contributing to the dowry of each.[148] Askiyà Dāwūd also donated two boubous, two turbans, two hats, a horse, and a dam to each of his sons on the occasions of their turbaning ceremonies.[149]

143 Houdas (ed. and trans.), *Tarikh es-Soudan*, Arabic text 35/French text 57; Hunwick, *Timbuktu and the Songhay Empire*, 49. On Aḥmad b. Muḥammad al-Sa'īd, see *ALA* IV, 15.

144 Houdas (ed. and trans.), *Tarikh es-Soudan*, Arabic text 43/French text 71; Hunwick, *Timbuktu and the Songhay Empire*, 62.

145 In this, I disagree with Levtzion, who locates Maḥmūd Ka'ti's birth "perhaps in the 1510s" (Levtzion, "A seventeenth-century chronicle," 575). This dating conforms to the one provided by the *Tārīkh Ibn al-Mukhtār*, which locates Maḥmūd Ka'ti's birth at the time of Askiyà Muḥammad's reign between 1493 and 1529.

146 *La chronique du chercheur*, Arabic text 109/French text 201. On the office of *askiyà-alfa*, see Hunwick, *Timbuktu and the Songhay Empire*, 338.

147 *La chronique du chercheur*, Arabic text 112–113/French text 205–207.

148 *La chronique du chercheur*, Arabic text 108–109/French text 200–201.

149 *La chronique du chercheur*, Arabic text 108–109/French text 200–201.

The *askiyà* also purchased a manuscript copy of the dictionary *al-Qāmūs al-muḥīt* (The All-Embracing Dictionary) by al-Fīrūzābādī (d. 1414–15) for Maḥmūd Ka'ti, for the price of eighty golden *mithqāls*.[150] On two occasions, Maḥmūd Ka'tī received from Askiyà Dāwūd a donation of land, as well as slaves to work it, seeds, and cattle.[151] A last piece of evidence pointing to Maḥmūd Ka'ti's close relationship with the *askiyà* is that Askiyà Dāwūd married his daughter, 'Ā'isha Kīmari, to him.[152]

In 1588 Maḥmūd Ka'ti was *qāḍī* in Tindirma, and had acquired enough influence and prestige to offer sanctuary (although only for a very short time) to Būkar, the governor of the region of Bāghana, who had rebelled against the Songhay king Askiyà Isḥāq I.[153] In 1591 Maḥmūd Ka'ti again returned to Gao as counselor of a king, this time Askiyà Isḥāq II, in the year when the Songhay faced the attack of the Moroccan army.[154] After the *askiyà*'s defeat Maḥmūd Ka'ti left to return to "his land" – most likely Tindirma – declining the king's request to remain with him and join him in his resistance against the Moroccan invaders.[155]

Maḥmūd Ka'ti eventually died in 1593 in Arkiya, in Gimmballa, as recorded by the *Tārīkh al-Sūdān*:

> Close to dawn on Monday, the first night of Muharram the Sacred which opened the year 1002/26 September 1593, the erudite scholar and jurist, Qāḍī Maḥmūd Ka'ti b. al-Ḥājj al-Mutawakkil 'alà Allāh, died in Arkiya. His body was brought to Timbuktu and the funeral prayer was said for him after the last *'ishā'* prayer on the eve of Tuesday, and he was buried immediately next to the grave of the jurist Aḥmad b. al-Ḥajj Aḥmad – may God have mercy on them both, and grant us benefit through their blessings. Amen.[156]

Maḥmūd Ka'ti left at least five sons and four daughters, as he himself said at one time to Askiyà Dāwūd.[157] The names of

150 *La chronique du chercheur*, Arabic text 108–109/French text 200–201.
151 *La chronique du chercheur*, Arabic text 108–109/French text 200–201.
152 *La chronique du chercheur*, Arabic text 118–119/French text 217.
153 Houdas (ed. and trans.), *Tarikh es-Soudan*, Arabic text 131/French text 209; Hunwick, *Timbuktu and the Songhay Empire*, 179 (Hunwick omitted the title *qāḍī* in his translation).
154 *La chronique du chercheur*, Arabic text 151/French text 271.
155 *La chronique du chercheur*, Arabic text 151/French text 271.
156 Houdas (ed. and trans.), *Tarikh es-Soudan*, Arabic text 211/French text 322; Hunwick, *Timbuktu and the Songhay Empire*, 260. The localization of Arkiya in Gimmballa is due to Hofheinz, "Goths in the Land of the Blacks," 180.
157 *La chronique du chercheur*, Arabic text 108/French text 200.

three sons are known: Ismāʿīl;[158] Muḥammad al-Amīn;[159] and Yūsuf.[160] As for his daughters, the only one who is mentioned is the mother of Ibn al-Mukhtār, but her name is not recorded in the *Tārīkh Ibn al-Mukhtār*.

In summary, the sources show that Maḥmūd Kaʿti was a scholar of stature. He is always given honorific titles pointing to his erudition. Sometimes the chroniclers call him *alfa*, a title derived from the Arabic *al-faqīh* (jurist) which refers, in the Songhay-speaking milieu, to "those men with a religious training, who were public exponents of the faith – *qāḍī*s, imams, *khaṭīb*s, and all manner of other holymen."[161] In some instances he is cited as a jurist, while at other times he is called *qāḍī*. His education and titles suggest that his main field was jurisprudence, but he also had an interest in history. The *Tārīkh Ibn al-Mukhtār* includes a section on Sonni ʿAlī that was recorded from "Maḥmūd Kaʿti, according to what has been written down by one of his disciples."[162] It also narrates a story concerning the 1591 battle of Tondibi copied from a piece of writing by Maḥmūd Kaʿti.[163]

It seems that this interest in history is what later attracted the attention of Nūḥ b. al-Ṭāhir.[164] As Kilito remarks, "the same discourse possesses different value depending on the person given credit for it. Thus it is essential to choose that person carefully, as the choice will determine the reader's response to the text."[165] As a renowned scholar with a passion for the past, Maḥmūd Kaʿti was chosen by Nūḥ b. al-Ṭāhir as the perfect candidate for this function, and was transformed into the apocryphal author of the *Tārīkh al-fattāsh*. However, the overall goal of Nūḥ b. al-Ṭāhir was to create a plausible narrative of Askiyà Muḥammad's reign, in order to serve as a frame for the legitimization of Aḥmad Lobbo. Therefore, to strengthen the basis for

[158] *La chronique du chercheur*, Arabic text 138–139/French text 72.

[159] *La chronique du chercheur*, Arabic text 89/French text 168.

[160] *La chronique du chercheur*, Arabic text 129/French text 236 and Arabic text 142/French text 257.

[161] Hunwick, *Timbuktu and the Songhay Empire*, lv.

[162] *La chronique du chercheur*, Arabic text 47/French text 236.

[163] *La chronique du chercheur*, Arabic text 152/French text 271–272.

[164] It might even be that the idea of making Maḥmūd Kaʿti the author of the *Tārīkh al-fattāsh* was ignited in Nūḥ b. al-Ṭāhir by the reference in the *Tārīkh Ibn al-Mukhtār* to a certain Katu (Yāʾī Katu), as one of the members of the entourage of Askiyà Muḥammad (*La chronique du chercheur*, Arabic text 64, n. 1/French text 124, n. 3).

[165] Kilito, *The Author and His Doubles*, 62.

his project, Nūḥ b. al-Ṭāhir transformed Maḥmūd Ka'ti into a contemporary of Askiyà al-Ḥājj Muḥammad, and made him a member of the entourage of scholars who went with the king on the Pilgrimage. To achieve this time-traveling feat, Nūḥ b. al-Ṭāhir wrote several passages to "prove" that Maḥmūd Ka'ti was a close associate of Askiyà Muḥammad – while in fact he was close, as underlined above, to Askiyà Dāwūd and Askiyà Isḥāq.

Maḥmūd Ka'ti is transformed, in the *Tārīkh al-fattāsh*, from a jurist and judge into a historian, expanding on the interest in that discipline that can be inferred from the seventeenth-century chronicles. His mastery of history is reiterated several times in the *Tārīkh al-fattāsh*, which stresses that it is only Maḥmūd Ka'ti who records the narrated events.[166]

However, being a masterful historian is not enough to be accepted as a reliable transmitter of the immediate events of Askiyà Muḥammad's reign. Therefore, Maḥmūd Ka'ti had to become a contemporary of the *askiyà*. Accordingly, Nūḥ b. al-Ṭāhir changed the date of Maḥmūd Ka'ti's birth to avoid anachronism. He achieved this task by ascribing to Maḥmūd Ka'ti the statement that he was only twenty-five in 1492–3, when Askiyà Muḥammad was aged fifty.[167] Maḥmūd Ka'ti's date of birth thus became set at 1468, more than half a century before the actual date. Then, so as not to contradict himself, Nūḥ b. al-Ṭāhir had to modify the section of the *Tārīkh Ibn al-Mukhtār* in which the birth of Maḥmūd Ka'ti is located during the reign of Askiyà Muḥammad. He did so by removing the name Maḥmūd Ka'ti from the list of the scholars born in the time of the Songhay king and replacing it with that of a fictional character called Māḥmūd SMB, most likely to be read as Sammba.[168]

The manipulation of the date of Maḥmūd Ka'ti's birth also resulted in the need for another substantial textual manipulation. The *Tārīkh al-fattāsh* refers to Maḥmūd Ka'ti as a native of Kourmina – most likely its most important center, Tindirma. However, this information created an inconsistency with the story of the town's foundation as recorded in the *Tārīkh Ibn al-Mukhtār*, which stated that Tindirma

166 *La chronique du chercheur*, Arabic text 92/French text 48 *et passim*.
167 *La chronique du chercheur*, Arabic text 58/French text 113.
168 Here again Houdas and Delafosse's intervention is particularly invasive, as they "fixed" the name provided by MS C back to Maḥmūd Ka'ti (*La chronique du chercheur*, Arabic text 82, n. 4).

was founded under Askiyà Muḥammad in 902/1496–7.[169] This would have resulted in an obvious anachronism: Maḥmūd Ka'ti could never have been born in Tindirma in 1468, because the city was only founded in 1496–7. In order to avoid this contradiction, Nūḥ b. al-Ṭāhir removed the story of the foundation as reported by the *Tārīkh Ibn al-Mukhtār* and replaced it with another story in which the same city is portrayed as an ancient site, the abode of an old Jewish community.[170] In this way, Nūḥ b. al-Ṭāhir makes it plausible that Maḥmūd Ka'ti was born in Tindirma well before the date of its foundation as related in the *Tārīkh Ibn al-Mukhtār*.

Once the date of Maḥmūd Ka'ti's birth had been established, Nūḥ b. al-Ṭāhir could make him part of the entourage of Askiyà Muḥammad. Maḥmūd Ka'ti is transformed into one of the three messengers sent to negotiate, in vain, the surrender of Sonni Bāru during the political unrest that led to the 1493 coup d'état.[171] However, despite the failure of this mission, his participation in the negotiation establishes a longstanding acquaintance between the scholar and the king that culminates with Maḥmūd Ka'ti going on the Pilgrimage with Askiyà Muḥammad: that he was among the *askiyà*'s companions during the trip is repeated twice in the *Tārīkh al-fattāsh*.[172] As part of the entourage, Maḥmūd Ka'ti is thereby made an eyewitness to the prophecy of Aḥmad Lobbo's advent, as foretold by Mūlāy al-'Abbās, al-Suyūṭī, and others. Maḥmūd Ka'ti is thus transformed into a "reliable" author who confirmed, in "his" *Tārīkh al-fattāsh*, the position of Aḥmad Lobbo as a legitimate West African authority of his time.

*****

Part I has demonstrated that one of the most extensively used sources for pre-colonial African history, *La chronique du chercheur*, is in fact a conflation of two chronicles: the seventeenth-century chronicle written by Ibn al-Mukhtār and the nineteenth-century *Tārīkh al-fattāsh*, written by Nūḥ b. al-Ṭāhir in support of Aḥmad Lobbo and the Caliphate of Ḥamdallāhi, but apocryphally ascribed to the sixteenth century and to Maḥmūd Ka'ti. This does not mean that Nūḥ b. al-Ṭāhir

[169] *La chronique du chercheur*, Arabic text 62/French text 119.
[170] *La chronique du chercheur*, Arabic text 62–63/French text 119–121.
[171] *La chronique du chercheur*, Arabic text 53/French text 103.
[172] *La chronique du chercheur*, Arabic text 16/French text 26 and Arabic text 65/French text 126.

composed his chronicle from scratch: the bulk of the texts included in the two chronicles overlap verbatim. Rather, Nuḥ b. al-Ṭāhir wrote his *Tārīkh al-fattāsh* by strategically altering the text of the earlier work of Ibn al-Mukhtār, to construct a chronicle with a new agenda. Ibn al-Mukhtār's work is a celebration of the Askiyà dynasty, which advocates for more space in the pāshālik for both the descendants of the *askiyà*s and the scholarly elite of Timbuktu. Nūḥ b. al-Ṭāhir's *Tārīkh al-fattāsh* represents a completely different political project. It is a metahistory built around an alleged prophecy recounted to Askiyà Muḥammad during his Pilgrimage to Mecca and witnessed by Maḥmūd Ka'ti, the "true" author of the chronicle. The prophecy foretold the advent of Aḥmad Lobbo and provided him with a basis for legitimacy as West African Muslim ruler.

Surely, crafting the *Tārīkh al-fattāsh* was a laborious task for Nūḥ b. al-Ṭāhir, the "real" author of the chronicle. His embedding of invented events into an older chronicle was such a sophisticated enterprise that the textual manipulation carried out by the Fulani scholar has escaped the full scrutiny of academics for more than a century, confirming Kilito's point that "a skillful master of the rules of forgery ... can disguise his handiwork so carefully that it becomes impossible to spot," or nearly so.[173] But what historical factors made the *Tārīkh al-fattāsh* project possible and necessary? The early nineteenth century was a time of great change in the Middle Niger. Aḥmad Lobbo, while a new and powerful actor on the scene, was an outsider to circles of power, both political and religious. Furthermore, he personifies the shift in the attitude of new West African Muslim scholarly elites, who abandoned their traditional position of political neutrality vis-à-vis the representative of the political authority, and turned instead to armed militancy. None of these changes went unopposed, and hence the *Tārīkh al-fattāsh* was crafted to respond to such challenges. In order to understand the motives, role, and impact of the chronicle, it is necessary to turn to the history of the Caliphate of Ḥamdallāhi, paying special attention to an issue that has escaped scholars' scrutiny so far: the establishment of Aḥmad Lobbo's authority and legitimacy at a time when the Middle Niger was a contested space of competing claims.

[173] Kilito, *The Author and His Doubles*, 33.

PART II

A Contested Space of Competing Claims

The Middle Niger, 1810s–1840s

O you who have believed, obey Allah and obey the Messenger and those in authority among you. And if you disagree over anything, refer it to Allah and the Messenger, if you should believe in Allah and the Last Day. That is the best way and best in result. (Qur'ān 4:59)

Saturday 13 Jumādà I 1233/21 March 1818. The annual flood of the River Niger was steadily retreating in Noukouma, where a thousand Fulani, Marka, Bozo, and other denizens of the Middle Niger had gathered around their leader, Aḥmad Lobbo.[1] Surrounding his supporters, and ready to annihilate them, was an enemy army twenty times their number. Aḥmad Lobbo is said to have addressed his followers:

There is no might nor power except in God. In your faces I see composure despite the danger that threatens us. The great day has arrived. Do not be discouraged by the confusion of your wives and the position of the enemy that seems to give them an advantage. Today is for us a new Badr.[2] Remember the victory that the Prophet won against the coalition of unbelievers. Did he not attack the enemies with only 313 fighters? Did he not gain a glaring victory? . . . We, in turn, have to rise above the events that threaten us and dominate the situation. Do not say, like some of the Jews who said, "There is no power for us today against Goliath and his soldiers [Qur'ān 2: 249]." Do as those others among them who said, "'How often has a small company has overcome a large company by permission of God. And God is with the patient.' And when they went forth to [face] Goliath and his soldiers, they said, 'Our Lord, pour upon us patience and plant firmly our feet and give us victory over the disbelieving people' [Qur'ān 2: 249–250]."

1 The following events are adapted from *L'empire peul*, 34–37.
2 In the battle of Badr, fought in the Ḥijāz in 624 CE, the Muslims led by Muḥammad defeated a larger army of Meccans.

Aḥmad Lobbo's supporters moved against their enemies, who fired their guns. The ground shook and Aḥmad Lobbo shouted: "The infidels have trembled!" A Mossi of Yatenga (Burkina Faso) named 'Abd al-Salām ran toward them and, when he got within range, fired an arrow that hit the war drum. A hail of bullets struck him. He fell down and cried out: *Lā ilāha illā Allāh*.[3]

The death of 'Abd al-Salām opened the battle of Noukouma, where Aḥmad Lobbo's partisans defeated the elites traditionally holding political power in the Middle Niger: the Bambara of Segou, overlords of the region, and the Fulani warrior elites of the Dikko and Sidibe. The battle also symbolically marks the birth of the Caliphate of Ḥamdallāhi. Its founder, Aḥmad Lobbo, was an outsider to both the religious and political elites of his time. As Last stresses, he "was born of a minor scholar family from one of the less important Fulbe clans."[4] He did not belong to any known family of *'ulamā'* in the Middle Niger or to any prominent family of political authority in the region. Yet his popularity increased exponentially in the second decade of the nineteenth century, and at the expense of the old elites. In Salvaing's words, he was the "*homo novus*" of the Middle Niger.[5] Eventually, this new man established one of the most important states in nineteenth-century West African history: the Caliphate of Ḥamdallāhi.

Part II continues the work of the previous section by performing, in Foucauldian terms, an archaeology of Nūḥ b. al-Ṭāhir's *Tārīkh al-fattāsh*.[6] This part is devoted to the study of the caliphate and, in particular, to the claims of authority on which Aḥmad Lobbo rested his role as a religious leader charged with the political power – a domain that had traditionally been a prerogative of the region's warrior elites. Based on a thorough analysis of mainly unexplored manuscripts, Part II examines the competing claims to authority in West Africa during the first half of the nineteenth century as the contexts that made the very existence of the chronicle possible and necessary or, in Foucault's words, its "conditions of possibilities."[7] It comprises three chapters

[3] "There is no deity worthy of worship, but God." This sentence represents the first part of the Declaration of Faith (*shahāda*).

[4] Last, "Reform in West Africa," 32. [5] Introduction to *Fatḥ al-Ṣamad*, 38.

[6] For a definition of "archaeology," see Foucault, *The Archaeology of Knowledge*, 7.

[7] Michel Foucault, *The Order of Things: An Archaeology of the Human Sciences* (London: Routledge, 2002), xiii–xiv.

that explore Aḥmad Lobbo's grounds for exercising legitimate authority, and how that legitimacy was contested by other actors in the region: the old Fulani warrior elites, who claimed political authority; the Kunta scholarly clan who, while accepting the political domination of Ḥamdallāhi in the Middle Niger, resisted Aḥmad Lobbo's claims in the religious sphere; and the Fodiawa leaders of the neighboring Sokoto Caliphate, who contested Aḥmad Lobbo's legitimacy in both political and religious domains.

3 *The Emergence of Clerical Rule in the Middle Niger*

This chapter describes the substantial shift that occurred in the relationship between political and religious authorities in the Middle Niger at the time of Ḥamdallāhi. The traditional order in which warrior elites were charged with political power and Muslim scholars were recognized as religious authorities was upset by the movement led by Aḥmad Lobbo. Like other Muslim scholars who headed revolutions in West Africa during the eighteenth and nineteenth centuries, Aḥmad Lobbo seized political power and joined it to his religious authority, to emerge as the ruler of the powerful Caliphate of Ḥamdallāhi.

Ahmad Lobbo's power rested on his political acumen, as well as on his status as an established scholar who had mastered the Islamic sciences, and especially jurisprudence (*fiqh*). This mastery is evidenced strongly in his writings, which have so far been neglected, or even been considered irrelevant, by previous scholars. In particular, this chapter will pay attention to Aḥmad Lobbo's *Kitāb al-Iḍṭirār* as testimony to the caliph of Ḥamdallāhi's erudition and ideology. Aḥmad Lobbo's authority, however, was not only expressed through his demonstrable mastery of Islamic jurisprudence. He was also perceived as a Friend of God (*walī*) known for his access to Divine Blessing, or *baraka*, as it emerges in sources that were produced at the time of his death.[1] This aspect of Aḥmad Lobbo's authority will be mainly explored through an analysis of the hagiography written by Muḥammad b. ʿAlī Pereejo, the *Fatḥ al-Ṣamad*. At the same time, however, the religious scholar's access to political authority, a novelty in the Middle Niger, was met with strong resistance by the local Fulani warrior elites of the Dikko of Masina and the Sidibe of Kounari, who would fight fiercely against Aḥmad Lobbo until their final defeat in the mid-1820s.

[1] For a detailed analysis of these terms, see M. Gaborieau, s.v. "Walī," *EI*[2], vol. 11, 109–125; G. S. Colin, s.v. "Baraka," *EI*[2], vol. 1, 1032.

The Middle Niger at the Dawn of Ḥamdallāhi: Warrior Elites and Muslim Scholars

In the early 1810s political power in the Middle Niger was in the hands of warrior elites. The region was policed by a series of Arma garrisons that exercised little control outside of urban areas. After the Arma of Timbuktu were defeated in the early 1770s, the Tuareg had become the virtually unchallenged masters of the Niger Bend.[2] South of Timbuktu, Djenné was the most important center, where the *Djenné-wéré* and the Arma *qā'id* both nominally recognized the overlordship of the *pāshā* of Timbuktu.[3] However, the strongest political influence in the region was exercised by the Fulani warrior elites and the Bambara *fama*s of Segou. The late eighteenth and early nineteenth centuries had witnessed a period of intense hostility between the Bambara and the Fulani, in particular the Dikko *arɗo*s of Masina, descendants of a foundational hero called Maghan Diallo, who had putatively arrived in the region around 1400, at the head of a group of nomads.[4] Subordinated first by the emperor of Mali and then by the Songhay *askiyà*s, the Fulani Dikko gradually gained more freedom under the decentralized Arma Pāshālik and formed what Sanankoua has described as the "Kingdom of Masina."[5]

The conflict between the people of Segou and the Dikko is recorded in the great Fulani oral epic of the Arɗo Silamaka, who lived at the time of either Fama Ngolo Diarra (r.1766–1797) or in the early years of the nineteenth century under Fama Da, which eventually witnessed the defeat of the Fulani leader.[6] The Dikko were reduced to the status of Bambara vassals and started collecting taxes on their behalf, and campaigning with the men of Segou.[7] However, while the power of the Dikko weakened with the emergence of the Bambara, another Fulani group rose to prominence on the right bank of the Niger, in

[2] See Abitbol, *Tombouctou et les Arma*, 225–231.
[3] On the city of Djenné, see Monteil, *Djénné*.
[4] The first name of the Fulani leader is sometime spelled without "n" in the oral traditions, but most of the time with a *nūn* in the Arabic sources. No recent works covers the history of the Fulani of Masina prior to the nineteenth century. I rely on Delafosse, *Haut-Sénégal-Niger*, vol. 2, 223–231; and Louis Tauxier, *Mœurs et histoire des Peuls: I. Origines ; II. Les Peuls de l'Issa-Ber et du Macina ; III. Les Peuls du Fouta-Djallon* (Paris: Payot, 1937), 156–163.
[5] Sanankoua, *Un empire peul*, 22. [6] Seydou, *Silâmaka*, 41 and 43.
[7] Brown, "The Caliphate of Hamdullahi," 101.

Kounari. Under the influence of the Sidibe, a Ferooɓe sub-clan, a Kounari-based polity emerged as a regional power in the second half of the eighteenth century under the leadership of Pereejo Hammadi Boɗeejo (Fulfulde "the red"), shortened to Hamboɗeejo, another hero of the Fulani oral traditions.[8] Hamboɗeejo married the daughter of Monzon (r. 1790–1808), another of the *fama*s of Segou, and managed, according to Sanankoua, to "exploit his privileged connection with Segou to consolidate his authority in his own kingdom and [at the same time] to exploit this very same authority to assert his independence from Segu."[9] Eventually, the Kounari *pereejo* bequeathed to his son, Gelaajo, a strong kingdom with capital in Goundaka. Consequently, Segou indirectly controlled the region by endorsing the Fulani military clans of the Dikko and the Sidibe, each of which enjoyed different degrees of autonomy.

Islam did not play any role in the legitimization of these warrior elites – as it did, for example, within the Songhay Empire.[10] Yet Islam had already started spreading among the Bambara of Segou, the Fulani warrior elites, and the Arma. While most scholarship takes it for granted that the Arma, descendants of North African soldiers, were Muslims, this is not necessarily the case for the Bambara and the Fulani. However, evidence does point to the spread of Islam among these populations before the emergence of Ḥamdallāhi. For example, as Monteil points out, Fama Ngolo Diarra, originally a crown slave of the Koulibaly, had been trained by Muslim scholars in Djenné and Timbuktu.[11] More generally, a crucial feature of the Segou state was its control over the economy, meaning control of crop production, which was largely in the hands of Muslim Marka farmers.[12] Similarly, Muslims held a monopoly over trade, namely the Marka traders and Somono boatmen.[13] Likewise, among the Fulani of the Middle Niger, Islam had already planted roots that extended back centuries, as evidenced by the Muslim names of most of the Fulani *arɗo*s recorded in several

8 The epic of Hamboɗeejo is narrated in Seydou, *La geste de Ham-Bodêdio*.
9 Sanakoua, *Un empire peul*, 27.
10 On the role of Islam in the legitimization of the Songhay Empire, see Bruce S. Hall, "Arguing for sovereignty in Songhay," *Afriques* 4 (2013): 2–17.
11 On these episodes of Ngolo Diarra's biography, see Monteil, *Les Bambara*, 47–49.
12 Roberts, *Warriors, Merchants, and Slaves*, 47–50.
13 Roberts, *Warriors, Merchants, and Slaves*, 51–75.

local traditions.[14] Such elites, however, also advertised their attachment to non-Islamic practices, such as the drinking of fermented beverages, which would become a mark of identity for such groups. For example, the Dikko prince Arɗo Giɗaaɗo would shout at one of Aḥmad Lobbo's students: "Mead is a drink held in contempt by the Qur'ān, but not by my ancestors. I will follow on their path and not on that of something else."[15]

A new idea of political-cum-Islamic authority was, simultaneously, emerging all over West Africa in the late eighteenth century. This is exemplified in the Middle Niger by the emergence of a prominent clan, of Arab–Berber origins, from Azawād during the second half of the eighteenth century: the Kunta.[16] This influence first manifested in the

[14] See for example the list of Fulani *arɗo*s provided in the *Tārīkh al-Sūdān* (Houdas [ed. and trans.], *Tarikh es-Soudan*, Arabic text 184–189/French text 281–288; Hunwick, *Timbuktu and the Songhay Empire*, 233–242).

[15] *L'empire peul*, 31. I translate the French "hydromel" literally, as "mead." However, in this passage, Hampaté Ba and Daget are most likely referring to a drink of fermented millet known in West Africa, among different names, including *dolo*.

[16] The Kunta occupied a very important role in the economic and intellectual history of West Africa during the eighteenth and nineteenth centuries. In spite of their relevance, no synthetic study has been produced on this important group of scholars and traders. An introduction to the history of the economic role of the Kunta is J. Genevière, "Les Kountas et leurs activités commerciale," *BIFAN* 12 (1950): 1111–1127; E. Ann McDougall, "The economics of Islam in the southern Sahara: The rise of the Kunta clan," in *Rural and Urban Islam in West Africa*, edited by Nehemia Levitzion and Humphrey J. Fisher (Boulder, CO: Lynne Rienner, 1987), 39–54.On the Kunta role as scholars and an introduction to the writings of the most important Kunta scholars, see *ALA* IV, 67–149. Monographic studies of the three most important scholars of the Kunta family are available in Batran's excellent Ph.D. dissertation, "Sīdī al-Mukhtār al-Kuntī," later published in a much-abridged version as Aziz A. Batran, *The Qadiriyya Brotherhood in West Africa and the Western Sahara: The Life and Times of Shaykh al-Mukhtar al-Kunti, 1729–1811* (Rabat: Institut des Études Africaines, 2001); and in Aziz A. Batran, "The Kunta, Sīdī al-Mukhtār al-Kuntī, and the office of Shaykh al-Ṭarīqa 'l-Qādiriyya," in *Studies in West African Islamic History*, vol. 1: *The Cultivator of Islam*, edited by John R. Willis (London: Frank Cass, 1976): 114–146; Wuld Daddah, "Šayh Sîdi Muhammed"; Abdelkader Zebadia, "The Career and Correspondence of Ahmad al-Bakkay of Timbuctu, from 1847 to 1866" (Ph.D. dissertation, University of London, 1974). See also Yahya Ould el-Bara, "The Life of Shaykh Sidi al-Mukhtar al-Kunti," in *The Meanings of Timbuktu*, edited by Shamil Jeppie and Souleymane B. Diagne (Cape Town: HSRC Press, 2008), 193–211; Mahmane Mahmoudou, "The Works of Shaykh Sidi al-Mukhtar al-Kunti," in *The Meanings of Timbuktu*, 213–229; Abdel Wadoud Ould Cheikh, "A man of

case of al-Mukhtār al-Kabīr, the teacher of Nūḥ b. al-Ṭāhir, the Kunta scholar who negotiated the surrender of the Arma of Timbuktu to the Tuareg after the siege of the city in 1771.[17] The Kunta soon emerged as one of the most influential scholarly networkers of West Africa, and their extensive influence extended to Muslim areas including Masina, the Western Sahara, and northern Nigeria, as well as Segou itself.

The Kunta never claimed political authority, although their status as Muslim scholars and saints gave them a great deal of power which had previously rested firmly in the hands of the Arma and the Tuareg. This relationship was a traditional one, characteristic among other cases in the Songhay Empire, which Hunwick describes as follows:

> the possibility of a genuine equilibrium ... achieved between secular powers and religious authorities. The secular power rules – [it] orders society, raises revenue, defends or expands the realm and provides security for its people. The religious authority remains to a great extent independent of the secular power and operates in a symbiotic fashion relative to it. Neither threatens the other, but each has the ability to put pressure on the other. The religious authorities do not dictate government policy, yet may influence it.[18]

More concrete evidence of this new concept of authority, which combined the political and the religious, was the collapse of these two spheres in the aftermath of Islamic revolutions in Fouta Toro and Fouta Djalon, and especially in the movement initiated by ʻUthmān b. Fūdī in Hausaland, which eventually set in motion the dynamics that led to the rise of Aḥmad Lobbo.

Scholars often argue that the Middle Niger was strongly affected by the Sokoto movement. However, as Abdullahi Smith underlined more than a half century ago, the precise repercussions of this movement in West Africa are still to be understood.[19] In the case of Ḥamdallāhi, there is evidence of ʻUthmān b. Fūdī's interest in expanding his influence into the Middle Niger in the form of a letter written to him by Muḥammad al-Kuntī, and datable to between 1813 and 1817.[20] In the

letters in Timbuktu: al-Shaykh Sidi Muhammad al-Kunti," in *The Meanings of Timbuktu*, 231–247.

[17] Abitbol, *Tombouctou et les Arma*, 228.

[18] Hunwick, "Secular power and religious authority," 178.

[19] Smith, "A neglected theme," 178.

[20] Partially translated in Wuld Daddah, "Šayh Sîdi Muhammed," 126–132. The date of the letter is inferred from the reference to the 1813 Egyptian conquest of Mecca from the Wahhabis of 1813 and the death of ʻUthmān b. Fūdī in 1817.

letter, Muḥammad al-Kuntī refers to previous correspondence between his father, al-Mukhtār al-Kuntī, and 'Uthmān b. Fūdī:

He [al-Mukhtār al-Kuntī], informed [me] about the interest you showed in Timbuktu, said that he really hoped that Alfa 'Uṯman ['Uthmān b. Fūdī] will rule over it, will end illegal taxes, established innovations and will restore the prosperity that the Arma power has destroyed. Since they established their authority over the Sudanese, the latter never stopped declining and getting poorer, a situation that has not improved after the Twâreg took over.[21]

Muḥammad al-Kuntī also endorses the possibility of expanding Sokoto's rule over Timbuktu and shows that he had actively promoted 'Uthmān b. Fūdī's cause with the people of the Middle Niger:

I wrote to all the Fulani chiefs: Funduk, Galâdio, the chiefs of the Sangâré and others, inviting them to come in support of the religion, join the Jihâd for the triumph of God's Word, get together against the enemies of Islam and to assist the one who has the destiny of Islam in his hands [i.e. 'Uthmān b. Fūdī]. They received my call with reservation. As for the Twâreg, they did not close the door to your cause, once I convinced them that your *da'wa* – propaganda – is in the name of God. I explained that was like that and they are not hostile anymore ... As for me, I love you for God's sake, and I am on your side longing for His reward.[22]

Apparently, 'Uthmān b. Fūdī not only asked for Kunta mediation, he directly sought support in the Middle Niger. Koullogo Diallo reports on a letter sent around 1814–15 by 'Uthmān b. Fūdī to *'ulamā'* of Masina and Gimmballa, exhorting them to prepare a revolution against the temporal leaders of the region: "1) Ahmed b. Abi Bakr, known as Walda Hoore Gooniya of Thioki; 2) Ahmed al-Mockhtar; 3) Ahmed Mohamed Boola; 4) Moodibo Maham Moodi; 5) Abdulaye Alfa Abba; 6) Ahmed Souleymane Bubu, or Aḥmad b. Alfagha;[23] 7) Alfa Amadou Foodiya Moussa."[24]

Written sources also record another attempt by Sokoto leaders to extend their influence in the Middle Niger. A certain jurist known only

[21] Wuld Daddah, "Šayh Sîdi Muhammed," 128.
[22] Wuld Daddah, "Šayh Sîdi Muhammed," 131–132.
[23] The name Alfagha is spelled in Arabic sources as "Alfaka"; the name seems to be of Moorish origin (see Charles C. Stewart, *Arabic Literature of Africa*, vol. 5: *The Writings of Mauritania and the Western Sahara* [Leiden and Boston: Brill, 2016], 294–299).
[24] Diallo, "Alpha Nuhu Taahiru," 225.

as Mallam Ibn Saʿīd came from Sokoto to Gimmballa in 1231/1815–16.[25] There, he obtained the support of the local population, which swore allegiance to him, and he thereafter fought against the Tuareg. However, Ibn Saʿīd's men were defeated and he retreated to Sokoto. This story is briefly reported in two local chronicles in almost identical passages: "And in the year 1232 arrived a man, a jurist, from the people of Sokoto, Mallam Ibn Saʿīd, to whom the inhabitants of Gimmballa pledged allegiance. He fought the Tuareg but was defeated and withdrew right away."[26]

Aḥmad Lobbo does not figure among ʿUthmān b. Fūdī's contacts in the region. However, it was Aḥmad Lobbo who successfully led a revolutionary movement in the Niger Bend; it was Aḥmad Lobbo whose victorious endeavors eventually overshadowed all the previous attempts in the region; and it was Aḥmad Lobbo who established a caliphate in the Middle Niger that remained independent from the neighboring state of Sokoto.

The Emergence of a Regional Leader

Little is known about Aḥmad Lobbo's early life and the beginning of his movement. As Brown emphasizes, his "birthplace is disputed ... but the weight of traditions among the *Shaykh*'s [Aḥmad Lobbo's] descendants favors Malangal as the likely site."[27] Malangal was a village situated on the left bank of the Diaka River, northeast of today's Ténenkou. As to the date of his birth, our sources disagree slightly. According to Hampaté Ba and Daget, he was born in 1189/1775–6, while Sanankoua simply gives his birth as "around 1773."[28] These two dates, variously repeated by later scholars, seem to be inaccurate. According to the pious hagiography *Fatḥ al-Ṣamad* which, as a contemporary source, may be the most reliable, Aḥmad Lobbo died in 1261/1845 at the age of seventy-one, pushing the date of his birth back to 1190/1771–2.[29]

Aḥmad Lobbo belonged to the Sangaré-Bari, a sub-clan of the Fulani Fittooɓe, which had emerged, by the beginning of the nineteenth

25 *Mallam* is an honorific title for Muslim scholars in Hausa-speaking contexts.
26 The quote is shared in *Dhikr*, p. 2; and *Mā waqaʿa*, p. 5.
27 Brown, "The Caliphate of Hamdullahi," 117.
28 *L'empire peul*, 20; Sanankoua, *Un empire peul*, 33.
29 *Fatḥ al-Ṣamad*, Arabic text 42/French text 91.

century, as a rather obscure scholarly lineage. An anonymous work, the *Maktūb fī bayān nasab shaykhinā amīr al-mu'minīn Aḥmad b. Muḥammad ilà Abī Bakr qāḍī Fūta Tūru* (Writing on the Explanation of the Genealogy of our *Shaykh*, the Commander of the Faithful Aḥmad b. Muḥammad back to Abū Bakr, Qāḍī of Fouta Toro) integrates information from the oral tradition surrounding the ancestors of Aḥmad Lobbo.[30] According to these sources, he was the son of Muḥammad (Hammadi II) [b.] Būbū (Boubou) b. Sa'īd (Seydou) b. al-Ḥājj (Alhadji II) b. Mūdi (Modi II) b. Ḥammad al-Ṣaghīr (Hammadoun Séghir) b. al-Ḥājj (Alhadji I) [b.] Mūdi (Modi I) [b.] Ḥammad (Hammadi I) [b.] Ghāraka (Ngarika) b. Hārūn b. Mūsà b. 'Abbās b. Jāj [Jaje] b. Maḥmūd b. Abī Bakr.[31] Many of his ancestors were Muslim scholars of limited fame. Muḥammad (Hammadi II) (d. ca. 1773–4), the father of the future caliph of Ḥamdallāhi, is remembered as a "wise" and "saintly" figure and his tomb in Yongo Siré, southwest of Mopti, was visited regularly by pilgrims until at least the 1950s, when Hampaté Ba and Daget recorded that information.[32] Three others, Mūdi (Modi II), Ḥammad al-Ṣaghīr (Hammadoun Séghir), and al-Ḥājj (Alhadji I), are mentioned as scholars and shepherds. In addition, the *Maktūb fī bayān* refers to two more of Aḥmad Lobbo's ancestors as scholars: Mūdi (Modi I) and a certain Mūsà, the first apparently the most famous, yet totally unknown today, of the family before Aḥmad Lobbo, recorded as "the great scholar" (*al-'ālim al-kabīr*). Furthermore, the forefather of the family, one Abū Bakr, was *qāḍī* in the region of Fouta Toro, confirming the oral traditions that describe the clan of Aḥmad Lobbo as originally from the valley of the Senegal River.[33]

Like some of his ancestors, Aḥmad Lobbo followed the traditional training of a local Muslim scholar.[34] He started learning the Qur'ān

[30] See IHERI-ABT 815; and *L'empire peul*, 20.

[31] I use the names in the form they appear in the Arabic text of the anonymous work on Aḥmad Lobbo's ancestors and in brackets the form of the names given in *L'empire peul*.

[32] *L'empire peul*, 24 and 24, n. 1.

[33] *L'empire peul*, 20. Brown records different oral traditions linking Aḥmad Lobbo's family to Arabia or to the east of Gao (Brown, "The Caliphate of Hamdullahi," 179, n. 17).

[34] For a description of a similar pattern of training, see Louis Brenner, *West African Sufi: The Religious Heritage and Spiritual Search of Cerno Bokar Saalig Taal* (London: C. Hurst, 1984), 74–79.

with his maternal grandfather Alfa Guuro, who also took care of him after his father's death. Later on, Aḥmad Lobbo continued pursuing Islamic knowledge, but he never studied with any prominent scholar, the most distinguished being Alfa Sammba Hammadi Bamma, a local scholar and the *qāḍī* of the region of Tyoubbi, with whom he completed the memorization of the Qur'ān.[35] Thereafter, unlike many other scholars who had left the region in pursuit of knowledge, Aḥmad Lobbo never left the southern Middle Niger.[36] He also studied Qur'ānic exegesis (*tafsīr*) with one Almamy Sono in Sebera.[37] Eventually, at the young age of twenty-two, Aḥmad Lobbo became a "well-known marabout."[38] He established himself and his students in Roundé Sirou, a village of northwest of Djenné, which was at the time the main cultural center of the area, after Timbuktu. From Roundé

[35] Tyoubbi is the region on the right side of the River Diaka, east of Ténenkou.

[36] A widespread historiographical myth exists, according to which Aḥmad Lobbo was among the students and soldiers of 'Uthmān b. Fūdī during the latter's campaigns in northern Nigeria (see, for example, Edward W. Bovill, *Missions to the Niger*, vol. 1: *The Journal of Friedrich Hornemann's Travels from Cairo to Murzuk in the Years 1797–98: The Letters of Alexander Gordon Laing 1824–26* [Cambridge: Cambridge University Press, 1964], 171). The origin of this assumption might be in the classical *Haut-Sénégal-Niger*, in which Delafosse reports that "he [Aḥmad Lobbo] accompanied in 1800 Ousmân da-Fodon ['Uthmān b. Fūdī] in his military expeditions in the Hausaland" before returning to his homeland and establishing himself close to Djenné (Delafosse, *Haut-Sénégal-Niger*, vol. 2, 232). Most likely expanding on this, Bugaje goes even further, describing Aḥmad Lobbo as a student of 'Uthmān b. Fūdī and the former's movement as an "extension" of Sokoto (Bugaje, "The Tradition of *Tajdid*," 218 and 220). However, no primary source supports this description of the Caliphate of Ḥamdallāhi as an offshoot of the Sokoto Caliphate, and it seems to be more an attempt to create continuity between Aḥmad Lobbo's movement and that of Sokoto as well as to enhance the prestige of Aḥmad Lobbo's teachers. Likewise, no evidence corroborates the statement of Willis according to which Aḥmad Lobbo went on Pilgrimage (Willis, "*Jihād fī sabīl Allāh*," 400).

[37] *L'empire peul*, 22.

[38] *L'empire peul*, 22. Although it is certainly widespread in West Africa, and used by West Africans themselves, the term "marabout" needs to be problematized, as the term in much scholarly literature echoes dichotomies between "orthodox" and "popular" Islam, as well as between a "center" and a "periphery" of the Muslim world. For a discussion of the term, see Mauro Nobili, "Book Review of *In the City of the Marabouts: Islamic Culture in West Africa*, by Geert Mommersteeg (Waveland Press, Long Grove, 2012)," *Journal of the American Academy of Religion* 82/3 (2014): 869–874. In this context, "marabout" is used as a synonym for scholar.

Sirou, Aḥmad Lobbo would have had regular access to the scholarly circuits of Djenné.

At this time, however, Aḥmad Lobbo was not looking to local scholars in the Middle Niger as sources of inspiration, but to the movement of ʿUthmān b. Fūdī. Although there is no proof of his active participation of ʿUthmān b. Fūdī's campaigns, what emerges from available sources is the more indirect influence of the Fūdīs, in keeping with Abdullahi Smith's conclusion that Aḥmad Lobbo's "greatest debt was clearly to Sokoto."[39] The strongest evidence for this is a set of replies (*ajwibat*) to eight questions posed by Aḥmad Lobbo to ʿAbd Allāh b. Fūdī, dated Shawwāl 1231/September–October 1816.[40] ʿAbd Allāh b. Fūdī introduces his responses by reproducing the original questions. The first two regard the Qur'ān, and specifically the problem of determining where each verse (*āya*) begins and ends, and the issue of abrogating and abrogated verses (*nāsikh* and *mansūkh*).[41] The next four questions concern Islamic law. Question three pertains to the status of the children of a female prisoner of war (*ma'sūra*), whether Muslim or not, and whether they are affected by their mother's enslavement.[42] The fourth question regards the status of property of unclear ownership.[43] Questions five and six relate to the call for prayer (*adhān*). One focuses on the issue of the positions of the muezzins in mosques.[44] Another refers to the appropriate limit to the number of people who can issue the call to prayer.[45] Question seven focuses on the Islamic sciences (*ʿulūm*) and comprises two sub-questions: the first regards the principles of religion (*uṣūl al-dīn*) as the best science and the second is on the subject of theology (*ʿilm al-kalām*) and the rejection of some of its aspects by early Muslim scholars.[46] Finally, the last question pertains to the *mahdī* and comprises two sub-questions. The first is about the name of the father of the *mahdī* and whether it would be Abū Bakr or al-Ḥasan, as reported by al-Shaʿrānī (d. 1565) on the authority of Ibn al-ʿArabī (d. 1240).[47] The second is a follow-up to a question that had been posed to ʿUthmān b. Fūdī and apparently left

[39] Smith, "A neglected theme," 179.
[40] IHERI-ABT 379. The manuscript also includes ʿAbd Allāh b. Fūdī's *Ḍiyā' al-umarā' fī-mā lahum wa ʿalayhim min al-ashyā'*, on which see *ALA* II, 93, item 28.
[41] IHERI-ABT 379, pp. 1–4. [42] IHERI-ABT 379, p. 4.
[43] IHERI-ABT 379, p. 4. [44] IHERI-ABT 379, pp. 4–5.
[45] IHERI-ABT 379, pp. 5–6. [46] IHERI-ABT 379, p. 6.
[47] IHERI-ABT 379, p. 6.

unanswered, about the internal and external characteristics (*khalq* and *kulq*) of the *mahdī*, in which Aḥmad Lobbo enquires about the validity of what al-Shaʿrānī had written on the topic.[48]

By the time ʿAbd Allāh b. Fūdī's replies reached Aḥmad Lobbo, the latter had started revealing his discontent with the behavior of the religious establishment of Djenné. The questions posed to the Fodiawa *shaykh* reflect some of the practices that Aḥmad Lobbo considered to be infringements on the Sunna, and that he would soon attack in his writings. They also reflect an interest in eschatological topics that would eventually be expanded by Nūḥ b. al-Ṭāhir in the *Tārīkh al-fattāsh*. Aḥmad Lobbo is reported to have complained that the "marabouts [of his time] dispute futile matters and close their eyes to practices that condone mortal sins."[49] Failing in their roles as spiritual guides for the local Muslim community, the *ʿulamāʾ* of Djenné were accused of allowing blameworthy practices that were contrary to Islam among the local population: the topic of a major work written by Aḥmad Lobbo, the *Kitāb al-Iḍṭirār*.

The *Kitāb al-Iḍṭirār*

This work is well known in West Africa, and appears to be the only lengthy treatise by Aḥmad Lobbo. As Brown convincingly argues, it was written before the establishment of the caliphate.[50] In the introduction, Aḥmad Lobbo refers to himself as "The one who is in need of God the Beneficent" (*al-faqīr ilà Allāh al-Ghaniyy*) instead of using the title Commander of the Faithful, which he would assume after the foundation of the caliphate.[51] The work is a manual of jurisprudence concerning "blameworthy innovations" (*bidaʿ*, sing. *bidʿa*). In it, Aḥmad Lobbo exposes what he calls the "satanic and psychological innovations" (*al-bidaʿ al-shayṭāniyya aw al-nafsiyya*) of West African Muslims, meaning ritual practices that diverge, according to the author, from the Qur'ān, the Sunna, and the Consensus.[52] The work is divided into an introduction and six chapters loosely organized according to themes.

[48] IHERI-ABT 379, p. 8. Al-Shaʿrānī is a major source ʿUthmān b. Fūdī's works on eschatology.

[49] *L'empire peul*, 23. [50] Brown, "The Caliphate of Hamdullahi," 21.

[51] *Kitāb al-Iḍṭirār*, Arabic text 21/French text 84.

[52] See J. Robson, s.v. "Bidʿa," *EI*², vol. 1, 1199.

In the introduction, Aḥmad Lobbo describes the circumstances that led to the composition of the book, namely his observation of the spread of *bid'a* among the people of the *bilād al-Sūdān*. The author continues by quoting several *ḥadīth*s against innovation before describing the practices he condemns. Chapters 1 and 2 focus on the call to prayer and the necessary conditions (*shurūṭ*) to be met by the muezzin and the appropriate places for the call. Chapter 3 describes the correct way of performing the prayer following the *imām* and includes a digression on prayer for women, arguing that it is better for them to do so at home than in the mosque. Chapter 4 is the longest in the work and focuses mainly on the mosque itself. It deals with the correct behavior to observe when inside, and the need to keep it clean. Then it describes the mosque's architectural features, addressing the correct way to build the pulpit (*minbar*) and the *miḥrāb*, also stipulating that the pillars have to be made of wood and not mud, as was custom in the region; the correct height of the mosque; and the condemnation of the custom of burying the dead inside it. This chapter concludes with more rules about appropriate dress in mosques. Chapter 5 continues this theme by describing the norms for the behavior of the *imām* during the Friday prayer. Chapter 6 focuses on the prayer during for the Festival of the Sacrifice (*'Īd al-Aḍḥà*) and the Festival of the Breaking of the Fast (*'Īd al-Fiṭr*). It also includes a discussion of whether there should be more than one mosque in the same village, a widespread practice which the author considers blameworthy. He concludes with two final remarks (*fā'ida*) on supererogatory prayers. The first is a warning against performing such prayers at particular times: the fifteenth night of the month of Sha'bān; the first Friday of Rajab (the so-called "prayer of *al-raghā'ib*"); the Night of Destiny (*Laylat al-Qadr*); and on the day of *'Āshūrā'* (10 Muḥarram). This first *fā'ida* continues with his censure of women's custom of visiting tombs. The second and last *fā'ida* is the enumeration of some supererogatory prayers ascribed to the Prophet and reported by al-Mukhtār al-Kunti in his *al-Kawkab al-waqqād fī sharḥ wird 'Abd al-Qādir al-Jīlānī* (The Shining Star in Comment on the *Wird* of 'Abd al-Qādir al-Jīlānī) – most likely the *al-Kawkab al-waqqād fī faḍl dhikr al-mashā'ikh wa-ḥaqā'iq al-awrād* (The Shining Star in Remembrance of the *Shaykh*s and the Truth of the *Wirds*).[53]

[53] *ALA* IV, 77, item 23.

The *Kitāb al-Idṭirār* follows the traditional style of works on *bida'*, and more specifically that of works on the topic by 'Uthmān b. Fūdī.[54] Usman M. Bugaje, for example, compares Aḥmad Lobbo's work with 'Uthmān b. Fūdī's *Bayān al-bida' al-shayṭāniyya allatī aḥdathahā al-nās fī abwāb al-milla al-Muḥammadiyya* (The Explanation of the Satanic Innovations that People have Introduced in the Domains of the Community of Muḥamma).[55] He stresses that some of the issues raised in the two works are very similar and that the formula *mimmā aḥdathūhu* ("among [the innovations] that they have introduced") employed systematically by 'Uthmān b. Fūdī is also used extensively by Aḥmad Lobbo in the *Kitāb al-Idṭirār*.[56] The affinity between these two works confirms Sokoto's influence on Ḥamdallāhi. However, Ahmad Lobbo's work needs to be understood in the context of the region of Djenné and as a statement of the tensions between Aḥmad Lobbo and the scholarly establishment of that city. It therefore inscribes itself within the "dialectic of legitimization and delegitimization" that characterized the nineteenth-century Islamic movements in West Africa.[57]

While most of the time there is no precise reference to the contexts in which these blameworthy innovations began to occur, Aḥmad Lobbo implicitly condemns the local *'ulamā'*, and is explicit in attacking their practice of reserving specific spaces for certain local notables in the mosque during communal prayer.[58] As Diakité underlines, this refers to an incident documented in oral traditions, in which Aḥmad Lobbo was once expelled from the Great Mosque of Djenné for having occupied a space reserved for scholars of high rank.[59] According to Hampaté Ba and Daget:

> One Friday, he [i.e. Aḥmad Lobbo] left the third row where he used to stand and moved to the second. The following Friday, he passed from the second row to the first one and occupied the place of one of those who assist the *imām* in the recitation of the prayers and whisper to him in case of memory failures. After the prayer, the council of notables met to discuss the measures to be taken against Amadou Hammadi [Aḥmad Lobbo], whose audacity, in

[54] Brown, "The Caliphate of Hamdullahi," 180, n. 21, 197, n. 27, 217, n. 32.
[55] Bugaje, "The Tradition of *Tajdid*," 218.
[56] Bugaje, "The Tradition of *Tajdid*," 218.
[57] Loimeier, *Muslim Societies in Africa*, 129.
[58] *Kitāb al-Idṭirār*, Arabic text 39–40/French text 92.
[59] *Kitāb al-Idṭirār*, French text 98, n. 396.

the opinion of all, exceeded the limits allowed. In such cases, the culprit would be summoned before a scholarly commission to justify his knowledge and precedence. However, this procedure would have given Amadou Hammadi the opportunity to show his strength and attract the attention of all. Thus, they dismissed the case as an attempt to introduce dissensions into the city. It was only decided to forbid Amadou Hammadi Boubou access to the mosque, under penalty of being beaten.[60]

A more overt condemnation is directed against the architectural features of the Grand Mosque of Djenné as being contrary to Islamic law. Aḥmad Lobbo explicitly cites it as the perfect example of the blameworthy innovation of building mosques of excessive height, whereas, "when His Prophet wanted to build his mosque, God the Most High ordered him to build it seven cubits in height."[61]

As a whole, the *Kitāb al-Iḍṭirār* can be read as a condemnation of the Muslim establishment of Djenné, collectively accused of not correcting these *bida'*. Indeed, Aḥmad Lobbo strongly censures the learned men who witnessed these innovations and did not correct them, via one *ḥadīth* quoted at the beginning of the work: "If dissention surfaces and my Companions are vilified, whoever has knowledge yet decides to conceal it is like the one who disbelieves in what has been revealed to Muḥammad – May God's blessings and peace be upon him."[62] Setting himself against the establishment of Djenné, Aḥmad Lobbo claims: "When I saw that some of the satanic and psychological innovations among many people of the Sudan, both in the countryside and in the cities, were so widespread as to become a part of regular worship, I could not bear them – and you know, O brethren, the negative effects of the innovations."[63] Unlike the *'ulamā'* of Djenné who tolerated these

[60] *L'empire peul*, 24.

[61] *Kitāb al-Iḍṭirār*, Arabic text 45/French text 102. The issue of the Grand Mosque of Djenné would remain a point of disagreement between Aḥmad Lobbo and the notables of Djenné. After the conquest of the city, sometime around 1830, the caliph ordered the destruction of the Great Mosque "because the Moroccans [i.e. the Arma] had soiled it with practices contrary to the tradition and the religion" (*L'empire peul*, 154). After complaints from the people of Djenné, Aḥmad Lobbo decided to remove the roof of the Great Mosque and to move the Friday prayer to another mosque (*L'empire peul*, 156). On the history of Djenné mosque, see Jean-Louis Bourgeois, "The history of the Great Mosques of Djenné," *African Arts* 20/3 (1987): 54–92.

[62] *Kitāb al-Iḍṭirār*," Arabic text 23/French text 85. The *ḥadīth* is cited by the fourteenth-century scholar al-'Abdarī (*Kitāb al-Iḍṭirār*, Arabic text 23, n. 36).

[63] *Kitāb al-Iḍṭirār*, Arabic text 21/French text 84.

blameworthy practices, Aḥmad Lobbo was compelled to act and, having been inspired by God after performing the prayer for advice (*ṣalāt al-istikhāra*), wrote his *Kitāb al-Iḍṭirār* to rectify Islamic practices in his region.

By exposing the misconduct of the religious leadership of this region, Aḥmad Lobbo was delegitimizing their role as valid representatives of religious authority. Although his attack on the *'ulamā'* of Djenné does not equate to a call for excommunication (*takfīr*), this work created the preconditions for the emergence of his movement of renewal. This sequence of actions is described, by Willis, as characteristic: "The first task of these revivalists was to create a climate of opinion favourable to their aims."[64] At this time, Aḥmad Lobbo was emerging as a scholar whose authority made him a viable alternative to the scholarly establishment of Masina.

Sources of Authority

The victory at Noukouma and the popular support mobilized during the first phase of Aḥmad Lobbo's movement raises the question of how he managed to gather such a large number of supporters. Willis argues that, for Aḥmad Lobbo as for other West African leaders of Islamic revolutions, "their chances for success depended on their reputation for sanctity and learning, their abilities as preachers, and – against almost inevitable opposition – their abilities as political organizers."[65] The political acumen of Aḥmad Lobbo has also been recognized by scholars such as Jean Gallais and Sanankoua, who have described in detail the effective administration of Ḥamdallāhi.[66] By contrast, however, scholars have completely neglected his role as scholar and saint.

The tendency to dismiss the depth of Aḥmad Lobbo's learning dates back to Abdullahi Smith's statement that Aḥmad Lobbo's "movement seems to have been much less learned than that of Sokoto."[67] Last, too, argues that "Ahmad Lobbo and his disciples ... seemed to have been distinguished more for their piety and zeal than for their scholarship."[68] By the same token, Sanankoua states that "Aḥmad Lobbo

64 Willis, "*Jiḥād fī sabīl Allāhi*," 401. 65 Willis, "*Jihād fī sabīl Allāh*," 406.

66 Jean Gallais, *Hommes du Sahel: espaces-temps et pouvoirs: le Delta intérieur du Niger 1960–1980* (Paris: Flammarion, 1984), 121–142; Sanankoua, "L'organisation politique," 121–299; Sanankoua, *Un empire peul*, 49–76.

67 Smith, "A neglected theme," 180. 68 Last, "Reform in West Africa," 32.

did not even finish the classical training cycle of the scholars of his time and his region"[69] and that "he did not contribute much to Islamic sciences and literature."[70] However, the assertion that Aḥmad Lobbo's followers did not count among their numbers any scholars of significance is inconsistent with the fame of Nūḥ b. al-Ṭāhir and Yirkoy Talfi (d. ca. 1864), two prolific scholars who stood out among the *'ulamā'* of Ḥamdallāhi and became known well beyond the borders of the caliphate.[71] Moreover, the picture of Aḥmad Lobbo as a leader of little erudition is not supported by the written sources, and contrasts with Hampaté Ba and Daget's description of him mastering, by the age of twenty-two, several disciplines, "such as Sources of Law [*uṣul al-fiqh*], Theology [*tawḥīd*], Rhetoric [*bayān*] etc."[72] A close analysis of Aḥmad Lobbo's early writings presents a picture that conforms with Hampaté Ba and Daget's findings concerning his high level of erudition. Later in his life, quite understandably, Aḥmad Lobbo seems to have been more concerned with the pragmatic issues of political administration; his writings from that era mainly consist of letters and dispatches that provide little information about his scholarly credentials.[73]

Aḥmad Lobbo was also acquainted with the works of a number of Muslim scholars, directly and indirectly, as indicated by his quotations of them and by his study of "derivative works."[74] Apart from the Qur'ān, he was familiar with the Sunna and classical collections of *ḥadīth*s. He quotes three of the six canonical collections (*al-kutub al-sitta*): Muḥammad b. Ismā'īl al-Bukhārī (d. 870), Abū Dāwūd, and al-Tirmīdhī (d. 892). Furthermore, he was acquainted with Mālik b. Anas's *Muwaṭṭā'*, as well as with Ibn Ḥajar al-'Asqalānī and his commentary on al-Bukhārī, the *Fatḥ al-bārī fī sharḥ Ṣaḥīḥ al-Bukhārī* (The Victory of the Creator Commenting on the Collection of al-Bukhārī). However, it was in the domain of

69 Sanankoua, *Un empire peul*, 34. 70 Sanankoua, *Un empire peul*, 52.

71 Brown, "The Caliphate of Hamdullahi," 104. As for Yirkoy Talfi, see Diakite, "al-Mukhtār b. Yerkoy Talfi."

72 *L'empire peul*, 22.

73 Exceptions are represented by a letter of advice to the people of Timbuktu, to which I will return in Chapter 4, and the polemical writings against Muḥammad Bello, discussed in Chapter 5.

74 I use the term "derivative work" with reference to Hall and Stewart, who talk of "abridgements and commentaries, exegeses and versifications" of a particular text (Hall and Stewart, "The historic 'core curriculum'," 114).

jurisprudence (*fiqh*) that Aḥmad Lobbo was especially well versed. He mastered classical works that appear as part of the "core curriculum" of West African scholars, such as the *Risāla* (The Epistle) of Ibn Abī Zayd al-Qayrawānī (d. 996) and the *Mukhtaṣar* of Khalīl b. Isḥāq, which he accessed most likely through the glosses (*ḥāshiyya*) of al-Sanhūrī (d. 1606) and al-Kharshī (d. 1690).[75] Less common were other sources quoted by Aḥmad Lobbo in *fiqh*, such as *al-Ḥawādith wa-l-bida'* (The Novelties and the Innovations) by al-Ṭurṭūshī (d. 1126); *al-Muḥkam* (The Complete Book) by Ibn Qutayba (d. 889); untitled works of al-Māzirī (d. 1141), al-Lakhmī (d. 1164–5),[76] and al-Ṭabarī (d. 923); as well as a work by Ibn Rushd al-Jadd (d. 1136), grandfather of Averroes, *al-Bayān wa-l-taḥṣīl wa-l-sharḥ wa-l-tawjīh wa-l-ta'līl fī masā'il al-Mustakhraja* (The Explanation, Collection, Commentary, Interpretation and Analysis of the Questions from the Extract), which is in turn a commentary on al-'Utbī (d. 869)'s *Mustakhraja min al-asmi'a al-ma'rūfa mimmā laysa fī al-Mudawwana* (Extract from the Known Oral Narrative not Reported in the *Mudawwana*). Aḥmad Lobbo was also familiar with 'Uthmān b. Fūdī's works on *bida'*, especially his *Bayān al-bida'*, which, as mentioned above, served as a model for the *Kitāb al-Iḍṭirār*. However, his chief sources on *fiqh* were the works of the Mālikī scholar al-'Abdarī (d. 1336) and especially his radical *Madkhal al-shar' al-sharīf 'alà al-madhā'ib* (Introduction to the Noble Law according to the Schools). This work, as Diakité calculated, is explicitly referenced twenty-three times in the *Kitāb al-Iḍṭirār*.[77]

Aḥmad Lobbo's mastery of *fiqh* is also demonstrated in his sermon (*khuṭba*) for *'Īd al-Aḍhà*.[78] After praises to God and salutations to the Prophet, he devotes the sermon to obligatory acts (*wājibāt*), praiseworthy recommended acts (*mustaḥabbāt*), blameworthy acts (*makrūhāt*), and prohibited acts (*muḥarramāt*). The sermon also cites differences of opinion (*khilāf*) on several issues related to the festival. Although his only explicit references are to Mālik b. Anas and Ibn Abī Zayd al-Qayrawānī, this text well

[75] Hall and Stewart, "The historic 'core curriculum'," 132.
[76] *Kitāb al-Iḍṭirār*, 40, n. 127. [77] Introduction to *Kitāb al-Iḍṭirār*, 80.
[78] IF, Fonds de Gironcourt, 2405 (28).

illustrates not only Aḥmad Lobbo's learning but also its public display.

In addition, Aḥmad Lobbo's acquaintance with the literature of Sufism (*taṣawwuf*) is evident in the *Kiṭāb al-Iḍṭirār*. This includes citations of such standard works as *Qūt al-qulūb fi mu'āmalat al-maḥbūb wa-waṣf ṭarīq al-murīd ilà maqām al-tawḥīd* (The Nourishment of Hearts in Dealing with the Beloved and the Description of the Seeker's Way to the Station of Declaring Oneness) by al-Makkī (d. 996), al-Sha'rānī's *al-Yawāqīt wa-l-jawāhir fī bayān aqā'd al-akbār* (The Pearls and Jewels in the Explanation of the Creeds of the Great People), and Ibn al-'Arabī's *al-Futuḥāt al-Makkiyya* (The Meccan Revelations).[79] He also makes reference to another Sufi author, al-Marjānī (d. 1300), but with no citation of a specific work. Furthermore, Aḥmad Lobbo was acquainted with the works of 'Abd al-Qādir al-Jīlānī (d. 1166), the founder of the Qādiriyya brotherhood, which he studied, according to oral traditions, with a certain Kabara Farma, in Djenné.[80] However, this does not necessarily mean that he was affiliated with the Qādiriyya, as often has been assumed.[81] Recently, Salvaing has noted the absence of any reference to the Qādiriyya in the *Fatḥ al-Ṣamad*, advancing the hypothesis that Aḥmad Lobbo might have been devoted to Sufi practices without any reference to a Sufi brotherhood, except for a loose allegiance to the Shādhiliyya.[82]

His familiarity with the literature on creed belief (*'aqīda*) is evinced by references to the works of Muḥammad b. Yūsuf al-Sanūsī and especially *'Aqīda al-sughrà* (The Small Creed).[83] On theology, Aḥmad Lobbo refers to *Ṭawāli' al-anwār min maṭāli'*

[79] Hall and Stewart, "The 'core curriculum'," 139–140. [80] *L'empire peul*, 22.

[81] The first reference I could find to Aḥmad Lobbo's affiliation to the Qādiriyya is in Marty, *La région de Tombouctou*, 179. The statement is often repeated, for example by Willis, "*Jihād fī sabīl Allāhi*," 400, n. 20.

[82] Introduction to *Fatḥ al-Ṣamad*, 28; Salvaing, "La question de l'influence de la Qādiriyya." For similar arguments regarding Sufi practices among West African Muslims, see Louis Brenner, "Muslim thought in eighteenth-century West Africa: The case of Shaykh Uthman b. Fudi," in *Eighteenth-Century Renewal and Reform in Islam*, edited by Nehemia Levtzion and John O. Voll (Syracuse: Syracuse University Press, 1987), 39–67, 56; and Charles C. Stewart and E. K. Stewart, *Islam and Social Order in Mauritania: A Case Study from the Nineteenth Century* (Oxford: Clarendon Press, 1973), 48–53.

[83] Hall and Stewart, "The historic 'core curriculum'," 137.

al-anẓār (The Manifestations from the Perspective of the Horizon) by al-Bayḍāwī (d. 1260) and unidentified writings of al-Rāzī (d. 1210), while in the domain of lexicography (*ma'ājim*) he makes reference to Abū 'Ubayd al-Qāsim b. Sallām (d. 838). Furthermore, apart from his general knowledge of exoteric sciences, Aḥmad Lobbo is remembered for his mastery of esoteric ones. In his *Fatḥ al-Ṣamad*, Muḥammad b. 'Alī Pereejo states: "As for the esoteric science [*'ilm al-bāṭin*] that is inspired by God's illumination, he was a pole of inner knowledge and light of the dawn."[84] Hampaté Ba and Daget, for example, describe Aḥmad Lobbo practicing occult sciences to kill Da, the *fama* of Segou.[85] Finally, in addition to his expertise in the works of scholars from outside West Africa, Aḥmad Lobbo was familiar with the writings of local scholars, as emerges from his reference to the works of al-Mukhtār al-Kuntī, 'Uthmān b. Fūdī, and 'Abd Allāh b. Fūdī.

Reports of Aḥmad Lobbo's erudition are found in several poems composed by West African scholars, both during the caliph's time and at the time of his death, which are included in Muḥammad b. 'Ali Peerejo's *Fatḥ al-Ṣamad*. For example, Muḥammad b. al-Ṭāhir Seyyouma, in his *al-Qaṣīda al-lāmiyya* (Poem with Rhyme in *Lām*), praised Aḥmad Lobbo during his lifetime as "reviver of the sciences."[86] A poem with rhymes in *alif* written by "the people of Walāta" celebrated Aḥmad Lobbo's erudition by saying:

> You made it [i.e. the Sunna] prosper by the sciences of *Sharī'a* that you teach,
> Until both the nomads and the townsfolk learnt it.[87]

'Alī b. Muḥammad Pereejo includes in the *Fatḥ al-Ṣamad* his own elegy, with rhyme in the letter *mīm*, composed at the time of Aḥmad Lobbo's death, which addresses him as "Sea of sciences" and says:

> How many problems in the discipline of Grammar, Arabic Language,
> And Logic he saved from being swallowed up by sea
> In every science he was the ocean
> who offers miracles by piety and wisdom.[88]

84 *Fatḥ al-Ṣamad*, Arabic text 20–21/French text 69.
85 *L'empire peul*, 141.
86 *Fatḥ al-Ṣamad*, Arabic text 36/French text 84.
87 *Fatḥ al-Ṣamad*, Arabic text 39/French text 89.
88 *Fatḥ al-Ṣamad*, Arabic text 43/French text 93.

A scholar named Aḥmad Abū Bakr al-Māsinī, in his *al-Qaṣīda al-nūniyya* (Poem with Rhyme in *Nūn*) praises Aḥmad Lobbo as

> Reviver of Sharī'a and of the sciences all,
> Especially of Grammar and [Sciences of] the Qur'ān.
> And even, every knowledge he acquired through his
> beautiful quintessence,
> And provided us the best of the explanations.[89]

One of his disciples, Aḥmad b. Muḥamma, says in a *Qaṣīda al-dāliyya* (Poem with Rhyme in *Dāl*):

> The gatherings [for the study] of the sciences of
> Grammar and Rhetoric are mourning
> For his loss with grief. Those of Theology
> and the *mihrābs* are also mourning,
> Like the gatherings for *dhikr* and acts of worship.[90]

This analysis of Aḥmad Lobbo's erudition supports Diakité's argument that his knowledge of Islamic sciences cannot be easily dismissed.[91] It is

[89] *Fatḥ al-Ṣamad*, Arabic text 45/French text 95.

[90] *Fatḥ al-Ṣamad*, Arabic text 50/French text 101.

[91] Diakite, "al-Mukhtār b. Yerkoi Talfi," 29. In spite of this evidence, scholars have neglected the level of Aḥmad Lobbo's erudition. I ascribe this to the nature of the sources employed: Scholars have usually analyzed the caliphate from the point of view of his opponent. For example, Barth collected his information on Aḥmad Lobbo first from Gelaajo, the Fulani leader of Kounari who fled from the territories conquered by Ḥamdallāhi, and second from the Kunta who hosted the German traveler in Timbuktu, at the time when Aḥmad al-Bakkāy, the son of Muḥammad al-Kuntī, was openly hostile to Aḥmad III, the last caliph of Ḥamdallāhi (Barth, *Travels and Discoveries*, vol. 4, 255–257, and 402 *et passim.*). Others have made reference to the history of Ḥamdallāhi mainly on the basis of writings produced by the scholars of Sokoto, Ḥamdallāhi's most important rival in the region (Last, *The Sokoto Caliphate*; Last, "Reform in West Africa"; Ahmad M. Kani and Charles S. Stewart, "Sokoto–Masina correspondence," *Research Bulletin of the Centre of Arabic Documentation – Ibadan* 9–1/2 [1975]: 1–12; Charles C. Stewart, "Frontier disputes and problems of legitimation: Sokoto–Masina relations 1817–1837," *Journal of African History* 17/4 [1976]: 497–514; Charles C. Stewart, "Diplomatic relations in early nineteenth-century West Africa: Sokoto–Masina–Azaouad correspondence," in *Studies in the History of the Sokoto Caliphate*, edited by Y. B. Usman [Zaria: Ahmadu Bello University Press, 1979], 408–429.). Still other assessments of scholarship in Ḥamdallāhi have been drawn from the works written by al-Ḥājj 'Umar, the caliphate's final opponent, whose conquest of the capital city in 1862 marked the end to the history of the state (Mahibou and Triaud, *Voilà ce qui est arrivé*; Robinson,

particularly clear that Aḥmad Lobbo's authority was based on his mastery of Islamic jurisprudence. However, his scholarly authority was also combined with his perceptions as a Friend of God with access to *baraka*. These two levels of authority, scholarly and saintly, should not be misunderstood as pertaining only to scholars and Sufi masters. As Vincent Cornell underlines in his study of sainthood in Islamic contexts, "certainly not all Muslim saints are sufi."[92] On the contrary, he continues, "the most important saints … were legal specialists."[93] Indeed, as Stewart remarks, "prior to the present century this distinction between jurists and mystics was not an important one in West Africa."[94]

Oral traditions play a great role in framing Aḥmad Lobbo as a *walī*. Of course, the depiction of the caliph of Ḥamdallāhi as a saint could be dismissed as a later re-imagination – except that there is direct evidence of his saintly authority in the *Fatḥ al-Ṣamad*.[95] This work was completed on 27 Rabīʿ II 1261/4 May 1845, at the death of Aḥmad Lobbo, and therefore represents the perception of the caliph of Ḥamdallāhi during his lifetime. An entire section is devoted to the "the outstanding traits that were manifested to some of his students."[96] Twelve of these miracles are recorded as having been reported by trustworthy transmitters. The first resembles the episode of the village of Nareval, near Ténenkou, where, according to oral traditions, God punished those who wronged

The Holy War). All those sources thus shared an interest in downgrading the legitimacy of the leaders of Ḥamdallāhi.

92 Vincent J. Cornell, *Realm of the Saint: Power and Authority in Moroccan Sufism* (Austin: University of Texas Press, 1998), xxxv.

93 Cornell, *Realm of the Saint*, xxxv.

94 Stewart, *Islam and Social Order*, 2. See also Charles C. Stewart, "Southern Saharan scholarship and the *Bilad al-sudan*," *Journal of African History* 15/1 (1976): 73–93.

95 It is possible to read the oral traditions belittling Aḥmad Lobbo's level of learning in light of his construction as a "saint." For example, Hampaté Ba and Daget argue that his "inspiration was much higher that the knowledge he had acquired from books" (*L'empire peul*, 51). Oral sources construct a parallel between the state of illiterate (*ummī*) assigned to the Prophet by Islamic traditions and that of a semi-illiterate condition of the caliph of Ḥamdallāhi. This parallel between the caliph of Ḥamdallāhi and Muḥammad is rooted in the notion of *imitatio Muhammadi* that, in the words of Cornell, "helped [in] setting the paradigm for sainthood in the Muslim world" (Cornell, *Realm of the Saint*, 65).

96 *Fatḥ al-Ṣamad*, Arabic text 33–35/80–84.

Aḥmad Lobbo: here, it is a horse that dies after having struck the caliph and leaving a black mark on his face, a mark that God cures.[97] Two other narrators record that Aḥmad Lobbo's supplications were always accepted by God.[98] If, while the caliph was reading in the open air, it started raining, no drop of water would fall on him or on his books.[99] Another miracle dates back to the time before Aḥmad Lobbo became recognized as a *walī*: he used to study under a tree that would move its thorny branches to allow the future caliph to sit comfortably.[100] Other miracles include the multiplication of foodstuffs;[101] invisibility;[102] the presence of *jinn* at his side during battles;[103] the caliph's ability to dig wells and find water in dry, rocky, and sandy soils;[104] his capacity to teach for long periods without blowing his nose, expectorating, or spitting;[105] and a profound psychological ability to know what his followers and subordinates were thinking.[106] A final event is associated with the caliph's death: several of his followers maintain that they heard voices at the time of his demise.[107]

These sources depict Aḥmad Lobbo as a scholar but also as an authoritative figure modeled on classical images of Muslim saints. They present, in Salvaing's words, the caliph of Ḥamdallāhi as an "authentic model of sanctity."[108] It was Aḥmad Lobbo's role as scholar and saint that legitimized him as an authoritative figure in the eyes of his followers and made him capable of attracting a large number of people who, in turn, helped him to overthrow the political order of the Middle Niger in the aftermath of his victory at Noukouma.

97 *Fatḥ al-Ṣamad*, Arabic text 34–35/French text 83. The episode of Nareval is narrated in *L'empire peul*, 21–22.
98 *Fatḥ al-Ṣamad*, Arabic text 34/French text 81–82.
99 *Fatḥ al-Ṣamad*, Arabic text 34/French text 83.
100 *Fatḥ al-Ṣamad*, Arabic text 34/French text 82–83.
101 *Fatḥ al-Ṣamad*, Arabic text 35/French text 83.
102 *Fatḥ al-Ṣamad*, Arabic text 33–34/French text 80–81.
103 *Fatḥ al-Ṣamad*, Arabic text 34/French text 83. Hampaté Ba and Daget record that the warrior *jinn* Ali Soutoura was always with Aḥmad Lobbo in battle (*L'empire peul*, 19, n. 1).
104 *Fatḥ al-Ṣamad*, Arabic text 34/French text 82.
105 *Fatḥ al-Ṣamad*, Arabic text 34/French text 82.
106 *Fatḥ al-Ṣamad*, Arabic text 33/French text 82.
107 *Fatḥ al-Ṣamad*, Arabic text 34/French text 83.
108 Introduction to *Fatḥ al-Ṣamad*, 20.

The Resistance of the Old Fulani Elites

The emergence of Aḥmad Lobbo as a new leader in the southern Middle Niger, but also as new kind of ruler who claimed both Islamic and political authority, was met with resistance by the old elites of the region. In particular, the fiercest opponents of Ḥamdallāhi after the battle of Noukouma were the representatives of the Dikko of Masina and the Sidibe of Kounari. The great Arɗo Ngurori, who had not been personally involved at Noukouma, was pulled back into the dispute because the emergence of the Caliphate of Ḥamdallāhi was threatening control over the areas traditionally under the Dikko. Accordingly, he requested the support of Da, the king of Segou, in suppressing the emerging power of Aḥmad Lobbo, by sending his half-brother Buubu Arɗo Galo to the Bambara capital.[109] However, no sign of support arrived from Segou and, under the pressure of the notables of Masina, Arɗo Ngurori pledged allegiance to Aḥmad Lobbo in 1824.

Submitting to Ḥamdallāhi was not an option for Arɗo Ngurori's half brother, Buubu Arɗo Galo, hero of Fulani oral epics.[110] He took the place of Arɗo Ngurori at the head of the Dikko's resistance to Aḥmad Lobbo and, in 1824–5, rebelled against Ḥamdallāhi.[111] His revolt was eventually suppressed by an army sent by Aḥmad Lobbo, which defeated the rebels and killed Buubu Arɗo Galo near Ténenkou, an event that is very prominent in oral traditions. The death and beheading of Buubu Arɗo Galo is described in one of the most dramatic passages of all West African oral epics:

> He said, "Horseman of Sekou [i.e. Aḥmad Lobbo]"
> And they replied, "Yes sir."
> "Today I only want to die in one way."

109 The relationship between Arɗo Ngurori and Aḥmad Lobbo is described in *L'empire peul*, 103–114.

110 On Buubu Arɗo Galo's resistance, see *L'empire peul*, 119–120. Christiane Seydou has recorded several episodes of the epic of Buubu Arɗo Galo (Christiane Seydou, *L'epopée peule de Boûbou Ardo Galo: hèros et rebelle* [Paris: Karthala, 2010]). See another version in Bassirou Dieng and Ibrahima Wane, *L'épopée de Boubou Ardo: l'islamisation des traditions de l'Ouest Africain* (Amiens: Presses du "Centre d'Études Médiévales" de l'Université de Picardie – Jules Verne, 2004).

111 The date can be inferred by the simultaneity of Buubu Arɗo Galo's rebellion with the dated one of Gelaajo discussed below and Aḥmad b. Alfagha (*L'empire peul*, 120), on which see, respectively, below and Chapter 5.

And they said, "How is that?"
"Betit-Bai [i.e. the horse] has returned home alone, and I will not go back on foot.
The only sure thing is what my father told me,
That, unless it is [on] my head that you hit me,
I will never die."
So they hit his head with a spear,
And killed him.
They beheaded him and put the head in a purse attached to the saddle.
The body, they left it there.
It was the people of his village who salvaged the body and buried it.[112]

With the death of Arɗo Ngurori and the defeat of Buubu Arɗo Galo, the long line of *arɗo*s founded by Maghan Diallo was extinguished. A similar fate befell the other Fulani power of the region, Kounari. In 1824–5, at the same time as the resistance of the Dikko was being crushed, Gelaajo rebelled against Ḥamdallāhi.[113] The origin of the tension between them dates to the time when the *pereejo* of Kounari pledged allegiance to the caliph after having fled from Noukouma, allowing the annexation of his territories as a province of the emerging caliphate. In return, Gelaajo expected to be compensated for his allegiance by being confirmed as governor of the province; but instead, the cousins of Aḥmad Lobbo, al-Ḥājj Mūdi and then Guuro Malaaɗo, were awarded control.

While Gelaajo was planning his revolt, the news of his intentions reached Ḥamdallāhi, so the *pereejo* was summoned and found guilty of insurrection. A death sentence was handed down, but oral traditions record that Gelaajo remained free and under surveillance in the capital, awaiting his execution, until he managed to escape on the day of the Festival of Sacrifice and return to his capital at Goundaka.[114] A new military encounter then took place between the armies of the Caliphate of Ḥamdallāhi and Kounari, the former led by Ousman Bokari and the latter by Gelaajo's brother, 'Uthmān. The battle took place very close to Ḥamdallāhi, and resulted in a victory for the caliphate. Eventually, Gelaajo managed to escape from the territory controlled by Aḥmad

[112] Seydou, *L'épopée peule de Boûbou Ardo Galo*, 273.
[113] The rebellion of Gelaajo is described in *L'empire peul*, 114–128. For the date of the rebellion, see *Dhikr*, p. 2; and *Mā waqaʿa*, p. 5.
[114] On the role of Muḥammad al-Kuntī in mediating between Aḥmad Lobbo and Gelaajo, see Chapter 4.

Lobbo. He crossed the Béléhédé River, which marked the border with the Sokoto Caliphate, and eluded an army that was sent for him. In the territory controlled by Muḥammad Bello, Gelaajo settled close to Say (Niger), where he founded Wouro Guéladio, in a region that become later known as New Kounari.

Scholarship based on oral traditions has framed the conflict between Aḥmad Lobbo and the old Fulani elite as a war between Muslims and non-Muslims. For example, oral traditions transform Buubu Arɗo Galo's rebellion into an existential resistance of Fulani against Islam, as epitomized in the following verses:

> It was the time
> When all Masina had converted
> Boubou Arɗo Galo declared that he would never convert
> That he will never eat the millet obtained from charity.[115]

In fact, the situation was more complex. The Fulani of the region were already Muslims by the early nineteenth century, and regarded Muslim scholars as authoritative figures in the religious sphere. For example, Gelaajo went to Timbuktu to consult with Muḥammad al-Kuntī and to seek support and legitimization for his revolt against Aḥmad Lobbo, in either 1234/1818–19 or 1235/1819–20.[116] This mission was a failure, yet it shows the recognition of the Kunta *shaykh*'s authority by the Kounari prince. The issue at stake, then, is not the religious affiliations of the old Fulani elite, but the disputed role of Muslim scholars and their relationship with political power. The accepted position of clerics is exemplified by a statement of Arɗo Giɗaaɗo, the Fulani prince who triggered the Simay incident, who in a moment of anger, said: "I want Amadou Hammadi Boubou [Aḥmad Lobbo] to know that the role of a marabout must be to bless marriages, to wash the body of the dead, to baptize the newborn, and, above all to live off handfuls of food begging here and there, door by door, in the villages, but nothing more."[117] Consequently, the very fact that a Muslim scholar could have mobilized the people of the Middle Niger and established a theocracy such as the Caliphate of Ḥamdallāhi represented the final checkmate to the traditional power represented by the old Fulani military elites, which

[115] Dieng and Wane, *L'épopée de Boubou Ardo*, 21.
[116] *Dhikr*, p. 2; and *Mā waqa'a*, p. 5.
[117] *L'empire peul*, 29–30. Compare with similar examples from Fouta Toro and Gonja (Ghana) reported in Levtzion, "Islam in West African politics," 336.

was based on kinship and warfare. At stake was a very different concept of authority.

When the old Fulani warrior elites were defeated, and the scholars emerged victorious, the latter contributed to the formulation of a new kind of narrative of the Fulani's past.[118] The oral traditions that circulated from Ḥamdallāhi's time onward homogeneously portray the heroes and the events dating to before the emergence of Aḥmad Lobbo as belonging to a past of "paganism" or, to use a local term, "ignorance" – hence the name given in Fulfulde to this pre-Ḥamdallāhi'era, *jahiliyaku*, from the Arabic *jāhiliyya* or the "period of ignorance," a concept used in Islamic discourses to refer to the time preceding the mission of the Prophet Muḥammad. These traditions do not discredit the value attached to classic *pulaaku* or the "ideal way of being Fulani."[119] However, they portray a substantial break with the values traditionally attached to the old Fulani warrior elites by projecting it back into a stigmatized pseudo pre-Islamic past. But one should not mistake this representation of Fulani history before Ḥamdallāhi as a factual narrative of a past in which Islam was not spread among the Fulani. These traditions are the deliberate result of the state-sponsored circulation of an official narrative celebrating the new order that emerged after the victory of Aḥmad Lobbo.

This manipulation of the past via oral traditions is epitomized by the story of the last days of Arɗo Ngurori. In the aftermath of his submission to Aḥmad Lobbo, traditions report that the last *arɗo* moved to Ḥamdallāhi after what they described as a "conversion to Islam, where he devoted the rest of his life to studying Islamic sciences with Aḥmad Lobbo."[120] Eventually, when Arɗo Ngurori died, traditions collected

118 As Brown argues, the available traditions are "essentially dynastic and political, and intimately connected with a state structure . . . This history legitimizes the privileged position which the scholarly class still enjoy in traditional society" (Brown, "The Caliphate of Hamdullahi," 8).

119 Seydou explains the term *pulaaku*, or "Fulanity," as a "socio-ethical code, the ideal and distinctive way of being a Fulani [including] courage, constancy, self-control, discretion, modesty, intelligence in its dimension of good judgment (μῆτις), pride, sense of honor" (Christiane Seydou, "L'épopée chez les Peuls du Massina (Mali): une approche ethnopoétique," *Cahiers d'études Africaines* 55 [2015]: 29–43, 32). For a historiographical analysis of the term *pulaaku* and a critique of the above definition, see Anneke Breedveld and Mirjam E. de Bruijn, "L'image des Fulbe: analyse critique de la construction du concept de 'Pulaaku'," *Cahiers d'études africaines* 36/144 (1996): 791–821.

120 *L'empire peul*, 112.

by Hampaté Ba and Daget narrate that Aḥmad Lobbo descended into the grave during Arɗo Ngurori's funeral to receive the corpse of the *arɗo* and, "at the very moment of laying the body down in its final abode, he said: '*Dugga*! The first *arɗo* to enter the Paradise of God!'"[121] In other words, this tradition, instead of providing an accurate depiction of the spread of Islam among the Fulani, describes the end of an era: that of the *arɗo*s, traditionally repositories of political power, and the emergence of a new figure, Aḥmad Lobbo, who personifies the new conflation of political and Islamic authority. However, the resistance of the old Fulani military aristocracy was not the only challenge that Aḥmad Lobbo encountered within the territories conquered by Ḥamdallāhi. From the Niger Bend and the Azawād, loosely controlled by the caliphate, a subtler challenge emerged among the leaders of the Arab–Berber Kunta clan.

[121] *L'empire peul*, 114. "Dugga" is a Fulfulde exclamation used to refer to the first person who receives something in this case, Islam (*L'empire peul*, 114, n. 1).

4 *Aḥmad Lobbo, Timbuktu, and the Kunta*

This chapter analyzes how Aḥmad Lobbo's claims to authority were received by the Arab–Berber Kunta clan. Since the late eighteenth century, Kunta scholars from the Niger Bend and the Azawād had represented the dominant religious authority in the Middle Niger. Their counsel and mediation were sought from the Western Sahara as far as the Central Sudanic region and the Nilotic Sudan. Likewise, their commercial networks extended from the Middle Niger to the Atlantic shores of the desert and Sokoto. However, by the late 1810s the establishment of the Caliphate of Ḥamdallāhi would challenge this order. The imposition of Ḥamdallāhi's dominion on the Niger Bend resulted in the Kunta's de facto recognition of Aḥmad Lobbo's rule, but this acceptance did not imply that the Kunta *shaykh*s also recognized his religious authority, a domain over which they continued to claim a monopoly. This struggle came to the fore over the issue of tobacco's legality in Islam; it was also fueled by Muḥammad al-Kuntī's failure to intercede with Aḥmad Lobbo on behalf of the rebels Gelaajo and Aḥmad b. Alfagha (one of the local scholars, mentioned in Chapter 3, who were sought out by 'Uthmān b. Fūdī as potential leaders of a revolution in the Middle Niger and who at first joined Aḥmad Lobbo).

The relationship between Ḥamdallāhi and the Kunta is a complex feature of nineteenth-century West African history. As Diakité posits it, "there is a controversy on the nature of the relationship between the Kunta and the Dīna."[1] Some scholars have claimed that the Kunta had always been hostile to Ḥamdallāhi, a position exemplified by the narrative of Hampaté Ba and Daget, who describe the Kunta as consistently plotting against Aḥmad Lobbo.[2] This narrative assumes a racialized tone, exemplified by their description of the Kunta's motives for confronting Hamdallahi: "This family, which had spread

[1] Diakite, "al-Mukhtār b. Yerkoy Talfi," 189. [2] *L'empire peul*, 211–231.

Islam in these regions, and which had a considerable number of saints, could not allow themselves to be supplanted without reaction by Fulani shepherds only converted the day before."[3] Hampaté Ba and Daget neglect to mention that, most of the time, the Kunta officially supported Aḥmad Lobbo, as I will demonstrate below. By contrast, other scholars have depicted the relationship between Ḥamdallāhi and the Kunta as one of continuous support: a position held especially by Abdallah Wuld Maulûd Wuld Daddah.[4] He overtly criticizes Hampaté Ba and Daget's conclusions, arguing that the Kunta leader "Š. Sîdi Muḥammed was in support of the State of Macina [Ḥamdallāhi], to which he never spared moral support nor the advantage of his prestige."[5] A more balanced and nuanced story emerges from my analysis of a large corpus of correspondence, which confirms the position of Ali Sanakare, who posits in his study on the topic that the relationships between Ḥamdallāhi and the Kunta have to be understood as "varied and contradictory."[6] They are also tied up with Ḥamdallāhi's expansionism in the Niger Bend, which started immediately after Noukouma.

Expansionism in the North

While Ḥamdallāhi's armies were busy crushing the last resistance of the Dikko and the Sidibe in Masina, Aḥmad Lobbo was also expanding his influence in the areas of the Erg of Bara. Establishing control over this land was challenging, yet it was crucial for the Caliphate of Ḥamdallāhi: it was used to graze the Fulani cattle in the rainy season, when the southern pastures were inundated by flooding. Furthermore, securing the territories of the Erg of Bara also created a buffer zone between the caliphate and the areas controlled by the Tuareg, who would move into the area to pasture their animals during the dry season and often threatened the northern frontiers of the caliphate.[7]

It is possible to infer that Aḥmad Lobbo had attempted to extend his control to the Erg of Bara at a very early stage, albeit unsuccessfully.

3 *L'empire peul*, 211.
4 Introduction to *Fatḥ al-Ṣamad*, 33, n. 3; and Diakite, "al-Mukhtār b. Yerkoy Talfi," 190–191.
5 Wuld Daddah, "Šayh Sîdi Muhammed," 84.
6 Ali Sankare, "Rapports entre les Peul du Macina et les Kounta (1818–1864)," *Sankore* 3 (1986): 1–58, 26.
7 See, for example, *L'empire peul*, 83, where there is reference to the efforts of one Sambourou Kolado to protect the region from Tuareg raids.

The anonymous chronicle called the *Tārīkh Walāta* (Chronicle of Walāta) refers to the defeat suffered by a Fulani army, most likely soldiers of Aḥmad Lobbo, at the hands of the Tuareg in late 1818: it was a disastrous rout, with 1,770 Fulani killed and only one Tuareg.[8] A new intervention by the Ḥamdallāhi forces in the Erg of Bara began in 1822–3, when a mission led by al-Ḥājj b. Sa'īd, a cousin of Aḥmad Lobbo, destroyed the movement of the Diawando scholar al-Ḥusayn Koita, who had rebelled against Aḥmad Lobbo in Fittouga, the region east of Niafounké.[9]

The campaign against al-Ḥusayn Koita was also the beginning of an effective northward expansionist phase for the Caliphate of Ḥamdallāhi. According to a narrative provided by Hampaté Ba and Daget, Aḥmad Lobbo entrusted Aḥmad b. Alfagha with the task of gaining the support of the population living north of Lake Débo.[10] However, the relationship between the caliph and his appointed deputy was soon to degenerate. Aḥmad b. Alfagha was a scholar from the Erg of Bara who had already started gaining a following of his own in the region, before the emergence of the caliphate, and he easily cultivated support there, especially among sedentary populations and the Fulani. In response, a group of Tuareg, led by one Woyfan, rejected the rule of the caliphate and attacked Aḥmad b. Alfagha at his headquarters in Thioki, west of the Issa Ber. The Tuareg were defeated and fled to the north, but it was not long before they joined forces with the ambitious Aḥmad b. Alfagha to free the area from Ḥamdallāhi's influence.

According to oral traditions, Aḥmad b. Alfagha delivered the following speech in the mosque on a certain Friday:

> God decided that one Amadou would raise the banner of the Dina in the Niger Bend. For descent, knowledge, and wealth, I am that Amadou, the most qualified for this effort. Amadou Hammadi Boubou [i.e. Aḥmad

[8] Raḥāl Bū Barīk (ed.), *al-Madīna fī mujtama' al-badāwa: al-Tārīkh al-ijtimā'ī li-Walāta khilāla al-qarnayn 18 wa-19 ma'a taqdīm wa-nashr tārīkh Walāta* (Rabaṭ: Manshūrāt Ma'hd al-Dirāsāt al-Ifrīqīya, 2002), 53.

[9] *Dhikr*, p. 2; *Mā waqa'a*, pp. 5–6. Diawando (pl. Diawambe) is a term that refers to individuals belonging to a group of ambiguous status, between an endogamous group and an ethnicity, which live in the areas inhabited by the Fulani. Devoted to different subsistence activities, the Diawambe are often associated to the Fulani, for whom they act as counselors and ambassadors. In the Arabic sources, Diawando appears as *zaghrānī* (see Tamari, *Les castes*, 102–106).

[10] On these events, see *L'empire peul*, 199–204.

Lobbo] is a usurper. If he wants peace and to enjoy his victories, he should entrust the northern territories to me. I will leave him the ones in the south and we will live in good agreement. In any case, he will see what I am capable of.[11]

Aḥmad Lobbo, informed about the insurrection in the north, sent an army to take Tyouki. Aḥmad b. Alfagha and the Tuareg chief Woyfan were defeated in what traditionalists remember as the battle of the "millet stalks," since Aḥmad Lobbo had allegedly ordered his soldiers not to use weapons but only pointed stalks of millet to avoid the spilling of Muslim blood.[12] No source dates the rebellion of Aḥmad b. Alfagha, but it must have occurred in 1824–5, as can be inferred by the fact that it happened at the same time as that of Gelaajo.[13]

The military expedition that defeated Aḥmad b. Alfagha opened the way for Ḥamdallāhi's conquest of the Niger Bend. In order to secure the northern part of the Middle Niger, Aḥmad Lobbo sent the bulk of his army to occupy the inner part of the Niger Bend, between the river and Lake Do. There, his army defeated another group of Tuareg in a series of battles near Bambara Maoundé. This success is known as the battle of Ndukkuwal in Fulfulde, meaning "luck that was unhoped for and considerably profitable," thanks to the Fulani's seizure of 4,000 cattle and 15,000 horses, as well as silver, gold, and captives – including Adya, the wife of the Tuareg supreme chief, Ṣirim.[14] Undated in the detailed accounts gleaned from oral tradition, this event occurred in 1825–6, as written sources testify.[15] After the battle, the northern territories pledged allegiance to Aḥmad Lobbo, who thus became the sovereign of a fragile state extending from the southern shores of the Niger's Inland Delta as far downriver, oral sources claim, as Gao.[16] The overall region was put under the authority of a military chief named Aamadu Alkaali, the first in a series of appointments made by the caliph of Ḥamdallāhi.

[11] *L'empire peul*, 201. [12] *L'empire peul*, 202. [13] *L'empire peul*, 119.

[14] On Ndukkuwal, see *L'empire peul*, 204–205.

[15] *Dhikr*, p. 3; *Mā waqa'a*, p. 6.

[16] In the oral tradition, the events that led to the allegiance of the Tuareg, who had in fact put together a large coalition to avenge Ndukkuwal, are unclear and follow a seemingly mythical event involving the young son of Aḥmad Lobbo, Hamidou, entering the enemy's camp and facing Ṣirim alone (see *L'empire peul*, 206–211).

As for the city of Timbuktu, Aḥmad Lobbo confirmed the Arma *pāshā*, 'Uthmān b. al-Qā'id Būbakar al-Rāmī, henceforth Pāshā 'Uthmān, as governor.[17] The French explorer credited with the "discovery" of Timbuktu, René Caillié (d. 1838), was received in the city by Pāshā 'Uthmān and left a very vivid description of the governor, an account almost unparalleled in our written sources:

> They [the Arab merchants of Timbuktu] have considerable influence over the native inhabitants of Timbuctoo, whose king or governor is a negro. This prince, who is named Osman, is much respected by his subjects. He is very simple in his manners: his dress is like that of the Moors of Morocco; and his house is no better furnished than those of the Moorish merchants. He is himself a merchant, and his sons trade with Jenné. He inherited a considerable fortune from his ancestors and is very rich. He has four wives, beside an infinite number of slaves, and is a zealous Mahometan ... The king appeared to be of an exceedingly amiable disposition; his age might be about fifty-five, and his hair was white and curly. He was of the middling height, and his colour was jet black. He had an aquiline nose, thin lips, a grey beard, and large eyes, and his whole countenance was pleasing; his dress, like those of the Moors, was composed of stuff of European manufacture. On his head was a red cap, bound round with a large piece of muslin in the form of a turban. His shoes were of morocco, shaped like our morning slippers, and made in the country.[18]

Aḥmad Lobbo appointed one of his local supporters to be *imām* of the Djinguereber Mosque, which was chosen as the only Friday mosque of the city – harking back to the caliph's earlier critique of blameworthy innovations.[19] This *imām*, Muḥammad b. Muḥammad b. 'Uthmān, known as San Shirfi (d. 1863), was a member of the family which would play a great role in the history of the *Tārīkh al-fattāsh* after the decline of Ḥamdallāhi.

[17] *L'empire peul*, 212.

[18] Caillié's narrative was first published as René Caillié, *Journal d'un voyage à Temboctou et à Jenné, dans l'Afrique Centrale, précédé d'observations faites chez mes Maures Braknas, les Nalous et d'autres peuples pendant les années 1824, 1825, 1826, 1827, 1828* (Paris: Imprimerie Royale, 1830). I used René Caillié, *Travels through Central Africa to Timbuctoo and Across the Great Desert, to Morocco, Performed in the Years 1824–1828*, trans. Edme-François Jomard, 2 vols. (London: Henry Colburn and Richard Bentley, 1830). The quote comes from Caillié, *Travels through Central Africa*, vol. 2, 53–54.

[19] *L'empire peul*, 212.

Despite these apparent successes, the events that followed the battle of Ndukkuwal are difficult to reconstruct, and there is evidence that the people of the north had not been entirely subdued. In particular, in the words of Hampaté Ba and Daget: "The Arma and all the people of the region of Timbuktu resisted fulfilling the religious prescriptions of Ḥamdallāhi."[20] This resistance took the form of refusals to pay *zakāt* (alms tax) to the caliphate and, after Ḥamdallāhi's attempts to enforce the payment, an open rebellion in Dire that spread throughout the region. At the same time, the Tuareg of Ṣirim seized this opportunity to withdraw their allegiance to Ḥamdallāhi, which in turn required an army to be sent to regain control of the north.[21]

These developments turned out to favor Aḥmad Lobbo. Muḥammad b. Muḥammad b. Muḥammad b. 'Uthmān San Shirfi, in a chronicle called *Tārīkh al-fūtāwī* (Chronicle of the Futanke Invasion), describes in detail the victorious entry which the caliph's general, al-Ḥājj Mūdi, made into Timbuktu when he was sent to take control of the city – most likely as a consequence of unreported victorious engagements in the north:

In 1241/1825–6, the *amīr* al-Ḥājj Mūdi arrived in Timbuktu at the head of a big army with a dispatch from *al-shaykh* Aḥmad [Lobbo]. There al-Ḥājj Mūdi called the *pāshā* of the place, 'Uthmān b. al-Qā'id Būbakar al-Rāmī and read him the dispatch. Pāshā 'Uthmān pledged allegiance and agreed to abandon the use of wax candles, the drums and other unlawful practices and changed all the reprehensible practices that they were doing before the arrival of the *amīr* [al-Ḥājj Mūdi].[22]

The conquest of Timbuktu in 1826 is also confirmed by a letter by the Scottish explorer Major Alexander Gordon Laing (d. 1826), written just a few days before his death in the Sahara.[23] He had arrived in

[20] *L'empire peul*, 212. [21] On these events, see *L'empire peul*, 211–217.

[22] IF, Fonds de Gironcourt, 2406 (72), Muḥammad b. San Shirfi, *Tārīkh al-fūtāwī* (henceforth *Tārīkh al-fūtāwī*). This work is a very important chronicle of Timbuktu, unpublished and incomplete. Three fragments of this chronicle were copied for de Gironcourt, and they record (1) the history of city from the emergence of Aḥmad Lobbo to 1863 (IF, Fonds de Gironcourt 2406 [72]); (2) the conquest of Ḥamdallāhi by al-Ḥājj 'Umar in 1862 (IF, Fonds de Gironcourt 2406 [71]); and (3) a skirmish between the army led by Aḥmad al-Bakkāy and that of al-Ḥājj 'Umar on 8 January 1863 (IF, Fonds de Gironcourt 2406 [70]).

[23] Letter quoted in Bovill, *Missions to the Niger*, vol. 1, 312. The early 1826 conquest of Timbuktu is also confirmed by Barth, *Travels and Discoveries*, vol. 4, 458.

Timbuktu on 13 August 1826. In his last correspondence with the British consul in Tripoli, Hanmer Warrington (d. 1847), dated 21 September, he writes: "My situation in Tinbūctū [has been] rendered exceedingly unsafe by the unfriendly disposition of the Foolahs [Fulani] of Massina, who have this year upset the dominion of the Tuaric and made themselves patrons of Tinbūctū, and whose Sultan has expressed his hostility towards me in no unequivocal terms."[24] Once again Timbuktu had pledged allegiance to Aḥmad Lobbo. The expansion of Ḥamdallāhi in the Niger Bend put Aḥmad Lobbo in close contact with the influential Kunta family.

Early Connections with the Kunta

While al-Mukhtār al-Kabīr had mainly conducted business from his camp in the Azawād, his son and successor, who had become leader in 1811, moved his headquarters to Timbuktu in either 1818–19 or 1819–20.[25] However, Aḥmad Lobbo's connections with the Kunta had begun much earlier, in what Ali Sankare's study refers to as "the friendly debut."[26] Indeed, the first correspondence that has survived between Aḥmad Lobbo and a Kunta representative is a letter that Muḥammad al-Kuntī wrote on 8 April 1818, just a few weeks after the battle of Noukouma.[27] The letter follows the "mirrors for princes" genre of literature, consisting of advice (*naṣīḥa*) from a scholar to a high-ranking administrator or ruler, which was widespread both in medieval and early modern Europe as well as in the Islamic world until the nineteenth century.[28] As Abdel Wadoud Ould Cheikh observes, these letters follow a standard formula in which the scholar would first recommend "moderation and balance, associated with the fundamental values of fairness (*'adl*), within the strict adherence to the legal standards defined in Sunnite Islam."[29] In this specific letter,

[24] Letter quoted in Bovill, *Missions to the Niger*, vol. 1, 312.
[25] Ismā'īl b. al-Mukhtār b. Wadī'at Allāh records the date 1818–19 (*Mā wāqa'a*, p. 4); al-Muṣṭafà b. 'Abd Allāh locates Muḥammad al-Kuntī's settlement in Timbuktu to the following year (*Dhikr*, p. 2).
[26] Sankare, "Rapports entre les Peul du Macina," 26.
[27] IF, Fonds de Gironcourt 2405 (25), ff. 152a–159b.
[28] On the mirrors for princes genre in Islamic history, see Louise Marlow, "Surveying recent literature on the Arabic and Persian mirrors for princes genre," *History Compass* 7/2 (2009): 523–538.
[29] Ould Cheikh, "A Man of Letters in Timbuktu," 239.

Muḥammad al-Kuntī asks Aḥmad Lobbo to mediate on behalf of the "people of Timbuktu" concerning the inheritance of a certain al-Ḥājj Muḥammad, who had died in Djenné.[30] This correspondence also indicates that the inhabitants of Timbuktu had pledged allegiance to the Fulani leader as early as April 1818 – an allegiance most likely broken after the defeat of the Fulani army by the Tuareg mentioned in the *Tārīkh Walāta*.[31]

The good relationship between Aḥmad Lobbo and Muḥammad al-Kuntī in the early years of the caliphate is confirmed by another letter from the Kunta *shaykh*, written on the occasion of the Fulani conquest of Djenné and thus datable to either 1819 or 1821.[32] It asks Aḥmad Lobbo not to touch the Kuntas' wealth, agents, or the slaves residing in Djenné, Timbuktu, or Sansanding. This document is particularly relevant because it begins by congratulating Aḥmad Lobbo on his recent expansion of Fulani power, and addresses him as "caliph."[33] The use of this term signals Muḥammad al-Kuntī's endorsement or even flattery of Aḥmad Lobbo, and must be understood within the context of West African Islamic revolutions: by calling Aḥmad Lobbo a caliph, Muḥammad al-Kuntī was recognizing the Islamic legitimacy of his rule in contrast to that of previous rulers, Muslim or non-Muslim, such as the Fulani *ardo*s or the *fama*s of Segou, who were thus denigrated as oppressive and illegitimate.[34]

This early correspondence also suggests that Aḥmad Lobbo had been in contact with Kunta scholars before the eruption of the conflict with the *ardo*s and Segou in 1818. It is plausible to posit that the Fulani leader had sought advice from Muḥammad al-Kuntī in the formative period of his movement, as he did from 'Abd Allāh b. Fūdī and 'Uthmān b. Fūdī. This might also explain Zebadia's statement that the future caliph of Ḥamdallāhi was a student of the Kunta, a relationship that is nowhere corroborated.[35] Their alliance was also strengthened by the very presence of the Kunta student Nūḥ b. al-Ṭāhir at Aḥmad Lobbo's side. Indeed, the connection between Aḥmad Lobbo and the Kunta was

30 IF, Fonds de Gironcourt, 2405 (25).
31 IF, Fonds de Gironcourt, 2405 (25), p. 12.
32 Bibliothèque de manuscrits de Djenné, KAN1, MS 163. Djenné was conquered twice, in 1819 and 1821 (*L'empire peul*, 151–154).
33 Bibliothèque de manuscrits de Djenné, KAN1, MS 163, f. 1b.
34 Hiskett, *The Development of Islam*, 173.
35 Zebadia, "Career and Correspondence," 87.

beneficial for both parties. If receiving the endorsement of the influential Kunta *shaykh* helped to legitimize the Fulani reformer's role as a Muslim authority, the emergence of Ḥamdallāhi was beneficial from an economic standpoint on the Kunta side. Muḥammad al-Kuntī and, most likely, the traders of Timbuktu, had realized that Aḥmad Lobbo could provide renewed political stability in the southern Middle Niger following the decline of the pāshālik and the rise to prominence of the Tuareg after the defeat of the Arma in second half of the eighteenth century, which is described as a "period of anarchy" by the Timbuktu scholar Aḥmad Bābēr in his *al-Sa'āda al-abadiyya*.[36]

The Kunta were, in their own commercial interests, "constantly in favour of peace and stability in the area."[37] However, the expansion of Ḥamdallāhi territories to the north around 1825 threatened the interests of the Kunta, in particular through Aḥmad Lobbo's interdiction of the production, consumption, and commercialization of tobacco. Given this situation, the relationship between Muḥammad al-Kuntī and Ḥamdallāhi was destined to deteriorate. However, what Sankare calls "the road towards the tension" between the two was a long one, since the deterioration was slow.[38]

Smoking, Chewing, and Sniffing Tobacco

The ban on tobacco was a crucial aspect of Ḥamdallāhi's policy. Aḥmad Lobbo declared it illegal, according to oral traditions, in the third year of the caliphate, i.e. 1821.[39] So strong was the aversion of Ḥamdallāhi to tobacco that Muḥammad b. 'Abd Allāh Sa'īd al-Fūtī (d. 1852), a scholar related to the court, wrote a poem against its use, the *Qaṣīda fī taḥrīm sham al-tibgh* (Poem on Outlawing the Sniffing on Tobacco).[40] From its very introduction in Africa and the Middle East in the sixteenth century, the consumption of tobacco by smoking, chewing, or sniffing had generated great controversy among Muslim scholars.[41] The debate was particularly heated in Timbuktu and its

36 IHERI-ABT 2752, f. 10a. 37 Zebadia, "Career and Correspondence," 83.
38 Sankare, "Rapports entre les Peul du Macina," 29.
39 Sankare, "Rapports entre les Peul du Macina," 30.
40 IHERI-ABT 1224. For a biography of the author, see Diagayeté [Jakāyatī], "al-Fulāniyyūn," 111–112.
41 On the tobacco controversy, with a special focus on North and West Africa in the late sixteenth and early seventeenth century, see, Aziz A. Batran, *Tobacco Smoking under Islamic Law: Controversy over its Introduction* (Beltsville, MD:

region because tobacco first entered Muslim lands via the Sahara. Originally of American origin, it was introduced in West Africa by European traders, and eventually reached North Africa as consequence of the Moroccan invasion of the Songhay in 1591.[42]

Not surprisingly, then, the earliest *fatwà* ever recorded on the issue comes from West Africa. A late sixteenth-century *qāḍī* of Timbuktu, Muḥammad b. Aḥmad b. ʿAbd al-Raḥmān (d. 1608), declared tobacco illegal.[43] Although his original juridical opinion is not available, it is often referenced by other scholars.[44] Contrary to this opinion, among others, is that of Aḥmad Bābā, the influential Timbuktu scholar who issued a *fatwà* titled *al-Lamaʿ fī al-ishāra li-ḥukm al-tibgh* (The Luminous Rays Darting on the Legal Status of Tobacco).[45] Completed on 7 October 1607, while Aḥmad Bābā was on his way back from Timbuktu after several years spent as a prisoner in Marrakesh, this work asserts the legality of tobacco consumption on the basis that this substance is neither a fermented drink nor a narcotic. Eventually, Aḥmad Bābā expanded this argument in the *ʿAyn al-iṣāba fī ḥukm ṭāba* (Hitting the Target in the Ruling on Tobacco), which he sent to another legal authority who had declared tobacco illegal, the al-Azhar scholar al-Laqānī (d. 1631–2).[46]

In spite of the negative opinions of several legal authorities, the use of tobacco in West and North Africa spread "with phenomenal speed."[47] In the areas covered by Ḥamdallāhi, for example, sources describe the Bambara, as well as the Tuareg and the Arabs of the Sahara, as avid tobacco smokers.[48] By the time of Aḥmad Lobbo, tobacco had become one of the most important commodities traded across the Sahara, as Caillié asserts in his descriptions of Timbuktu and Arawān.[49] The French explorer also reports the cultivation of tobacco fields around the city, noting that the quality of local tobacco was inferior to that

Amana Publications, 2003). See also Dorrit van Dalen, *Doubt, Scholarship and Society in 17th-Century Central Sudanic Africa* (Leiden and Boston: Brill, 2016), 154–187.

42 Batran, *Tobacco Smoking*, 19. 43 Batran, *Tobacco Smoking*, 24.

44 Batran, *Tobacco Smoking*, 38, n. 29.

45 *ALA* IV, 24, item 29. Full translation of the *fatwà* is in Batran, *Tobacco Smoking*, 169–190.

46 *ALA* IV, 20, item 4. 47 Batran, *Tobacco Smoking*, 27.

48 See *L'empire peul*, 140; and Caillié, *Travels through Central Africa*, vol. 2, 58 and 67.

49 Caillié, *Travels through Central Africa*, vol. 2, 54 and 101–102.

from across the desert.[50] Among the merchants who benefited from trading in tobacco, most likely both locally produced and imported, were the Kunta, who counted it among their most important products.[51]

With Aḥmad Lobbo and the Kunta positioned on opposite sides of this debate, one might wonder if the ban on tobacco could have been an attempt by Aḥmad Lobbo to curtail the prosperity of the Kunta. By contrast, Muḥammad al-Kuntī composed a work, now lost, in support of tobacco's trade and consumption: *Jalā' al-abṣar wa-shifā' al-ṣudūr fī taḥrīr aḥkām al-sham wa-l-qahāwī w-l-ghūru* (The Clearing Eyes and the Cure of Breasts in the Clarification of Rulings on Sniffing Tobacco and Consuming Coffee and Kola).[52] He also addressed this issue in several letters to Aḥmad Lobbo. In particular, the Kunta *shaykh* makes his position explicit in a letter datable to around 1824–5 because it makes reference to Gelaajo's rebellion: "I advise you to allow traders and the public to trade as they wish among lawful products over which there is disagreement among the scholars, as the prohibitions cause harm to these traders. Keep in mind that the use of these products predates your arrival to power."[53] He concludes by saying that "tobacco is a herb and herbs are legal except for those that are [explicitly] prohibited by law."[54] This dispute was not the only instance in which disagreement arose between Muḥammad al-Kuntī and Aḥmad Lobbo. Differences are also evident in several cases involving the Kunta *shaykh*'s mediation on behalf of the rebels who rose against Ḥamdallāhi.

Mediating between Ḥamdallāhi and the Rebels

In their *L'empire peul du Macina*, Hampaté Ba and Daget portray Muḥammad al-Kuntī as supporting – even fomenting – rebellions against Aḥmad Lobbo in the north.[55] In fact, written sources show Muḥammad al-Kuntī supporting Ḥamdallāhi until just a few months before this death, when the relationship degenerated. Prior to this

[50] Caillié, *Travels through Central Africa*, vol. 2, 58.
[51] McDougall, "Economics of Islam," 53.
[52] The work is not known today to my best knowledge. It is referred to in IHERI-ABT 5163, p. 30.
[53] IHERI-ABT 10870, 10a (IHERI-ABT 461 is an incomplete copy of the same letter).
[54] IHERI-ABT 10870, 13b. [55] *L'empire peul*, 212.

rupture, Muḥammad al-Kuntī had performed the role of mediator in local disputes, a practice inaugurated by his father, al-Mukhtār al-Kabīr, on the occasion of the siege of Timbuktu in 1771.

The first time that Muḥammad al-Kuntī took a stand in favor of Ḥamdallāhi is related to the case of al-Ḥusayn Koita, the Diawando scholar who rebelled against Aḥmad Lobbo in 1820. In a letter addressed to the Diawando leader, Muḥammad al-Kuntī warned him "not to dispute the qualified emirs. And al-shaikh Alfa Ahmad Lebbu [*sic*] is the Amir in these areas."[56] Muḥammad al-Kuntī went on to mediate between Aḥmad Lobbo and his opponent: "We are going to write to al-shaikh Ahmad Lebbu [*sic*], recommending him to pay attention to you and to entrust you with the administration of the area," i.e. the Fittouga.[57] However, Aḥmad Lobbo seems not to have accepted this offer of mediation, and eventually al-Ḥusayn Koita was killed. Even so, Muḥammad al-Kuntī respected Aḥmad Lobbo's decision to neutralize the rebel, as a later letter of his testifies.[58] The tone of this letter is cordial, and Muḥammad al-Kuntī addresses Aḥmad Lobbo as "caliph of the caliphs."[59] He acknowledges that the Fulani leader's stance against the rebel was correct and quotes, in support of his decision, the Qur'ān and such *ḥadīth*s as "Whoever you see splitting away from the community or trying to create division among the Nation of Muhammad – Peace be upon him, then kill him, for the Hand of God is with the community, and the devil is with the one who splits away from the Islamic Nation, running with him."[60]

Around 1825, shortly after the end of al-Ḥusayn Koita's quashed revolt, the rebellions of Gelaajo and of Aḥmad b. Alfagha were also condemned by Muḥammad al-Kuntī, who attempted to persuade them not to break their alliance with Aḥmad Lobbo. In a letter to Gelaajo and his brother 'Uthmān, the Kunta leader explicitly discourages the

[56] Quoted in Stewart, "Frontier disputes," 505. Stewart interprets this letter differently, as a step towards Muḥammad al-Kuntī's support of the separatist movement of al-Ḥusayn Koita (Stewart, "Frontier disputes," 506).

[57] Quoted in Stewart, "Frontier disputes," 505.

[58] IF, Fonds de Gironcourt, 2405 (22–24)/II, ff. 151b–140b. A response to this letter by Aḥmad Lobbo survives in French translation, but with the wrong date, in Ibrahima M. Ouane, *L'Énigme du Macina* (Monte Carlo: Regain Ouane, 1952), 131–138.

[59] IF, Fonds de Gironcourt, 2405 (22–24)/II, f. 148b.

[60] IF, Fonds de Gironcourt, 2405 (22–24)/II, ff. 143a–142b.

Kounari prince from rebelling.[61] He urges "a sincere and total adhesion to God, the Prophet and your *amīr* [Aḥmad Lobbo]" and invites them "not to commit anything that can displease your just *amīr*, Aḥmad Lobbo."[62] In another missive addressed to Gelaajo and one al-Rashīd, Muḥammad al-Kuntī says that "obedience to the *amīr* [Aḥmad Lobbo] is obedience to God."[63] Likewise, it seems that Muhammad al-Kuntī also tried to convince Aḥmad b. Alfagha not to rebel. In a long letter addressing the virtues of *jihād*, Muḥammad al-Kuntī warns him against spilling Muslim blood and argues that obeying a tyrant is better than fighting against him if this would lead to violence against other Muslims.[64] This letter, although lacking any overt reference to Aḥmad Lobbo, seems nonetheless to suggest that Muḥammad al-Kuntī was discouraging rebellion against Ḥamdallāhi.

After both rebellions broke out, Muḥammad al-Kuntī continued playing the role of mediator. Several letters show him advising Aḥmad Lobbo to be lenient with Gelaajo and Aḥmad b. Alfagha.[65] In one of these exchanges we learn that Aḥmad b. Alfagha had even sought protection from Muḥammad al-Kuntī.[66] In another, the Kunta *shaykh* requested that Aḥmad Lobbo reinstate Aḥmad b. Alfagha to his position at the head of the Farimaké, the region west of the Lake Débo.[67] Likewise, he suggests that Aḥmad Lobbo should not remove Gelaajo from his position.[68]

Another letter sent from Muḥammad al-Kuntī, in mid-Rabīʿ II 1241/ November–December 1825, clarifies the circumstances surrounding Aḥmad Lobbo's sentencing of rebel leaders.[69] Aḥmad Lobbo had not accepted the mediation attempt, and declared that the rebellions of Aḥmad b. Alfagha and Gelaajo were tantamount to expressions of

[61] The original Arabic text of letter is not available. A partial translation in French exists in Wuld Daddah, "Šayh Sîdi Muhammed," 162–163.

[62] Wuld Daddah, "Šayh Sîdi Muhammed," 163.

[63] IHERI-ABT 2735, f. 1a. This letter also refers to some military engagements and to securing the territory, but no direct evidence exists that these military activities can be related to the conflict against Aḥmad Lobbo.

[64] IF, Fonds de Gironcourt, 2405 (39), ff. 210a–220b.

[65] IF, Fonds de Gironcourt, 2405 (22–24)/I; IF, Fonds de Gironcourt 2405 (22–24)/II; IHERI-ABT 289 (partially translated in Wuld Daddah, "Šayh Sîdi Muhammed," 135–156); IHERI-ABT 10870.

[66] IF, Fonds de Gironcourt, 2405 (22–24)/I.

[67] IF, Fonds de Gironcourt, 2405 (22–24)/II.

[68] IHERI-ABT 10870, f. 2a.

[69] Boutilimit 62, (an incomplete copy is IHERI-ABT 289; the latter is partially translated in Wuld Daddah, "Šayh Sîdi Muhammed," 135–156).

disbelief; consequently the two rebels were to be put to death.[70] In that letter, Muḥammad al-Kuntī had pleaded for their lives, comparing these cases to an event in early Islamic history, in Naḥrawān in 658, when a group of dissidents, the Khārijites, faced the army of the caliph ʿAlī b. Abī Ṭālib. After that battle, he argued, the surviving Khārijites were not declared infidels. Returning to the case of Gelaajo and Aḥmad b. Alfagha, Muḥammad al-Kuntī explains that their rebellions were caused by the misconception that Aḥmad Lobbo had paid allegiance to Sokoto and thus that his claims over the territories of the rebels were not sound.[71] The Kunta *shaykh* admits that Ḥamdallāhi has the legitimacy of an independent state.[72] Therefore, he acknowledges that the position of the rebels was wrong, but he reasons that their rebellions had been contained and that the unity of the caliphate was no longer in danger, so that it would be appropriate for Aḥmad Lobbo to show mercy and forgiveness to Gelaajo and Aḥmad b. Alfagha.[73]

The letter, however ineffectual, still shows the support of Muḥammad al-Kuntī for Aḥmad Lobbo, recalling his "joy" at the establishment of the caliphate and his hope for its lasting "eternity."[74] It calls the caliph of Ḥamdallāhi "the *amīr*, the righteous, the just, the one whom nobody can resist in the stage of the true caliph and the one of whom there is no equal in his state as an ascetic, in the position of sainthood, and in his rise to the position of caliph."[75] Consequently, the difference of opinion on the guilt of the rebels should not be read as Muḥammad al-Kuntī turning his back on Aḥmad Lobbo. In a contemporary document, the Kunta *shaykh* is explicit in emphasizing that the intercession of scholars with rulers is not meant to undermine their authority:

> The one who is offering intercession is not doing it out of disagreement about evil things, and it has nothing to do with leadership or claims . . . Intercession with the just *imām* is based on civility and generosity. The act of seeking intercession is in line with the rules of politics and leadership and enacts what the Prophet (Peace be upon him) has recommended in the meaning of intercession without a particular limit.[76]

[70] Boutilimit 62, 9, pp. 28–29.
[71] On the quarrel concerning Aḥmad Lobbo's allegiance to Sokoto, see Chapter 5.
[72] Boutilimit 62, 9, p. 27. [73] Boutilimit 62, 9, p. 28.
[74] Boutilimit 62, 9, p. 30. [75] Boutilimit 62, 9, p. 1.
[76] IHERI-ABT 10870, ff. 3a–3b.

Despite Muḥammad al-Kuntī's attempts to mollify him, Aḥmad Lobbo condemned Gelaajo to death – although the Kounari ruler managed to escape;[77] no information is available in the sources concerning the fate of Aḥmad b. Alfagha. However, the failed mediation of Muḥammad al-Kuntī shows the first signs of an increased tension between him and Aḥmad Lobbo, and the approach of a breakdown between Ḥamdallāhi and the Kunta.

A Breakdown

Given this history of cordial relations, what accounts for Muḥammad al-Kuntī's withdrawal of support for Aḥmad Lobbo? It seems likely that the war between the army of the caliph and the northern resistance disrupted the trade routes that were central to the interests of the Kunta. Moreover, the ban on tobacco was being enforced to the extent that, as Caillié reports, the people of Timbuktu did not consume tobacco during the mid-1820s.[78] These, then, were the factors that would eventually erode the *shaykh*'s support for the caliphate.

A letter from Muḥammad al-Kuntī, which might represent the last correspondence exchanged between the two, reflects a severely strained relationship.[79] The context seems to be the quarrel over *zakāt* that led to the northern revolt which was crushed by an army sent by Ḥamdallāhi and, eventually, to the conquest of Timbuktu in 1826. From this letter, it is possible to infer that Aḥmad Lobbo had asked the Kunta *shaykh* to help him rule over the newly conquered city. However, Muḥammad al-Kuntī defends the people of Timbuktu in the controversy over the payment of *zakāt* and refuses Aḥmad Lobbo's request for his help in governing the people of Timbuktu: "Regarding what you asked me, to govern Timbuktu [on your behalf], I already have another legacy that is not compatible with politics."[80] The Kunta *shaykh* contends that the spheres of religion and political power are different and that he sees himself as a religious leader. Yet, he recognizes, "We are obliged to collaborate, but everyone in his domain for the smooth running of Shari'a."[81] And he continues: "I have always

77 *L'empire peul*, 123–124.
78 Caillié, *Travels through Central Africa*, vol. 2, 58.
79 IHERI-ABT 5163.
80 IHERI-ABT 5163, p. 13.
81 IHERI-ABT 5163, p. 19.

assisted you with useful advice and I will continue it; but to govern the city, this I cannot, even if all of the kingdoms of the world are together."[82]

In this letter, the conciliatory tone of Muḥammad al-Kuntī is gone and the Kunta *shaykh* harshly criticizes Aḥmad Lobbo for having impoverished Timbuktu by the imposition of his interdiction of tobacco, which is described as more valuable than salt and kola (the two other major products of the time).[83] He compares the caliph's conservative attitude with that of the Moroccan sultan Mūlāy Sulaymān (d. 1822), who had also forbidden the use of tobacco but had reversed his position and declared it legal on the advice of the *'ulamā'*.[84] He continues: "You told me that you do not accept the authorization of tobacco in the region even if I [Muḥammad al-Kuntī] authorize it. You say you forbid it, but I strictly forbid you to do it."[85] And:

Regarding the ban on tobacco, I authorized its use and I do not accept that you have strictly prohibited it ... There is no explicit provision that prohibits tobacco. All the fundamental texts agree, the others that do not are all polemics. We did not hear *khulafā'* and those who came after them forbidding people anything that is lawful unless it contradicts the Consensus [*ijmā'*] and the Analogy [*qiyās*]. Tobacco is not of this order. It is a lawful herb, which God has authorized [us] to use ... Tobacco is not *ḥarām*.[86]

These events took place around the time when Muḥammad al-Kuntī fled Timbuktu, never to return.[87]

An account of the circumstances of Muḥammad al-Kuntī's death in May 1826 is included in the letter from Gordon Laing, written a few days before he himself was killed in the desert. The Scottish explorer had been in the Kunta camp, and describes it as having been decimated by a deadly disease:

About the time I last wrote to you [i.e. 10 May], when I was preparing (as I expected) to set off for Tinbuctoo, a dreadful malady something similar to yellow fever in its symptoms, broke out in this place ... Nearly half of the population have been swept away by its ravages, and among other Sidi

[82] IHERI-ABT 5163, p. 19. [83] IHERI-ABT 5163, p. 30.
[84] On Mūlāy Sulaymān's ban on tobacco, see Batran, *Tobacco Smoking*, 34.
[85] IHERI-ABT 5163, p. 10. [86] IHERI-ABT 5163, p. 28.
[87] *L'empire peul*, 215.

[Muḥammad b.] Mohtar [*sic*] himself, the Mrabot [*sic*] and *Shaykh* of the place.[88]

After the death of Muḥammad al-Kuntī, there was no representative of the Kunta in Timbuktu for almost a decade, during which time the city was subjected anew to the domination of Ḥamdallāhi. Muḥammad al-Kuntī's son and successor, al-Mukhtār al-Ṣaghīr b. Muḥammad b. al-Mukhtār b. Aḥmad b. Abī Bakr al-Kuntī (d. 1846), would not take up residence in city until 1833.

The Leadership of al-Mukhtār al-Ṣaghīr

Control over the region of Timbuktu remained a problem for Ḥamdallāhi throughout the lifetime of the caliph. After the conquest of Timbuktu in 1826 and until the early 1830s, control over the city and of the north was very limited. The real masters of the region continued to be the Tuareg under Ṣirim – to such an extent that some members of the Great Council complained, according to oral sources, that Ḥamdallāhi's authority in the north was merely "nominal."[89] This seems to be confirmed by Caillié's comment that Timbuktu was governed autonomously by Pāshā 'Uthmān and the fact that his references to Aḥmad Lobbo are limited to accounts of some Fulani attacks.[90]

To impose stricter control on the north and to subjugate the Tuareg, Aḥmad Lobbo engaged in a series of military activities in the year 1829–30. Written sources document an attack on Bamba, on the northern shore of the Niger close to Gao, led by al-Ḥājj Mūdi, the conqueror of Timbuktu.[91] According to the *Tārīkh al-fūtāwī*, al-Ḥājj Mūdi also led an attack against the Tuareg of Ṣirim, who were defeated and expelled from the region.[92] After these battles, Ḥamdallāhi established its own representatives in Timbuktu. Aḥmad Lobbo, according to the detailed account of the events in the *Tārīkh al-fūtāwī*, "appointed as *qāḍī* for the Ḥamdallāhi state in Timbuktu, the *sharīf* 'Abd al-Qādir b. Muḥammad al-Sanūsī b. Aḥmad Z.N.K., who made the Law

[88] Letter in Bovill, *Missions to the Niger*, vol. 1, 303. The year of Muḥammad al-Kuntī's death is confirmed in Arabic internal sources (*Dhikr*, f. 98b; *Mā waqa'a*, p. 5). Oral traditions collected by Hampaté Ba and Daget confirm the year of Muḥammad al-Kuntī's demise but have a different date, i.e. 2 Shawwāl 1241/12 March 1826 (*L'empire peul*, 217).

[89] *L'empire peul*, 218. [90] Caillié, *Travels through Central Africa*, vol. 2, 68.

[91] *Dhikr*, p. 3; *Mā waqa'a*, p. 5. [92] *Tārīkh al-fūtāwī*, p. 7.

undisputed there in the district. [In turn,] the *qāḍī* al-Sānūsī selected, under the authorization of Aḥmad Lobbo, San Shirfi as official scribe [*kātib al-wathā'iq*]" – the same San Shirfi who had already been chosen by Ḥamdallāhi as the *imām* of the Great Mosque.[93]

However, control in the north was never secured and, eventually, these efforts only exacerbated the tensions between the people of Timbuktu and Ḥamdallāhi. In 1833, Pāshā ʻUthmān once again broke his alliance with Aḥmad Lobbo and led an army against Ḥamdallāhi with the support of the Tuareg: an event that is well described in both oral and written sources.[94] The army reached the region of Diré, where it was defeated by Ḥamdallāhi's counter-offensive, led by Abū Bakr b. Mūdi and al-Qādir b. Saʻīd. The Arma were defeated over and over, Timbuktu reoccupied, Ṣirim fled to the desert, and Pāshā ʻUthmān was made prisoner in Ḥamdallāhi, where he remained for "two or more" years.[95]

These developments initiated a period of Ḥamdallāhi's "direct rule" over Timbuktu, in the words of Zebadia.[96] In place of Pāshā ʻUthmān, ʻAbd al-Qādir al-Sanūsī, who was already Ḥamdallāhi's *qāḍī* in Timbuktu, was chosen as *amīr* of the city and occupied this position for about three years.[97] Later, once Pāshā ʻUthmān was freed, he returned to his old position as *amīr*, replacing ʻAbd al-Qādir al-Sanūsī. In time, Pāshā ʻUthmān left the position to San Shirfi.[98] After ʻAbd al-Qādir al-Sanūsī, the position of *qāḍī* was occupied first by Alfa Saʻīd b. Bāba Gorko al-Fullānī.[99] Eventually, San Shirfi emerged as the most important representative of Ḥamdallāhi in Timbuktu, carrying the title of *amīr* and at the same time maintaining the positions of *qāḍī* and *imām* of the Great Mosque, as recorded in *al-Saʻāda al-abadiyya*.[100]

93 *Tārīkh al-fūtāwī*, pp. 6–7.
94 *L'empire peul*, 220–222; *Dhikr*, p. 3; *Mā waqaʻa*, p. 6; see also the detailed report of Ḥamdallāhi's campaign to regain Timbuktu written by some Fulani military leaders (IHERI-ABT 285).
95 Compare *L'empire peul*, 222, which reports that Pāshā ʻUthmān was killed during these skirmishes, with Muḥammad b. San Shirfi's *Tārīkh al-fūtāwī*, which reports his capture and imprisonment (*Tārīkh al-fūtāwī*, pp. 5–6). This latter information is confirmed by a detailed account of the time spent by the *pāshā* in Ḥamdallāhi, which dates his imprisonment until 1836/7, is IHERI-ABT 4253.
96 Zebadia, "Career and Correspondence," 86. 97 *Tārīkh al-fūtāwī*, p. 7.
98 *Tārīkh al-fūtāwī*, p. 7. 99 *Tārīkh al-fūtāwī*, p. 7.
100 IHERI-ABT 2752, ff. 18b–19a and 23.

The treatment that Aḥmad Lobbo decreed for the Arma of Timbuktu, who had masterminded the 1833 rebellion, was harsh. Muḥammad b. San Shirfi records that

> For those who had participated in the battle and have died, he took half of their wealth. For those who had participated, but have not died, he took all their wealth. For those who did not participate or kill anybody, he took one-third. This was the decision that Aḥmad Lobbo took regarding the wealth of the Arma.[101]

It seems that, at this time, Aḥmad Lobbo attempted again to secure the support of the Kunta under al-Mukhtār al-Ṣaghīr, who had succeeded his late father Muḥammad al-Kuntī as head of the clan in 1826.[102] Named after his grandfather, al-Mukhtār al-Kabīr, al-Mukhtār al-Ṣaghīr ("the Younger") maintained his headquarters far away from the Niger Bend and spent his first years as the leading *shaykh* of the Kunta in the Saharan camp of al-Ḥilla.

We can date a very important document, a long letter of advice sent by Aḥmad Lobbo to the people of Timbuktu, to this period.[103] It was written in 1244/1828–9, when there was no Kunta leader residing in Timbuktu, and it focuses on the need for reconciliation (*iṣlāḥ*).[104] In it, Aḥmad Lobbo counsels the inhabitants to recognize al-Mukhtār al-Ṣaghīr's role as the new leader of the Kunta, implying that there had been resistance to his acceptance. While the details of this controversy are not clarified, the letter indicates that Aḥmad Lobbo was trying, after his failed attempt with Muḥammad al-Kuntī, to convince a Kunta *shaykh* to help him control the city of Timbuktu and the recalcitrant inhabitants of Ḥamdallāhi's northern province.

It is not clear what role Aḥmad Lobbo actually played in the acceptance of al-Mukhtār al-Ṣaghīr by the people of Timbuktu, but this did eventually occur some five years later, in 1834.[105] However, by that

101 *Tārīkh al-fūtāwī*, p. 7.

102 Currently, no monographic study exists on al-Mukhtār al-Ṣaghīr. Boubacar Sissoko is completing a Ph.D. dissertation on the topic at the École normale supérieure in Lyon, but I have not had access to his work.

103 IHERI-ABT 25858. I thank Dr. Diagayeté for his help in understanding the context of the letter, which is in fact to an undisclosed recipient. However, the context strongly suggests that it is addressed to the people of Timbuktu (personal communication, 25 September 2017).

104 IHERI-ABT 25858, f. 20a.

105 *Dhikr*, p. 3; *Mā waqaʿa*, p. 5.

point the relationship between Aḥmad Lobbo and al-Mukhtār al-Ṣaghīr had become tense. Most likely, as Zebadia argues, al-Mukhtār al-Ṣaghīr moved to the city to mediate with the Fulani after the second conquest of Timbuktu in 1833. Confirming this, but with a faulty date, is Barth's statement that

> it was in consequence of this oppression, especially after a further increase of the Fúlbe party in the year 1831, that the Ghadámsíye people induced the Sheikh el Mukhtár, the elder brother of El Bakáy, and successor of Sídi Mohammed, to remove his residence from the hille, or hillet e' sheikh el Mukhtár, in A'zawád, half a day's journey from the well Bek Mehán, to Timbúktu.[106]

The harsh punishment of the Arma, the establishment of Aḥmad Lobbo's direct control over Timbuktu, and the continuing hostility between Ḥamdallāhi's army and the Tuareg were all threatening the prosperity of the region and, ultimately, the Kunta's commercial interests. For example, the *Tārīkh al-fūtāwī* states that, after the conquest of Timbuktu in 1833, one of the most important decisions taken by Aḥmad Lobbo was the enforcement of the ban on tobacco and kola in the city.[107] Further confirmation of this comes from a letter written by Aḥmad Lobbo to the *qāḍī* of Timbuktu, 'Abd al-Qādir al-Sanūsī, in which the caliph orders, among other things, the destruction of tobacco and declares that any profit deriving from the commercialization of this product would be treated as *ribā*, illegal gain.[108]

In this context, and consistent with the role of his Kunta predecessors, al-Mukhtār al-Ṣaghīr approached Aḥmad Lobbo to mitigate the crisis. In two long letters written within two days (13 Ṣafar 1250/20 June 1834 and 15 Ṣafar 1250/22 June 1834), al-Mukhtār al-Ṣaghīr defends himself from what he characterizes as false accusations that he sided with the Arma and Tuareg rebels.[109] He also affirms his recognition of Aḥmad Lobbo's authority, calling him "*Imām* of the Muslims and Commander of the believers" and the "trustworthy *amīr* and *imām* of exalted position" in the first letter;[110] and in the second he is described as "powerful *imām*, noble *shaykh*, and Commander of the believers."[111] He then excoriates the Arma chief Pāshā 'Uthmān for having revolted against Ḥamdallāhi.

106 Barth, *Travels and Discoveries*, vol. 4, 434. 107 *Tārīkh al-fūtāwī*, p. 7.
108 IHERI-ABT 2885. 109 BnF, ms. Arabe 5259, ff. 1–18; IHERI-ABT 282.
110 BnF, ms. Arabe 5259, f. 1a. 111 IHERI-ABT 282, p. 1.

In both letters the Kunta *shaykh* asks Aḥmad Lobbo to have mercy on Timbuktu and maintain it as the pillar of the Sudan and the leading city of learning and trade. The two letters also deal extensively with the Tuareg resistance against Ḥamdallāhi's domination. In one, al-Mukhtār al-Ṣaghīr asks the caliph to approach the Tuareg gently, because without their collaboration it would be impossible to pacify the region and return it to its previous prosperity.[112] In the other, he discusses in depth the conditions that Aḥmad Lobbo had offered to the Tuareg in order to settle the ongoing conflict: (1) return of their stolen wealth; (2) reparations to be paid by them; (3) their surrender to him; and (4) their renunciation of tobacco. Al-Mukhtār al-Ṣaghīr maintains that the Tuareg would never accept these conditions, and suggests that Aḥmad Lobbo find a way to settle his disputes with the Tuareg chief Ṣirim, considered the key person to win over. Without Ṣirim's consent, al-Mukhtār al-Ṣaghīr argues, no Tuareg would ever accept Ḥamdallāhi's rule.[113]

Evidently, al-Mukhtār al-Ṣaghīr's mediation was successful; at least temporarily. A letter from Aḥmad Lobbo begins by confirming the hostile attitude of Ḥamdallāhi toward the Tuareg, with the caliph stating that he had previously made a firm, irrevocable decision not to collaborate with the Tuareg, but to destroy them or force them to implement Ḥamdallāhi's rulings. However, Aḥmad Lobbo writes that the mediation of al-Mukhtār al-Ṣaghīr, and the respect of Ḥamdallāhi for the Kunta family, has allowed him to find the best solution for settling the dispute with the Tuareg.[114] It seems that his mediation was effective, since a period of tranquility followed. This period corresponds to the timing of a letter in which the relationship between Aḥmad Lobbo and Ṣirim appears to be good, and the caliph requests that the people of Timbuktu accommodate the Tuareg chief.[115]

Collectively, these letters reveal the position that the Kunta *shaykh* took with Ḥamdallāhi after the 1833 crisis and the occupation of Timbuktu, up until the death of Aḥmad Lobbo: one of consistent recognition of the caliph's authority. The situation had changed dramatically from the time of his father, Muḥammad al-Kuntī, who had led the Kunta at a time when Aḥmad Lobbo's authority in the region of Timbuktu was either nonexistent or, at a later stage, precarious. By

[112] BnF, ms. Arabe 5259, ff. 1–18. [113] IHERI-ABT 282, p. 22.
[114] IHERI-ABT 3654. [115] IHERI-ABT 5747.

contrast, in the time of al-Mukhtār al-Ṣaghīr, Ḥamdallāhi controlled the Niger Bend, and all the decisions of the Kunta *shaykh* need to be understood, as Diakité underscores, in the context of Aḥmad Lobbo's political domination.[116]

Several other documents bear witness to the cordial and supportive relationship between al-Mukhtār al-Ṣaghīr and Aḥmad Lobbo up to the death of the caliph. For example, a letter from Aḥmad Lobbo shows his explicit support for one of al-Mukhtār al-Ṣaghīr's juridical decisions, contrary to the criticism of other local scholars.[117] In another, al-Mukhtār al-Ṣaghīr intervenes in support of the *qāḍī* of Timbuktu, Sa'īd b. Bāba, and asks that Aḥmad Lobbo help his *qāḍī*, who was financially strapped.[118] Yet another document shows Aḥmad Lobbo asking the *qāḍi* Sa'īd b. Bāba to intervene in a dispute that took place between al-Mukhtār al-Ṣaghīr and one Mikā'īl.[119] A last letter contains a request from Aḥmad Lobbo to one 'Umar b. Ḥammadi, to work with al-Mukhtār al-Saghīr on an undisclosed matter relating to the women of the Arma.[120] Together, these letters convey that al-Mukhtār al-Ṣaghīr was in good and collegial standing with Aḥmad Lobbo and that he helped the caliph to secure control over Timbuktu.

Other letters also show that the role of the Kunta as mediators continued despite their subordinate position. The recognition of Aḥmad Lobbo's authority did not mean a passive acceptance of the caliph's rulings, especially regarding the ongoing debate over the permissibility of tobacco that would not be settled even after the death of Aḥmad Lobbo, as later documents confirm that it was also contentious at the time of Aḥmad II.[121] Al-Mukhtār al-Ṣaghīr explicitly attacks Ḥamdallāhi on the topic: "The biggest sedition you see is caused by banning tobacco and enforcing laws in the wrong way."[122] He complains about the market supervisors appointed by the authority of Ḥamdallāhi in Timbuktu, citing their brutal treatment of people suspected of tobacco consumption. It may be the result of al-Mukhtār al-Ṣaghīr's complaints that, in another letter, Aḥmad Lobbo scolded his own governor for his harsh measures.[123] Elsewhere, al-Mukhtār al-Ṣaghīr admits to being a consumer of tobacco himself: "As for my

116 This is also emphasized by Diakite, "al-Mukhtār b. Yerkoy Talfi," 192–193.
117 IHERI-ABT 3656. 118 IHERI-ABT 8948. 119 IHERI-ABT 9544.
120 IHERI-ABT 5748 (I).
121 See, for example, IHERI-ABT 9538/II; IHERI-ABT 11521.
122 IHERI-ABT 282, p. 8. 123 IHERI-ABT 2884.

consumption of tobacco, I am not the first innovator, but there are those who are better than me who have preceded me [in the use of tobacco]."[124] In his defense, he references writings of other Kunta *shaykhs*, including his grandfather al-Mukhtār al-Kabīr's book *al-Burd al-muwashshà* (The Adorned Garment).[125] In this treatise, al-Mukhtār al-Kabīr argues that there is disagreement among the *'ulamā'* concerning the consumption of tobacco and, consequently, it should be not declared illegitimate.[126] In the same letter, al-Mukhtār al-Ṣaghīr also makes reference to his "paternal uncle," one Ḥabīb Allāh, who had written in support of the consumption of tobacco for medical purposes.[127]

The picture that emerges from these documents is that relations between the Kunta and Aḥmad Lobbo were normalized and cordial at the time of al-Mukhtar al-Ṣaghīr. This is confirmed by a eulogy of Aḥmad Lobbo written by the Kunta *shaykh* at the time of his death.[128] It is also affirmed by the colonial administrator, Lieutenant Péfontan, who in his history of Timbuktu described al-Mukhtār al-Ṣaghīr as a "precious auxiliary" of Ḥamdallāhi.[129]

Aḥmad al-Bakkāy and Ḥamdallāhi

When al-Mukhtār al-Ṣaghīr was the head of the Kunta clan, his younger brother, Aḥmad al-Bakkāy b. Muḥammad b. al-Mukhrār al-Kuntī (d. 1865), was also actively involved in the affairs of the Kunta.[130] According to Zebadia, in the years "1829–1845 Sīdī Aḥmad Al-Bakkāy was frequently in touch with the rulers of Ḥamdullāhi both in religious and political affairs."[131] Unfortunately, not many documents corroborate Zebadia's statement and only a little evidence points to this direct connection. However, there is an almost one-hundred-page response to the caliph by Aḥmad al-Bakkāy, entitled *Dhakhīra al-sarmad fī jawāb al-shaykh Aḥmad Lobbo* (The Treasury

124 IHERI-ABT 282, p. 12.
125 IHERI-ABT 282, p. 12. On this work, see *ALA* IV, 73, item 8.
126 IHERI-ABT 282, p. 12. 127 IHERI-ABT 282, p. 12.
128 IHERI-ABT 7803.
129 Lieutenant Pefontan, "Histoire de Tombouctou de sa fondation à l'occupation Française (XIIe siècle–1893)," *Bulletin du Comité d'Études Historiques et Scientifiques de l'Afrique Occidentale Française* 5/1 (1922): 1–25, 25.
130 Zebadia, "Career and Correspondence," 107.
131 Zebadia, "Career and Correspondence," 110.

of Eternity in the Response to Shaykh Aḥmad Lobbo), which, after a long section of advice on good governance, deals mainly with the issue of tobacco.[132] Following in the footsteps of other Kunta leaders, Aḥmad al-Bakkāy advises Aḥmad Lobbo to acknowledge the permissibility of tobacco consumption. Aḥmad al-Bakkāy also wrote another letter in response to the concerns of the caliph, this time on repentance.[133] Finally, in correspondence between him and an unnamed representative of Ḥamdallāhi in Timbuktu, the connection between Aḥmad Lobbo and Aḥmad al-Bakkāy is confirmed via the description of a controversy that took place in Timbuktu over the selling of a slave and involved the Arma chief Pāshā ʿUthmān.[134]

The first real evidence of al-Bakkāy's political skills in dealing with Ḥamdallāḥi dates to the period immediately after the death of Aḥmad Lobbo. The tension between the Tuareg, led by Ṣirim, and Ḥamdallāhi had exploded again into open hostility in the early 1840s.[135] The Tuareg defeated the Aḥmad Lobbo's army at Goundam, in 1840–1, and took more than seven hundred slaves.[136] Then, in the following year, Aḥmad II led a revenge campaign and chased the army of Ṣirim away from Timbuktu.[137] However, this was only a temporary defeat for the Tuareg, who returned after having mobilized all their men "from Bourem to Mabrūk and from Mabrūk to Arawān."[138] Similarly impressive was the army put together by Aḥmad Lobbo, who mustered a force of 50,000 soldiers.[139] The final and decisive battle took place in Toya, southwest of Timbuktu, in 1841–2. These events left a vivid memory in the Fulani traditions, and their story is chanted to celebrate the deeds of the Fulani hero Aamadu Sambuuru Koolaaɗo.[140] However, in this epic the outcome of the battle is reversed, and the Fulani are described as victorious.[141] In fact, Toya was a harsh defeat for the

132 https://memory.loc.gov/cgi-bin/query/D?malibib:2:./temp/~intldl_YVwf. On the website, the letter is coupled with another one that is described as being a shorter version, while in fact it is a totally different document – a letter to Aḥmad II. IHERI-ABT 2883 is copy of the first two pages of the letter.

133 Cited in Zebadia, "Career and Correspondence," 111.

134 IHERI-ABT 8979.

135 These events are described in detail in *L'empire peul*, 222–231.

136 Dhikr, p. 3; *Mā waqa*ʿa, p. 7; *Tārīkh al-fūtāwī*, pp. 7–8.

137 *Tārīkh al-fūtāwī*, p. 8.

138 *L'empire peul*, 223.

139 The final clash between the Fulani and the Tuareg is described in *L'empire peul*, 222–231.

140 See Seydou, *Les guerres du Massina*, 316–351.

141 Seydou, *Les guerres du Massina*, 314.

Fulani: the army of Ḥamdallāhi was crushed, with 2,005 soldiers killed and 3,152 injured, leading to the Tuareg regaining control of the northern part of the Middle Niger.[142]

Unable to maintain control of the Timbuktu region, Ḥamdallāhi developed a new strategy to bring the city to its knees: an economic blockade.[143] The north was literally starved. The best description of the event comes from Barth, who most likely collected his information from Aḥmad al-Bakkāy: "The Tawárek drove the Fúlbe completely out of the town, about the year 1844, when a battle was fought on the banks of the river, in which a great number of the latter were either slain or drowned."[144] However, he adds, "the victory only plunged the distracted town into greater misery; for, owing to its peculiar situation on the border of the desert tract, Timbúktu cannot rely upon its own resources, but must always be dependent upon those who rule the more fertile tracts higher up the river."[145] In this, Barth confirms the observation that Caillié had made almost half a century before:

> Timbuctoo, though one of the largest cities I have seen in Africa, possesses no other resources but its trade in salt, the soil being totally unfit for cultivation. The inhabitants procure from Jenné every thing requisite for the supply of their wants, such as millet, rice, vegetable butter, honey, cotton, Soudan cloth, preserved provisions, candles, soap, allspice, onions, dried fish, pistachios, &c.[146]

In consequence of rebellions in Timbuktu, Barth writes, "the ruler of Másina had only to forbid the exportation of corn from his dominions to reduce the inhabitants of Timbúktu to the utmost distress."[147]

Under these circumstances, Aḥmad al-Bakkāy fulfilled the role of mediator in a time of crisis between the capital and Timbuktu, implying the Kunta's continued recognition of Ḥamdallāhi. The blockade was lifted after the death of Aḥmad Lobbo, and Timbuktu was put under a sort of "indirect rule," described by Barth as follows:

> [Timbuktu] should be dependent on the Fúlbe without being garrisoned by a military force, the tribute being collected by the two kádhis, one Púllo, and the other Songhay, who should themselves decide all cases of minor

142 *L'empire peul*, 230. 143 *L'empire peul*, 231.
144 Barth, *Travels and Discoveries*, vol. 4, 435.
145 Barth, *Travels and Discoveries*, vol. 4, 435.
146 Caillié, *Travels through Central Africa*, vol. 2, 57.
147 Barth, *Travels and Discoveries*, vol. 4, 435.

importance, the more important ones being referred to the capital. But, nevertheless, the government of the town, or rather the police, as far as it goes, is in the hands of one or two Songhay mayors, with the title of emir, but who have scarcely any effective power, placed as they are between the Fúlbe on the one side and the Tawárek on the other, and holding their ground against the former though the two kádhis, and against the latter by means of Sheikh el Bakáy.[148]

Later in his life, however, the Kunta *shaykh* distanced himself from the caliphate. Indeed, Aḥmad al-Bakkāy completely dismissed the authority of the descendants of Aḥmad Lobbo and denied their legitimacy. In a long letter to Aḥmad III, dating to the period of Barth's stay in Timbuktu in 1853–4, al-Bakkāy wrote:

You are not the *Imām* of the Muslims. However, the *Imām* of the Muslims is his excellency 'Abdurraḥmān or the Sulṭān 'Abdulmajīd, because his excellency 'Abdurraḥmān is religiously the sanctioned leader, and the Sulṭān 'Abdulmajīd is the greatest and the most extensive in the domain whereas you are an Amīr from Ḥamdullāhi to Timbuktu, five days' journey, at the most extreme end of the land of the Sudān in the West.[149]

This argument relates to the actual territorial extent of the Caliphate of Ḥamdallāhi, whose limited domain is contrasted with the much more extensive territory of explicitly powerful Muslim states, represented by the Ottoman Empire under Sultan 'Abd al-Majīd (d. 1861) and the Moroccan kingdom under Mūlāy 'Abd al-Raḥmān (d. 1859).

In another letter, quoted by al-Ḥājj 'Umar in his *Bayān mā waqa'a baynanā wa-bayna amīr Māsina Aḥmad b. Aḥmad b. al-Shaykh Aḥmad b. Muḥammad Lobbo* (What Happened between us and the Emir of Masina Aḥmad b. Aḥmad b. Aḥmad b. Muḥammad Lobbo), al-Bakkāy advances a different argument against Ḥamdallāhi's legitimacy, asking a rhetorical question about how he could ever be under allegiance to a "black Fulani" – Aḥmad III.[150] As Amir Syed has pointed out, "al-Bakkāy's reference to Aḥmad III as a both a *sūdānī* [black] and a Fulani rests on historically rooted racial idioms in the Sahara" and Sahel.[151] The racial argument had been already used in

148 Barth, *Travels and Discoveries*, vol. 4, 435–436.
149 Cited in Zebadia, "Career and Correspondence," 195 (Arabic text) and 196 (English text).
150 Mahibou and Triaud (eds.), *Voilà ce qui est arrivé*, 14b/104.
151 Syed, "al-Ḥājj 'Umar Tāl," 203.

a previous correspondence addressed to Nūḥ b. al-Ṭāhir and Muḥammad b. ʻAlī Pereejo at the time of Aḥmad II, when al-Bakkāy bluntly states that "blacks do not belong to the community of our Prophet Muhammad."[152] In this context, blackness is equated with unbelief, as Hall has argued in his history of ideas of race in Western Africa over a *longue durée.*[153]

However, a closer look at al-Bakkāy's arguments reveals yet another dimension to his assertion that blacks do not belong: "the community of the Prophet is the Qurāysh and the imamate and the allegiance only belongs to them and cannot be rightfully given to anybody but them."[154] This view is reiterated in al-Bakkāy's statement: "I would never follow or be under the authority of a non-Arab."[155] In short, al-Bakkāy, who claimed Arab descent (as did as all the Kunta), is "playing the race card" to justify his refusal to recognize the authority of Ḥamdallāhi. This occurred in a specific moment of crisis, during the time of tension surrounding the Barth "affair" of 1853–4, when the German traveler Barth was hosted and protected in Timbuktu by the Kunta, despite Aḥmad III's requests to hand him over to Ḥamdallāhi.

In other circumstances, by contrast, al-Bakkāy assumed a conciliatory attitude toward "black authorities." For example, his relationships with the Fodiawa in Sokoto were excellent.[156] Likewise, for many years his relationship with Aḥmad II was one of "mutual understanding," in the words of Zebadia.[157] He had even written a poem in praise of the two sons of Aḥmad II, Aḥmad III (his future inveterate enemy when the Barth incident exploded) and ʻAbd Allāh.[158] Likewise, al-Bakkāy's words and actions cannot be understood as a single-mindedly hostile attitude toward the family of Aḥmad Lobbo. The *shaykh*'s rhetoric certainly reflects the Arabs' assumption of racial superiority over the Fulani, in particular, and black Africans, in general. However, it also reveals a pragmatic approach to the power of Ḥamdallāhi, an approach that was renegotiated several times.

Aḥmad al-Bakkāy's multifaceted relationship with Aḥmad Lobbo, like those of his father Muḥammad al-Kunti and his elder brother al-

152 IHERI-ABT 8969, f. 1a. 153 Hall, *A History of Race.*
154 Aḥmad b. Muḥammad b. al-Mukhtār al-Kuntī, *Risāla ilà ikhwatihi min al-Fulāni*, IHERI-ABT 8969, f. 1a.
155 Mahibou and Triaud (eds.), *Voilà ce qui est arrivé*, 14b/104.
156 Zebadia, "Career and Correspondence," 92.
157 Zebadia, "Career and Correspondence," 165. 158 IHERI-ABT 3543.

Mukhtār al-Ṣaghīr, prove that the Kunta alliance with the Caliphate of Ḥamdallāhi must be understood as the product of historical contingencies and changing political contexts, rather than static positions of perpetual support or inveterate resistance. The real differences between Ḥamdallāhi and the Kunta were their attitudes toward power. The Kunta continued in the local tradition of distancing themselves from politics, although in their roles as advisors and mediators they attempted to influence political rulers. However, they did so as scholars, claiming a different kind of religious authority. By contrast, Aḥmad Lobbo claimed authority in both the political and religious spheres, disrupting the traditional embodiment of these two domains in different elites. That is why the Kunta could accept and even collaborate with Aḥmad Lobbo as the ruler of Timbuktu and the Niger Bend but – at the same time – question him on issues such as tobacco consumption, payment of ritual alms, and anathemization of enemies. A more comprehensive denial of Aḥmad Lobbo's authority would come from Ḥamdallāhi's powerful neighboring rival, the Fodiawa of Sokoto.

5 *Fluctuating Diplomacy: Ḥamdallāhi and Sokoto*

This chapter's analysis of the relationship between the caliphates of Ḥamdallāhi and Sokoto contributes to our hitherto very limited knowledge of pre-colonial West African diplomacy.[1] In so doing, it follows in the footsteps of Charles C. Stewart's pioneering research on the topic.[2] Stewart focused on the period between the battle of Noukouma until about 1837 and the death of Muḥammad Bello, describing the relationship between the two theocracies as having "vacillated, being in turn amicable (1815–17), abruptly broken (1817–21), then regularized but

[1] The topic received some interest mainly in the 1970s, but has not substantially developed since, with the exception of the recent contributions by Rémi Dewière on Borno (Rémi Dewière, "A struggle for Sahara: Idrīs ibn 'Alī's embassy to Aḥmad al-Manṣūr in the context of Borno–Morocco–Ottoman relations, 1577–1583," *Annual Review of Islam in Africa* 12/1 [2014]: 85–91; and Rémi Dewière, *Du Lac Tchad à La Mecque: le sultanat du Borno et son monde (XVIe–XVIIe siècle)* [Paris: Éditions de la Sorbonne, 2017]). See the introductory works Robert Smith, "Peace and palaver: International relations in pre-colonial West Africa," *Journal of African History* 14/4 (1973): 599–621; and Thomas Hodgkin, "Diplomacy and diplomats in the western Sudan," in *Foreign Relations of African States*, edited by K. Ingman (London: Butterworths, 1974), 1–24. Case studies on the topic are A. D. H. Bivar, "Arabic documents of northern Nigeria," *Bulletin of the School of Oriental and African Studies* 22/2 (1959): 324–349; Adeleye, *Power and Diplomacy*; A. Adu Bohanen, "Fante diplomacy in the eighteen century [plus Discussion]," in Ingman (ed.), *Foreign Relations of African States*, 25–51; Graham W. Irwin, "Precolonial African diplomacy: The example of Asante," *International Journal of African Historical Studies* 8/1 (1975): 81–96; John E. Lavers, "The diplomatic relations of the Sokoto Caliphate: Some thoughts and a plea," in *Studies in the History of the Sokoto Caliphate: The Sokoto Seminar Papers*, edited by Y. B. Usman (Zaria: Department of History, Ahmadu Bello University, for the Sokoto State History Bureau, 1979), 379–391; M. A. al-Hajj, "Contribution to the study of the international relations of Bornu in the reign of Sultan Idrīs ibn 'Alī, known as Aloma," in *Studia Arabica et Islamica, Festschrift for Ihsân 'Abbâs*, edited by W. al-Qadi (Beirut: American University in Beirut, 1981), 183–194; Dramani-Issifou, *L'Afrique noire*.

[2] Kani and Stewart, "Sokoto–Masina correspondence"; Stewart, "Frontier disputes"; Stewart, "Diplomatic relations."

formal between 1821 and 1837."[3] Extending the chronology of Stewart's argument, this chapter takes into consideration the period before Noukouma, when Aḥmad Lobbo sought the advice of the Sokoto leaders, and continues to trace that relationship to the death of the caliph in 1845. It shows that changing historical circumstances, as well as the different personalities and motivations of the various political actors, informed the fluctuations of diplomacy between Ḥamdallāhi and Sokoto.

A consistent feature of this relationship, on Sokoto's side, was the rejection of Aḥmad Lobbo's claims to legitimate authority. However, the tension between Ḥamdallāhi and Sokoto never erupted into military confrontation, and this stands in stark contrast to the ways in which Ḥamdallāhi dealt with internal dissent, which was crushed by military means; it also contrasts with the military engagements that characterized the caliphate's relations with the neighboring Bambara polities of Segou and Kaarta. In the case of Sokoto, the tensions took the shape of dialectical disputes over Aḥmad Lobbo's claims to rule a sovereign Islamic state independent of Sokoto: tensions which escalated after the caliph of Ḥamdallāhi withdrew the pledge of allegiance that he had sworn to 'Uthmān b. Fūdī prior to his victory at Noukouma.

It was this debate that generated the historical context in which the *Tārīkh al-fattāsh* has to be located. In fact, the chronicle only appears in a late correspondence between Aḥmad Lobbo, Nūḥ b. al-Ṭāhir, and the Fodiawa, in which Sokoto is urged to pledge allegiance to Ḥamdallāhi. But this is only one of the last pieces of a decades-long diatribe that dates to the very emergence of Aḥmad Lobbo's movement.

The Early Years: Before Noukouma

Between 1818, the year of the battle of Noukouma, when the foundations of the caliphate were laid, and the death of Aḥmad Lobbo in 1845, Ḥamdallāhi could be counted as one of the most powerful Islamic states in West Africa. As such, the caliphate established diplomatic relations with the most important Islamic theocracy of the region: the Sokoto Caliphate. Founded by 'Uthmān b. Fūdī in 1804, the Sokoto Caliphate consisted of a series of emirates loosely connected

[3] Stewart, "Frontier disputes," 498.

to the capital city. Its leaders had showed interest in expanding to the Middle Niger since its very inception, well before the emergence of Aḥmad Lobbo, as proven by existing correspondence between 'Uthmān b. Fūdī and the Kunta, as well as by the mission of Mallam Ibn Sa'īd in the 1810s, discussed in Chapter 3. However, the emergence of Ḥamdallāhi and the formation of an independent theocracy frustrated the expansionist aims of Sokoto.

Before Noukouma, Aḥmad Lobbo had sought advice from the Fodiawa *shaykh*s in several instances, as proven by the letter to 'Abd Allāh b. Fūdī mentioned in Chapter 3. That Aḥmad Lobbo had further looked to Sokoto as a source of inspiration and legitimacy is proven by his request to 'Uthmān b. Fūdī for support in the imminent war against the coalition led by Segou: he had sent a delegation to Sokoto consisting, according to oral sources, of his brother Bokari Hammadi and one Hammadi Juulde.[4] The delegation pledged allegiance to 'Uthmān b. Fūdī, who in turn authorized Aḥmad Lobbo to wage war against his enemies and invested him with his authority, represented by a flag.[5] This system was typical of Sokoto, where 'Uthmān b. Fūdī and his successors would appoint commanders to lead expeditions beyond the core regions of the state, vesting them with such flags. Once these expeditions had established emirates, they were governed by lieutenants who would loosely recognize the central authority of Sokoto via their pledge of allegiance.[6]

This was most likely 'Uthmān b. Fūdī's plan in sending the flag to Aḥmad Lobbo: to create a Sokoto-dependent emirate in the Middle Niger. The emergence of Aḥmad Lobbo seemed to fulfill the plans of the early days of Sokoto. However, the death of 'Uthmān b. Fūdī and the unexpected series of early Fulani victories in Masina, including that at Noukouma, resulted in Ahmad Lobbo's emergence as a powerful actor in the Middle Niger, who did not require any external support. In Brown's words, "the death of Shaykh 'Uthman would have rendered it [the pledge of allegiance and the flag sent from Sokoto] somewhat meaningless – and the victory of Noukouma even more so."[7]

An extensive correspondence seems to have taken place at this time between Ḥamdallāhi, Sokoto, and Gwandu, the capital of the western

4 *L'empire peul*, 36. 5 *L'empire peul*, 40–41.
6 On this system, see Last, *The Sokoto Caliphate*, 46–57.
7 Brown, "The Caliphate of Hamdullahi," 21.

territories ruled by the Fodiawa, but unfortunately most of these letters are not available.[8] However, two documents include extensive quotations from these exchanges and serve to illuminate the early phases of diplomacy between the two theocracies. The first and most famous of these is a response by Abū Bakr al-ʿAtīq (d. 1842), the third ruler of Sokoto, to a missive from Aḥmad Lobbo, known as the Abu Bakr Atiku Manuscript – following the name given to it by Stewart, the first to attract attention to it.[9] This manuscript can be internally dated to around 1838, since the author mentions the death of Muḥammad Bello as having occurred "last year," i.e. 1837.[10] Accordingly, in Stewart's words, it represents a "review of Masina–Sokoto correspondence" up to the late1830s.[11]

At the time when Stewart studied it, however, the second of these two documents was unknown: the letter from Aḥmad Lobbo which had prompted Abū Bakr al-ʿAtīq to send his response. This document has now been recovered: a long missive from Aḥmad Lobbo to notables within the Fodiawa circle, including the third emir of Sokoto, Abū Bakr al-ʿAtīq; the emir of Gwandu and the son of ʿAbd Allāh b. Fūdī, Ibrāhīm al-Khalīl b. ʿAbd Allāh (d. 1860); and others.[12] It therefore adds new details to our picture of these early diplomatic exchanges, supplementing those revealed by the Abū Bakr Atiku Manuscript.

[8] An exception is represented by a letter from Muḥammad Bello to Aḥmad Lobbo (Kaduna, NA, O/AR1/19).

[9] IFAN, Fonds Brevié, Mauritania 7. Although this is the main copy I use and cite, I have also consulted two other copies of this letter: Sokoto, Waziri Junaidu Collection 6/55 (I have accessed the photocopy in Kaduna, NA, P/ARI/28/4), and Djenné Library, Alfady Traore 77. The letter does not report the name of the sender, which is given as Abu Bakr al-ʿAtīq by Waziri Junaidu on the frontispiece of his copy of the manuscripts (Sokoto, Waziri Junaidu Collection, 6/55, p. 1) and in turn reproduced by Stewart and Kani (Kani and Stewart, "Sokoto–Masina correspondence," 10; Stewart, "Frontier disputes," 497; Stewart, "Diplomatic relations," 409). The absence of the name of the author, who was indeed Abū Bakr al-ʿAtīq, as it emerges from the context, is explained by the fact that all the three manuscripts of the letter are copies and not the original. In the original correspondence generated from the Sokoto chancery, the name of the sender is on the seal that records the name of the current *amīr al-muʾminīn*, as can be observed in Bivar, "Arabic documents." Therefore, in the three available copies the copyist only reproduced the main text and left out the actual name of the sender, Abū Bakr al-ʿAtīq, included in the seal of the original letter.

[10] IFAN, Fonds Brevié, Mauritania 7, p. 1.

[11] Kani and Stewart, "Sokoto–Masina correspondence," 2.

[12] MAMMP, Reel 6.

From Allegiance to Tension (1817–1821): 1. The Abu Bakr Atiku Manuscript

The Abu Bakr Atiku Manuscript includes the full text of a very important letter from Aḥmad Lobbo to Muḥammad Bello.[13] This letter includes a clear justification for the independence of Ḥamdallāhi from Sokoto in response to a previous, lost, missive, in which Muḥammad Bello had asked for an explanation for Aḥmad Lobbo's withdrawal of his allegiance to Sokoto. Aḥmad Lobbo never denies having paid allegiance to 'Uthmān b. Fūdī, but explains the reasons for his withdrawal of allegiance to Sokoto, arranged in neat chronological order.

First, the caliph of Ḥamdallāhi takes strategic advantage of the crisis that had followed the death of 'Uthmān b. Fūdī, when Muḥammad Bello and 'Abd Allāh b. Fūdī had struggled for power. According to the established narrative of Sokoto history, 'Abd Allāh b. Fūdī, the most recognized scholar of the region and brother of 'Uthmān b. Fūdī, had gone to the capital after the death of his brother with the intention of laying claim to the caliphate; but he found the doors of the city closed so that he could not intervene while Muḥammad Bello, his nephew, was elected.[14] After this event, which amounted to a coup d'état, 'Abd Allāh "returned ... to Gwandu where he cut all communication with Sokoto and began to handle Gwandu affairs without reference to Sokoto."[15]

With reference to these events, Aḥmad Lobbo argues that he withdrew his allegiance from Sokoto after having received requests for allegiance from both Muḥammad Bello and 'Abd Allāh b. Fūdī.[16] "'Abd Allāh sent Mālik to me with a letter in his own handwriting, asking for allegiance and declaring himself to be the *amīr al-mu'minīn*, whereas I had heard differently" – that is, he had heard that Muḥammad Bello was the *amīr al-mu'minīn* of Sokoto.[17] Having two individuals claiming authority in the same land is tantamount to

[13] IFAN, Fonds Brevié, Mauritania 7, pp. 11–12.
[14] S. A. Balogun, "The position of Gwandu in the Sokoto Caliphate," in *Studies in the History of the Sokoto Caliphate: The Sokoto Seminar Papers*, edited by Y. B. Usman (Zaria: Department of History, Ahmadu Bello University, for the Sokoto State History Bureau, 1979), 278–295, 283.
[15] Balogun, "The position of Gwandu in the Sokoto Caliphate," 283.
[16] IFAN, Fonds Brevié, Mauritania 7, p. 11.
[17] IFAN, Fonds Brevié, Mauritania 7, p. 12.

fitna or civil strife, to which Aḥmad Lobbo refers in other letters cited in the Abu Bakr Atiku Manuscript.[18] Therefore, Aḥmad Lobbo claims, he decided to withdraw his allegiance to Sokoto because of this controversy over authority, "for the greater good of the Muslims, and not aspiring to power."[19]

The tension between the two Fūdī leaders was settled, eventually, in the aftermath of the battle of Kalembaina in 1821. On this occasion, an army led by Muḥammad Bello rescued his uncle ʿAbd Allāh b. Fūdī, who had been virtually under siege for two years by a coalition of rebels: a battle that resulted in the victory of Sokoto and marked, in Last's words, "the reconciliation between nephew and uncle."[20] However, as one reads in the Abu Bakr Atiku Manuscript, the dispute between Sokoto and Ḥamdallāhi did not end. "After I heard about the settling of the affair between you,"[21] Aḥmad Lobbo writes, he continued to assert his independence from Sokoto, this time on the basis of sound jurisprudence. Cleverly, Aḥmad Lobbo uses ʿAbd Allāh b. Fūdī's own *Ḍiyāʾ al-ḥukkām fī mā lahum wa-ʿalayhim min al-aḥkām* (The Illumination of Rulers on the Legal Rulings to which they are Entitled and which are Due from Them.) to justify his independence. From this work, Aḥmad Lobbo cites the opinion of al-Nafarāwī (d. 1713), who wrote, in his *al-Fawākih al-dawānī ʿalà Risālat Ibn Abī Zayd al-Qayrawānī* (The Collected Fruits on the Commentary of the Epistle of Ibn Abī Zayd al-Qayrawānī), that "the multiplicity [of rulers] is not permissible according to the consensus of the scholars, except if the distance between the two places does not allow the authority of the [first] *imām* to reach the other place."[22] Then Aḥmad Lobbo proceeds to ask a rhetorical question about whether Muḥammad Bello could argue "objectively" that his rule has reached the Middle Niger since the death of ʿUthmān b. Fūdī. He adds: "Be fair, your jurisdiction has not reached us since the death of our lamented Shaykh ʿUthmān. If you accept my argument that your authority has not reached us, then is it not permissible to have more than one authority? In fact, [you cannot claim authority over us] except if you claim that lands such

[18] IFAN, Fonds Brevié, Mauritania 7, p. 9.
[19] IFAN, Fonds Brevié, Mauritania 7, p. 12.
[20] Last, *The Sokoto Caliphate*, 70. [21] IFAN, Fonds Brevié, Mauritania 7, p. 12.
[22] IFAN, Fonds Brevié, Mauritania 7, p. 12.

as al-Andalus and Khurāsān are also attached to your jurisdiction."[23]

Aḥmad Lobbo also uses al-Zurqānī's (d. 1688) commentary (*Sharḥ*) on the *Mukhtaṣar Khalīl* to explain the conditions under which two places can be considered separate. "The condition is that [a territory] is one, according to al-Māzarī, except if the distance across the land is such [so far] that it is not possible to send a representative of the ruler – in this case a multiplication of rulers is permissible."[24] To this, Aḥmad Lobbo adds that "it is known that you have not been able to send any representative since the demise of our lamented *shaykh* ['Uthmān b. Fūdī] until today due to apostasy in the lands, the highway robbery, and the distance [between our lands]." Thus, concludes Aḥmad Lobbo, "as for the modality of my withdrawal [of allegiance from Sokoto], it has happened following the Book, the Sunna, the [principles of] 'fighting in the path of God' and of 'commanding good and forbidding wrong' [*amr bi-l-maʿrūf wa-nahī ʿan al-munkar*] according to one's ability. All this happened with God's favor and mercy, not for my boastfulness, pride, arrogance, or self-gratification."[25] In this way, Aḥmad Lobbo justifies his independence from Sokoto in the post-Kalembaina context when the argument about civil strife would no longer be effective.

From the manuscript, it emerges that 'Abd Allāh b. Fūdī accepted Aḥmad Lobbo's arguments concerning his independence from Sokoto: "When you explained your reasons 'Abd Allāh accepted it completely and said that he knew of no additional legal precedent beyond what you had written according to Islamic law and customs."[26] Apparently, other authorities, who are left unnamed, also accepted the decision of Aḥmad Lobbo: "And I asked some scholars about the issue of the allegiance to you and they forbade that to me and said to me 'If you do that, God will ask you about it on the Day of Resurrection.'"[27] However, it seems that Muḥammad Bello did not accept Aḥmad Lobbo's arguments, and "inappropriate words" were exchanged.[28]

[23] IFAN, Fonds Brevié, Mauritania 7, p. 12.

[24] IFAN, Fonds Brevié, Mauritania 7, p. 12. Al-Zurqani's commentary on the *Mukhtaṣar al-Khalīl* was very widespread in West Africa (see Hall and Stewart, "The historic 'core curriculum'," 133).

[25] IFAN, Fonds Brevié, Mauritania 7, p. 12.

[26] IFAN, Fonds Brevié, Mauritania 7, p. 9.

[27] MAMMP, Reel 6, p. 3.

[28] IFAN, Fonds Brevié, Mauritania 7, p. 9.

From Allegiance to Tension (1817–1821): 2. The *Maktūb fī radd masāʾil ʿan Aḥmad Lobbo*

Muḥammad Bello's denial of Ḥamdallāhi's independence seems to have generated a lengthy controversy between him and Aḥmad Lobbo, which is referenced in the Abu Bakr Atiku Manuscript.[29] During this period, according to Aḥmad Lobbo, Muḥammad Bello had also attempted to undermine his position as legitimate ruler of the Middle Niger, by fomenting dissent in his lands, i.e. the rebellions of al-Ḥusayn Koita, Aḥmad b. Alfagha, and Gelaajo.[30] The controversy is also recounted in an untitled work by Muḥammad Bello; although classified as a response to Aḥmad Lobbo, it is in fact a "Treatise in Response to some Questions from Aḥmad Lobbo" (*Maktūb fī radd masāʾil ʿan Aḥmad Lobbo*).[31] The treatise is an extremely important summary of the points of contention between Muḥammad Bello and the caliph of Ḥamdallāhi, and it seems to have been written after the quarrel between them was terminated.

Muḥammad Bello begins the document, after pious opening formulas, with an explanation of how the exchange came about. "After I read what our master [i.e. ʿAbd Allāh b. Fūdī] has written commenting on my answer to Sayyid Aḥmad Lobbo,"[32] the author had initially decided not to intervene but he was incited by "some brothers" to intervene and "to explain the truth" – and not "for sake of argument."[33] From there on, the treatise is a point-by-point refutation of Aḥmad Lobbo's arguments in defense of Ḥamdallāhi's independence. It consists of fifteen statements that relate to four major issues: the relationship between Ḥamdallāhi and Sokoto; Sokoto's claims to be a caliphate; the legitimacy of Muḥammad Bello as successor of ʿUthmān b. Fūdī; and the status of some territories claimed by both Ḥamdallāhi and Sokoto.

In this text, Muḥammad Bello describes the territory of Ḥamdallāhi and Sokoto as "one country or one land" and in another place as "one region."[34] The core question was whether or not Ḥamdallāhi could be considered as part of the Sokoto state, and consequently whether or not Aḥmad Lobbo had legitimately declared independence. Aḥmad Lobbo's main argument is that "our community [i.e. Ḥamdallāhi] has

[29] IFAN, Fonds Brevié, Mauritania 7, p. 9. [30] MAMMP, Reel 6, p. 3.
[31] Kaduna, NA, A/AR50. [32] Kaduna, NA, A/AR50/2, f. 1a.
[33] Kaduna, NA, A/AR50/2, f. 2a. [34] Kaduna, NA, A/AR50/2, ff. 3a, 5b.

never been united to yours [i.e. Sokoto], so they cannot be divided."[35] Muḥammad Bello rejects this argument on the grounds of the "agreement by word," meaning that Ḥamdallāhi had previously pledged allegiance to Sokoto and this was, in itself, a binding action.[36] Subsequent breach of this pledge was therefore an attempt to disrupt the unity of the Muslim community, for which "there is no excuse" as underlined in a *ḥadīth* reported by al-Nawawī (d. 1277).[37] Muḥammad Bello also rejects Aḥmad Lobbo's point that "your jurisdiction did not reach us. What did reach us was your letters and scattered travelers."[38] Muḥammad Bello continues, "The arrival of their letters containing the pledge of allegiance is already enough for the [abovementioned] agreement by word, and it implies that they [those who sent the allegiance] will have to obey the orders and the prohibitions on religious and worldly matters [of the one to whom allegiance was sworn]." Muhammad Bello then backs up his statement with authoritative sources.[39]

The basic argument made by Aḥmad Lobbo rested on the concepts of "distance and interruption," and cites the example of the case of al-Andalus and Khurasān at the time of the Rightly Guided Caliphs and the Umayyads.[40] According to Aḥmad Lobbo, distance was not a reason for having two rulers, so long as there was unity within the caliphate; but after the death of 'Umar b. al-Khaṭṭāb there was a fragmentation of this original unity.[41] Muḥammad Bello corrects Aḥmad Lobbo's knowledge of history by quoting from books that state how al-Andalus, where the first schism of the caliphate emerged, was conquered under al-Walīd b. 'Abd al-Malik b. Marwān, thus after the death of 'Umar b. al-Khaṭṭāb.[42] In this way, he reveals a historical error that would, from his point of view, weaken the credibility of the caliph of Ḥamdallāhi's contention. But Aḥmad Lobbo had argued that it was not mere distance that gave rise to two caliphs, but the "interruption" of communication between the two.[43] To this Muḥammad Bello responds that he has never heard of any leading scholar arguing for that when talking about "a distance for which there is not possibility of contact." This, in any case, does not apply to Sokoto and

[35] Kaduna, NA, A/AR50/2, ff. 2a–2b. [36] Kaduna, NA, A/AR50/2, f. 2b.
[37] Kaduna, NA, A/AR50/2, f. 2b. [38] Kaduna, NA, A/AR50/2, f. 2b.
[39] Kaduna, NA, A/AR50/2, f. 2b. [40] Kaduna, NA, A/AR50/2, f. 3a.
[41] Kaduna, NA, A/AR50/2, f. 3b. [42] Kaduna, NA, A/AR50/2, f. 3b.
[43] Kaduna, NA, A/AR50/2, f. 3b.

Ḥamdallāhi.[44] Muḥammad Bello continues by providing several proofs for his point and concludes that, if interruption of communication were considered sufficient to justify the addition of Imāms, this would lead to multiple Imāms, which is not permissible, as made clear by a famous *ḥadīth* on the action to be taken in the case of two Imāms: the Prophet had said, "kill the second."[45]

In any event, Aḥmad Lobbo considered the discussion to be futile, since all the rulings that had been cited "only apply to the caliphs" and "not to the emirs of the lands, like us" – showing that Aḥmad Lobbo was rejecting the very concept of caliphate in the early phase of his tenure as ruler of Ḥamdallāhi.[46] Aḥmad Lobbo also adds that there was already a caliph in Egypt, so there could be none in West Africa.[47] Muḥammad Bello counters by correcting Aḥmad Lobbo's statement about the existence of a caliphate in North Africa, pointing out that there was now only "a governor of the ruler of Istanbul" in Egypt – which was, anyhow, very far from West Africa.[48] Furthermore, he argues that his father, "our *shaykh*," presented himself as a caliph and, although not everybody had agreed, "it will be not legitimate to anybody in this land to claim the caliphate after his appearance."[49] Aḥmad Lobbo had argued explicitly against the notion that 'Uthmān b. Fūdī had ever claimed the position of caliph: "I have not heard that utterance nor I have ever read it in any book – and concealment was not in his nature."[50] Muḥammad Bello quickly dismisses this by saying that "he [Aḥmad Lobbo] was not present in the gathering when 'Uthmān b. Fūdī said it."[51] He also corrects Aḥmad Lobbo by pointing out that in his book *Naṣīḥat ahl al-zamān* (Admonition to the People of the Time), 'Uthmān b. Fūdī made reference to the Prophetic traditions on the twelve caliphs (the same one employed in the *Tārīkh al-fattāsh*), saying: "I hope I am the first of the awaited two [that remains of the twelve], and the *mahdī* is the last."[52] It also appears that Muḥammad Bello had claimed that his father was the first West African caliph, to which Aḥmad Lobbo had responded by citing the precedent of Askiyà

44 Kaduna, NA, A/AR50/2, f. 3b.

45 Kaduna, NA, A/AR50/2, f. 3b. Muslim, *Saḥīḥ*, edited by Huda Khattab (Riyadh: Dār al-Salām, 2007), vol. 5, 186–187, no. 1853.

46 Kaduna, NA, A/AR50/2, ff. 2b–3a.

47 Kaduna, NA, A/AR50/2, f. 3a.

48 Kaduna, NA, A/AR50/2, f. 3a. At this time, Muḥammad 'Alī (d. 1849) was the governor of Egypt, while the Ottoman sultan was Maḥmūd II (d. 1839).

49 Kaduna, NA, A/AR50/2, f. 3a.

50 Kaduna, NA, A/AR50/2, f. 6a.

51 Kaduna, NA, A/AR50/2, f. 6a.

52 Kaduna, NA, A/AR50/2, f. 6b.

Muḥammad, who had already been recognized as a caliph in West Africa.[53] In response, Muḥammad Bello defends himself by clarifying that he meant "the first to emerge in our era."[54]

A heated part of the discussion focuses on the doubts cast by Aḥmad Lobbo on the legitimacy of Muḥammad Bello's claims to be the successor of 'Uthmān b. Fūdī, on the grounds that 'Uthmān b. Fūdī had made a sworn pact with him. In the words of Aḥmad Lobbo, "[as for] this pact, I do not know anything of it, nor has anybody that was present [when it happened] told me anything about it."[55] Muḥammad Bello's argument is that the mere fact that it was not made public does not mean that the event did not take place.[56] As for Aḥmad Lobbo not having heard of the event, Muḥammad Bello claims to be surprised since "those who were present did write to him about the fact that the pact was concluded while excusing themselves for not having waited for him." According to M. T. M. Minna, this obscure passage can be explained: "Before the Shehu's death there was a covenant written for Bello's succession which was confirmed in the presence of those who, presumably, came from Masina to receive the permission and the flag of the Shehu, on behalf of Aḥmad Lobbo, for the Jihad in Masina."[57] Aḥmad Lobbo, however, insists that he would have been informed about the choice of Muḥammad Bello by 'Uthmān b. Fūdī himself, because the *shaykh* ['Uthmān] would have not concealed something so important. He adds that being informed about the succession "is obligatory on the one who is given allegiance to the one who [has] pledged it."[58] Muḥammad Bello responds that "the mere absence of knowledge of the fact is not tantamount to absence of the fact itself."[59] And he adds that the Imam is not bound to inform the one who had pledged allegiance, while it is still obligatory for the latter to obey, as stated by Aḥmad Zarrūq (d. 1494) in his *'Umdat al-murīd al-ṣādiq* (Pillar of the Sincere Wayfarer).[60]

The last point debated in the treatise concerns disputed lands which both Ḥamdallāhi and Sokoto claimed as part of their territories: Fittouga, Hayre, and the surrounding areas. Aḥmad Lobbo had advanced claims that the inhabitants of these regions had paid allegiance to him. On the contrary, Muḥammad Bello argues that "the

[53] Kaduna, NA, A/AR50/2, f. 6a. [54] Kaduna, NA, A/AR50/2, f. 6a.
[55] Kaduna, NA, A/AR50/2, f. 5b. [56] Kaduna, NA, A/AR50/2, f. 5b.
[57] Minna, "Sultan Muhammad Bello," 110. [58] Kaduna, NA, A/AR50/2, f. 6a.
[59] Kaduna, NA, A/AR50/2, f. 6a. [60] Kaduna, NA, A/AR50/2, f. 6a.

people of Fittouga, those descendants of 'Alī Māna [i.e. the people of Hayre], and those close to them had first paid allegiance to him even though they might have later sworn it to Ahmad Lobbo."[61]

In the end, it is not clear from this treatise how this heated dispute between Aḥmad Lobbo and Muḥammad Bello was resolved. According to the Abu Bakr Atiku Manuscript, a letter of apology was sent from Sokoto to Ḥamdallāhi at some point.[62] This missing letter seems to have concluded this phase of tension between Aḥmad Lobbo and the Fodiawa, and to have inaugurated a period of a cordiality.

The Intermediate Period: Ḥamdallāhi and Sokoto Reconciled (1821–1838)

After the reconciliation between Aḥmad Lobbo and Muḥammad Bello, Ḥamdallāhi emerged from the dispute as a locally recognized theocracy, independent from Sokoto. For example, in 1825–6 Muḥammad al-Kuntī explicitly took the side of Aḥmad Lobbo and insisted that his claim to independence was sound: "It is well known that you [Aḥmad Lobbo] conducted the jihad, not with the armies of 'Uthmān b. Fūdī's emirs nor with their supplies, or with the support of any of the provinces that are under his authority."[63] Similarly, al-Mukhtār al-Ṣaghīr explicitly supports the legitimacy of Aḥmad Lobbo vis-à-vis Sokoto in a letter to the caliph of Ḥamdallāhi:

Some argue that Shaykh Aḥmad cannot claim the title of *shaykh* since he had pledged allegiance to Shaykh 'Uthmān b. Fūdī. However, these forget that when Shaykh Aḥmad pledged allegiance, he did it as a poor and weak person, who did not have authority over anybody. Instead of being under the authority of the unbelievers and of the bad Muslims who used to reign at the time on the land, the river and the fields, he chose to submit to one of the biggest *shaykhs* of his time, making clear he wanted to free himself from the above [evil authorities]. After the wars Aḥmad Lobbo waged and the death of Shaykh 'Uthmān, and after having set in place substantial and deep reforms, in reviving the Sunna and fighting the innovation ... he became undisputedly the biggest reformer of Islam in the land of the Sūdān.[64]

[61] Kaduna, NA, A/AR50/2, f. 6b. I thank Diakite for his help in identifying the descendants of 'Alī Māna with the people of Hayre.
[62] IFAN, Fonds Brevié, Mauritania 7, p. 9.
[63] Wuld Daddah, "Šayh Sîdi Muhammed," 152.
[64] Translated in Sanankoua, *Un empire peul*, 59–60.

Few documents better describe a regularized relationship between Aḥmad Lobbo and Sokoto after the post-1821 recognition of the independence of Ḥamdallāhi.

In a letter to the Arma *qā'id* of Timbuktu, Pashā 'Uthman, written to mark the arrival of the Scottish explorer Alexander Gordon Laing in Timbuktu, in August 1826, Aḥmad Lobbo writes:

> Having heard that a Christian traveller desires to visit our country, but not knowing whether he is arrived or not, you are to endeavour to prevent his entry, if not already come, and if he is come, endeavour to send him away, and take from him all hope of remaining into our dominions. For I have just received a letter from Bello Danfoda [Muḥammad Bello], full of wholesome advice, by which I am instructed to prevent Europeans from visiting the Musliman [*sic*] country of the Soudan. This was caused by a letter he received from Egypt, in which the abuses and corruptions the Christians have committed in that country are mentioned, as well as Andalusia and other countries in former times.[65]

This letter documents a relationship between Ḥamdallāhi and Sokoto in which the rulers of the two theocracies exchanged information as equals, and there is no sign of tension between them.

These amicable relations are further confirmed by other correspondence. The Abu Bakr Atiku Manuscript refers to a letter of condolence from Aḥmad Lobbo to the people of Sokoto following the death of Muḥammad Bello.[66] Cordial relations are also proven by a contemporary missive to Aḥmad Lobbo from one of the most important representatives of the Sokoto state, 'Uthmān b. Abī Bakr b. 'Umar b. Aḥmad, better known as Giɗaaɗo ɗan Laima (d. 1851).[67] Giɗaaɗo ɗan Laima was a close associate of 'Uthmān b. Fūdī and the *wazīr* of Sokoto under Muḥammad Bello and Abū Bakr al-'Atīq, occupying a position of power second only to that of the *amīr al-mu'minīn* of the region.[68] Giɗaaɗo ɗan Laima's letter is dated 10 Ṣafar 1255/ 25 April 1839, addresses Aḥmad Lobbo as "the master, the distinguished, the *shaykh*, the scholar, the God-fearing, the ascetic, the pious, the *mujāhid*," and remarks on the good relationship existing between

[65] Translated in Bovill, *Missions to the Niger*, vol. 1, 311. Some scholars have cast doubt on the authenticity of this letter (Minna, "Sultan Muhammad Bello," 111–115).

[66] The text of this letter has not been found, but reference to it is made in IFAN, Fonds Brevié, Mauritania 7, p. 1.

[67] BnF 6112, f. 57a. [68] On Giɗaaɗo ɗan Laima, see *ALA* II, 185–187.

the sender and the recipient. Giɗaaɗo ɗan Laima also makes reference to two books he is sending, most likely along with the letter: his biographies of the two seminal figures of Sokoto, ʿUthmān b. Fūdī and Muḥammad Bello, respectively the *Rawḍ al-jinān fī dhikr baʿḍ manāqib al-shaykh ʿUthmān* (The Meadows of Paradise in Remembrance of some of the Miracles of Shaykh ʿUthmān) and the recently completed *al-Kashf wa-l-bayān ʿan baʿḍ aḥwāl al-sayyid Muḥammad Bello b. al-shaykh ʿUthmān* (Unveiling and Elucidation of some Facts regarding the Master Muḥammad Bello, the son of Shaykh ʿUthmān).[69]

The letter from Giɗaaɗo ɗan Laima, however, also represents the conclusion of cordial diplomacy between the courts of Ḥamdallāhi and Sokoto. After the death of Muḥammad Bello in 1837, the tensions between Aḥmad Lobbo and the new Sokoto leaders, the *amīr al-mu'minīn* Abū Bakr al-ʿAṭīq and the emir of Gwandu, Ibrahīm al-Khalīl, escalated.

Later Years: Tensions Reemerge (1838–1845)

The balance of power that marked the settling of the dispute between Muḥammad Bello and Aḥmad Lobbo was disrupted by the emergence of a younger generation of Fodiawa leaders in Sokoto and Gwandu. Muḥammad Bello's brother, Abū Bakr al-ʿAtīq, became the new *amīr al-mu'minīn* of Sokoto in a climate of political instability. A challenger to his position was his elder brother Muḥammad al-Bukhārī, who was, in the words of Kani, "the strongest contender for the office of Caliph."[70] Eventually, the office fell to Abū Bakr al-ʿAtīq because of a severe injury suffered by Muḥammad al-Bukhārī prior to his nomination.[71] However, it seems that Muḥammad al-Bukhārī did contest the election of his younger brother. A letter that Aḥmad

[69] This is not the only time that books were sent from Sokoto to Ḥamdallāhi. According to oral traditions recorded by Hampaté Ba and Daget, Aḥmad Lobbo had asked for books to equip Ḥamdallāhi's library after the establishment of the caliphate (*L'empire peul*, 62).

[70] Ahmed M. Kani, "The intellectual and political contribution of Muhammad al-Bukhari (d. 1258 AH) to the Sokoto Caliphate," in *Studies in the History of the Sokoto Caliphate: The Sokoto Seminar Papers*, edited by Y. B. Usman (Zaria: Department of History, Ahmadu Bello University, for the Sokoto State History Bureau, 1979), 223–237, 232.

[71] Kani, "The intellectual and political contribution," 232.

Lobbo sent to Muḥammad al-Bukhārī, referenced in the Abu Bakr Atiku Manuscript, indicates that the latter did not pledge allegiance to his brother, the new caliph.[72]

Aḥmad Lobbo was close to Muḥammad al-Bukhārī. In one letter, for example, he refers to Muḥammad al-Bukhārī as his "dearest beloved in the path of God."[73] On the other side, Muḥammad al-Bukhārī is credited with a poem in praise of the caliph of Ḥamdallāhi.[74] It is reasonable to conclude that Aḥmad Lobbo had hoped that his friend and supporter would become the caliph of Sokoto and thus extend the decade-and-a-half of peace between the two theocracies. The election of Abū Bakr al-'Atīq might therefore have disillusioned Aḥmad Lobbo. The events that followed are unclear, but it seems that Aḥmad Lobbo took the opportunity created by the temporary vacancy in Sokoto to send a request that the Fodiawa recognize him as a legitimate authority for both Ḥamdallāhi and Sokoto. This much can be inferred from the Abu Bakr Atiku Manuscript.[75]

As expected, the leaders of Sokoto did not grant Ḥamdallāhi's request. Their response was entrusted to the powerful emir of Gwandu, Ibrāhīm al-Khalīl b. 'Abd Allāh (d.1860), who had occupied his position for two years before Abū Bakr al-'Atīq's ascension to the caliphate. Ibrāhīm al-Khalīl's response is not available, but a reply from Aḥmad Lobbo cites this document:

> I believe that obedience to us [Sokoto] is your duty as you have entered under the allegiance of our *shaykh*, the light of the time, the *amīr al-mu'minīn*, 'Uthmān b. Fūdī, who has brought back to us his blessings, *amīn*, and to his deputies. Now know that his successor, the *amīr al-mu'minīn* Muḥammad Bello, joined his Lord, God may have mercy on him and be pleased with him, and met his father in Paradise, *amīn*. The people who matter agreed upon his brother, sibling from both parents, 'Atīq, and positioned him in the place of his brother who is caliph now and we pledged allegiance to him. May God help him in this.[76]

Aḥmad Lobbo responded to this request by rejecting Ibrāhīm al-Khalīl's claims. He refers to the events of the so-called Second Civil

[72] IFAN, Fonds Brevié, Mauritania 7, pp. 14–15. See also Last, *The Sokoto Caliphate*, 81, n. 89.
[73] IFAN, Fonds Brevié, Mauritania 7, pp. 1 and 14.
[74] Kani and Stewart, "Sokoto–Masina correspondence," 7, item 7.
[75] IFAN, Fonds Brevié, Mauritania 7, p. 10.
[76] MAMMP, Reel 6, Aḥmad Lobbo, p. 10.

War in early Islamic history (680–692).[77] In this context, Aḥmad Lobbo compares himself to the rebel 'Ibn al-Zubayr because he had pledged allegiance to 'Uthmān b. Fūdī, just as Ibn al-Zubayr had to Mu'āwiya. However, since al- Zubayr considered his allegiance to the Umayyads dissolved upon the death of Mu'āwiya and the selection of Yazīd b. Mu'āwiya as caliph, Aḥmad Lobbo likewise felt he was freed from any obligation to Sokoto with the death of 'Uthmān b. Fūdī, and therefore not obliged to reaffirm his pledge to the latter's successor, Muḥammad Bello.[78] Indeed, Aḥmad Lobbo states explicitly: "Know that I have never entered in allegiance with any of his successors."[79]

Accordingly, Aḥmad Lobbo concludes, the new leaders of Sokoto should just accept Ḥamdallāhi's independence:

> The truth is, *amīr al-mu'minīn* al-'Atīq and Khalīl, the son of the jurist 'Abd Allāh b. Fūdī, you should be content with what satisfied your father the jurist 'Abd Allāh b. Fūdī and your elder brother, *amīr al-mu'minīn* and exemplary scholar Muḥammad Bello. Indeed, if they are not above you in knowledge and piety, they are surely not below you, and my opinion and that of other people is that you are clearly below them. It is not appropriate for a person of intellect to debate with somebody who is above him on a matter that the person who is above did not venture into.[80]

In response to these arguments, Abū Bakr al-'Atīq reinforced Ibrāhīm al-Khalīl's position. After a long analysis of previous letters from Aḥmad Lobbo, Abū Bakr al-'Atīq upholds the arguments of Ibrāhīm al-Khalīl on the obligatory nature of the former's allegiance to Sokoto: "What he [Ibrāhīm al-Khalīl] mentioned is the truth of the matter."[81]

What happened after this exchange of letters is unknown. However, it seems that the issue was reopened again in another correspondence that can be dated to 1840–1.[82]At this stage, Aḥmad Lobbo made

77 MAMMP, Reel 6, Aḥmad Lobbo, pp. 12–14.

78 After the death of Mu'āwiya, al- Zubayr, a prominent Companion from among the Qurāysh, did not renew his allegiance to the son and successor of Mu'āwiya, Yazīd I. He declared himself caliph and challenged the authority of the Umayyads, by extending his authority from the Arabian Peninsula to Iraq and Egypt, only to be eventually defeated and killed in 692 by al-Ḥajjāj b. Yūsuf after the siege of Mecca, al- Zubayr's capital.

79 MAMMP, Reel 6, p. 15. 80 MAMMP, Reel 6, p. 4.

81 IFAN, Fonds Brevié, Mauritania 7, p. 13.

82 IHERI-ABT/I. This letter (other copies are BnF, 5695, ff. 57a–58a; and MAMMP Reel 10), which is part of a miscellanea IHERI-ABT 4104, can be dated to 1840–1, as it was sent by Aḥmad Lobbo along with his condolences on

another request that allegiance be paid to him by the Fodiawa's leaders, as was ordered by an enigmatic and unidentified Maḥmūd, "*walī* among the *walī*s of the desert who came to us last year once and ordered that I send a request so that you can pledge allegiance to me."[83] This request generated at least three answers from Fodiawa leaders that have survived: all negative, as might be anticipated. First, Abū Bakr al-'Atīq abruptly rejected Aḥmad Lobbo's request and declared that it was not for the caliph to request allegiance – leaving it to be understood that it is up to the subjects to pledge it.[84] Aḥamd Lobbo should know, continues Abū Bakr al-'Atīq, what is permissible according to books "on the subject of imamate," as well as to various *ḥadīth*s, which he also quoted.[85] A second answer is included in a letter from Ibrāhīm al-Khalīl, who also rejected the request, explaining that he was already under allegiance to another emir, i.e. Abū Bakr al-'Atīq.[86] Breaking an existing allegiance is not permissible, adds Ibrāhīm al-Khalīl, who quotes the Qur'ān, the *ḥadīth*s, 'Abd Allāh b. Fūdī's *Ḍiyā' al-sulṭān wa-ghayrihi min al-ikhwān fī aham mā yaṭlabu 'ilmuhi fī umūr al-zamān* (Illumination of the Sultan and Others from among the Brethren in the Vital Issues Required of his Knowledge of the Affairs of the Time), and a poem in Fulfulde by 'Uthmān b. Fūdī.[87]

Ibrāhīm al-Khalīl's letter is extremely important for another reason: in listing the recipients to whom it was sent, the response introduces another crucial actor: "to the *amīr* of Māsina *al-shaykh* Aḥmad [Lobbo], to the scholar Nūḥ b. al-Ṭāhir, and those with them."[88] This is the first appearance of the author of the *Tārīkh al-fattāsh* in the debate between Aḥmad Lobbo and the Sokoto leaders concerning the legitimacy of Ḥamdallāhi. Explicitly addressed to Nūḥ b. al-Ṭāhir, along with Aḥmad Lobbo, is another response, this time from one of the most important scholars of Sokoto, 'Abd al-Qādir b. al-Muṣṭafà

the death of Muḥammad al-Bukhārī (IHERI-ABT 4104/II, f. 1b). The death of Muḥammad al-Bukhārī comes from an elegy in Hausa by Nana Asmā'u titled *Sonnori Buhari* (Boyd and Mack, *Collected Works*, 120, work 18).

83 IHERI-ABT 4104.

84 IHERI-ABT 4104/III, pp. 3–4; the name of the sender of this letter is absent in this manuscript, as in the Abu Bakr Atiku Manuscript, since it was most likely present in the seal (see note 9).

85 IHERI-ABT 4104/III, p. 3.

86 IHERI-ABT 4104/II, p. 1.

87 IHERI-ABT 4104/III, pp. 1–2.

88 IHERI-ABT 4104/III, p. 1.

al-Turūdī (d. 1864).[89] In this, 'Abd al-Qādir al-Turūdī, to whom I will return in Chapter 6, argues:

If the request of you two [i.e. Aḥmad Lobbo and Nūḥ b. al-Ṭāhir] is directed to the people, it is an issue of sin because you are asking them to be disobedient as you are asking them to break allegiance with their *imām*, and to part from the community of the Muslims is forbidden according to sound *ḥadīth*s.[90]

Thus, according to 'Abd al-Qādir al-Turūdī, Aḥmad Lobbo's request to the people of Sokoto is illegal. Furthermore, it would also be illegal to request the Sokoto ruler to send his allegiance to Ḥamdallāhi. Then 'Abd al-Qādir al-Turūdī continues with a second possible interpretation of Aḥmad Lobbo's request: "If it is directed to our *imām*, the one who makes such demands must display perfection that the other lacks; he must better fulfill the conditions of the caliphate; and he must be very close to being just."[91] However, according to 'Abd al-Qādir al-Turūdī, Aḥmad Lobbo does not display these qualities, thus being simply "among the oppressors."[92]

Most importantly, apart from containing another refusal of Aḥmad Lobbo's claims, this letter refers to a third document, penned by Nūḥ b. al-Ṭāhir, which was sent to the Fodiawa along with the request for allegiance and the condolences on the occasion of Muḥammad al-Bukhārī's death:

We paid attention, O brother, to the letter and the writing you sent to us regarding your Imām, Shaykh Aḥmad. We read what you wrote in it concerning the issue of the twelve caliphs mentioned in the *ḥadīth* and that [you claim] al-Shaykh Aḥmad is the twelfth of them, after which the *mahdī* will come, according to what is written in the *Tārīkh al-fattāsh*.[93]

[89] IHERI-ABT 4104/IV, pp. 2b–3b. This letter is incomplete, but a photocopy of a different, complete manuscript is preserved in Zaria, at Northern History Research Scheme (henceforth NHRS) 192/19, 'Abd al-Qādir b. al-Muṣṭafà, *Risāla ilà Aḥmad Lobbo*. From now on, I use this latter copy. I thank Salisu Bala and Mohammad Shareef for having shared with me pictures of this document. On 'Abd al-Qādir, see Ahmed M. Kani, "The private library of 'Abd al-Qadir b. al-Muṣṭafā (d. 1864)," in *Sixth Interim Report, 1979–1981* (Zaria: Northern History Research Scheme, 1987); *ALA* II, 221–30; and John O. Hunwick, "A supplement to Infāq al-maysūr: The biographical notes of 'Abd al'Qādir b. al-Muṣṭafā," *Sudanic Africa* 7 (1996): 35–51.

[90] NHRS 192/19, p. 3. [91] NHRS 192/19, p. 3. [92] NHRS 192/19, p. 3.

[93] NHRS 192/19, p. 1.

With these words, the *Tārīkh al-fattāsh* makes its entrance on the stage of the debate over Aḥmad Lobbo's legitimacy.

This crucial letter from 'Abd al-Qādir al-Turūdī is the only explicit evidence that connects the chronicle to a particular moment in the history of the Caliphate of Ḥamdallāhi, the early 1840s. Although it is possible that the chronicle had been produced at an earlier time, it is unlikely that it would have been left unused and unnoticed if it had already been in existence. It is much more plausible that the *Tārīkh al-fattāsh* was produced in the very years when the legitimacy Caliphate of Ḥamdallāhi was being contested, from within and without. The last years of Aḥmad Lobbo's life coincided with several military engagements of Ḥamdallāhi's army in Kaarta, and more intensely in and around the Niger Bend. Meanwhile, the relationship with Sokoto deteriorated, both at the time of Abū Bakr al-'Atīq and Ibrāhīm al-Khalīl, as documented in this chapter, but also at the accession of the next ruler, 'Alī b. Bello (d. 1859). Although no correspondence is available for this period in the early 1850s, Barth noted in that, "even at the present time [1853–4], there are no amicable relations whatever subsisting between the courts of Sókoto and Gando [Gwandu], on the one hand, and that of Hamda-Alláhi on the other."[94] There would have been no better time to reinforce Aḥmad Lobbo's authority as ruler, Muslim scholar, and saint, with an extra level of legitimacy, the triple-layered one provided by the *Tārīkh al-fattāsh* that made the ruler of Ḥamdallāhi Sultan, Caliph, and the Renewer of the Faith.

*****

Part II has analyzed the history of the emergence of Aḥmad Lobbo as a new ruler of the Middle Niger. A member of a minor scholarly clan from the rural areas of the southern Middle Niger, Aḥmad Lobbo rose from anonymity and emerged as an influential religious leader whose authority was based on his wisdom and sanctity. He managed to overthrow the Dikko and the Sidibe Fulani nobility, who were ruling the area of the floodplain up to the Bandiagara cliff on behalf of the powerful kingdom of Segou. By seizing political power, Aḥmad Lobbo united two spheres of authority that had traditionally been separate in the area – the political and the religious. Thereafter, he founded a powerful theocracy, the Caliphate of Ḥamdallāhi, that

[94] Barth, *Travels and Discoveries*, vol. 4, 257.

expanded further into the northern Middle Niger, including the region of Timbuktu.

However, his claims to authority were challenged time and time again. First, Aḥmad Lobbo faced the resistance of the old Fulani elite, who were eventually vanquished in battle. He also had to resist challenges from the influential Kunta family, residing in the Niger Bend and in the Azawād, who resisted the idea of giving up their religious authority to the caliph of Hamdallāhi, advocating a more traditional balance of power and separation of the secular and religious spheres of authority. A wholesale rejection of Aḥmad Lobbo's authority came from the Fodiawa family, rulers of Sokoto. The Fodiawa rejected any claim to authority from Hamdallāhi and continued claiming Ḥamdallāhi's submission, on the basis of an earlier pledge of allegiance by the future caliph of Ḥamdallāhi to the founder of Sokoto, ʿUthmān b. Fūdī.

This world of competing claims is the one in which the *Tārīkh al-fattāsh* project emerged. The chronicle written by Nūḥ b. al-Ṭāhir was meant to intervene by equipping Aḥmad Lobbo with unassailable legitimacy based on the prophecy purportedly recorded by Maḥmūd Kaʿti. However, several questions remain unanswered. How did the chronicle construct its argument for Aḥmad Lobbo's authority? How were the claims of the chronicle's narrative implemented on the ground? How were they publicized? And furthermore, how were such claims received by the people of the Middle Niger? Finally, it also remains to explore how the project of the *Tārīkh al-fattāsh* resisted the test of the time and acquired a new kind of legitimacy when Western scholars "discovered" and analyzed it.

PART III

The Circulation and Reception of the Tārīkh al-fattāsh, *1840s–2010s*

Some books are like a wadi, those capricious and ephemeral rivers in the North African desert, which mysteriously appear and disappear after months and miles, irrigating oasis and leaving behind stony grounds, without any manifest reason. Their public presence, on the surface, is never considerable nor prolonged enough to leave any significant track. But their absence is not sufficient to rule out the possibility of a future reincarnation.

Graziano Krätli, "Un viaggiatore danese e musulmano nella Libia del generale Graziani," Studi piacentini – Rivista dell'Istituto storico della Resistenza e dell'età contemporanea *27 (2000), 58.*

In the first half of the nineteenth century the Middle Niger was a world of competing claims to authority. After the swansong of the old Fulani warrior elites, the Dikko and the Sidibe, Aḥmad Lobbo emerged as a regional leader and founder of the Caliphate of Ḥamdallāhi. His authority, which rested on both religious and political claims, was firmly established in the southern Middle Niger. Further north, in the Niger Bend, the Tuareg continued raiding the northern borders of the caliphate, and the Arma were sporadically resistant to Ḥamdallāhi's rule in major centers, such as Timbuktu. Aḥmad Lobbo exercised his control over these areas by a combination of coercion, the appointment of local representatives, and the installation of functionaries sent from the capital; but also by seeking, with varying degrees of success, the cooperation of the powerful Kunta scholarly clan of the Niger Bend and Azawād. However, while the Kunta had accepted the rule of Ḥamdallāhi, their support for Aḥmad Lobbo was only partial, and limited to the political domain. The Kunta never gave up their role as the ultimate religious authority of the region, and tension flared at times between them and Ḥamdallāhi, as in the case of the never-resolved tobacco dispute and that of the Kunta's mediation with rebels such as Gelaajo and Aḥmad b. Alfagha. East of Ḥamdallāhi, contestation of Aḥmad Lobbo's authority was even more bitter. The Fodiawa leaders of the Sokoto Caliphate constantly questioned the role of Aḥmad Lobbo as both a religious and political authority, even claiming sovereignty over Ḥamdallāhi. The *Tārīkh al-fattāsh*, which was a political project disguised as a historical work, took shape in the 1840s as response to these challenges.

Part III's focus returns to the *Tārīkh al-fattāsh*. Consisting only of one chapter, it explores how the chronicle affected the political history of the Middle Niger in the nineteenth century and describes how the work was circulated and received from the time of its production up to the present day. By focusing on the reception of the chronicle, my analysis first pays attention to the strategies and the structure that enabled the efficient dispersion of propaganda materials derived from the *Tārīkh al-fattāsh*. Then, I move to the reception of the chronicle itself and concentrate on the debates that it generated in the Middle Niger and beyond. I conclude by following the decline of the political project that the chronicle was designed to support, which occurred with the disappearance of the Caliphate of Ḥamdallāhi in the 1860s, and the later repurposing of the chronicle during the colonial period. At this point, the *Tārīkh al-fattāsh* began to serve another political project: that of production of knowledge for the use of French colonial administrators who wanted to better understand the past of the colonized peoples in order to control them more effectively.

6 *The* Tārīkh al-fattāsh *at Work*

This chapter approaches the *Tārīkh al-fattāsh* from the perspective of what McKenzie describes as a sociology of texts: "The discipline that studies texts as recorded forms, and the processes of their transmission, including their production and reception."[1] Accordingly, I deal with the social life of the *Tārīkh al-fattāsh* during the heyday of Ḥamdallāhi and in its afterlife following the decline of the caliphate, exploring how the chronicle, a skillfully crafted work written by Nūḥ b. al-Ṭāhir, was effectively circulated within and beyond the caliphate. A lengthy narrative, consisting of about a hundred manuscript folios, the *Tārīkh al-fattāsh* was employed as an authoritative source for citation in shorter works of political propaganda or in administrative documents. These documents were put in circulation through already established administrative and diplomatic channels, in line with Donald Crummey's argument that literacy was "one of the tools of Sudanic state power."[2] As a result, the claims of the *Tārīkh al-fattāsh* were circulated in West Africa, especially in Sokoto, but also in Timbuktu and in the Western Sahara. Moreover, this study of the *Tārīkh al-fattāsh*'s reception shows that it resonated with contemporary political, scholarly, and racial discourses, all of which were shaped by an epistemological context in which prophecies, divine appointments, and eschatological insecurities were current.

The legacy of the *Tārīkh al-fattāsh*, however, long outlasted Aḥmad Lobbo and his caliphate. The caliph of Ḥamdallāhi died in 1845, only a few years after the chronicle's completion. While there is evidence that the work continued to be used during the time of Aḥmad II and

[1] McKenzie, *Bibliography and the Sociology of Texts*, 12.

[2] Donald Crummey, "Land, literacy and the state in Sudanic Africa," in *Land, Literacy and the State in Sudanic Africa*, edited by Donald Crummey (Trenton, NJ: Africa World Press, 2005), 1–18. See also Anaïs Wion, Sébastien Barret, and Aïssatou Mbodj-Pouye (eds.), *L'écrit pragmatique africain*, special issue of *Afriques* 7 (2016) (https://journals.openedition.org/afriques/1870).

afterward, the caliphate itself fell apart under the advance of al-Ḥājj 'Umar, just twenty years after the claims of the *Tārīkh al-fattāsh* were first circulated. Thereafter, the chronicle's original project became obsolete, a vestige of the past splendor of Ḥamdallāhi to which only the Timbuktu-based family of the San Shirfis remained attached.

Ironically, it would be the interests of French colonizers that gave new life to the *Tārīkh al-fattāsh*. The French project was not geared toward producing knowledge per se. Rather, it aimed to produce, in Said's words, "effective knowledge": information to be used in dominating colonial subjects.[3] French "scholar-administrators," hearing rumors of a valuable ancient chronicle, started looking for it.[4] Eventually, the chronicle – or, as I have shown in Part I, copies of both the *Tārīkh Ibn al-Mukhtār* and the *Tārīkh al-fattāsh* – were found, and then edited and translated in the conflated text produced by Houdas and Delafosse in 1913. At this point, a new colonial text was born, *La chronique du chercheur*, which in turn, as will be detailed below, "gave birth" to a new textual tradition in West Africa, when manuscript copies of their printed Arabic text were transcribed by local copyists.[5] But this would be only the last phase of the complex history of the chronicle's circulation and reception.

The Letter on the Appearance of the Twelfth Caliph

The chronicle written by Nūḥ b. al-Ṭāhir and ascribed to Maḥmūd Ka'ti fulfilled the need for a (pseudo-) historical work legitimizing the authority of Aḥmad Lobbo. However, despite Nūḥ b. al-Ṭāhir's genius in producing a coherent text, the circulation of the entire manuscript might have revealed his historical manipulations. In the words of Simone Simonini, the skilled forger who is the main character of one of the last works by Italian novelist Umberto Eco: "Where possible, the original must not be seen but only talked about, without reference to any precise source, as happened with the Three Kings, whom only Matthew mentions in a couple of verses, not saying what they were

3 Said, *Orientalism*, 38.
4 The name "scholar-administrators" is derived from Christopher Harrison, *France and Islam in West Africa, 1860–1960* (Cambridge and New York: Cambridge University Press, 1988).
5 I borrowed the concept of "giving birth" to textual traditions from Luciano Canfora, *Il copista come autore* (Palermo: Sellerio, 2002), 26.

called, or how many they were, or that they were kings, and all the rest is tradition."[6] Moreover, the chronicle must have been a manuscript of about hundred leaves – MS A/IHERI-ABT 3927, for example, is an incomplete copy of the *Tārīkh Ibn al-Mukhtār* and yet consists of seventy-seven folios. Therefore, it is unlikely that the *Tārīkh al-fattāsh* was circulated as a complete chronicle, both because sustained scrutiny might raise doubts about its claims and because its length was not conducive to rapid circulation in multiple copies.

My research in West African manuscript collections suggests, in fact, that the *Tārīkh al-fattāsh* may have existed in only a single manuscript copy, the matrix from which Brévié had MS C copied in Kayes (see Chapter 1). No other copy of the chronicle has surfaced so far.[7] However, the existence of this manuscript in Kayes, far from the centers of Ḥamdallāhi's power, is significant in itself. Oral traditions point to the preservation of the chronicle in the so-called *Beembal dewte* or "granary of books" – Ḥamdallāhi's library – where books were accessible for consultation and copying.[8] Most likely, with al-Ḥājj 'Umar's conquest of the city in 1862, the original manuscript of the *Tārīkh al-fattāsh* ended up in Segou, along with many documents that were taken from the city, according to information collected by Yattara.[9] The book would then have been seized by Archinard at the time of the

6 Umberto Eco, *The Prague Cemetery* (New York: Houghton Mifflin Harcourt, 2010), 200.

7 All the published catalogues of West African libraries as well as several unpublished lists of manuscripts from Malian collections have been analyzed in preparation of this work. The copies found so far, as shall be explained at the end of this chapter, are copies of the Arabic text of *La chronique du chercheur*. The copies referred to in Bābā Yūnus Muḥammad and 'Ali 'Abd al-Muḥsin al-Zakī, *Fihris makhṭūṭāt maktabāt Ghāna/Catalogue of Manuscripts in the Ghana Libraries* (London: al-Furqan Islamic Heritage Foundation, 2000) and Bābā Yūnus Muḥammad, *Fihris al-makhṭūṭāt al-islāmiyya bi-dār al-wathā'iq al-waṭāniyya bi-dawlat Sāhil al-'Āj/Catalogue of Islamic Manuscripts in the National Library of Côte d'Ivoire*, 2 vols. (London: al-Furqan Islamic Heritage Foundation, 2014) do not exist – in fact, most of the entries of these catalogues seem to have been fabricated (see Mauro Nobili and Mohamed Diagayeté, "The manuscripts that never were: In search of the *Tārīkh al-fattāsh* in Côte d'Ivoire and Ghana," *History in Africa* 44 [2017]: 309–321).

8 *L'empire peul*, 62; Sanankoua, "L'organisation politique," 149. Sanankoua provides a list of the books that were present in the library based on information offered by A. K. Diallo (Sanankoua, "L'organisation politique," 155).

9 Yattara and Salvaing, *Almamy*, vol. 2, 214.

French conquest of Segou in April 1890, along with others from the same library, and eventually moved to Kayes. French archival documents reveal that the colonial authorities did not really know what to do with these books, and left them in a pile for a few months until 2 September 1890.[10] If so, it is not unlikely that the copy of the *Tārīkh al-fattāsh* was extracted from the manuscripts stored by the French, and that it remained in Segou while the other documents were eventually shipped to France.

Whether or not this plausible reconstruction of the *Tārīkh al-fattāsh*'s manuscript history is accurate, my examination of extant manuscript collections shows that other documents containing several passages from the chronicle were widespread throughout West Africa. These documents show how effectively the claims contained in the *Tārīkh al-fattāsh* were circulated. The most important, surviving in at least twenty manuscript copies, is a very famous document also authored by Nūḥ b. al-Tāhir: the so-called Letter on the Appearance of the Twelfth Caliph or *Risāla fī ẓuhūr al-khalīfa al-thānī 'ashar* (henceforth *Risāla*). Arguably, this was the most widely reproduced text in pre-colonial West Africa.[11] Indeed, the *Risāla* is none other than the propaganda pamphlet found by Dubois during his trip to Timbuktu (Chapter 1). Couched in the form of a circular letter, it opens with the following lines:

> In the name of God, the Most Gracious, the Most Merciful. May God's blessings and perfect peace be on our master, Muḥammad His Prophet, his household and his companions. "God summons to the Abode of Peace [Qur'ān 10: 25]." "And vie with one another, hasting to forgiveness from your Lord, and to a garden whose breadth is as heavens and earth [Qur'ān 3: 133]." O brethren, from the needy Nūḥ b. al-Ṭāhir b. Abī Bakr b. Mūsà, the student of *shaykh sīdī* al-Mukhtār al-Kuntī – Allah guides you and guides through you those who are not with you among nations.[12]

[10] Archives nationales d'outre-mer, Soudan I: 2 *bis. Ségou 1890–1892, Bulletin d'expédition*. I thank Amir Syed for having shared this document.

[11] The text of the *Risāla* is edited and translated into English in Nobili (ed. and trans.), "Letter on the appearance of the twelfth caliph." The list of copies of this document provided in *ALA* is incomplete (*ALA* IV, 213, item 1). Nobili, "A propaganda document" lists seventeen manuscripts of this letter, but since the article was published more copies have emerged in West African libraries.

[12] Nobili (ed. and trans.), "Letter on the appearance of the twelfth caliph."

This letter exists in two versions, which differ only in their lists of named recipients and a short passage added to the end of one.[13] The first is addressed to Moorish tribes of the Western Sahara:

Ahl ʿAli ʿAmār and their wards and the brethren from among the Awlād Mbārak, Hannūna Būsayf, Awlād ʿAllūsh, and the Awlād Muhammad, to the Znaga all the way to Trārza and those from al-Ḥawḍ, in towns such as Niʿma, Walāta, and Tishīt, and in the desert areas of Aghlāl, the Idaw Bilāl, the Tinwāj, the Burtayl, the [I]daybusāt, the Zummān, the Kunta, the Idaw ʿAli, the Awlād Bār Kull [or Kulla], Awlād Dulaym, all the way to Wadān, the home of palm groves, and surrounding areas extending to the Ocean.[14]

The second version is addressed to anonymous leaders of cities and countries, including an anachronistic al-Andalus:

The Sultan of the West in Fes and Marrakesh, and his wards in Timbuktu, Araouane, Boujbeiha, Taoudenni, the people of the far and hither Sousse, Touat, Ghadamis, all the way to Tunis, Algiers and Berber, to Egypt, Kairouan, Tlemcen, al-Andalus, until the far end of the abode of Islam.[15]

In both versions there follows a clear announcement of Aḥmad Lobbo's status as the legitimate authority of the Middle Niger:

After the fullest and most complete greetings of peace, the all-encompassing and perfect honor, know that *shaykh*, the Commander of the Believers Aḥmad b. Muḥammad b. Abī Bakr [i.e. Aḥmad Lobbo], the one who stood up to revive the religion of God the Most High and *jihād* in His path in the land of Masina and its surrounding territories to the east, west, south and north, is the twelfth caliph and renewer of the faith after whom the *mahdī* will emerge.[16]

Here enters the *Tārīkh al-fattāsh*, as Nūḥ b. al-Ṭāhir substantiates this claim for Aḥmad Lobbo's authority by revealing that it is based on an older text, written by Maḥmūd Kaʿti:

13 One of the two versions has the following *explicit* that is missing in the other: "Always peace. The one who has the power to make the letter of the *askiyà* to the *amīr al-mu'minīn* Aḥmad b. Muḥammad b. Abī Bakr has also the power to allow my writing to reach those it was written for, by the baraka of the shaykh. Amīn. End" (Nobili [ed. and trans.], "Letter on the appearance of the twelfth caliph").

14 Nobili (ed. and trans.), "Letter on the appearance of the twelfth caliph."

15 Nobili (ed. and trans.), "Letter on the appearance of the twelfth caliph."

16 Nobili (ed. and trans.), "Letter on the appearance of the twelfth caliph."

If it was asked where is the source [for this statement], I would say it is documented in the *Tārīkh al-fattāsh fī akhbār al-buldān*, by the *shaykh*, jurist, and scholar, Maḥmūd Ka'ti, from Kurmina but resident in Timbuktu, of Soninke origin – God the Most High have mercy on him and benefit us through him, through the likes of him, and through all those of high rank. *Amīn.*[17]

References to remote regions such as Egypt or the Maghreb, or to no-longer-extant entities such as al-Andalus, are most likely a flamboyant literary embellishment designed to add further prestige to Aḥmad Lobbo's claims. These claims are all supported by quotations from the *Tārīkh al-fattāsh* and, as described in Chapter 2, represent Aḥmad Lobbo as a West African sultan, inheritor of a long and unbroken line of legitimate rulers dating back to the first millennium CE; the last of a series of twelve caliphs mentioned in a *ḥadīth* of the Prophet; and as renewer of the faith: the leader who is expected to come each century, according to another prophetic tradition, in order to revive Islam and prevent its degeneration.

The more immediate audience of the letter seems to be the Muslim communities of West Africa. Interestingly, the text even offers indications of how the document was circulated in the region:

I, Nūḥ b. al-Ṭāhir, urge and press all those who receive this letter of mine to make a copy of it and to send it to everybody who they think did not receive what is included in it. For him [is valid] the admonishment of God and of his Prophet – and they are the two most trustful ones who said, "The believers are indeed brothers" [Qur'ān 49:10] and "the religion is an admonishment." I also urge and press the carrier of the letter to gather the Muslims of the towns, the villages and hamlets that he passes through and he thinks did not hear of it to read the letter to them or to tell them what is in it, according to his capability.[18]

Copies were most likely sent to different towns and villages via couriers, and local chiefs were in turn asked to have the document copied and circulated. The couriers were also charged with reading the document in public.

Reading letters and dispatches in public was a very common practice in nineteenth-century West Africa. Hampaté Ba and Daget record that

[17] Nobili (ed. and trans.), "Letter on the appearance of the twelfth caliph."
[18] Nobili (ed. and trans.), "Letter on the appearance of the twelfth caliph." For the *ḥadīth*, see Abū Dāwūd, *Sunan*, vol. 5, 331, no. 4944.

a very important position established by Ḥamdallāhi was that of *goolowo* (Fulfulde): a "town crier" who would read written texts to those who did not have direct access to literacy.[19] A very lively description of this practice is narrated by Caillié, who witnessed it during his stay in Fouta Djalon:

I went to the evening prayer where, contrary to custom, I found a great number of Mandingoes assembled. On leaving the mosque they all formed a circle round the old chief. He made a short speech, informing them that a messenger had arrived from Timbo with a circular letter, which should be read to them, and to which he requested them to pay attention. A marabout who was seated beside him then read the letter aloud.[20]

The availability of multiple copies of the *Risāla* testify that the document was indeed effectively disseminated in West Africa, especially within the borders of the caliphate. Its extensive circulation was made possible by the very efficiency of Ḥamdallāhi's administrative networks.

Ḥamdallāhi's Administration and Literacy

Ḥamdallāhi developed as a highly centralized state that extended along the River Niger. The "administrative units" of the caliphate were villages and towns called *ngenndi*s (Fulfulde "ancient town").[21] A conglomeration of *ngenndi*s formed a canton, in Fulfulde *leppi leydi* (sing. *lefol leydi*).[22] Cantons were grouped together to form provinces (Fulfulde *leyde*, sing. *leydi*).[23] Each province was governed by an *amīr* chosen by the Great Council, who could in turn be removed

19 *L'empire peul*, 74. 20 Caillié, *Travels through Central Africa*, vol. 1, 218.

21 Sanankoua, on the basis of information collected by traditionalist Arskoula, records the exorbitant number of 67,000 *ngenndi*s (Sanankoua, *Un empire peul*, 66) – an unlikely figure given that if each village had only, say, one hundred inhabitants, that would make the entire population of the caliphate amount to almost 7 million people.

22 *L'empire peul*, 73.

23 According to Sanankoua the provinces were Masina, Jenneri (between the Niger and the Bani Rivers from Sanari to Fakala and from Murari to Sebera), Kounari, Fakala (between the Bani River and the Bandiagara cliff) and Gimmballa (Sanankoua, "L'organisation politique," 231–252; Sanankoua, *Un empire peul*, 66–76). In addition to these five provinces, the regions of Timbuktu and the Dyilgodyi "had a special status although [they] recognized the authority" of the caliphate's – very limited – control over these regions, in time and depth, and mainly characterized by a semi-independence involving the payment of taxes

from his position by the same body.[24] The *amīr* combined military and administrative roles. He oversaw a garrison of soldiers stationed in the province that he commanded on behalf of Ḥamdallāhi.[25] He was also in charge of collecting taxes.[26] The *amīr* was accompanied in his duties by a *qāḍī*, also selected by the Great Council, whose duties were to administer justice according to the Mālikī school.[27]

The centralization of Ḥamdallāhi was possible due to the substantial development of literacy in the region, which resulted from a process that can be characterized – borrowing from Konrad Hirshler's study of medieval Arabic lands – as "textualization," i.e. the process by which "the role of the written word significantly increased."[28] The textualization of the Middle Niger depended on both technological and human factors. The technological revolution that took place in West Africa during the eighteenth and nineteenth centuries resulted in the more extensive availability of paper. While inks and pens had always been produced locally, paper-making technology was not developed in West

(Sanankoua, *Un empire peul*, 72). A slightly different list of provinces is provided by Hampaté Ba and Daget, who anachronistically date this structure of the caliphate to just after the battle of Noukouma when Aḥmad Lobbo would have divided the first hundred scholars who formed the members of the Great Council into five commissions according to their provenances and eventually decided to transform these regions into five administrative divisions of the caliphate (*L'empire peul*, 59). Written evidence suggests that this description is a later attempt to create an image of the caliphate as having a clear-cut regional organization. For example, an anonymous poem mentions the great provincial rulers of Ḥamdallāhi and contradicts the organization of Ḥamdallāhi into provinces, as sketched in oral sources collected by Hampaté Ba, Daget, and Sanankoua. This manuscript comes from a series of pictures taken by Salvaing in the Malian town of Dalla, close to Duenza. I thank Salvaing for having shared this manuscript with me.

24 *L'empire peul*, 74. The title is ambiguous as *amīr*s were also governors of towns (*L'empire peul*, 73).

25 For a description of the military structure of Ḥamdallāhi's army, see *L'empire peul*, 68–73.

26 Sanankoua, *Un empire peul*, 106. For an introduction to these taxes, see also *L'empire peul*, 67. Johnson, "Economic foundations," 486–488, provides a more detailed analysis of the finances of the caliphate.

27 *L'empire peul*, 65. However, regional *qāḍī*s were limited in their capacities. They would mainly act as a court of reconciliation and, in cases of violence, the decisions had to be confirmed by the *qāḍī* of Ḥamdallāhi, and the execution of punishments could only take place there in the capital: *L'empire peul*, 65.

28 Konrad Hirschler, *The Written Word in the Medieval Arabic Lands: A Social and Cultural History of Reading Practices* (Edinburgh: Edinburgh University Press, 2013), 5.

Africa until the colonial period.[29] From the seventeenth century onward, paper started to figure among the goods imported from North Africa south of the Sahara.[30] However, the availability of this writing support increased on an unparalleled scale only in the nineteenth century, and "the large availability of paper in the nineteenth century goes a long way in explaining the remarkable growth in scholarly production and library collection in this period."[31]

Once the technological infrastructure became readily available in the Middle Niger, Arabic literacy became the crucial tool for the development of an administrative apparatus based on orders that emanated from the capital and circulated through a capillary system of letters and dispatches to the different local administrative units. This process placed the local *'ulamā'*, linked to Aḥmad Lobbo, in an unprecedented position of administrative power. Literacy became not only a tool by which Ḥamdallāhi governed the provinces of the caliphate, but also a prerequisite for accessing power.[32] In this regard, the response that Aḥmad Lobbo gave to Gelaajo, after the latter complained about not having been chosen as *amīr* of Kounari, is telling:

> The Council decided to monitor the security and the good administration of the Dina, so nobody unable to read, write and understand the meaning of a document written in Arabic characters can govern a territory that extends for more than five days' walk ... The Council does not contest your illustrious birth, nor your military achievements. However, it would be an issue to give you an office in which neither military merit nor origin matter. From administrators we require piety and science. And, without insulting you, your piety is mild, and your science is non-existent.[33]

[29] Jonathan M. Bloom, "Paper in Sudanic Africa," in *The Meanings of Timbuktu*, edited by Shamil Jeppie and Souleymane B. Diagne (Cape Town: HSRC Press, 2008), 45–57, 45.

[30] Terence Walz, "The paper trade of Egypt and the Sudan in the eighteenth and nineteenth centuries and its re-export to the Bilād as-Sūdān," in *The Trans-Saharan Book Trade: Manuscript Culture, Arabic Literacy, and Intellectual History in Muslim Africa*, edited by Graziano Krätli and Ghislaine Lydon (Leiden and Boston: Brill, 2011), 73–107, 97.

[31] Ghislaine Lydon, "Inkwells of the Sahara: Reflections on the production of Islamic knowledge in Bilād Shinqīṭ," in *The Transmission of Learning in Islamic Africa*, edited by Scott S. Reese (Leiden and Boston: Brill, 2004), 39–71, 56.

[32] *L'empire peul*, 73. [33] *L'empire peul*, 118.

Oral sources make ample reference to such Arabic documents. Hampaté Ba and Daget record that, after the foundation the capital city of Ḥamdallāhi around 1819, Aḥmad Lobbo sent a circular instructing that all the owners of pirogues under his control should send their boats to help relocate the inhabitants of Noukouma, the ancient capital, to the new one.[34] Manuscripts of these letters sent from Ḥamdallāhi to the provinces also exist in relatively large numbers.[35] One such document, for instance, is a letter concerning punishment for immoral conduct:

In the name of God the Most Merciful and the Most Compassionate. Following on with peace. From the *shaykh amīr al-mu'minīn* Aḥmad [Lobbo] b. Muḥammad to the *amīr*s and the *qāḍī*s of the land telling them: God willing, you will see our messengers to oversee [correct] dress-code which is our concern. Everybody who is found guilty of immorality in dress-code is to be fined two thousand shells if he is able to pay the amount; otherwise he will be punished with twenty lashes. Also, everybody who is found guilty of talking with an unrelated woman in a non-permitted circumstance, he and the woman will be fined two hundred and forty shells. Whosoever fails to follow this rule after he has heard of it is guilty of sin. End.[36]

Another addresses the issue of the dowry and other matters of jurisprudence.[37] Very widespread too were *fatwà*s issued by Aḥmad Lobbo in response to the requests of scholars and administrators in the provinces. For example, one was issued for one Bāba b. 'Uthmān concerning the sharing of profits with his spouses;[38] two to a certain Abū Bakr b. Samūd, the first on pastures and the second on six other juridical issues;[39] and several others, responding to questions asked by different scholars, concerning slavery.[40]

[34] *L'empire peul*, 45.
[35] Specifically, the Gironcourt collection is particularly rich in such documents.
[36] IF, Fonds de Gironcourt, 2406 (66).
[37] IF, Fonds de Gironcourt, 2405 (31–35)/V.
[38] IF, Fonds de Gironcourt, 2405 (31–35)/IV, (another copy is IF, Fonds de Gironcourt, 2406 [69]).
[39] IF, Fonds de Gironcourt, 2406 (46–60)/XI; and IF, Fonds de Gironcourt, 2405 (31–35)/III.
[40] IF, Fonds de Gironcourt, 2406 (46–60)/II; IF, Fonds de Gironcourt, 2406 (46–60)/V; IF, Fonds de Gironcourt, 2406 (46–60)/VII (which is in turn a response to IF, Fonds de Gironcourt, 2406 (46–60)/VI); IF, Fonds de Gironcourt, 2406 (46–60)/VIII; IF, Fonds de Gironcourt, 2406 (46–60)/IX; IF, Fonds de Gironcourt, 2406 (46–60)/X.

The issue of slavery in the region is also closely linked to the story behind *Tārīkh al-fattāsh*. Several of the passages written by Nūḥ b. al-Ṭāhir suggest that the chronicle was also intended to justify the imposition of slave status on different endogamous groups of the Middle Niger (see Chapter 1). The most extensive passage, which is quoted verbatim in the *Risāla*, is the one narrating that Askiyà Muḥammad was in possession of "twelve tribes" inherited as slaves of the crown from the Sonni kings:

Then the *askiyà* also asked about the issue of the twenty-four tribes that he had found at hand of Shī [Sonni] Bāru as bond people, who had in turn inherited them from his ancestors. The *shaykh* asked him, "Describe them" and he did. Then the *shaykh* told him: "Half of them belong to you by right. As for the second half, it is better that you leave them because there is doubt about them." Then the *shaykh* added: "The first is Jindèkèta, a tribe [spelled] with *jīm* and *dāl* both with *kasra* and a *nūn* with *sukūn* in between, and then with *kāf* and *tā'* with *fatḥa*. The second is Jām Walé, with *jīm* with elongated *fatḥa* and *mīm* with *sukūn*, and then *wāw* with *fatḥa* and *lām* with elongated *kasra*. The third is Jam Téné; the fourth Komé; and the fifth Sorobanna; the sixth are the infidels Bambara descending from Diarra Kur Bukari; the seventh descends from Tankara Tibi; the eighth from Kasambara; the ninth from Samasiku; the tenth is called Sorko; the eleventh Gorongoy; and the twelfth Arbi.[41]

The chronicle continues with Askiyà Muḥammad enforcing his rule over the members of the "twelve tribes," which he had "inherited" from the previous Songhay king, after al-Maghīlī confirmed the juridical opinion of al-Suyūṭī- a passage that is also verbatim repeated in the text of the *Risāla*.[42] Therefore, following Nūḥ b. al-Ṭāhir's argument, Aḥmad Lobbo, inheritor of Askiyà Muḥammad's authority, also inherited ownership of these tribes' descendants.

The way the claims made in the *Tārīkh al-fattāsh* concerning the servile status of these groups were circulated closely resembles those of the passages concerning the legitimacy of the caliph of

[41] *La chronique du chercheur*, Arabic text 14/French text 20–21. For the identification of these groups, see *La chronique du chercheur*, French text 20, nn. 1–9, 21, nn. 1–6; Bambā (ed.), *Tārīkh al-fattāsh*, 97–98; Maiga et al. (eds.), *Tārīkh al-fattāsh*, 54. Some of these groups are discussed in Tamari, *Les castes*.

[42] *La chronique du chercheur*, Arabic text 15/French text 22.

Ḥamdallāhi. An undated *fatwà* by Aḥmad Lobbo, attempting to reduce one such endogamous group to the status of slaves, quotes the *Tārīkh al-fattāsh*:

In the name of God, the Most Gracious, the Most Merciful. After that, may God's blessings [be on Muḥammad His Prophet]. For all the *walī*s and *qāḍī*s who receive this letter, know that the *shaykh*, the Commander of Believers, Aḥmad b. Muḥammad has ordered [what follows], on the basis of what is in the *Tārīkh al-fattāsh* regarding the enslavement of the Zanj in general, meaning whether or not their mothers are free. According to the *Tārīkh al-fattāsh*: 'Then Askiyà [Muḥammad] asked the abovementioned *shaykh* [al-Suyūṭī]: "What is the condition of someone from these tribes who claims to be the son of a free man or a free woman?" The *shaykh* replied: "For one who is certain that his father is free and his mother is from one of these tribes, he is your property by right. As for somebody who is certain that his mother is free and his father is from one of these tribes, if he stays in his father's house and works his father's job, he belongs to you." End of quote. This applies in any case, except someone who is freed from slavery based on a different perspective among which is that his status is that of the son of a free woman, who has not been raised in his father's house, but in that of his maternal uncles, or who does not work his father's job which makes him an unbeliever, and it is obligatory on this person to make public repentance with those who are present with them, leave the job of unbelief, according to what is stated in the *Tārīkh al-fattāsh*: "if he leaves the house of the father to go to the mother's house, he is not your property anymore." It is also stated, "As for every woman who marries a man from these tribes, she gives birth and wants freedom for her son, she has to make him leave the house of her husband and go to her own father's house. However, if he stays at the husband's house and works his job, he, meaning the child, will be my property" – in case what is intended here is that the work of the husband is a work of unbelief and nothing else. As for all those Zanj who claim freedom for lack of applicability of the conditions of mentioned by the *askiyà*, you should listen to his claim and if it is established according to *sharīʿa*, he is left free, while if not he remains in slavery.[43]

In this case, the *Tārīkh al-fattāsh*, a pseudo-historical work, creates a fictitious juridical precedent in order to enforce the slave status of certain groups, and also sets up the conditions for their freedom.

[43] IF, Fonds de Gironcourt, 2406 (45–60)/XVI.

The chronicle, therefore, was designed to aid Aḥmad Lobbo and his deputies in their attempts to restructure the society of the region. This project also involved the regulation and militarization of the traditional routes for Fulani transhumance.[44] Even more spectacularly ambitious was the successful attempt to enforce Fulani sedentarism, which resulted in the foundation of several towns that still sprinkle the Middle Niger. Apart from Ḥamdallāhi, the most remarkable results of this endeavor were the foundation of Ténenkou, the "capital" of the Masina province, and the relocation of the inhabitants of Mopti from the old seat of the city to the island where it stands today.[45]

While this project of social reconstruction is beyond the scope of the present book, the actual imposition of slave status on some of the peoples of the Middle Niger highlights how effectively the *Tārīkh al-fattāsh* worked in the region. In December 1853 Barth met a crowd of people who were leaving the territories controlled by Ḥamdallāhi and noted: "They belonged to the tribe of the Surk [i.e. Sorko], who, from being the indigenous tribe on that part of the Niger which extends on both sides of the lake Debu, had been degraded, in the course of the time, to the condition of serfs, and were threatened by the fanatical Sheikho A'hmedu with being sold into slavery."[46]

Barth's encounter with the Sorko refugees proves that the *Tārīkh al-fattāsh* was a work whose historical agency was strong enough to propel entire groups of people away from their homes – and not just a textual abstraction that had very little impact on the nineteenth-century Middle Niger.

The *Tārīkh al-fattāsh*'s effective circulation confirms Sanankoua's argument that the "use of the writing as instrument of propaganda and of consolidation of power" became a "crucial innovation of the Dina in a region traditionally attached to orality."[47] However, to further understand the impact of the chronicle in the nineteenth century, it is also necessary to investigate how its claims – circulated in pamphlets, circular letters, and *fatwà*s – were received in the Middle Niger and beyond.

44 See the description of the regulation of transhumance in *L'empire peul*, 81–101. Muḥammad Bello started a similar policy in Sokoto; see Omar Bello (trans.), *Ballo's Fatwā on Urbanization of Nomads* (Sokoto: Islamic Academy, 2000).

45 *L'empire peul*, 79.

46 Barth, *Travels and Discoveries*, vol. 4, 504.

47 Sanankoua, *Un empire peul*, 84.

A Sokoto Answer to Ḥamdallāhi's Claims

The most explicit answer to Ḥamdallāhi's claims to have surfaced in West African archives comes from Sokoto. Nūḥ b. al-Ṭāhir's *Risāla* was most likely attached to the request for allegiance that Aḥmad Lobbo sent to Sokoto around 1842 (Chapter 5). From Sokoto, the response was formulated by Nūḥ b. al-Ṭāhir's alter ego there: the abovementioned 'Abd al-Qādir al-Turūdī.

As Hunwick shows, little is known about 'Abd al-Qādir al-Turūdī's life.[48] He was born in 1804, as can be inferred from his *Kashūfāt rabbāniyya* (The Divine Unveilings), in which he mentions that he was thirteen at the time of 'Uthmān b. Fūdī's death in 1817.[49] His father, al-Muṣṭafà b. Muḥammad b. Muḥammad al-Tūrūdī, known as Mallam Tafa (d. 1845), was also a famous scholar belonging to the Qādiriyya order.[50] He was a close associate of 'Uthmān b. Fūdī, whose eldest daughter, Khadīja bt. 'Uthmān b. Muḥammad Fodiye (d. 1856), the future mother of 'Abd al-Qādir al-Turūdī and a renowned scholar herself, he married.[51] 'Abd al-Qādir al-Turūdī intermarried with 'Uthmān b. Fūdī's family, marrying the daughter of Muḥammad Bello, who was also called Khadīja. Muḥammad Bello was not only 'Abd al-Qādir al-Turūdī's maternal uncle and father-in-law, but also one of his celebrated teachers, along with his father, Muḥammad Sambo b. 'Uthmān b. Muḥammad Fodiye (d. 1826); Muḥammad al-Bukhārī; Muḥammad Giɗaaɗo b. Aḥmad b. Abī Bakr b. Ghārī; a certain Mudi, tentatively identified by Hunwick as Mūdi Māmār; and one Muḥammad Yero.[52]

'Abd al-Qādir al-Turūdī never occupied any official position in Sokoto. According to oral sources collected by Last, the caliph Aḥmad b. Abī Bakr 'Atīq (d. 1866) had decided to appoint 'Abd al-Qādir al-Turūdī as *wazīr* of Sokoto in the late 1850s, but the pressure of the powerful Giɗaaɗo family made the caliph choose Ibrāhīm Khalīl b. 'Abd al-Qādir (d. 1874), nephew of Giɗaaɗo ɗan Laima, for the

48 *ALA* II, 221.
49 Kani, "The private library of 'Abd al-Qadir," 20. On the *Kashufāt al-rabbāniyya*, see *ALA* II, 223, item 21.
50 No substantial research has been devoted to Mallam Tafa; for a short introduction, see *ALA* II, 220–221.
51 On Khadīja bt. 'Uthmān b. Muḥammad b. Fūdī, see *ALA* II, 161.
52 Hunwick, "A supplement to *Infāq al-maysūr*," 47, n. 31.

position in his stead.[53] Yet, in the words of Kani, 'Abd al-Qādir al-Turūdī was "one of the most outstanding scholars of the Central *bilād al-sūdān*."[54]

The fame of 'Abd al-Qādir al-Turūdī is confirmed by Barth. During the latter's stay in Katsina in February 1853, a *faqīh* from Tuwāt by the name of 'Abd al-Raḥmān drew Barth's attention to "Abd el Káder dan Taffa (meaning, the son of Mústapha)" who was "the most learned of the present generation of the inhabitants of Sókoto."[55] In April of the same year Barth met with 'Abd al-Qādir in Wurno, and his expectations about the latter's knowledge were immediately confirmed:

> He paid me a visit in the evening, and furnished me immediately with some positive data with regard to the history of the dynasty of the Asáki, or A'skiya, the rulers of Songhay, which he had perfectly in his head, and which were of the greatest importance in giving me an insight into the historical relation of the western countries of these regions with that of the Central Negroland.[56]

From his headquarters in Salame (northeast of Sokoto), 'Abd al-Qādir al-Turūdī contributed extensively to the field of history. For example, his untitled work – usually referenced as *Rawḍāt al-afkār* (The Sweet Meadows of Contemplation) – is an important history of West Africa up to 1824.[57] He also wrote several biographical notes on his teachers, such as the *Waraqa 'an al-muta'akhkhirīn min 'ulamā' bilādina* (Note on the Most Recent Scholars of our Land) or the *Salwat al-aḥzān fī dhikr ba'd 'ulamā' al-khawāṣṣ min ahl hādhā al-zamān* (Comfort for the Grieving in Remembrance of the Prominent Scholars from the People of our Time).[58]

However, historical writing was not his only talent. Among his extant works are contributions to other Islamic sciences that were widespread in West Africa, such as Sufism, grammar, Qur'ānic

53 Last, *The Sokoto Caliphate*, 162–163.
54 Kani, "The private library of 'Abd al-Qadir," 20.
55 Barth, *Travels and Discoveries*, vol. 4, 101–102.
56 Barth, *Travels and Discoveries*, vol. 4, 183.
57 See *ALA* II, 227–228, item 33. The *Rawḍāt al-afkār* was first translated by Palmer, who, however, misattributes the work to Muḥammad Bello (H. R. Palmer, "Western Sudan history: The raudthåt' ul afkåri," *African Affairs* 15/59 [1916]: 261–273, 261). A more recent edition and translation in English by Abu Alfa Muhammad Shareef bin Farid is available at https://siiasi.org/shaykh-dan-tafa/rawdatl-afkaar/.
58 *ALA* II, 230, item 48 and *ALA* II, 228, item 36.

exegesis, and esoteric sciences, as well as writings on disciplines less common in the region. For example, he wrote a work of geography, a rare topic in West Africa, entitled *Qaṭā'if al-jinān fī dhikr aḥwāl arḍ al-Sūdān* (The Fruits of the Heart in Reflection about the Earth of Sudan).[59] He also devoted himself to the study of philosophy, a discipline that had not featured in the scholarly production of the region before, and composed works such as the *Kulliyāt al-ʿālam al-sitta* (The Sixth World Faculty) and the *ʿUhūd wa-mawāthīq* (Covenants and Treaties).[60] Many of his works were preserved in a large library which he had gathered, but it was pillaged by the sultan of Gobir Mayaki (*fl.* ca. 1847), according to a history of Sokoto written by al-Ḥājj Saʿīd (d. after 1861–2).[61] What was left of this collection was "discovered" on 26 December 1981 by Kani, who found the manuscripts with Mallam Tahir, grandson of ʿAbd al-Qādir al-Turūdī.[62]

Among these manuscripts is the *Jawāb min ʿAbd al-Qādir al-Turūdī ilà Nūḥ b. al-Ṭāhir* (Abd al-Qādir al-Turūdī's response to Nūḥ b. al-Ṭāhir, henceforth *Jawāb*), an explicit response to the *Risāla* and a refutation of its claims.[63] After the *basmala* and the salutations to the Prophet, and the indicator of the sender and recipient of the letter, ʿAbd al-Qādir al-Turūdī highlights the conditions of writing: "We have received, O brother, your letter and your words along with the writing of your Imām, Shaykh Aḥmad [Lobbo]. We read what you mentioned in it about the issue of the twelve caliphs mentioned in the *ḥadīth* and that Shaykh Aḥmad [Lobbo] is the twelfth of them, after which the *mahdī* will come."[64] Then ʿAbd al-Qādir summarizes the contents of Nūḥ b. al-Ṭāhir's *Risāla*.

After this introduction, ʿAbd al-Qādir al-Turūdī refutes the arguments of the *Risāla* meticulously. He first denies that Aḥmad Lobbo

[59] *ALA* II, 227, item 32. For a discussion of geography in post-*jihād* northern Nigeria and an analysis of the *Qaṭā'if al-jinān*, see Stephanie Zehnle, "A Geography of Jihad: Jihadist Concepts of Space and Sokoto Warfare (West Africa, ca. 1800–1850)" (Ph.D. dissertation, Universität Kassel, 2015), 85–89.

[60] *ALA* II, 223, item 20 and *ALA* II, 230, item 47.

[61] Al-Ḥājj Saʿīd, *Taqāyīd mimmā waṣala ilaynā min aḥwāl ʿumarā' al-muslimīn salāṭīn Ḥawsa*, in Houdas (ed. and trans.), *Tedzkiret en-nisiān*, 342.

[62] See Kani, "The private library of ʿAbd al-Qadir," 20–21, item 18. This was part of the effort of collecting Arabic sources for the history of northern Nigeria by the NHRS, Ahmadu Bello University, Zaria, on which see Suleiman, "The Nigerian History Machine," 93–96.

[63] NHRS 192/19. [64] NHRS 192/19, p. 1.

could be one of the caliphs mentioned by the Prophet: "If you mean, by referring to these caliphs, the twelve rightly guided Imāms that are mentioned in the *ḥadīth*, [know that] they are twelve, not other than that, and one of them is the *mahdī*, the last one."[65] Since Nūḥ b. al-Ṭāhir ascribes the prophecy to al-Suyūṭī, 'Abd al-Qādir al-Turūdī resorts to al-Suyūṭī's own writings to reject the claim that Aḥmad Lobbo was the twelfth caliph: "O brother, know that your words are contrary to what was mentioned by al-Suyūṭī in his famous books."[66] To prove his point, 'Abd al-Qādir quotes passages from al-Suyūṭī's *Tārīkh al-khulafā'* concerning the different versions and interpretations of the *ḥadīth* on the twelve caliphs. Then he concludes synthetically by saying that al-Suyūṭī could never have prophesied the arrival of a twelfth caliph other than the *mahdī*: "This is what al-Suyūṭī said in his book *Tārīkh al-khulafā'*. He wrote that the *mahdī* is the twelfth [caliph] because there is nobody left but the last of them. However – O brother Nūḥ – you made Shaykh Aḥmad [Lobbo] the twelfth."[67] Therefore, concludes 'Abd al-Qādīr, "Either you are making the claim of *mahdiyya* for him, with its obvious contradiction in the description of the *mahdī* in attributes and place; or you remove the *mahdī* from this number [of caliphs] after establishing his mention from among them in the referred *ḥadīth*s. Reflect on that."[68] Having rejected the possibility that Aḥmad Lobbo could have been the twelfth caliph, 'Abd al-Qādir al-Turūdī explores the second of Nūḥ b. al-Ṭāhir's claims, that of Aḥmad Lobbo as renewer of the faith:

> If you were meaning that these caliphs are the *'ulamā'*, renewers of the faith of this community, following in the famous footsteps of al-Bayhaqī, al-Ḥākim [al-Nīshābūrī] and others, on the authority of Hurayra, [know] that the Prophet – may God honor him and grant him peace – said: "God will raise for this community at the end of every hundred years someone who will renovate its religion for it."[69]

Based on the *ḥadīth*, 'Abd al-Qādir al-Turūdī excludes the possibility that Aḥmad Lobbo could be considered a renewer of the faith on more than one ground. First, Aḥmad Lobbo could not be the twelfth of the renewers "because he did not emerge in the twelfth century" of the Islamic calendar (1699–1785).[70] Indeed, Aḥmad Lobbo was only a teenager when the twelfth century closed. However, he cannot be

[65] NHRS 192/19, p. 1. [66] NHRS 192/19, p. 1. [67] NHRS 192/19, p. 2.
[68] NHRS 192/19, p. 2. [69] NHRS 192/19, p. 2. [70] NHRS 192/19, p. 2.

considered a renewer at all, not even of the thirteenth century, continues ʻAbd al-Qādir, "since the condition of the renewer is that he emerges by the end of the century in which he will be the renewer and will enter the following."[71] In this case, ʻAbd al-Qādir also uses al-Suyūṭī as an authority, namely his *Urjūza fī mujaddidīn al-Islām* (Poem in Verse *Rajaz* on the Renewer of Islam), in which he says that "the condition for that [i.e. for being a renewer] is that the century has to pass and he is alive, but this condition also does not apply."[72] ʻAbd al-Qādir implies that Aḥmad Lobbo could have never been alive by the end of the thirteenth century hijrī (1785–1883 CE), thus he does not fulfill the requirements to be the renewer of the thirteenth century.

Last, ʻAbd al-Qādir al-Turūdī dismisses the claim that Aḥmad Lobbo could be the heir of Askiyà Muḥammad, thus rejecting his legitimacy as sultan, inheritor of that legitimate line of rulers dating back to the dawn of West African history, invented by the seventeenth-century chroniclers and attached by Nūḥ b. al-Ṭāhir to the ruler of Ḥamdallāhi via the prophecy. He simply makes the case that everything that is transmitted regarding Askiyà Muḥammad does not apply to anybody else, thus negating any possible connection between Aḥmad Lobbo and the Songhay king:

> Regarding what you mentioned on the investiture of the just Imām Askiyà al-Ḥājj [Muḥammad] with power, on which this piece that you wrote was written, there is nothing wrong with it by reason or by law. However, this was a particular caliphate for a particular place. Where did you get [the idea] that [what applied to him] could apply to someone else?[73]

ʻAbd al-Qādir al-Turūdī's response was sent along with the Fodiawa's rejection of the request for allegiance from Aḥmad Lobbo. These documents show how the *Tārīkh al-fattāsh* was not successful in winning followers for Aḥmad Lobbo in Sokoto – which, intriguingly, was not mentioned among the recipients of the *Risāla*. Paradoxically, it is more difficult to understand, or even guess, how the debate generated by the *Risāla* unfolded in the areas of the Niger Bend and the southern Sahara, which had been explicitly targeted by Nūḥ b. al-Ṭāhir.

[71] NHRS 192/19, p. 2. [72] NHRS 192/19, p. 2. [73] NHRS 192/19, p. 2.

Distant Echoes of the Debate

Although no copies of the *Risāla* have surfaced in northern Nigeria, the debate between Nūḥ b. al-Ṭāhir and ʻAbd al-Qādir al-Turūdī is direct evidence of the circulation of this document, and of the contestation of its claims, in the territories controlled by the Fodiawa. The opposite happens in other regions of West Africa, especially in the Middle Niger. Here, the widespread availability of multiple copies of the *Risāla* testifies that the document was effectively disseminated, but only vague echoes of the debates surrounding it can still be discerned.

These echoes emanate from Timbuktu, the very place where Aḥmad Lobbo's authority was indeed contested. Its population had broken out into open rebellion against Ḥamdallāhi several times after the conquest of 1826. The Kunta *shaykh*s had rejected the religious authority of the caliph of Ḥamdallāhi, although they had never openly rejected his political power. These factors made the city a plausible target of Aḥmad Lobbo's propaganda, via the *Risāla*.[74] However, only a single a posteriori comment, in a letter by Aḥmad al-Bakkāy to Aḥmad III, refers to the circulation of Aḥmad Lobbo's claims. Aḥmad al-Bakkāy completely dismisses the legitimacy of Aḥmad III's nephew by mocking the Fulani people in general, saying that "if somebody tells them that the twelfth caliph of the Quraysh is among them, they will believe it."[75] The Kunta leader's comment thus overtly references one of the claims couched in the *Tārīkh al-fattāsh* and circulated via the *Risāla*.

Further west, the region of Tīris (Mauritania) was an area never claimed by Ḥamdallāhi but explicitly targeted by the *Risāla*, as is clear from the list of recipients mentioned in the first of the two versions. Here, Aḥmad Lobbo's propaganda campaign also penetrated the discourses of Saharan scholars, who displayed resistance and skepticism. This emerges explicitly from a *fatwà* issued by al-Mukhtār al-Kuntī al-Ṣaghīr, in which he is asked by one Aḥmad b. Ḥamā' Allāh whether Moorish merchants trading in the land controlled by the

[74] There are eight copies at the IHERI-ABT alone (IHERI-ABT 479, IHERI-ABT 4220, IHERI-ABT 4840, IHERI-ABT 8783, IHERI-ABT 8967, IHERI-ABT 8996, IHERI-ABT 9728, IHERI-ABT 11098). All the copies preserved in France were also collected in Timbuktu: see BnF, Arabe 5259 (74a–75b), Arabe 5259 (79a–84b), Arabe 6756 (31a–42b), and IF, Fonds de Gironcourt, 2405(2)/I, 2405(2)/II, 2406(73).

[75] Mahibou and Triaud (eds.), *Voilà c'est qui est arrivé*, French text 104/Arabic text 15 recto.

Caliphate of Ḥamdallāhi are supposed to swear allegiance to Aḥmad Lobbo.[76] The same issue seems to be at stake in an earlier *fatwà* issued by Muḥammad al-Kuntī, who was asked by an anonymous questioner, most likely from among the Western Saharan Arab-speaking tribes self-identifying as "white," about the necessity of paying allegiance to a "black ruler," most likely Aḥmad Lobbo.[77]

By contrast, the evidence also shows that many other Saharan groups were very willing to collaborate with Ḥamdallāhi, if not to pay allegiance. The important intellectual and commercial city of Walāta, for example, had strong mercantile ties to the caliphate.[78] Its population seems to have enjoyed a very good relationship with Aḥmad Lobbo, as testified by three poems written by unnamed Walāta scholars that are quoted in the *Fatḥ al-Ṣamad*.[79] These poems might reflect a partnership between the inhabitants of the city in the southern Sahara and Aḥmad Lobbo, which is further confirmed by an anecdote also recorded in the *Fatḥ al-Ṣamad*: after an unspecified conflict between Ḥamdallāhi and Segou, some of the Walāta traders' goods were taken as part of the booty, but promptly returned by Aḥmad Lobbo when he discovered their true owners.[80] Likewise, a local chronicle concerning the Western Sahara, *al-Ḥaswa al-bīsāniyya fī al-ansāb al-ḥasāniyya* by Muḥammad Ṣāliḥ b. ʻAbd al-Wahhāb al-Nāṣirī (d. 1855), relates that some families from Tishīt (Mauritania) left their homeland in the Western Sahara as a consequence of internal disputes and sought refuge under Aḥmad Lobbo – further evidence of the recognition of the caliph of Ḥamdallāhi among prominent families of desert dwellers.[81]

An even more explicit position in favor of Aḥmad Lobbo was taken by al-Shaykh Muḥammad al-Māmī b. al-Bukhārī al-Bārikī (d. 1875; henceforth al-Māmī), author of the highly original book of jurisprudence, the *Kitāb al-bādiyya* (The Book of the

76 Hall, *A History of Race*, 98–101.
77 Ghislaine Lydon, *On Trans-Saharan Trails: Islamic Law, Trade Networks, and Cross-Cultural Exchange in Nineteenth-Century Western Africa* (Cambridge and New York: Cambridge University Press, 2009), 309–310.
78 Timothy Cleaveland, *Becoming Walāta: A History of Saharan Social Formation and Transformation* (Portsmouth, NH: Heinemann, 2002), 91.
79 *Fatḥ al-Ṣamad*, French text 67/Arabic text 18.
80 *Fatḥ al-Ṣamad*, French text 88–91/Arabic text 39–41.
81 Boutilimit 76/20–77/1 (another copy is Boutilimit 82/3).

Desert).[82] This work is an attempt to reconcile Islamic jurisprudence with nomadic Saharan customs, and includes a discussion of the implementation of Qur'ānic punishments, considered to be a criterion for the evaluation of a ruler's legitimacy:

> If someone [from the inhabitants of these areas] seizes power, obedience to him is mandatory, even if he is a slave . . . as for those [areas] where no such self-proclaimed ruler exists, their inhabitants are the people of the intermediate land situated between the two Imāmic states. Therefore, the application of Quranic punishments is dependent on the emergence of such a ruler, if there is no notable council powerful enough to prevent disorder, such as the Ahl Būṣayba or the people of Fes.[83]

In this section, al-Māmī explicitly refers to Aḥmad Lobbo as one of those leaders whose legal decisions must be considered legitimate:

> In what concerns those [areas] ruled by a leader, such as Aḥmad Lobbo, the Almāmī Abū Bakr [of Fouta Toro], or by a notable council powerful enough to prevent disorder, their legal decisions are to be regarded as identical to those issued by the Imām, regardless of whether [their inhabitants] are nomads or sedentary people; and I personally saw the Almāmī Abū Bakr implementing the Qur'ānic punishments.[84]

Although the book cannot be dated with certainty, al-Māmī's positive position regarding the legitimacy of Aḥmad Lobbo may well have reflected the local effects of the *Risāla*'s circulation in the region.

In sum, what emerges from these sources is the existence of lively local debates over the legitimacy of Aḥmad Lobbo among the people of the Western Sahara, making it likely that this region, too, was targeted by Ḥamdallāhi's propaganda. This strongly suggests that there was a broader West African debate over the legitimacy of the Caliphate of Ḥamdallāhi and its ruler, ranging from the Central Sudan to the Western Sahara. In Sokoto, seat of a powerful rival caliphate, the scholars of the court strongly rejected any such claims. Yet scholars in the Sahara were willing to validate them, possibly to serve their own political and commercial ends. However, in order to understand how these discourses were meaningful to the West Africans who were the

82 Muḥammad al-Māmī al-Bārikī, *Kitāb al-bādiyya* (Nuwakshūṭ: Zāwiya al-Shaykh Muḥammad al-Māmī, 1428/2007). On al-Māmī and his *Kitāb al-bādiya*, see *ALA* V, 322–334 (esp. *ALA* V, 331, item 71).

83 al-Māmī, *Kitāb al-bādiya*, 249.

84 al-Māmī, *Kitāb al-bādiya*, 249.

intended audience of the *Tārīkh al-fattāsh*, one must account for its intersection with local Islamic epistemologies, taking into consideration the role of prophecy in this region, and the belief that the End of the World was nigh.

Prophecies and the Eschaton

Although the scholarly debates over the legitimacy of Aḥmad Lobbo were influenced by political, economic, and racial dynamics, the prophetic character of the *Tārīkh al-fattāsh* was perhaps the most timely and powerful aspect of its message. The plausibility of the prophecy was never questioned by the West African actors whose voices are recorded in the available sources. Indeed, mystical events endorsing, predicting, or justifying political claims were very common in the region. For example, just a few years before the emergence of the Caliphate of Ḥamdallāhi, 'Uthmān b. Fūdī's movement was endorsed by a vision in which he was given "the Sword of Truth" by 'Abd al-Qādir al-Jilānī, the founder of the Qādiriyya brotherhood.[85] 'Uthmān b. Fūdī's work known alternatively as *Wird* (The Litany) or *Lammā balaghtu* (When I Reached) tells of the author's encounter with the Prophet and the Rightly Guided Caliphs, Abū Bakr, 'Umar, 'Uthmān, and 'Alī, as well as al-Jilānī: "He [al-Jilānī] sat me down, and clothed me and enturbaned me. Then he addressed me as the 'Imam of the saints' and commanded me to do what is approved of and forbade me to do what is disapproved of; and he girded me with the Sword of Truth, to unsheathe it against the enemies of God."[86]

Likewise, Muḥammad al-Kuntī, in the hagiography of his father, the *al-Ṭarā'if wa-l-Talā'id min karāmāt al-shaykhayn al-wālida wa-l-wālid* (The Marvelous and Exceptional Examples of Miracles of the Two *Shaykhs*, the Mother and the Father), reports the divine investiture that al-Mukhtār al-Kabīr had received directly from the Prophet: "I saw al-Muṣṭafà [i.e. Muḥammad] really in a vision, He told me a good news and drew me close to him. And told me: 'You are a true messenger, to renovate my Sunna, be patient.'"[87] In a similar fashion, later in the nineteenth century, the Sudanese *mahdī* Muḥammad

[85] See W. Braune, s.v. "'Abd al-Qādir al-Djīlānī," *EI*², vol. 1, 69–70.
[86] Quoted in Hiskett, *The Sword of Truth*, 66. On the *Wird/Lammā balaghtu*, see *ALA* II, 79–80, item 102.
[87] Quoted in Batran, "Sīdī al-Mukhtār al-Kuntī," 172.

Aḥmad b. ʻAbd Allāh (d. 1885) states that, in a vision, the Prophet "appointed me as his successor by seating me on his chair in the presence of the caliphs, the hierarchy of saints, and [Qur'ānic figure] al-Khiḍr ... and the Prophet girded me with his sword, in addition he supported me with ten angels and ʻAzrā'īl [the angel of death] will always accompany me."[88]

In the Middle Niger, a prophecy such as the one foretelling the advent of Aḥmad Lobbo – as allegedly disclosed to Askiyà Muḥammad more than three hundred years before Ḥamdallāhi – was an extraordinary event, but not an inconceivable one. Furthermore, one must take into consideration that the thirteenth century of the Islamic calendar (1785–1883 CE) was charged with eschatological anxieties. As the scholar Muhammad A. al-Hajj points out, in the one of the few existing studies of eschatology in West Africa, the expectation that the world was coming to an end reached high levels in that century. This was due to the intermingling of the two Prophetic traditions, that of the Twelve Caliphs and that of the Renewer of the Faith, the very same traditions that were invoked by Nūḥ b. al-Ṭāhir in his construction of Aḥmad Lobbo's legitimacy.[89] In al-Hajj's words, "the tradition about the 'twelve caliphs' has been linked with the concept of reform or revival of the Faith" in West Africa.[90] Merging this tradition with that of the Renewer of the Faith, West African scholars calculated the date of the Hour's coming, positing that after 1,200 years the Muslim community would face a period of anarchy and disorder, the tumultuous era during which the awaited *mahdī* would be expected to come, just before the End of the World. Thus, the thirteenth century of the Islamic calendar was interpreted by West African scholars as the last age before the Eschaton.

Most evidence about the millenarian turmoil that invested West Africa at this period comes from the writings of the Fodiawa, which have been explored in a systematic and extensive way by scholars.

88 Quoted in Kim Searcy, *The Formation of the Sudanese Mahdist State: Ceremony and Symbols of Authority, 1882–1898* (Leiden: Brill, 2010), 57. The original texts is in the *mahdī*'s *al-Athār al-kāmila li-l-imām al-Mahdī*, on which see R. S. O'Fahey and John O. Hunwick, *Arabic Literature of Africa*, vol. 1: *The Writings of Eastern Sudanic Africa to c. 1900* (Leiden: Brill, 1994), 307–308.

89 See Muhammad A. al-Hajj, "The Mahdist Tradition in Northern Nigeria" (Ph.D. dissertation, Abdullahi Bayero College – Kano, 1973); and al-Hajj, "The thirteenth century in Muslim eschatology."

90 Al-Hajj, "The thirteenth century in Muslim eschatology," 108.

Eschatology occupies a special place in the writings of ʿUthmān b. Fūdī. For example, as al-Hajj has argued with reference to the *Muddat al-dunyā* (The Duration of the Earthly World) and the *Tanbīh al-umma ʿalà qurb hujūm isahrāt al-sāʿa* (Awakening the *Umma* on the Close Manifestations of the Signs of Time), "traditions about the approach of the End of Time were copiously quoted without any attempt to distinguish between 'authentic' and 'spurious' ... in order to instill in his followers the love of martyrdom and the renunciation of this transitory world."[91] While eschatology seems to be absent from the works of ʿAbd Allāh b. Fūdī, Muḥammad Bello wrote extensively on this topic.[92] Likewise, other authors of Sokoto contributed to eschatological literature in the nineteenth century.[93]

But eschatological expectations did not remain limited to the learned elite who were able to understand Arabic. They also circulated widely among the non-literate. Indeed, the spread of these prophecies in Hausaland was surely propelled by their propagation in Fulfulde and Hausa, the local languages. It seems that ʿUthmān b. Fūdī engaged in discussions on eschatological matters in Fulfulde, as reported in his *Taḥdhīr al-ikhwān min iddiʿā' al-mahdiyya al-mawʿūda ākhir al-zamān* (A Warning to the Brothers against Claiming the Mahdiyya Promised at the End of Time).[94] A work he wrote in Fulfulde on the topic of the *mahdī* is lost today, but exists in a Hausa translation by his son ʿĪsā b. ʿUthmān b. Muḥammad Fodiye (d. 1872): the *Sifofin Shehou* (Attributes of

[91] Al-Hajj, "The thirteenth century in Muslim eschatology," 108. On the *Muddat al-dunyā* and the *Tanbīh al-umma ʿalà qurb hujūm ʿashrāt al-sāʿa*, see *ALA* II, 66, item 44 and 75, item 81. After 1808, when the revolution he led was virtually completed, ʿUthmān b. Fūdī expressed the need to strengthen his reign. His position on the coming of the Hour then radically changed. In later works he "categorically rejected all prophecies about the End of the World as false and unsupported by the Sunna of the Prophet" (al-Hajj, "The thirteenth century in Muslim eschatology," 110).

[92] See, for example, his *Tanbīh al-fāhim ʿalā anna al-mahdī huwa khitām* and *Waṯīqa ilā al-shaykh Ḥāmid b. Aḥmad qāḍī al-Sayyid Muḥammad b. al-Mukhtār b. Aḥmad Bābā fī mā yuʿtamad ʿalayhi fī amr al-mahdī*; on these works, see *ALA* II, 140, item 93, and 143, item 109.

[93] For example, Hunwick stresses that "essays reflecting expectations of the Mahdī" are the main literary production of nineteenth-century rulers of Kano (*ALA* II, 258).

[94] See *ALA* II, 72–73, item 71.

the *Shaykh*).[95] However, it was 'Uthmān b. Fūdī's daughters who became deeply involved in the effort of translating into Hausa works originally written in Arabic or Fulfulde, to reach a broader audience of Hausa-speaking people who were only partially literate in Arabic. His daughter Khadīja bt. 'Uthmān b. Muḥammad Fodiye (d. 1856), for instance, is remembered as the translator of one poem into Fulfulde.[96] Another of his daughters, Maryam bt. 'Uthmān b. Muḥammad Fodiye (d. after 1880), rendered her own contributions in Arabic on the topic into Hausa texts.[97]

From these sources it appears that the ferment over the coming of the Hour, widely encouraged by the Sokoto leaders' propaganda, was so widespread that it was having very real effects. Since the central point of many prophecies concerning the coming of the Hour is that the *mahdī* will appear in the East, their "outcome [was] the migration of hordes of people" towards the East.[98] Indeed, many episodes recorded in oral and written traditions concern individuals who tried to lead huge waves of migrants to the East. Abū Bakr al-'Atīq, for example, wrote a proclamation intended to debunk the imminent arrival of the Hour and dissuade people from the necessity of emigration.[99] In 1856 or 1857, during his Pilgrimage, a certain Ibrāhīm Šarīf al-Dīn gathered such a huge following that he clashed with the ruler of Bagirmi, 'Abd al-Qādir, killing him and being in turn murdered by local people.[100] About twenty years later, in 1878, another Muslim leader from the region of Kano, Mallam Yāmūsa, initiated a new movement that closely resembled the one inspired by Ibrāhīm Šarīf al-Dīn. However, the caliph Mu'ādh b. Muḥammad Bello (r. 1877–1881) caught and deported the man, putting an end to his initiative.[101] Roughly at the same time, Maryam bt. 'Uthmān wrote a letter to her son Muḥammad Bello b. Ibrāhīm Dabo (r. 1882–1893), the ruler of

95 F. H. El-Masri et al., Sifofin Shehu: An autobiography and character study of 'Uthmān b. Fūdī in verse," *Research Bulletin – Center for Arabic Documentation of the University of Ibadan* 2/1 (1966): 1–36.

96 This poem is not mentioned in *ALA* II but in Jean Boyd and Murray Last, "The role of women as 'agents religieux' in Sokoto," *Canadian Journal of African Studies/Revue canadienne des études africaines* 1/3 (1985): 283–300, 293.

97 Boyd and Last, "The role of women," 293.

98 Al-Hajj, "The thirteenth century in Muslim eschatology," 109.

99 See *ALA* II, 161, item 8.

100 Al-Hajj, "The Mahdist Tradition," 94–95.

101 Al-Hajj, "The Mahdist Tradition," 95–96.

Kano, reassuring him and his people that the rumors about the arrival of the End of the World were false.[102]

Eventually, the most spectacular of the millenarian outbreaks in African history would take place in the Sudan, with the emergence of Mahdī Muḥammad Aḥmad. However, scholars have stressed that the origins of the Sudanese Mahdiyya should be traced back to peoples and ideas emerging in West Africa.[103] Testimony to the resilience of millenarian expectations in the region is the impact of the Mahdiyya in West Africa is the establishment by Ḥayāt al-Dīn b. Saʿīd b. Muḥammad Bello (d. 1898) and Jibrīl Gaini (d. after 1902) of two states founded in Adamawa (divided among today's Nigeria, Cameroon, Chad, and the Central African Republic) and in the Gombe (Nigeria) that pledged allegiance to the Sudanese *mahdī*.[104]

The Mahdiyya is the last and most famous manifestation of millenarian turmoil in pre-colonial African history.[105] However, it was also the culmination of a century of eschatological expectations that can be traced back to the two Prophetic traditions employed by Nūḥ b. al-Ṭāhir in the *Tārīkh al-fattāsh*. The fervency of belief in these traditions explains Nūḥ b. al-Ṭāhir's decision to use them as the backbone for his construction of Aḥmad Lobbo's authority. They were already widely held beliefs among his intended audience, as proven by the effects of eschatological expectations throughout West Africa, the writings of the Fodiawa, and the waves of emigration to the East, as well as the resonance of the Mahdiyya in Adamawa and Gombe.

The Decay of the *Tārīkh al-fattāsh* Project

When Nūh b. al-Ṭāhir's *Risāla* arrived in Sokoto in 1842, Aḥmad Lobbo was about seventy years old. According to oral sources recorded

[102] See Mauro Nobili, "*Risāla min Maryam bint Fudī ilà al-ibn*: A brief contribution to the study of 19th-century Nigerian eschatology," in *Collectanea Islamica*, edited by Nicola Melis and Mauro Nobili (Rome: Aracne, 2012), 71–86.

[103] Saburi Biobaku and Muhammad A. al-Hajj, "The Sudanese Mahdiyya and the Niger–Chad Region," in *Islam in Tropical Africa*, edited by I. M. Lewis (London: Oxford University Press, 1966), 425–441; John Hunwick et al., "Between the Niger and the Nile: New light on the Fulani Mahdist Muḥammad al-Dādārī," *Sudanic Africa* 8 (1997): 85–108.

[104] Al-Hajj, "The Mahdist Tradition," 109–144.

[105] For millenarian expectations in the colonial period, see P. B. Clarke, "Islamic millenarianism in West Africa: A 'revolutionary' ideology?" *Religious Studies* 16/3 (1980): 330–337.

by Hampaté Ba and Daget, the caliph had realized that his days were numbered, and so, in 1843 or 1844, he asked the Great Council to suggest a successor. The Council settled on two possible candidates: Aḥmad II, the elder son of Aḥmad Lobbo; and Baalobbo, an experienced military leader and cousin of the caliph. Eventually, the piety and learning of Aḥmad II carried more weight in the decision, and Aḥmad Lobbo's son was nominated successor. Representative notables from Djenné and from Timbuktu also agreed to the nomination.[106] On 12 Rabīʿ I 1261/19 March 1845 Aḥmad Lobbo passed away, and his son became the second caliph of Ḥamdallāhi.[107]

The death of Aḥmad Lobbo might have made the *Tārīkh al-fattāsh* obsolete, but it seems that the text was still being used at the time of Aḥmad II. Immediately after he became caliph, the Kunta *shaykh* Aḥmad al-Bakkāy visited the capital to discuss lifting the embargo on Timbuktu. Both oral traditions and written texts record that he arrived in Ḥamdallāhi with a list of requests and a series of juridical questions. Along with the perennial request to allow the commercialization of tobacco, he asked for permission to ally with Segou, and also that he himself, rather than San Shirfi, might be assigned to the government of Timbuktu. Then, among other questions, the *shaykh* asked Aḥmad II to explain why the Dogon from the Bandiagara cliff and the Somono were considered slaves.[108] In response, Aḥmad II argued:

> The Dogon and the Somono were enslaved before Ḥamdallāhi. It was Muslim scholars from the ancient times who listed the people of the Sudan who are bound to servitude. The *Tārīkh al-fattāsh* lists them … Since the list was established neither by our rulings nor our instructions, we are not responsible for it, but we cannot also apply any change to it.[109]

The same argument is repeated in a letter to Ghūrū b. Saʿīd, the ruler of So (near Konna), in which Aḥmad II summarizes the terms of his

[106] On the designation of Aḥmad b. Aḥmad as second caliph of Ḥamdallāhi, the only available information comes from oral sources recorded in *L'empire peul*, 248–250.

[107] *Fatḥ al-Ṣamad*, French text 91/Arabic text 42. Aḥmad Lobbo's memory was celebrated by several elegies, many of which are quoted in *Fatḥ al-Ṣamad*, French text 91–102/Arabic text 42–51.

[108] *L'empire peul*, 277.

[109] *L'empire peul*, 280.

meeting with Aḥmad al-Bakkāy.[110] Regarding the Dogon and the Somono, the second caliph of Ḥamdallāhi stated:

> Then he [Aḥmad al-Bakkāy] asked me six questions concerning the enslavement of the People of the Mountain [i.e. the Dogon] and the Zanj [i.e. the Somono] ... The People of the Mountain have been enslaved because of unbelief, and unbelief is the origin of slavery. As for the Zanj, we found them already owned by the rulers of this region, therefore we own them since they were owned by al-Ḥajj Muḥammad Askiyà, as we found in the *Tārīkh al-fattāsh*. The ownership of them is also based on [their] unbelief.[111]

These sources point to the continued citation of the *Tārīkh al-fattāsh* as an authoritative text during the time of Aḥmad II. However, its authority could not transcend the death of Aḥmad Lobbo, which precipitated the deterioration the Caliphate of Ḥamdallāhi, whose slow decline under Aḥmad II accelerated dramatically with the third and last caliph, Aḥmad III.[112]

The seeds of this decline were planted in what Sanankoua defines as the unresolved problem of succession.[113] Many members of the Ḥamdallāhi elite were afraid that the election of Aḥmad II meant the "confiscation of power by Seeku Aamadu [Aḥmad Lobbo] to the benefit of his own family."[114] The nomination of Aḥmad II by his father and the endorsement of influential members of the Great Council, such as Nūḥ b. al-Ṭāḥir, resulted in a smooth transition of power, but the problem of succession reemerged even more strongly with the death of Aḥmad II in 1853, after only eight years as ruler. The best candidates to succeed him were, again, Baalobbo and another of Aḥmad Lobbo's sons, Allay. The latter, born in 1819 after the battle of Noukouma, was a pious and renowned scholar, close to the Kunta. He

110 IF, Fonds de Gironcourt, 2405 (36); another copy is IF, Fonds de Gironcourt, 2405 (38).

111 IF, Fonds de Gironcourt, 2405 (36), f. 200b. The notion that "unbelief" is the source of slavery, although not to be found in normative sources, was very widespread in the Islamic world (Rudolph T. Ware, "Slavery in Islamic Africa, 1400–1800," in *The Cambridge World History of Slavery*, edited by David Eltis and Stanley L. Engerman [Cambridge, Cambridge University Press, 2011], vol. 3, 47–80, 50). This is, for example, the position of Aḥmad Bābā in his famous *fatwà* on slavery (Hunwick and Harrak [ed. and trans.], *Miʿrāj al-ṣuʿūd*, 23).

112 For accounts of the reigns of Aḥmad II and Aḥmad III, see Robinson, *The Holy War*, 282–316; and Sanankoua, *Un empire peul*, 115–161.

113 Sanankoua, *Un empire peul*, 115.

114 Sanankoua, *Un empire peul*, 116.

also occupied military positions, serving as *amīr* of the region of Farimaké, and was also *amīr* ad interim of Masina in once instance. As in the previous succession crisis, the Great Council dismissed Baalobbo's claims and selected Allay as the third caliph; but this time Baalobbo did not accept the decision, and threatened a civil war against his cousin. However, he also offered an alternative to warfare: he would abandon his claims if Aḥmad III was chosen instead of Allay – counting on his ability to manipulate his young nephew and rule through him. The Great Council endorsed Baalobbo's proposition, which should have established a patrilineal succession system and avoided future disputes.

Civil war was thereby avoided, but the reign of Aḥmad III would be characterized by a series of "serious fissures."[115] These include grievances of the local population, disunity in the ruling family, and the disastrous disintegration of the governmental structures put in place by Aḥmad Lobbo. Aḥmad III inaugurated a less austere form of government in Ḥamdallāhi that was harshly criticized by his contemporaries. He also centralized all the power that had been divided between the caliph and the Great Council. In this way, he alienated the veteran leaders of the caliphate, transforming the Great Council into a mere mechanism for approving the caliph's decisions. Hence, most of its members abandoned both Aḥmad III and the Great Council. At the same time, Aḥmad III lost the support of the Kunta when Aḥmad al-Bakkāy broke off his relationship with Ḥamdallāhi. With little support from inside the capital or from Timbuktu, Aḥmad III initiated a policy of rapprochement with the rulers of Segou. This attracted the attention of the expanding movement of al-Ḥājj 'Umar, who fought against Aḥmad III and his army until the final defeat of the caliphate at Cayawal in 1862, after which 'Umar completed the conquest of the capital.

As Ḥamdallāhi fell apart, the knowledge of the *Tārīkh al-fattāsh* and the rationale for its creation faded in the southern part of the Middle Niger. Only the family of San Shirfi, the Timbuktu notable who had been raised to prominence after Aḥmad Lobbo's conquest of Timbuktu, kept it from disappearing altogether. Muḥammad b. San Shirfi, about whom nothing is known except that he was *qāḍī* in Timbuktu shortly before French colonization, wrote the *Tārīkh al-fūtāwī*, a chronicle extensively used

115 Robinson, *The Holy War*, 284.

throughout the present book. This chronicle begins by recording the prophecy foretelling the arrival of Aḥmad Lobbo, often quoting verbatim from the *Tārīkh al-fattāsh*.[116]

The involvement of San Shirfi's family in the preservation of the memory of Ḥamdallāhi and of the *Tārīkh al-fattāsh* is further confirmed by the role of San Shirfi's sons. Copies made from fragments of the *Tārīkh al-fūtāwī* were provided to de Gironcourt by 'Abd al-Raḥmān b. San Shirfi (d. 1913–14), one of these sons, a scholar and *qāḍī* of Timbuktu.[117] Another son played an even greater role in the story of the *Tārīkh al-fattāsh*: Aḥmad b. San Shirfi (d. 1921–2) who, according to the *al-Sa'āda al-abadiyya*, was also *qāḍī* of Timbuktu.[118] Most importantly, he was the local informant of Dubois, the one who attracted the attention of French journalist to the *Tārīkh al-fattāsh* and provided information about the chronicle, and so indirectly triggered the interest of Westerners.

All of these later phases in the chronicle's preservation stem from San Shirfi's strong connection with Aḥmad Lobbo. He had been appointed *qāḍī* of Timbuktu, the first in a long line, as noted by Aḥmad Lobbo himself in 1257/1841–2; and he remained in that position for twenty-four years until he died in 1280/1863–4, during the war against al-Ḥājj 'Umar.[119] San Shirfi was an exception among the scholars in Timbuktu's history, having occupied the positions of *qāḍī*, *amīr*, and *imām* of the Djinguereber Mosque at the same time. Due to the importance of Aḥmad Lobbo's role in establishing and fostering the fortunes of San Shirfi's family, it is not difficult to see why he and his sons remained partisans of Ḥamdallāhi in Timbuktu. The founder of the family owed his prestige to Aḥmad Lobbo and, by extension, to Aḥmad Lobbo's quest to establish his legitimacy. Maintaining the memory of that legitimacy, and the text that had advanced it, were thus key to maintaining the status of San Shirfi's descendants during the late pre-colonial period and the early days of French rule. Elsewhere, the memory of the *Tārīkh al-fattāsh* had almost disappeared.

116 *Tārīkh al-fūtāwī*, pp. 2–5.

117 On 'Abd al-Raḥmān, see Aḥmad Bābēr's *al-Sa'āda al-abadiyya* (IHERI-ABT 2752, ff. 19a and 23a).

118 On Aḥmad b. San Shirfi, *al-Sa'āda al-abadiyya* (IHERI-ABT 2752, ff. 23a–b). This information is confirmed by Saad, *Social History of Timbuktu*, 235.

119 *Tārīkh al-fūtāwī*, f. 75a. See also *al-Sa'āda al-abadiyya* (IHERI-ABT 2752, ff. 18b–29a and 23a) and *ALA* IV, 51–52.

The Resurgence of the *Tārīkh al-fattāsh* as *La chronique du chercheur*

The death of Aḥmad Lobbo, the decline of the caliphate, and the conquest of Ḥamdallāhi by the army of al-Ḥājj ʿUmar led to the slow disappearance of the *Tārīkh al-fattāsh*. Eventually, by the 1890s, very little was left of it but the memory of the propaganda circulated via Nūḥ b. al-Ṭāhir's *Risāla*. Nothing would ever have suggested that, in just a few years, the chronicle was going to reemerge, like a phoenix from the ashes, to become one of the most famous historical sources produced in pre-colonial Africa.

The resurgence of the *Tārīkh al-fattāsh*, in the problematic guise of *La chronique du chercheur*, had little to do with the chronicle itself and much more to do with the imposition of French colonial rule at the end of the nineteenth century. As Pekka Masonen, among others, has observed, the early colonial period produced "a new kind of need for historical and ethnological studies about African peoples."[120] The main aim was to "produce practical information that would facilitate effective government of the new colonies."[121] France, as a powerful colonial empire, excelled in this politico-academic effort, which Edmund Burke III refers to as "scientific imperialism."[122] The opening paragraph of the classic work *Les empires du Mali* by Charles Monteil, himself an influential French scholar-administrator, is telling:

> In West Africa, we rule populations of Negroes on which our colonizing mission in this country is centered and aimed. To be effective and successful, our action has necessarily to be based on the past, which preserves the memory of the political systems most appropriate for these people. Indeed, the old great empires witness the inclination towards political organization among the Negroes.[123]

A major focus of these inquiries were the West African Muslim communities, often perceived as a threat that needed to be understood and controlled, due to the persistent fear of possible Islamic or pan-Islamic

120 Pekka Masonen, *The Negroland Revisited: Discovery and Invention of the Sudanese Middle Ages* (Helsinki: Finnish Academy of Science and Letters, 2000), 426.
121 Masonen, *The Negroland Revisited*, 427.
122 Edmund Burke III, *The Ethnographic State: France and the Invention of Moroccan Islam* (Oakland: University of California Press, 2014), 6.
123 Monteil, *Les empires du Mali*, 1.

upheavals that characterized official French policy toward their Muslim subjects. As Christopher Harrison stresses in *France and Islam in West Africa, 1860–1960*: "Throughout the colonial period successive administrators, scholars and interested spectators produced a constant stream of works which were designed both to document Islam [in Africa] and to suggest what policies should be adopted towards France's [African] Muslim subjects."[124]

For instance, on 1 August 1913 the governor-general of the French Federation of West Africa (AOF), William M. Ponty (d. 1915), issued a circular in which the connection between production of knowledge and control over the territory is made explicit:

> It is our duty to study the Muslim society of our colonies in West Africa in the minutest detail. It is a study which demands almost a scientific method. It presupposes special studies, a previous documentation and a serious knowledge of the sociological laws of Islam which the great Orientalists of France and of Europe have now virtually succeeded in establishing ... [The study] will seem very attractive to many because of the scientific interest attached to it. But above all it is interesting for political and administrative reasons ... It is this understanding of native society which, alone, will enable a peaceful and profound action on the minds of the people. It is, therefore, in this study ... that we will find the surest bases and the most suitable directions for our Muslim policy.[125]

This policy, in the context of French colonialism, dates back to the conquest of Algeria and the establishment of the *bureaux arabes* in 1844. Notwithstanding their disappearance by the 1870s, the *bureaux arabes* "had nonetheless established a tradition of detailed administrative research" that was to be reproduced elsewhere in French colonies.[126] This model, and the type of knowledge that resulted from it, was exported to French West Africa by Louis Faidherbe (d. 1889).[127] However, it was Clozel who is best remembered for his investment in producing knowledge put to use in the interest of

[124] Harrison, *France and Islam*, 1.

[125] Quoted in Harrison, *France and Islam*, 107.

[126] Harrison, *France and Islam*, 18.

[127] Jacques Frémeaux, "Des bureaux arabes à Maurice Delafosse," in *Maurice Delafosse. Entre Orientalisme et Ethnographie: l'itinéraire d'un Africaniste, 1870–1926*, edited by Jean-Loup Amselle and Emmanuelle Sibeud (Paris: Maisonneuve et Larose, 1998), 193–209, 202; Jean Schmitz, "L'Afrique par défaut ou l'oubli de l'Orientalisme," in Amselle and Sibeud (eds.), *Maurice Delafosse. Entre Orientalisme et Ethnographie*, 107–121, 107.

French colonialism, with respect to both Islamic and non-Islamic societies. As the lieutenant-governor of the Côte d'Ivoire colony in 1901, Clozel asked local administrators to collect the ethnographic data on local customs that allowed him to publish, with Roger Vallamur, *Les coutumes indigènes de la Côte d'Ivoire.*[128] While posted in the Upper Senegal and Niger in 1908, Clozel replicated his efforts in order to collect information about the conquered peoples by sending a circular, dated 12 January 1909, which requested a survey of local cultures by all local administrators.[129] It was this "considerable amount of documentation, of very different quality" – in Clozel's words – that was reshaped by Delafosse, along with the latter's extensive knowledge of the region, to write his *Haut-Sénégal-Niger.*[130]

French scholar-administrators were particularly interested in collecting and translating Arabic manuscripts that were believed to contain crucial information vital to understanding the colonized peoples and to supporting effective colonial government, reflecting the era's assumption that written records were the only reliable sources for studying the past.[131] Specifically, the *Tārīkh al-Sūdān*, known in Europe since the 1850s, and the *Tārīkh al-fattāsh*, first mentioned by Dubois, had attracted the interest of French colonial authorities. A letter sent by an unnamed French author to the *qāḍī* of Timbuktu, Aḥmad Bābā b. Abī al-'Abbās b. 'Umar b. Zayyān, asked the judge to send, via an interpreter called "Moríké Konaré," information on the *Tārīkh al-fattāsh* and the *Tārīkh al-Sūdān*, and to inform the writer if there were copies of these chronicles available, along with other "books

128 François J. Clozel and Roger Villamur, *Les coutumes indigènes de la Côte d'Ivoire* (Paris: Challamel, 1902).

129 The dispatch is annexed, along with others, to Delafosse, *Haut-Sénégal-Niger*, 18–24.

130 Clozel, Introduction to Delafosse, *Haut-Sénégal-Niger*, 1.

131 The French were not alone in this effort of collecting Arabic sources. Germans and British were likewise involved in very similar projects, for example in the territories of Gonja, split between what is today Ghana and Togo (Ivor Wilks, Nehemia Levitzion, and Bruce M. Haight, *Chronicles from Gonja: A Tradition of West African Muslim Historiography* [Cambridge and New York: Cambridge University Press, 1986], 28). The greatest effort of collecting manuscripts by the British took place in Nigeria, were scholar-administrators devoted extensive work to locating and translating Arabic manuscripts; see, for example, Herbert R. Palmer, *Sudanese Memoirs: Being Mainly Translations of a Number of Arabic Manuscripts Relating to the Central and Western Sudan* (Lagos: Government Printer, 1928).

explaining the origins of the Sūdān and of its past nations."[132] The letter is not dated, but it was arguably written around 1896 – just after Dubois first reported the existence of the *Tārīkh al-fattāsh* but before the 1898 publication of Houdas' edition of the *Tārīkh al-Sūdān*.

Eventually, the *Tārīkh al-fattāsh* was "found" and edited, in a process that heavily involved the French colonial apparatus. Firstly, two colonial administrators were responsible for "finding" the copies of the *Tārīkh Ibn al-Mukhtār* and the *Tārīkh al-fattāsh* that Houdas and Delafosse collated to produce the conflated edition of *La chronique du chercheur*: They were Bonnel de Mézières, who was an experienced traveler in Africa on behalf of the French government, and Brévié, a colonial office who also became governor-general of the AOF (1930–1936).[133]

Furthermore, the West Africans who provided their manuscripts also held official positions in the colonial structure. The owner of MS A/ IHERI-ABT 3927 was Muḥammad b. Muḥammad b. al-Suyūṭī (d. 1928–9), a prominent scholar of Timbuktu and local representative (*muqaddam*) of the Tijāniyya Sufi order.[134] Muḥammad b. Muḥammad b. al-Suyūṭī was very close to the French administration, being a teacher at the French *medersa* of Timbuktu and a member of the Comité consultatif des affaires musulmanes.[135] Also close to the French administration was the West African scholar who provided Brévié with a copy of the *Tārīkh al-fattāsh* and copied it for him,

132 IHERI-ABT 4613.

133 Broc, *Dictionnaire illustré*, 35–36; Cornevin, "Jules Brévié."

134 A sketch on Muḥammad b. al-Suyūṭī is found in Marty, *La région de Tombouctou*, 15–17 (under Imam Soyouthi, fils de Mohammed); Abdel-Rahman ben Essayoû tî, "Sidi Muhammad al-Imam ben Essayoû tî," in *Culture et civilisation islamiques: Le Mali*, edited by Abdelhadi Boutaleb (Casablanca: Organisation islamique pour l'éducation, les sciences et la culture, 1408 [1988]), 263–265; and *ALA* IV, 53. See also the early twentieth-century IHERI-ABT 2752, Aḥmad Bābēr, *al-Sa'āda al-abadiyya*, f. 19b, under "al-Suyūṭī b. Muḥammad" (on the *al-Sa'āda al-abadiyya*, see *ALA* IV, 63). His descendants in Timbuktu still own one of the most important private libraries of the town, on which see Abdelkader Haïdara, "An overview of the major manuscript libraries in Timbuktu," in *The Trans-Saharan Book Trade: Manuscript Culture, Arabic Literacy, and Intellectual History in Muslim Africa*, edited by Graziano Krätli and Ghislaine Lydon (Leiden and Boston: Brill, 2011), 256–259 and Abdelqader Haïdara and Safa Akhavan, *Catalogue de la bibliothèque Imam Essayouti* (Qom: Grand Library of the Ayatullah al-Uzma Marashi Najafi, 2010) [catalogue].

135 Ben Essayoûtî, "Sidi Muhammad al-Imam ben Essayoûtî," 265.

producing MS C: Wāli Bah.[136] A trader and Tijānī scholar, he was the first "president" of the Muslim Tribunal established by the French in Kayes in 1905.[137]

Lastly, as scholars and colonial administrators, Houdas and Delafosse were heavily involved in the intellectual enterprise of producing "effective knowledge." Houdas was born in France but raised in Algeria, where he occupied several official positions thanks to his mastery of the Arabic language, especially spoken Arabic. He served in positions ranging from official translator to instructor in French schools to inspector of local *medersas*.[138] The case of Delafosse is even more interesting. He had started studying medicine, but became interested in Africa at a young age after enlisting in the Institut des frères armés du Sahara, a group founded by Cardinal Charles-Martial Allemand Lavigerie (d. 1892) and devoted to combating the slave trade in the Sahara. Even though his membership in the Frères armés was short-lived, this experience inspired Delafosse to study Arabic. After graduation in 1904, he began a long career as colonial administrator in the Côte d'Ivoire, Liberia, Sudan, and Senegal. Like Houdas, Delafosse combined his duties as colonial officer (he became a *chevalier* of the Legion of Honor in 1903) with that of academic.[139]

Delafosse's masterpiece *Haut-Sénégal-Niger* is a perfect example of the intertwining of the exigencies of colonial administration and scholarship. This work was produced by using data provided by the colonial infrastructure and, along with many of his other writings, was used to instruct colonial administrators.[140] For instance, *Haut-Sénégal-Niger* was included in the 1925 *Manuel à l'usage des troupes employées outre-mer*.[141] Delafosse himself was an overt supporter of colonization, firmly believing in the importance of local knowledge for

136 On Wāli Bah, see Marty, *La région de Kayes*, 7–8. On his term as *qāḍī* of the French Muslim tribunal (1905–6), see Rebecca A. Shereikis, "Customized Courts: French Colonial Legal Institutions in Kayes, French Soudan, c. 1880–c. 1913 (Mali)" (Ph.D. dissertation, Northwestern University, 2003), xx.

137 Shereikis, "Customized Courts," 81.

138 Triaud, "De la coutume à l'histoire," 213–215.

139 Delafosse, *Maurice Delafosse*.

140 Filippo M. Zerrilli, "Maurice Delafosse, entre science et action," in *Maurice Delafosse. Entre Orientalisme et Ethnographie: l'itinéraire d'un Africaniste, 1870–1926*, edited by Jean-Loup Amselle and Emmanuelle Sibeud (Paris: Maisonneuve et Larose, 1998), 144–165, 148.

141 Frémeaux, "Des bureaux arabes à Maurice Delafosse," 107.

orienting the application of colonial policies on the ground.[142] For example, he describes A. Richer's book *Les Oulliminden: les Touareg du Niger (région de Tombouctou-Gao)* (1924) as a crucial tool for control of the turbulent Saharan region.[143] This work, in Delafosse's words, makes it possible for the colonial authorities to discover "the past of the people with whom they deal, the past relationship between them and us, the different tribes and their chiefs and important personalities, and to provide them also [with] a solid foundation on which it will became possible, in the future, to build a reasonable and definitive policy."[144] In the obituary written for Delafosse by the sociologist René Maunier (d. 1951), he was aptly described as a "man of science" and a "man of action" at the same time.[145]

Once published in Paris, *La chronique du chercheur* found its way back to West Africa. In a letter from Muḥammad b. Muḥammad b. al-Suyūṭī, dated April 1914, the *imām* of the Great Mosque of Timbuktu thanks Houdas for having sent him a copy of the book.[146] Clozel also sent several copies to other notables of Timbuktu.[147] Having arrived in Timbuktu, these books were transcribed back into manuscripts by local copyists. Thus *La chronique du chercheur* began a new life when it transmigrated from the medium of printed book into manuscript, a sort of textual metempsychosis resulting from the initiatives of West African scribes who copied Houdas and Delafosse's Arabic text and placed those handwritten copies in local libraries.[148] Ironically, the

[142] Zerrilli, "Maurice Delafosse, entre science et action," 146.
[143] Frémeaux "Des bureaux arabes à Maurice Delafosse," 204.
[144] Quoted in Frémeaux, "Des bureaux arabes à Maurice Delafosse," 204.
[145] Quoted in Zerrilli, "Maurice Delafosse, entre science et action," 157.
[146] IHERI-ABT 608.
[147] Ben Essayoûtî, "Sidi Muhammad al-Imam ben Essayoûtî," 264.
[148] In fact, the distinction between printed and handwritten materials is a very artificial one in places where manuscript traditions are alive, such as in West Africa. The case of *La chronique du chercheur* proves to be a very interesting one that shows how texts did move from manuscript to print, but the contrary was true as well. So it is not unusual to find in West African collections, for example, a history of the spread of tea in Maghreb in manuscript format that is a copy of an article published in the Moroccan newspaper *al-Sa'āda* (Happiness), issue 8096, Jumādà II 1370/1 March 1951 (Maktabat Mamma Ḥaydara al-Tidhkāriyya, 125; I thank Shamil Jeppie for attracting my attention to this manuscript); or a handwritten copy of the *Ta'rīf al-'ashā'ir wa-l-khillān bi-shu'ūb wa-qabā'il al-Fullān*, a history of the Fulani written by a nephew of al-Ḥājj 'Umar Tall, Muḥammad al-Hāshimī b. Aḥmad b. Sa'īd, better known as Alfa Hāshim (d. 1931–2), which was copied from a printed book published

original texts of the *Tārīkh Ibn al-Mukhtār* and of the *Tārīkh al-fattāsh* remained very rare, while several copies of the conflated text derived from *La chronique du chercheur* started circulating extensively under the misleading title *Tārīkh al-fattāsh*. Of the nine copies listed as *Tārīkh al-fattāsh* in existing catalogues and handlists of West African manuscripts today, both published and unpublished, all but two are in fact copies of *La chronique du chercheur*.[149] The two that are not copies of that conflated text are none other than MS A/IHERI-ABT 3927 and MS B/BnF 5561.

Eventually, the abundance of Arabic manuscript copies of *La chronique du chercheur* spurred the emergence of a *hysteron proteron*: handwritten copies of that edition became accepted – and are still accepted – as manuscripts reflecting the *pre-edition* stage of the text. This misunderstanding reached its apex in 2014, with the publication of a new edition of the *Tārīkh al-fattāsh* by the IHERI-ABT team.[150] This edition was supposed to provide scholars with a more reliable text of the chronicle and to overcome the problems of the text created by Houdas and Delafosse. However, of the four manuscripts collated to create the IHERI-ABT edition, three are actually copies of *La chronique du chercheur* and the other is MS A/IHERI-AB 3927 – the one used by Houdas and Delafosse themselves.

*****

Part III has followed the social life of the *Tārīkh al-fattāsh*, focusing on its circulation and reception. It has traced the strategies through which a lengthy chronicle of about a hundred manuscript leaves was effectively disseminated in West Africa during the late period of Aḥmad Lobbo's rule over the Caliphate of Ḥamdallāhi. The *Tārīkh al-fattāsh* was quoted in shorter documents that promulgated the claims made by the chronicle, proclaiming Aḥmad Lobbo's political legitimacy and supporting a project of social engineering in the Middle Niger, which involved the transformation of several endogamous groups into slaves

in Mecca in 1354/1936 (IHERI-ABT 431; on Alfa Hāshim and this work, see *ALA* IV, 223–225, esp. item 6).

149 IHERI-ABT 2, IHERI-ABT 64, IHERI-ABT 2934, IHERI-ABT 8387, IHERI-ABT 11752, IRSH 2569 (I thank Shamil Jeppie for having taken pictures of this manuscript with the permission of the NHRS staff), Boukhary Library, Banikan Village, 54 (I thank Mohamed Diagayeté for sharing pictures of this last manuscript with me).

150 Maiga et al. (ed. and trans.), *Tārīkh al-fattāsh*.

of the caliph and of the sedentarization of nomads. Further evidence of the reception of the *Tārīkh al-fattāsh* is supplied by the writings of the Sokoto leaders who explicitly rejected these claims, which were also questioned by the Kunta and debated in the Western Sahara. None of these debates, however, concerned the plausibility of divine investiture, ancient prophecies, or the approaching End of the World. These events fit perfectly within the Islamic epistemology of nineteenth-century Middle Niger and worked to advance the chronicle's political project.

Part III has also described the afterlife of the *Tārīkh al-fattāsh* and its mobilization as a part of another, very different, political project. While the decline of the Caliphate of Ḥamdallāhi led to the chronicle's obsolescence, the arrival of French colonial domination led to its resurgence in the fictive edition of Houdas and Delafosse's *La chronique du chercheur*. For over a century thereafter, this confected text prevented scholars from understanding the original *Tārīkh al-fattāsh* as a source witnessing the construction of political legitimacy in nineteenth-century West Africa.

Conclusion

This book has contributed to two different historiographies: that of the *Tārīkh al-fattāsh*, one of the most important sources for precolonial African history; and that of the Caliphate of Ḥamdallāhi and other West African Islamic revolutions. By uncovering the inextricable histories of the chronicle and of the caliphate, I have analyzed how the *Tārīkh al-fattāsh* legitimized Aḥmad Lobbo against the challenges to his position as a new ruler in the Middle Niger. His emergence represented a break with local tradition because his claims to power rested on both political and religious (Islamic) authority. Moreover, the founding leader of Ḥamdallāhi was an outsider to both groups that traditionally occupied these spheres of authority. He was not a member of any of those Fulani warrior elites who ruled the southern Middle Niger on behalf of Segou, such as the Dikko or the Sidibe. Likewise, he did not belong to any established family of *'ulamā'*, such as the Kunta or the Fodiawa, nor to the circles of scholars in the main centers of learning of his time, like Timbuktu or Djenné. Aḥmad Lobbo was therefore the new man of the Middle Niger, with new ideas of governance that combined political and religious authority in the person of one ruler: the caliph of Ḥamdallāhi.

While Aḥmad Lobbo's political authority rested mainly on his political and administrative acumen as well as on his military might, this book has mainly focused on his claims to religious authority, as they emerge from study of the extensive but heretofore unexplored written sources left behind by Ḥamdallāhi's elite, especially Nūḥ b. al-Ṭāhir's *Tārīkh al-fattāsh* and the writings of the caliph himself. My study confirms Hunwick's argument that, in Islamic contexts,

> authority may be derived *inter alia* from the ability to interpret the texts (especially the Qur'ān and legal texts), in the case of the *'ulamā'*, or from the ability to have access to divine power through "miraculous" acts (*karāmāt*),

in the case of "Friends of God" (*awliyā'* [sing. *walī*]), or through [a] direct mandate from heaven, as in the case of those who claim to be the Mahdi.[1]

Aḥmad Lobbo wielded all of these forms of authority in Ḥamdallāhi. He had risen to be a scholar of stature vis-à-vis more well-known and recognized *'ulamā'* of his era. At the same time, he was recognized as a *walī* by his contemporaries. However, these forms of authority proved insufficient to legitimize Aḥmad Lobbo's rule, especially in the regions remote from Ḥamdallāhi – whether at the peripheries of the caliphate or in the neighboring areas, such as Timbuktu, Sokoto, and the Western Sahara. Another level of legitimacy was thus required. Although Aḥmad Lobbo never pretended to be the *mahdī*, the eschatological Muslim leader who is awaited to rule the Muslim community before the Day of Judgment, he was invested with a "mandate from heaven." Apart from being presented as sultan of the Middle Niger and heir to a long line of legitimate rulers dating back to the late first millennium CE, he was also identified as the twelfth of the caliphs under whom the Islamic community would thrive, according to a *ḥadīth* ascribed to the Prophet, and so to be the *mujaddid* or "renewer" of Islam.

These claims came to rest on a sophisticated manipulation of local historiography and the invention of a series of events associated with the Pilgrimage of the late fifteenth-/early sixteenth-century Songhay king Askiyà Muḥammad. These events, culminating in a prophecy foretelling the arrival of Aḥmad Lobbo, are narrated in the famous *Tārīkh al-fattāsh*: a chronicle whose origins, authorship, and contents have been fundamentally misunderstood by scholars for over a century, both in West Africa and abroad. Rather than being recognized as a crucial source for the study of the Caliphate of Ḥamdallāhi and its wider world, it had been regarded as a sixteenth- or seventeenth-century work. In actuality, as this study has proved, the chronicle is a nineteenth-century work written by Ahmad Lobbo's talented advisor, Nūḥ b. al-Ṭāhir, who transformed an earlier seventeenth-century chronicle, the *Tārīkh Ibn al-Mukhtār*, into a meta historical narrative which bestowed upon Aḥmad Lobbo a multi-layered source of legitimacy as sultan, caliph, and the renewer of the faith.

This study of the connected histories of the *Tārīkh al-fattāsh* and the Caliphate of Ḥamdallāhi also calls for further reflection on three

[1] Hunwick, "Secular power and religious authority," 176.

broader issues that face scholars working on African Islamic history: the political nature of history writing; the extant "vibrancy" and "agency" of African Muslim intellectuals and their participation in the wider Islamic discursive tradition; and the importance of literacy in pre-colonial African history.

History Writing as Political Projects

The first lesson of the book, which emerges especially from Part I, concerns the nature of history writing in West Africa. A superficial reading of the Islamic Library of West Africa might suggest that chronicles make up the lion's share of writings by local Muslim scholars. Almost every scholar casually familiar with African historiography is aware of the existence of the *Tārīkh al-Sūdān*, the *Tārīkh Ibn al-Mukhtār* – hitherto subsumed beneath the tricky format of *La chronique du chercheur* – and the *Tadhkirat al-nisyān*, all of which were edited and translated into French at the very beginning of the colonial period. However, these works are not representative of the works of the Islamic Library of West Africa. As Hall and Stewart prove, in their study of the "core curriculum" used by West African scholars, the topic of history "was not one of widespread study judging from the contents of West African collections."[2] They continue by positing that "the histories we find tend to be local or regional works."[3] Most likely, they refer to the many scanty accounts of historical events organized by year in the form of annals, the likes of the *Tārīkh al-fūtāwī*, the *Mā waqa'a fī al-Takrūr al-sūdāniyya*, or the *Dhikr mā waqa'a*, extensively used throughout this book.

That history remained a marginal interest for West African Muslim scholars might be explained by the fact that the memory of the past seems to have remained the domain of a different type of "specialist" in the region: the griots.[4] Therefore, when confronted with a lengthy and sophisticated chronicle like the *Tārīkh al-fattāsh*, one must recognize that the writer of such a work was stepping far beyond the most common literary genres of his time and was not following in the

2 Hall and Stewart, "The historic 'core curriculum'," 128.
3 Hall and Stewart, "The historic 'core curriculum'," 128.
4 For the diverse functions, including that of historian, that the griots occupy in West Africa, see Thomas A. Hale, *Griots and Griottes* (Bloomington: Indiana University Press, 1998), 18–58.

footsteps of a locally established tradition. As de Moraes Farias has demonstrated, the writing of chronicles emerges in West Africa at a very late date: "Something special happened in Timbuktu in the second half of the seventeenth century AD/eleventh century *hijri*: the emergence of a literary genre. This was the Timbuktu *tarikh* genre."[5] This genre, de Moraes Farias continues, is characterized by a sort of "plenitude effect," a strategy of filling in the gaps in the author's historical knowledge in order to create complete narratives of the past.[6] These chronicles served a particular purpose: "The *tarikh*s works were … implicitly centred on a novel political project, which expressed a will to power."[7] The seventeenth-century chronicles were a project devoted to claiming space for older religious and political elites within the new Arma state. Consequently, de Moraes Farias concludes that "the *tarikh* genre was short lived" and did not survive the test of time when the political circumstances of the Niger Bend changed at the end of the seventeenth century.[8]

Of course, the changing of the political context in post-seventeenth-century West Africa might have rendered these political aims outdated and moot. However, if one understands *tārīkh*, in line with de Moraes Farias, as a genre characterized by lengthy and all-encompassing chronicles that reshape the events of the past in a way that supports new political understandings of the present, it clearly did not die in the seventeenth century. As I have demonstrated elsewhere, there are other works that display these same features in the Middle Niger well after this era.[9] The *Tārīkh al-fattāsh*, created in the mid-nineteenth century, is one of them. Another is the twentieth-century *Kitāb al-turjumān fī tārīkh al-Saḥrā' wa-l-Sūdān wa-balad Tinbuktu wa-Shinqīṭ wa-Arawān* (The Manual of Guidance on the History of the Sahara and the Sudan and the lands of Timbuktu, Shinqīt and Arawān) by Muḥammad Maḥmūd b. al-Shaykh b. Abī Bakr b. Aḥmad al-Ḥasanī al-Sūqī al-Arawānī al-Tinbuktī (d. 1973), a history of the Niger Bend from the sixteenth century up to the time of French colonialism.[10] It

5 De Moraes Farias, "Intellectual innovation," 95.
6 De Moraes Farias, "Intellectual innovation," 100.
7 De Moraes Farias, "Intellectual innovation," 97.
8 De Moraes Farias, "Intellectual innovation," 98.
9 Nobili, "New reinventions of the Sahel."
10 On Muḥammad Maḥmūd b. al-Shaykh's *Kitāb al-turjumān*, see *ALA* IV, 58–59, item 7.

portrays the region as belonging to "white" Arab and Tuareg groups, thereby supporting the political claims of those leaders lobbying for an independent Saharan state in the event of independence during the 1950s: a period of upheaval comparable in its impact to the fall of the Songhay state after the Moroccan invasion.[11] Further east, in Air, the so-called Chronicles of Agadez display similar features, and support the claims of specific Tuareg groups immediately after the beginning of French colonialism, as recently shown by Benedetta Rossi.[12] Not surprisingly, 'Abd Allāh b. Fūdī and Muḥammad Bello set out to write large chronicles such as the *Tazyīn al-waraqāt bi-ba'ḍ mā lī min al-abyāt* (The Adornment of Pages from Some of my Authored Verses) and *Infāq al-maysūr fī Tārīkh Bilād al-Takrūr* (The Easy Accessible Outlay on the History of Takrūr) in order to advance the cause of the Sokoto Caliphate.[13]

In short, when encountering lengthy historical texts, a scholar has to be on the alert: there is a political project at stake. To extend de Moraes Farias's insight, as I argue elswhere, "scholars from the Niger Bend [and elsewhere in West Africa] did not only produce, by resorting to works belonging to the *tārīkh* genre, a new idea of the Sahelian past *in* the 17th century ... West African historians, by composing *tārīkh*s, have been cyclically engaged in producing new reinventions of the Sahel *since* the seventeenth century."[14]

West Africa and the Islamic Discursive Tradition

Throughout this book, and especially in Part II, words that tend to occur most frequently are "scholars" and "knowledge." For a long time, the association of these two terms with any place in sub-Saharan Africa would have been impossible. As Reese points out in the introduction to his pivotal edited collection *The Transmission of Learning in Islamic Africa*, studies of African Islamic societies have been characterized, for decades if not centuries, by the assumption of

11 Nobili, "New reinventions of the Sahel."

12 Benedetta Rossi, "The Agadez Chronicles and Y Tarichi: A reinterpretation," *History in Africa* 43 (2016): 95–140.

13 Paul J. Naylor, "From Rebels to Rulers: Religious and Political Legitimacy in the Arabic Writings of the Sokoto Fodiawa, 1804–1837" (Ph.D. dissertation, University of Birmingham, 2018), 13. On the *Tazyīn al-waraqāt* and *Infāq al-maysūr*, see *ALA* II, 109–110, item 87, and *ALA* II, 119, item 21.

14 Nobili, "New reinventions of the Sahel," 216–217.

marginality, both spatial and intellectual.[15] According to this paradigm, African Muslims were cut off from the rest of the Islamic world and, at the same time, had neither access to the intellectual achievements of their coreligionists elsewhere nor any active role in producing original contributions within the global space of Islamic knowledge.

This double marginality has a long genealogy in the historiography of African Muslim societies. It dates back to the colonial period and is associated with the paradigm of *Islam noir* or African Islam – to which ample space has been devoted and upon which I will not dwell here.[16] A shift in this paradigm took place in the early 1990s.[17] However, it was Reese's volume that constituted a declaration for a new type of scholarship on African Islamic societies, built around the insistence on the "continued intellectual vibrancy of African *'ulamā'*" and "the interconnectedness of Africa's Muslims to their co-religionists in the wider *umma*."[18]

This book has contributed to the growing body of scholarly literature that substantiates Reese's arguments. African Muslims have indeed been always in contact, both physically and intellectually, with other Muslims living outside sub-Saharan Africa, as recent studies have proved.[19] True, none of the main actors featured in the present book seems to have traveled extensively outside West Africa. Nūḥ b. al-Ṭāhir, the author of the *Tārīkh al-fattāsh*, most likely left the Middle

15 Scott S. Reese, "Islam in Africa: Challenging the perceived wisdom," in *The Transmission of Learning in Islamic Africa*, edited by Scott S. Reese (Leiden and Boston: Brill, 2004), 1–14, 1.

16 See, for example, the story of the genesis of this notion and its continued resonance in Jean-Louis Triaud, "Giving a name to Islam south of the Sahara: An adventure in taxonomy," *Journal of African History* 55/1 (2014): 3–15.

17 The excellent Robert Launay, *Beyond the Stream: Islam and Society in a West African Town* (Berkeley: University of California Press, 1992) is often considered as the contribution that inaugurated a new way of studying African Muslim societies.

18 Reese, "Challenging the perceived wisdom," 4.

19 See for example, Ghislaine Lydon's study of the trans-Saharan trading networks (Lydon, *On Trans-Saharan Trails*); Anne K. Bang's analysis of the Indian Ocean connections that brought about the emergence of the 'Alawiyya Sufi brotherhood in East Africa (Anne K. Bang, *Sufis and Scholars of the Sea: Family Networks in East Africa, 1860–1925* [London: Routledge, 2014]); or Ahmed Chanfi's work on West African scholars in Saudi Arabia and their contribution to the emergence of contemporary Salafism (Ahmed Chanfi, *West African 'Ulamā' and Salafism in Mecca and Medina: Jawāb al-Ifrīqī – The Response of the African* [Leiden and Boston: Brill, 2015]).

Niger only to go so far as Sokoto. Aḥmad Lobbo, the caliph of Ḥamdallāhi, was even less widely traveled: there is no trace of him even on the peripheries of his own caliphate. Yet, as I have proved, the intellectual connections of these scholars to the wider world were made by traveling virtually, *in absentia*, through writing, diplomacy, and the forging of networks that enabled both. Furthermore, they mastered knowledge produced in every corner of the Islamic world, making it impossible to sustain the fiction that West Africa was a remote and isolated backwater.

Moreover, Aḥmad Lobbo and Nūḥ b. al-Ṭāhir, like the Kunta and the Fodiawa, produced scholarship of relevance and sophistication. As proven by my analysis of their writings, the scholars of Ḥamdallāhi mastered several works representing the different branches of Islamic knowledge, with a special focus on jurisprudence and history. Consequently, this book enriches the existing scholarship that has, in past years, highlighted the depth and vibrancy of African Muslim scholars' contributions to the fields of, for example, Sufism and jurisprudence;[20] or their active role in furthering education in their communities and in forming relationships with different pre-colonial, colonial, and post-colonial ruling elites.[21] What is peculiar to this present study, however, is that it has revealed not only the mastery over Islamic knowledge attained by the scholars of Ḥamdallāhi and neighboring areas, but their creative and successful use of that knowledge for political purposes.

20 Scott S. Reese, *Renewers of the Age: Holy Men and Social Discourse in Colonial Benaadir* (Leiden: Brill, 2008); Rüdiger Seesemann, *The Divine Flood: Ibrāhīm Niasse and the Roots of a Twentieth-Century Sufi Revival* (New York: Oxford University Press, 2011); Anne K. Bang, *Islamic Sufi Networks in the Western Indian Ocean (c. 1880–1940): Ripples of Reform* (Leiden: Brill, 2014); Zachary V. Wright, *Living Knowledge in West African Islam: The Sufi Community of Ibrāhīm Niasse* (Leiden: Brill, 2015); Aharon Layish, *Sharīʿa and the Islamic State in 19th-Century Sudan: The Mahdī's Legal Methodology and Doctrine* (Leiden: Brill, 2016); Ismail Warscheid, *Droit Musulman et société au Sahara premodern: la justice islamiques dans les oasis du grand Touat (Algérie) aux XVIIe–XIXe siècles* (Leiden: Brill 2017).

21 Muhammad Sani Umar, *Islam and Colonialism: Intellectual Responses of Muslims of Northern Nigeria to British Colonial Rule* (Leiden: Brill, 2006); Roman Loimeier, *Between Social Skills and Marketable Skills: The Politics of Education in 20th Century Zanzibar* (Leiden: Brill, 2009); Ware, *The Walking Qur'an.*

This book also provides a vivid example of African Muslims' interaction with the Islamic discursive tradition. As Loimeier underlines, "specific aspects and interpretations of the canon have to be linked with the respective realities of a Muslim society to acquire social, political and religious relevance."[22] In the case of the *Tārīkh al-fattāsh*, the canonical *ḥadīth*s of the twelve caliphs and of the renewer of the faith were taken from the broad corpus of Prophetic traditions. However, they were adapted to a context in which they were particularly meaningful and useful: the thirteenth century of the Islamic calendar, fully loaded with millenarian expectations. Therefore, the impact of the belief in the approach of the Eschaton also proves how "'the unseen' possesses an agency that directly impacts the material world."[23] Likewise, the tropes of political authority employed by Aḥmad Lobbo and Nūḥ b. al-Ṭāhir, such as the role of the caliph and the position of the scholar vis-à-vis political authority, were drawn from the larger Islamic canon and applied in a local context. In this endeavor, I align with Reese's argument that "the Islamic canon constitutes a living body of knowledge continuously employed and interpreted by the believers of a particular place and time to provide guidance and solutions to the problems of their day."[24] At the same time, the contestation of such knowledge by other actors, such as the Kunta or the Fodiawa, shows that ideas employed to make sense of historically contingent contexts were objected, disputed, resisted, and rebuked, confirming Asad's observation of the contested and dialectic nature of Islamic discursive tradition.[25]

Islamic West Africa as a Mosaic of Literacy-Aware Societies

A third lesson, emerging in particular from Part III, is the important role of literacy in the nineteenth-century Middle Niger. My study argues strongly that writing was both a prerequisite for accessing power in Ḥamdallāhi and a tool for governing the territories of the caliphate. Because literacy was an indispensable precondition for all administrators, Ḥamdallāhi became a state run by scholars. This does not mean that all the administrator of the caliphate were sophisticated

[22] Loimeier, *Between Social Skills and Marketable Skills*, 5.
[23] Reese, *Imperial Muslims*, 10. [24] Reese, "Africans and Islam," 19.
[25] Asad, *Anthropology of Islam*, 16.

'ulamā'. Last's division of Sokoto's scholars into two types also seems to fit those of Ḥamdallāhi. The first were "those that were good preachers but relatively poor Arabists; they provided local ritual services as well as medicines and amulets."[26] They served as bridge between more highly trained literary scholars and the people at large. There were also those well-trained scholars, including the scholars who served as members of the Great Council, including Nūḥ b. al-Ṭāhir and Aḥmad Lobbo himself: "good Arabists, [and] by contrast, [they] were bookmen-teachers who owned or memorised books, and taught them to students."[27]

Cultivating this apparatus of literati allowed Aḥmad Lobbo and his Great Council to govern the territories of the caliphate from Ḥamdallāhi, so breaking with the traditional de-centralization of West African states. Therefore, the Caliphate of Ḥamdallāhi resembles what Brinkley Messick has defined as a "calligraphic state."[28] For Messick, who focuses on eighteenth- and nineteenth-century Yemen, "the calligraphic state was both a political entity and a discursive condition";[29] or, in other words, it was "a phenomenon anchored in the complex authority relations of a spectrum of writings and associated institutions."[30]

Describing the Caliphate of Ḥamdallāhi as a calligraphic state does not imply that all its subjects were literate in Arabic. In fact, it is unlikely that many people could read and write beyond primary Qur'ānic education. Nevertheless, the picture that emerges from my study of the caliphate's documentation challenges the traditional paradigm of "oral societies" usually applied to sub-Saharan Africa (the *griot paradigm*). This paradigm, often accepted in both scholarly and non-scholarly circles, is epitomized by the statement of the famous historian Jan Vansina, that "the African civilizations in the Sahara and south of the desert were to a great extent civilizations of

[26] Murray Last, "The book and the nature of knowledge in Muslim Northern Nigeria, 1457–2007," in *The Trans-Saharan Book Trade: Manuscript Culture, Arabic Literacy, and Intellectual History in Muslim Africa*, edited by Graziano Krätli and Ghislaine Lydon (Leiden and Boston: Brill, 2011), 175–212, 201.

[27] Last, "The book and the nature of knowledge," 202.

[28] Brinkley Messick, *The Calligraphic State: Textual Domination and History in a Muslim Society* (Berkeley and Los Angeles: University of California Press, 1992).

[29] Messick, *The Calligraphic State*, 1.

[30] Messick, *The Calligraphic State*, 257.

the spoken word."[31] Although Vansina leaves space for the existence of writing, he insists that "even where the written word existed, as it did in West Africa from the sixteenth century onward … only very few people knew how to write and the role of the written word was often marginal to the essential preoccupations of a society."[32]

Here, Vansina implicitly references Jack R. Goody's influential notion of "restricted literacy," first advanced in 1963, in an article co-authored by Ian Watt, and then expanded in several other publications.[33] Goody specifically applied it to Islamic West Africa in his contribution to the edited collection *Literacy in Traditional Societies*, in 1968:

> Literacy was restricted in its diffusion, its content and its implications largely because it was a religious literacy, dominated by the study of the Holy Book. Indeed, learning to read at all meant learning a foreign language, Arabic, and the actual techniques of teaching were often more appropriate to oral than to written cultures. But the main factor in restricting the developments in the cognitive sphere was the association of the book with magic and religion, an exclusive, all-embracing cult that claimed it had the single road to the truth. It is above all the predominantly religious character of literacy that, here as elsewhere, prevented the medium from fulfilling its promise.[34]

Goody adds that only a very small percentage of the population had access to writing techniques, with literacy becoming the specialized craft of literati who were interested in protecting their exclusive monopoly on it; Goody describes these societies as "oligoliterate."[35]

The assumption that systems of learning in Islamic West Africa, and the use of writing in general, were relegated to "magical" and therapeutical purposes has been studied elsewhere.[36] Like the stereotypes

31 Jan Vansina, "Oral tradition and its methodology," in *General History of Africa*, vol. 1: *Methodology and Africa Prehistory*, edited by Joseph Ki-Zerbo (Berkeley: UNESCO/University of California, 1981), 142–165, 142.

32 Vansina, "Oral tradition," 142.

33 Jack R. Goody and Ian Watt, "The consequences of literacy," *Comparative Studies in Society and History* 5/3 (1963): 304–345.

34 Jack R. Goody, "Restricted literacy in northern Ghana," in *Literacy in Traditional Societies*, edited by Jack R. Goody (Cambridge: Cambridge University Press, 1968), 199–264, 241.

35 Goody and Watt, "The consequences of literacy," 313.

36 As for the topic of "magic" in the Islamic world, see, among others, Constant Hamès, *Coran et talismans: textes et pratiques magiques en milieu musulman* (Paris: Karthala, 2007); and the recent Jean-Charles Coulon, *La*

concerning the deficiency of so-called "traditional Islamic learning," it has been strongly challenged in recent studies.[37] Here, I specifically want to challenge Goody's notion of West Africa as an "oligoliterate society." First, how many societies were not "oligoliterate" prior to the mid-nineteenth century? From this angle, it is interesting to underline the remarks of the first European explorers and colonial administrators who visited West African Muslim societies and were impressed by the level of literacy. For example, Baron Jacques-François Roger (d. 1849), governor of the French colony of Saint-Louis (on the mouth of the Senegal River) in the 1820s, found in his region "more negros who could read and write in Arabic in 1828 than French peasants who could read and write French."[38]

A much more useful paradigm suited to Islamic West Africa is that of the "literacy aware society," first coined by C. A. Bayly with respect to nineteenth-century north India and imported to the West African context by Hall.[39] Bayly defines this as a society in which there is easy "access to literate people" and where almost everyone understands the full "meaning and power of writing."[40] In a literacy aware society, adds Hall with reference to West Africa, "the number of people who participated in larger intellectual conversations connected to literacy was much higher than the five to ten percent of the population that could read and write."[41] The example of the circular letters and decrees sent from Ḥamdallāhi to the different regions of the caliphate – like the *Risāla* of Nūḥ b. al-Ṭahir, which were to be read publicly – points to this degree of access to literacy among illiterate or semi-literate people. Another example of literacy awareness among non-literati of the Middle Niger is the widespread usage of manumission documents.[42]

magie en terre d'islam au Moyen Âge (Paris: Éditions du Comité des travaux historiques et scientifiques, 2017).

37 Excellent recent studies that reevaluate the role of such system of learning are Ware, *The Walking Qur'an*; and Hannah Hoechner, *Quranic Schools in Northern Nigeria: Everyday Experiences of Youth, Faith, and Poverty* (Cambridge: Cambridge University Press, 2018).

38 Quoted in Kane, *Beyond Timbuktu*, 7.

39 See C. A. Bayly, *Empire and Information: Intelligence Gathering and Social Communication in India, 1780–1870* (Cambridge: Cambridge University Press, 1996), 39; Hall, *A History of Race*, 21.

40 Bayly, *Empire and Information*, 36. 41 Hall, *A History of Race*, 21.

42 See, for example, the many documents of manumission contained in the online database "Slavery and manumission manuscripts of Timbuktu" (www.crl.edu/slavery-and-manumission-manuscripts-timbuktu).

Only a limited number of slaves could read at an advanced level, such as those described by Hall in his work on slaves who acted as commercial agents in the Middle Niger and the Sahara.[43] Yet a written document of manumission literally meant freedom to a person who was unable, most likely, to read the text itself. In other words, the Middle Niger was characterized by the presence of literacy that impacted on the lives of everyone, regardless of the individual's capacity to read or write.[44]

*****

In conclusion, *Sultan, Caliph, and the Renewer of the Faith* emphasizes Meikal Mumin's argument that "Africa is not a continent without writing. Rather, it is a continent without studies on writing."[45] My study is thus an open invitation to engage with the philological study of these writings, mostly still in manuscript form. However, contrary to old philological approaches, I have argued that the analyses of these manuscripts should not be confined to the texts themselves, but need to be located within their historical contexts of production, circulation, and reception. In this way, as my book has demonstrated, focusing on the writings of African Muslim intellectuals will enable scholars to write deeper histories of these societies from within. By extension, efforts toward seriously taking into consideration local epistemologies, such as the one carried on in *Sultan, Caliph, and the Renewer of the Faith*, will also contribute to the decolonization of knowledge about African societies at large.

43 Bruce Hall, "How slaves used Islam: The letters of enslaved Muslim commercial agents in the nineteenth-century Niger Bend and Central Sahara," *Journal of African History* 52/3 (2011): 279–297.

44 Approaching literacy in a broader sense is not uncommon in other geographical areas; see, for example, Steven Justice, *Writing and Rebellion: England in 1381* (Berkeley and Los Angeles: California University Press, 1994).

45 Meikal Mumin, "The Arabic script in Africa: Understudied literacy," in *The Arabic Script in Africa: Studies in the Use of a Writing System*, edited by Meikal Mumin and Kees Verteegh (Leiden and Boston: Brill, 2014), 41–76.

Index

African Studies Series

1. *City Politics: A Study of Leopoldville, 1962–63*, J.S. La Fontaine
2. *Studies in Rural Capitalism in West Africa*, Polly Hill
3. *Land Policy in Buganda*, Henry W. West
4. *The Nigerian Military: A Sociological Analysis of Authority and Revolt, 1960–67*, Robin Luckham
5. *The Ghanaian Factory Worker: Industrial Man in Africa*, Margaret Peil
6. *Labour in the South African Gold Mines*, Francis Wilson
7. *The Price of Liberty: Personality and Politics in Colonial Nigeria*, Kenneth W. J. Post and George D. Jenkins
8. *Subsistence to Commercial Farming in Present-Day Buganda: An Economic and Anthropological Survey*, Audrey I. Richards, Fort Sturrock, and Jean M. Fortt (eds)
9. *Dependence and Opportunity: Political Change in Ahafo*, John Dunn and A. F. Robertson
10. *African Railwaymen: Solidarity and Opposition in an East African Labour Force*, R. D. Grillo
11. *Islam and Tribal Art in West Africa*, Rene´ A. Bravmann
12. *Modern and Traditional Elites in the Politics of Lagos*, P. D. Cole
13. *Asante in the Nineteenth Century: The Structure and Evaluation of a Political Order*, Ivor Wilks
14. *Culture, Tradition and Society in the West African Novel*, Emmanuel Obiechina
15. *Saints and Politicians*, Donal B. Cruise O'Brien
16. *The Lions of Dagbon: Political Change in Northern Ghana*, Martin Staniland
17. *Politics of Decolonization: Kenya Europeans and the Land Issue 1960–1965*, Gary B. Wasserman
18. *Muslim Brotherhoods in the Nineteenth-Century Africa*, B. G. Martin
19. *Warfare in the Sokoto Caliphate: Historical and Sociological Perspectives*, Joseph P. Smaldone
20. *Liberia and Sierra Leone: An Essay in Comparative Politics*, Christopher Clapham
21. *Adam Kok's Griquas: A Study in the Development of Stratification in South Africa*, Robert Ross
22. *Class, Power and Ideology in Ghana: The Railwaymen of Sekondi*, Richard Jeffries
23. *West African States: Failure and Promise*, John Dunn (ed)

24. *Afrikaaners of the Kalahari: White Minority in a Black State*, Margo Russell and Martin Russell
25. *A Modern History of Tanganyika*, John Iliffe
26. *A History of African Christianity 1950–1975*, Adrian Hastings
27. *Slaves, Peasants and Capitalists in Southern Angola, 1840–1926*, W. G. Clarence-Smith
28. *The Hidden Hippopotamus: Reappraised in African History: The Early Colonial Experience in Western Zambia*, Gywn Prins
29. *Families Divided: The Impact of Migrant Labour in Lesotho*, Colin Murray
30. *Slavery, Colonialism and Economic Growth in Dahomey, 1640–1960*, Patrick Manning
31. *Kings, Commoners and Concessionaries: The Evolution of Dissolution of the Nineteenth-Century Swazi State*, Philip Bonner
32. *Oral Poetry and Somali Nationalism: The Case of Sayid Mahammad 'Abdille Hasan*, Said S. Samatar
33. *The Political Economy of Pondoland 1860–1930*, William Beinart
34. *Volkskapitalisme: Class, Capitals and Ideology in the Development of Afrikaner Nationalism, 1934–1948*, Dan O'Meara
35. *The Settler Economies: Studies in the Economic History of Kenya and Rhodesia 1900–1963*, Paul Mosely
36. *Transformations in Slavery: A History of Slavery in Africa,1st edition*, Paul Lovejoy
37. *Amilcar Cabral: Revolutionary Leadership and People's War*, Patrick Chabal
38. *Essays on the Political Economy of Rural Africa*, Robert H. Bates
39. *Ijeshas and Nigerians: The Incorporation of a Yoruba Kingdom, 1890s-1970s*, J. D. Y. Peel
40. *Black People and the South African War, 1899–1902*, Peter Warwick
41. *A History of Niger 1850–1960*, Finn Fuglestad
42. *Industrialisation and Trade Union Organization in South Africa,1924–1955*, Stephen Ellis
43. *The Rising of the Red Shawls: A Revolt in Madagascar 1895–1899*, Stephen Ellis
44. *Slavery in Dutch South Africa*, Nigel Worden
45. *Law, Custom and Social Order: The Colonial Experience in Malawi and Zambia*, Martin Chanock
46. *Salt of the Desert Sun: A History of Salt Production and Trade in the Central Sudan*, Paul E. Lovejoy

47. *Marrying Well: Marriage, Status and Social Change among the Educated Elite in Colonial Lagos*, Kristin Mann
48. *Language and Colonial Power: The Appropriation of Swahili in the Former Belgian Congo, 1880–1938*, Johannes Fabian
49. *The Shell Money of the Slave Trade*, Jan Hogendorn and Marion Johnson
50. *Political Domination in Africa*, Patrick Chabal
51. *The Southern Marches of Imperial Ethiopia: Essays in History and Social Anthropology*, Donald Donham and Wendy James
52. *Islam and Urban Labor in Northern Nigeria: The Making of a Muslim Working Class*, Paul M. Lubeck
53. *Horn and Crescent: Cultural Change and Traditional Islam on the East African Coast, 800–1900*, Randall L. Pouwels
54. *Capital and Labour on the Kimberley Diamond Fields, 1871–1890*, Robert Vicat Turrell
55. *National and Class Conflict in the Horn of Africa*, John Markakis
56. *Democracy and Prebendal Politics in Nigeria: The Rise and Fall of the Second Republic*, Richard A. Joseph
57. *Entrepreneurs and Parasites: The Struggle for Indigenous Capitalism in Zaire*, Janet MacGaffey
58. *The African Poor: A History*, John Iliffe
59. *Palm Oil and Protest: An Economic History of the Ngwa Region, South-Eastern Nigeria, 1800–1980*, Susan M. Martin
60. *France and Islam in West Africa, 1860–1960*, Christopher Harrison
61. *Transformation and Continuity in Revolutionary Ethiopia*, Christopher Clapham
62. *Prelude to the Mahdiyya: Peasants and Traders in the Shendi Region, 1821–1885*, Anders Bjorkelo
63. *Wa and the Wala: Islam and Polity in Northwestern Ghana*, Ivor Wilks
64. *H.C. Bankole-Bright and Politics in Colonial Sierra Leone, 1919–1958*, Akintola Wyse
65. *Contemporary West African States*, Donal Cruise O'Brien, John Dunn, and Richard Rathbone (eds)
66. *The Oromo of Ethiopia: A History, 1570–1860*, Mohammed Hassen
67. *Slavery and African Life: Occidental, Oriental, and African Slave Trades*, Patrick Manning
68. *Abraham Esau's War: A Black South African War in the Cape, 1899–1902*, Bill Nasson

69. *The Politics of Harmony: Land Dispute Strategies in Swaziland*, Laurel L. Rose
70. *Zimbabwe's Guerrilla War: Peasant Voices*, Norma J. Kriger
71. *Ethiopia: Power and Protest: Peasant Revolts in the Twentieth-Century*, Gebru Tareke
72. *White Supremacy and Black Resistance in Pre-Industrial South Africa: The Making of the Colonial Order in the Eastern Cape, 1770–1865*, Clifton C. Crais
73. *The Elusive Granary: Herder, Farmer, and State in Northern Kenya*, Peter D. Little
74. *The Kanyok of Zaire: An Institutional and Ideological History to 1895*, John C. Yoder
75. *Pragmatism in the Age of Jihad: The Precolonial State of Bundu*, Michael A. Gomez
76. *Slow Death for Slavery: The Course of Abolition in Northern Nigeria, 1897–1936*, Paul E. Lovejoy and Jan S. Hogendorn
77. *West African Slavery and Atlantic Commerce: The Senegal River Valley, 1700–1860*, James F. Searing
78. *A South African Kingdom: The Pursuit of Security in the Nineteenth-Century Lesotho*, Elizabeth A. Elredge
79. *State and Society in Pre-colonial Asante*, T. C. McCaskie
80. *Islamic Society and State Power in Senegal: Disciples and Citizens in Fatick*, Leonardo A. Villalón
81. *Ethnic Pride and Racial Prejudice in Victorian Cape Town: Group Identity and Social Practice*, Vivian Bickford-Smith
82. *The Eritrean Struggle for Independence: Domination, Resistance and Nationalism, 1941–1993*, Ruth Iyob
83. *Corruption and State Politics in Sierra Leone*, William Reno
84. *The Culture of Politics in Modern Kenya*, Angelique Haugerud
85. *Africans: The History of a Continent, 1st edition*, John Iliffe
86. *From Slave Trade to 'Legitimate' Commerce: The Commercial Transition in Nineteenth-Century West Africa*, Robin Law (ed)
87. *Leisure and Society in Colonial Brazzaville*, Phyllis Martin
88. *Kingship and State: The Buganda Dynasty*, Christopher Wrigley
89. *Decolonialization and African Life: The Labour Question in French and British Africa*, Frederick Cooper
90. *Misreading the African Landscape: Society and Ecology in an African Forest-Savannah Mosaic*, James Fairhead, and Melissa Leach
91. *Peasant Revolution in Ethiopia: The Tigray People's Liberation Front, 1975–1991*, John Young

92. *Senegambia and the Atlantic Slave Trade*, Boubacar Barry
93. *Commerce and Economic Change in West Africa: The Oil Trade in the Nineteenth Century*, Martin Lynn
94. *Slavery and French Colonial Rule in West Africa: Senegal, Guinea and Mali*, Martin A. Klein
95. *East African Doctors: A History of the Modern Profession*, John Iliffe
96. *Middlemen of the Cameroons Rivers: The Duala and Their Hinterland, c.1600–1960*, Ralph Derrick, Ralph A. Austen, and Jonathan Derrick
97. *Masters and Servants on the Cape Eastern Frontier, 1760–1803*, Susan Newton-King
98. *Status and Respectability in the Cape Colony, 1750–1870: A Tragedy of Manners*, Robert Ross
99. *Slaves, Freedmen and Indentured Laborers in Colonial Mauritius*, Richard B. Allen
100. *Transformations in Slavery: A History of Slavery in Africa, 2nd edition*, Paul E. Lovejoy
101. *The Peasant Cotton Revolution in West Africa: Côte d'Ivoire, 1880–1995*, Thomas E. Basset
102. *Re-imagining Rwanda: Conflict, Survival and Disinformation in the Late Twentieth Century*, Johan Pottier
103. *The Politics of Evil: Magic, State Power and the Political Imagination in South Africa*, Clifton Crais
104. *Transforming Mozambique: The Politics of Privatization, 1975–2000*, M. Anne Pitcher
105. *Guerrilla Veterans in Post-War Zimbabwe: Symbolic and Violent Politics, 1980–1987*, Norma J. Kriger
106. *An Economic History of Imperial Madagascar, 1750–1895: The Rise and Fall of an Island Empire*, Gwyn Campbell
107. *Honour in African History*, John Iliffe
108. *Africans: A History of a Continent*, 2nd edition, John Iliffe
109. *Guns, Race, and Power in Colonial South Africa*, William Kelleher Storey
110. *Islam and Social Change in French West Africa: History of an Emancipatory Community*, Sean Hanretta
111. *Defeating Mau Mau, Creating Kenya: Counterinsurgency, Civil War and Decolonization*, Daniel Branch
112. *Christianity and Genocide in Rwanda*, Timothy Longman
113. *From Africa to Brazil: Culture, Identity, and an African Slave Trade, 1600–1830*, Walter Hawthorne

114. *Africa in the Time of Cholera: A History of Pandemics from 1817 to the Present*, Myron Echenberg
115. *A History of Race in Muslim West Africa, 1600–1960*, Bruce S. Hall
116. *Witchcraft and Colonial Rule in Kenya, 1900–1955*, Katherine Luongo
117. *Transformations in Slavery: A History of Slavery in Africa*, 3rd edition, Paul E. Lovejoy
118. *The Rise of the Trans-Atlantic Slave Trade in Western Africa, 1300–1589*, Toby Green
119. *Party Politics and Economic Reform in Africa's Democracies*, M. Anne Pitcher
120. *Smugglers and Saints of the Sahara: Regional Connectivity in the Twentieth Century*, Judith Scheele
121. *Cross-Cultural Exchange in the Atlantic World: Angola and Brazil during the Era of the Slave Trade*, Roquinaldo Ferreira
122. *Ethnic Patriotism and the East African Revival*, Derek Peterson
123. *Black Morocco: A History of Slavery and Islam*, Chouki El Hamel
124. *An African Slaving Port and the Atlantic World: Benguela and Its Hinterland*, Mariana Candido
125. *Making Citizens in Africa: Ethnicity, Gender, and National Identity in Ethiopia*, Lahra Smith
126. *Slavery and Emancipation in Islamic East Africa: From Honor to Respectability*, Elisabeth McMahon
127. *A History of African Motherhood: The Case of Uganda, 700–1900*, Rhiannon Stephens
128. *The Borders of Race in Colonial South Africa: The Kat River Settlement, 1829–1856*, Robert Ross
129. *From Empires to NGOs in the West African Sahel: The Road to Nongovernmentality*, Gregory Mann
130. *Dictators and Democracy in African Development: The Political Economy of Good Governance in Nigeria*, A. Carl LeVan
131. *Water, Civilization and Power in Sudan: The Political Economy of Military-Islamist State Building*, Harry Verhoeven
132. *The Fruits of Freedom in British Togoland: Literacy, Politics and Nationalism, 1914–2014*, Kate Skinner
133. *Political Thought and the Public Sphere in Tanzania: Freedom, Democracy and Citizenship in the Era of Decolonization*, Emma Hunter
134. *Political Identity and Conflict in Central Angola, 1975–2002*, Justin Pearce

135. *From Slavery to Aid: Politics, Labour, and Ecology in the Nigerian Sahel, 1800–2000*, Benedetta Rossi
136. *National Liberation in Postcolonial Southern Africa: A Historical Ethnography of SWAPO's Exile Camps*, Christian A. Williams
137. *Africans: A History of a Continent*, 3rd edition, John Iliffe
138. *Colonial Buganda and the End of Empire: Political Thought and Historical Imagination in Africa*, Jonathon L. Earle
139. *The Struggle over State Power in Zimbabwe: Law and Politics since 1950*, George Karekwaivanane
140. *Transforming Sudan: Decolonisation, Economic Development and State Formation*, Alden Young
141. *Colonizing Consent: Rape and Governance in South Africa's Eastern Cape*, Elizabeth Thornberry
142. *The Value of Disorder: Autonomy, Prosperity and Plunder in the Chadian Sahara*, Julien Brachet and Judith Scheele
143. *The Politics of Poverty: Policy-Making and Development in Rural Tanzania*, Felicitas Becker
144. *Boundaries, Communities, and State-Making in West Africa: The Centrality of the Margins*, Paul Nugent
145. *Politics and Violence in Burundi: The Language of Truth in an Emerging State*, Aidan Russell
146. *Power and the Presidency in Kenya: The Jomo Kenyatta Years*, Anaïs Angelo
147. *East Africa after Liberation: Conflict, Security and the State since the 1980s*, Jonathan Fisher

CPSIA information can be obtained
at www.ICGtesting.com
Printed in the USA
LVHW031047080622
720784LV00010B/354

9 781108 789820